The Last Days of George Armstrong Custer

—◦◦◦—

Also by Thom Hatch

The Last Days of George Armstrong Custer

The Last Days of
George Armstrong Custer

Thom Hatch

ST. MARTIN'S PRESS
New York

www.stmartins.com

LIBRARY OF CONGRESS CATALOGING-IN-PUBLICATION DATA

Hatch, Thom, 1946–
    The last days of George Armstrong Custer: the true story of the Battle of the Little Bighorn /
by Thom Hatch.—First edition.
        pages cm
    Includes bibliographical references.
    ISBN 978-1-250-05102-8 (hardcover)
    ISBN 978-1-4668-5197-9 (e-book)
    1. Little Bighorn, Battle of the, Mont., 1876.   2. Custer, George A. (George Armstrong),
1839–1876.   I. Title.

E83.876.H3713 2015
973.8'2—dc23

                                                                    2014033624

St. Martin's Press books may be purchased for educational, business, or promo-
tional use. For information on bulk purchases, please contact the Macmillan Corpo-
rate and Premium Sales Department at 1-800-221-7945, extension 5442, or write
to specialmarkets@macmillan.com.

First Edition: February 2015

10   9   8   7   6   5   4   3   2   I

To Lynn and Cimarron,
the most incredible wife and daughter
any man could wish for

Contents

If I were an Indian, I often think I would greatly prefer to cast my lot among those of my people adhered to the free open plains rather than to submit to the confined limits of a reservation, there to be the recipient of the blessed benefits of civilization, with its vices thrown in without stint or measure.

—GEORGE ARMSTRONG CUSTER

THE BATTLE OF THE LITTLE BIGHORN
June 25, 1876

Deep Coulee

Medicine Tail Coulee

Custer Hill

Calhoun Hill

Battle Ridge

Keogh Companies F, J, & L

Reno-Benteen Defense Site

Weir Point

Custer's Advance

Gall's Attack

Deep Ravine

Crazy Horse's Attack

Yates/Custer Companies C & E

Little Bighorn River

Reno's Valley Fight

RENO'S VALLEY FIGHT

Reno-Benteen Defense Site

✝ Dr. DeWolf

2nd Lt. Hodgson

✝ Isaiah Dorman

Little Bighorn River

✝ Charley Reynolds

✝ Bloody Knife

Reno's Advance

✝ 1st Lt. McIntosh

Skirmisher Line

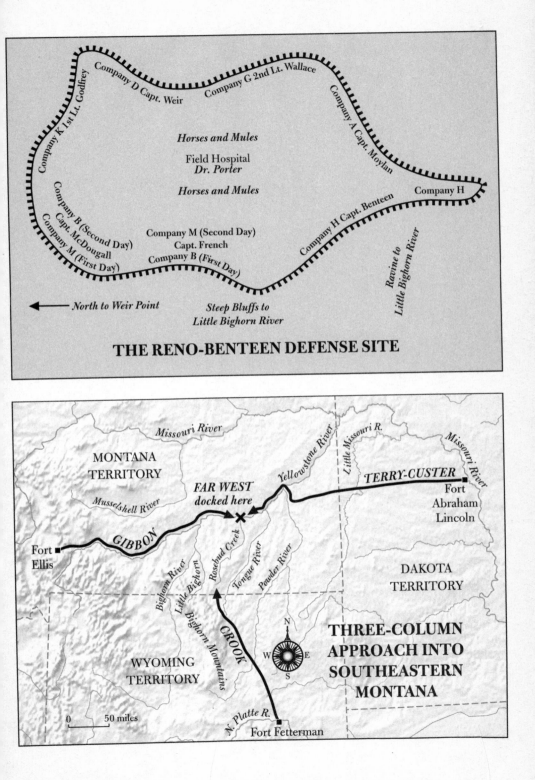

Company D Capt. Weir

Company G 2nd Lt. Wallace

Company K 1st Lt. Godfrey

Company A Capt. Moylan

Horses and Mules

Field Hospital
Dr. Porter

Horses and Mules

Company H

Company B (Second Day)
Capt. McDougall

Company M (First Day)

Company M (Second Day)
Capt. French

Company B (First Day)

Company H Capt. Benteen

Ravine to
Little Bighorn River

← *North to Weir Point*

Steep Bluffs to
Little Bighorn River

THE RENO-BENTEEN DEFENSE SITE

Missouri River

MONTANA
TERRITORY

Yellowstone River

Little Missouri R.

Missouri River

TERRY-CUSTER

Fort
Abraham
Lincoln

Musselshell River

FAR WEST
docked here

✕

GIBBON

Bighorn River

Little Bighorn

Rosebud Creek

Tongue River

Powder River

Fort
Ellis

DAKOTA
TERRITORY

Bighorn Mountains

CROOK

N
W E
S

THREE-COLUMN
APPROACH INTO
SOUTHEASTERN
MONTANA

WYOMING
TERRITORY

0   50 miles

N. Platte R.

Fort Fetterman

The Last Days of
George Armstrong
Custer

Introduction

One of the greatest, if not the most enduring, myths in American history is that George Armstrong Custer made a tactical blunder in the Battle of the Little Bighorn and consequently sacrificed the lives of over two hundred men. This invention has been so oft repeated over the years that it has virtually become fact, and most historians are quite comfortable embracing that position.

What would happen if this litmus test for any aspiring historian was proven to be untrue? What if the battle plan that Custer had designed was actually brilliant and could have—should have—brought about success? Would the world of history tip on its axis and threaten to topple everything sacred if this mistake was revealed?

Brace yourself for the unthinkable. You are now hot on the trail of the holy grail of American history and it is not going to look like you thought it might when finally you come face-to-face with it. At last, here is a book of bare-knuckle history, where you will encounter unexpected ideas, opinions, and conclusions.

This book assuredly is not a read for the thin-skinned or fainthearted who cannot handle blunt statements, harsh judgments, barbed-wire criticism, or graphic details and need their history doled out in warm and fuzzy familiarity. It is time to cast aside this Custer myth and allow the evidence to lead us to a proper and plausible verdict.

The Last Days of George Armstrong Custer provides an enlightening, innovative, exciting, and yes, highly controversial, approach to this battle. Every fact, theory, or accusation has been confronted and put to the test, and every piece of the Little Bighorn puzzle has been slotted into place to reveal the entire picture.

I hope the reader will sense the drama of the moment as I conjure up visions of chilling war whoops, barrages of rifle and pistol fire, sizzling arrows, shouted orders, blinding smoke and dust, cries of panic and agony, thundering horse hooves and terrified whinnies, and—lastly—a deathly silence on a battlefield where over two hundred American soldiers lay dead.

To understand why the death of Custer in the Valley of the Little Bighorn had such an impact on the country that it has been the subject of countless stories and legends, I first briefly examine the events in the life of George Armstrong Custer and the mood of the United States leading up to this historic moment in time. Custer was a dominant national figure of his era, whose popularity shined like a meteor streaking across the sky—until abruptly burning out at age thirty-six. The man and the legend are often one and the same.

What was it really like for those cavalrymen who rode with Custer that day? How could such a tragedy have occurred to such an elite regiment? What really happened on June 25, 1876, in the Valley of the Little Bighorn?

This book is the next best thing to having been there.

One

The Wrath of President Grant

It was May 1876, springtime in Washington, D.C. The trees along Pennsylvania Avenue in the nation's capital were sprouting with fresh green leaves and the beds of flowers that lined the street were blooming with an eye-pleasing explosion of rainbow colors. The White House lawn had been trimmed and manicured with an elegance befitting a royal palace.

No doubt the cottonwoods and wildflowers that grew along the Missouri River near Fort Abraham Lincoln out in Dakota Territory were also showing signs of waking from their long winter's dormancy.

Lieutenant Colonel George Armstrong Custer, however, at the moment failed to appreciate the splendorous emergence of the foliage. If given his choice, he would be enjoying the rites of spring at his post in Dakota Territory. Instead, he anxiously waited in the anteroom outside the Oval Office in the White House for an audience with President of the United States Ulysses S. Grant.

This particular visit by Custer was not for the purpose of reminiscing about Civil War battles or discussing strategies for the upcoming campaign in Montana against the Sioux and Cheyenne. In fact, Custer had not been invited to the White House—and Grant had thus far refused to see him. Custer was not a patient man and the wait must have been torturous, especially given the reason for his presence.

Custer had been unwittingly lured into a dangerous political situation that threatened public humiliation, if not severe damage to his military career. The president had denied the lieutenant colonel permission to accompany the Seventh Cavalry on the upcoming Montana expedition as punishment for a perceived slight. Custer now hoped to persuade the president in a face-to-face meeting to reverse his order and allow Custer to lead his troops on this perilous mission.

Scandal was nothing new to the administration of Ulysses S. Grant. Although the president personally was a man of unquestioned integrity, associates of his had taken advantage of their positions near the seat of power to pad their personal fortunes. One such scandal involved Grant's secretary of war, William W. Belknap. This alleged wrongdoing captured the full attention of the press and the public for one specific reason—a national hero by the name of George Armstrong Custer had been called to testify before the congressional hearing investigating the secretary.

It had been an open and dirty little secret for years around the War Department and western military posts that certain high-ranking government officials were profiting from kickbacks in the awarding of post traderships. Those who had suspicions or were aware of this corruption had simply looked the other way—with one exception.

George Armstrong Custer refused to ignore this criminal activity. He had investigated circumstances at Fort Abraham Lincoln and concluded that this corruption went right to the top—Secretary of War William W. Belknap was conspiring with a local trader in a kickback scheme. Custer, disgusted by his findings, had in effect snubbed the secretary when he visited Fort Abraham Lincoln during the summer of 1875.

The manner in which information of this sort found its way to the *New York Herald* newspaper, an ardent Grant administration critic, would be a matter of speculation. Competing newspapers pointed to the likelihood that Custer, who was a political friend of James Gordon Bennett, Jr., the newspaper's publisher, had been supplying details as an informant—perhaps even paid for his material. This accusation against Custer has never been proven. Regardless, the February 10, 1876, edition of the *Herald* accused Secretary Belknap of selling traderships and receiving kickbacks and further implicated Orville Grant, the president's brother.

This scandal was not particularly new, but revelations in this particular editorial were seized upon by the Democrat-controlled Congress as an ideal opportunity to embarrass Republican president Grant. Heister Clymer, chairman of the House Committee on Expenditures in the War Department, announced that hearings would be held to investigate the matter, which could possibly result in the impeachment of Belknap.

Belknap, without admitting guilt, resigned as secretary of war on March 2, but Clymer continued his hearings. On March 9, Orville Grant admitted that his brother had given him license to four posts in 1874 and he had acted as a middleman in awarding these traderships. In addition, supplies that were supposed to have been delivered to authorized recipients had been diverted and resold elsewhere. The profits had been split; Belknap's share was funneled to his wife.

Custer would have preferred not to testify at the hearing, but he was a high-profile witness whose presence would generate great publicity for the Democrats. His popularity in early 1876 can be evidenced by the fact that the Redpath Lyceum Bureau, a Boston talent agency, had offered him a contract calling for lectures five nights a week for four to five months at two hundred dollars per night. He could earn more than ten times his annual army salary in less than half a year merely by speaking—not to mention adding to his popularity and fame as the country's premier Indian fighter. Custer, however, turned down the lucrative offer because it would interfere with preparations for the upcoming campaign in Montana against hostile Sioux and Cheyenne Indians.

Custer was called before the committee for the first time on March 29. The public paid close attention to what this national hero had to say. His personal integrity was unquestioned, and his experience with the Cheyenne, Sioux, and other tribes gave him a credibility unmatched by any other army field officer. He candidly related that soon after he had assumed command at Fort Lincoln he had requested the removal of the trader S. A. Dickey for various infractions, including introducing alcohol to the Indians. The new trader, Robert C. Siep, subsequently had confessed to Custer that he had been delivering two-thirds of his profits to Belknap. Custer's concern was that this practice resulted in increased prices on goods at frontier posts, which caused a hardship on the troops.

Contrary to popular belief, an examination of the transcript does not show that Custer directly implicated Orville Grant by name in the scheme but does reveal that he only hinted at the possibility of complicity. His hearsay testimony concluded on April 4, and Custer at that time expected to return to Fort Lincoln and prepare his troops for the upcoming campaign in Montana against the Sioux and Cheyenne.

Although Custer's testimony provided more in publicity than substance, he was not without critics. Cynics pointed out that Custer saw nothing contradictory about fighting Indians as well as those who cheated them. Editorials seeking any reason to discredit Custer questioned his intentions when defending the Indians against being cheated by the same government that was now prepared to go against them in battle.

The most damaging blow, however, was delivered by his commander in chief. President Grant was infuriated by Custer's testimony—Belknap was a close personal friend of the president. Grant decided to punish his impudent officer by denying him permission to lead the Seventh Cavalry on the spring campaign. And so Custer sat outside the Oval Office, hoping that the president would at least hear an explanation that would satisfy him and restore Custer to duty.

Custer, to say the least, was devastated by the decision of the president to deny his participation in the campaign. While the Seventh Cavalry prepared for the march—temporarily under the command of Major Marcus A. Reno—Custer marked time in the White House anteroom, uninvited, feeling lost and confused as he hoped for an audience with Grant.

This forlorn and humbling state of mind may have provoked thoughts within Custer of the days when he did not have such prestige and popularity and to consider that the President of the United States would even acknowledge him would be regarded as an unattainable dream. He was a perfect example of what could be called nothing less than a truly remarkable American success story. He had been born of low social standing and had risen by his own ambition and abilities to the point where everyone in the country recognized his name and most had a favorable impression of him.

George Armstrong Custer had entered the world on December 5, 1839, in the back room on the first floor of a house in New Rumley, Harrison County, Ohio, the first child of Emanuel Henry and Maria Ward Kirkpatrick Custer. Although he was formally named George Armstrong, the family would call him Armstrong. As he learned to talk, his childlike way of pronouncing his name, "Autie," became his nickname.

Both of Armstrong's parents had lost a spouse and each had brought two children to their marriage, which was beset by tragedy in the early years. Within five months of his marriage to Maria in February 1836, Emanuel's three-year-old son, John, died. Two other children born to the couple died in infancy before five healthy children, beginning with George Armstrong, survived. Three boys followed: Nevin Johnson, Thomas Ward, and Boston; and later a daughter, Margaret Emma (Maggie).

Emanuel, the village blacksmith, had helped found the New Rumley Methodist Church, served as a prominent member of the New Rumley Invincibles, the local militia, regarded his fidelity to the Democratic Party to be as sacred as his church membership, and had been New Rumley's justice of the peace for twelve years.

Maria was often referred to as being in ill health or an invalid for much of her life. It is probable that Armstrong, who was an only child for his first three years, was her favorite. Custer adored his mother throughout his life and never quite severed that invisible umbilical cord that linked them together. Custer's future wife, Libbie, once related that the hardest trial of her husband's life was parting with his mother. Libbie told about how when parting Armstrong would leave his mother's side and throw himself into their carriage in tears.

The Custer family was not by any means well-to-do, but Emanuel and Maria compensated for the lack of material possessions by creating a home full of love and family unity. The children from the three families bonded together with loyalty and affection, and the Custer household was said to be always in a happy uproar. This unrestrained atmosphere was engendered by Emanuel, who acted like a big kid when he was around his children. He would romp, wrestle, and play aggressively, making them the target of his practical jokes, which became a lifelong practice between them, and dodging their mischief in return.

From an early age, Autie enjoyed hanging around his father's blacksmith shop listening to the friendly banter and watching his father work. The boy would test ride the newly shod horses, an experience that enabled him to develop an early skill in horsemanship. Young Autie would also attend militia musters and parades, always wearing the little uniform made especially for him and carrying a toy musket or a wooden sword. Emanuel would show off his son by having Autie execute the manual of arms.

The Custer children attended school in New Rumley, and Autie became known as a boy who loved pranks and was not afraid to take chances. Armstrong may have been a rather bad boy in school, but he always completed his work and valued learning.

In 1849, Emanuel sold his shop in town and moved his family to an eighty-acre farm on the outskirts of New Rumley, where Armstrong began attending Creal School. For reasons unknown—perhaps financial—Armstrong was soon apprenticed to a furniture maker in Cadiz. This arrangement did not work out, and the boy was sent to live with his half sister, Lydia Ann Reed. Ann, as she was known, had married David Reed, a drayman, farmer, and real estate investor, and had subsequently moved to Monroe, Michigan. Ann became a surrogate mother and trusted confidante to Custer, a relationship that would continue throughout his life.

Armstrong attended New Dublin School, then Alfred Stebbins's Young Men's Academy in Monroe. His deskmate at the academy told about Armstrong's penchant for sneaking adventure novels into class and reading them instead of his textbooks. His favorite titles included *Tom Burke of "Ours,"* *Jack Hinton,* and *Charles O'Malley, the Irish Dragoon*—the latter a childhood favorite of future Seventh Cavalry member Captain Myles W. Keogh.

The young man was hardly a bookworm, however, but a spirited and fun-loving youngster who was a natural-born leader. He was remembered by the minister of the Methodist church in Monroe as the main instigator of mischief and minor disruptions during services.

At age sixteen, Armstrong returned to New Rumley and attended McNeely

Normal School in Hopedale, where he became quite a favorite with the young ladies. One classmate remembered that Custer "was kind and generous to his friends; bitter and implacable towards his enemies."

Armstrong interrupted his own education in 1856 to teach at the Beech Point School in Athens Township for twenty-eight dollars a month. The young teacher was known as a "big-hearted, whole-souled fellow," which made him extremely popular.

Armstrong, however, did not intend to teach forever. He arrived at the conclusion that—due to his family's poor economic situation—he would require some sort of assistance in order to further his education. To that end, he wrote to the district's Republican representative, John A. Bingham, and requested an appointment to the U.S. Military Academy at West Point.

This audacious act demonstrates the determination that would be Custer's lifelong hallmark. The odds that a son of an outspoken Democrat such as Emanuel could gain political patronage from a Republican were beyond comprehension.

Many stories have been written about why Armstrong Custer was even considered for such a prestigious appointment from a man whose politics were contrary to those of the staunchly Democratic Custer family. Bingham later related—after Custer had become famous—that the "honesty" of the young man's letter "captivated" him. Perhaps that was true, but another story appears to have gained more credibility. Historians have speculated that the father of a girl with whom Custer was romantically involved used his influence with the congressman in order to remove Custer from his daughter's life.

While teaching at Beech Point, the seventeen-year-old Custer had boarded at the home of a prosperous local farmer and fallen in love with his daughter, Mary Holland. The couple traded correspondence—he even wrote her a poem that began: "I've seen and kissed that crimson lip"—but Mary's father was not thrilled in the least about having this happy-go-lucky amateur poet as a family member and likely set out to remove Custer from his daughter's life.

Regardless of the circumstances, in January 1857 seventeen-year-old George Armstrong Custer received notification that he had been awarded an appointment to West Point that would take effect in June. Emanuel mortgaged his farm in order to raise the two hundred dollars necessary to pay for his son's expenses and admission fee.

On July 1, 1857, Armstrong Custer and sixty-seven other plebes reported for duty as the class of 1862 at the U.S. Military Academy at West Point, New York.

The blue-eyed Armstrong Custer stood nearly six feet tall, weighed about 170 pounds, and was called Fanny by his classmates due to his wavy, blond hair and fair complexion. Students were organized into sections according to their academic abilities, and Armstrong found himself for the most part among the Southerners and Westerners, who were generally academically inferior to the New Englanders.

Therefore, Custer's closest friends were those with Southern roots—Kentuckians William Dunlop and George Watts, Mississippian John "Gimlet" Lea, Georgian Pierce M. B. Young, and Lafayette "Lafe" Lane, a Southern sympathizer from Oregon. Custer's best friend was Virginia-born Texan Thomas L. Rosser, who roomed next door.

Custer's fun-loving nature was immediately at odds with the strict Academy code of conduct, which was calculated by a system of demerits—called skins by the cadets—issued for various offenses. One hundred skins in a six-month period would be grounds for dismissal from the Academy.

At the end of his first year, Fanny Custer ranked fifty-second in mathematics and fifty-seventh in English—in a class of sixty-two. His placement was due in part to the fact that he had accumulated 151 demerits, the highest number in his class. His less-than-glowing academic record was not the result of a lack of intelligence on his part, rather his propensity for pranks and devil-may-care attitude. Fellow cadet Peter Michie wrote: "Custer was always in trouble with the authorities. He had more fun, gave his friends more anxiety, walked more tours of extra guard, and came nearer to being dismissed more often than any other cadet I have ever known."

Although his "boyish, but harmless frolics kept him in constant hot water," one area in which Custer excelled was popularity and leadership. "He was beyond a doubt," one cadet wrote, "the most popular man in his class." Another reported: "West Point has had many a character to deal with, but it may be a question whether it ever had a cadet so exuberant, one who cared so little for its serious attempts to elevate and burnish, or one on whom its tactical officers kept their eyes so constantly and unsympathetically searching as upon Custer. And yet how we all loved him."

Custer, however, was disciplined enough when his total of demerits would reach levels of dismissal to behave for long periods of time or choose to work off minor infractions by walking extra guard duty. Also to his credit, he was never assessed a skin for fighting or for an altercation with another cadet throughout his West Point career.

A check of his four-year record reveals, among others, offenses for making a boisterous noise in his sink, talking and laughing in class, throwing snowballs outside, throwing bread in the mess hall, being late for parade, swinging his arms in formation, not keeping his eyes to the front, throwing stones on post, not properly carrying his musket during drill, having cooking utensils in the chimney, and gazing about in ranks.

Armstrong's second year showed little improvement over the first. He accumulated 192 demerits—only 8 short of the 200 that would have resulted in his dismissal. His class standing was fifty-sixth out of sixty. He did, however, prove his skill as a horseman by, according to tradition, executing the highest jump of a hurdle ever at the Academy while slashing at a dummy with his saber.

Custer's third year at West Point was another poor performance. He earned 191 demerits, 1 fewer than the preceding year, and ranked at the bottom of his class.

For the 1860–61 academic year at the Academy, Congress voted to reduce the school term from five to four years. The reason for this change was the threat of war between the North and the South, as new officers might be required to fight to preserve the Union. And, indeed, the Southern cadets vowed to resign from West Point when their states seceded. "You cannot imagine," Custer wrote to sister Ann Reed, "how sorry I will be to see this happen as the majority of my friends and all my roommates except one have been from the South."

The formation of the Confederate States of America in February 1861 had a profound effect on the cadets. This separation of loyalties became evident at the Academy with impromptu good-natured contests of regional pride. As winter turned into spring, however, these rivalries more often than not escalated into arguments that resulted in blows being exchanged.

On April 12, when Southern artillery opened up on Fort Sumter in Charleston Harbor, thirty-seven cadets, including Custer's best friend, Tom Rosser, departed from the Academy to offer their services to the Confederacy. In spite of his friendship with Southern classmates, Custer vowed to honor the oath of allegiance to which he had sworn upon entering West Point and offer his services to the governor of Ohio.

The class of 1861 was graduated early on May 6. Custer's class, which was subjected to an abbreviated curriculum that would supplant the final year of studies, was scheduled to graduate on June 24.

Perhaps amazingly to many instructors and fellow cadets, Fanny Custer had satisfactorily completed his studies and was commissioned a second lieutenant. He had racked up an additional 192 demerits during the year, which gave him an impressive four-year total of 726. Nevertheless, the class clown who excelled in horsemanship and athletic prowess but lagged behind in academics had overcome his own outrageous antics to qualify for graduation from West Point.

Perhaps predictably, Custer's military career was in trouble before the ink had dried on his diploma. On June 29, he was Officer of the Guard when a fistfight broke out between two cadets. Inexplicably, Custer disregarded his duty to break up the fight and instead told the assembled crowd to "stand back, boys; let's have a fair fight."

The Officer of the Day, First Lieutenant William B. Hazen, a West Point instructor and future Custer critic, happened along and placed Custer under arrest. While his classmates departed from the Academy and proceeded to Washington for further orders, Custer was detained to await a court-martial, which would convene on July 5.

On that date, nine officers listened to evidence pertaining to charges of neglect of duty and "conduct to the prejudice of good order and military discipline." Custer was found guilty on both counts. His punishment, however, was the ruling that he only be "reprimanded in orders." In other words, a black mark would be listed in his service record book, but he would suffer no other penalty.

Under normal circumstances, Custer probably would have been dismissed from the service. "Custer's Luck," the term that Custer and others would employ to characterize the favorable events that occurred to him throughout his life, had saved his military career. He was now free to apply the lessons that he had learned at the Academy on the battlefields of the Civil War.

And now, as Custer impatiently whiled away his time in the Oval Office anteroom that May 1876 day, he was certainly disappointed in his treatment by Grant. Custer may even have experienced a twinge of bitterness or resentment that the president had apparently dismissed him as being less than a significant and irreplaceable cavalry commander.

Aside from Grant, William T. Sherman, and Philip H. Sheridan, few active officers serving in the Army of the Potomac had more to do with bringing that war to a conclusion than George Armstrong Custer. He had risked his life on countless occasions and met every seemingly impossible challenge with heroic actions meant to secure victory for the Union. The Civil War had defined him as a leader of men and made him a national hero, and now Grant threatened to tarnish that stellar reputation over an honest testimony. Custer would not have even tendered the notion of speaking out against the president, however. He would be the loyal army officer no matter the cost.

For the time being, however, George Armstrong Custer could only cool his heels and hope that the president would take into consideration that service in the Civil War that had propelled him from an ordinary soldier to a genuine American hero.

Two

━━◆◉◆━━

Glorious War

I n his time, George Armstrong Custer was not a symbol of defeat but a national hero on a grand scale due to his amazing achievements in the Civil War. He captured the first enemy battle flag taken by the Union army and accepted the Confederate white flag of surrender at Appomattox. In between those notable events exists a series of intrepid acts of almost unbelievable proportion as he personally led electrifying cavalry charges that earned the flamboyant general the admiration of his men and captured the fancy of newspaper reporters and the public.

Custer's active military career, however, had a somewhat inauspicious beginning. Nevertheless his ambition and flair for being in the thick of the fight was always evident. On July 21, 1861, just three days out of West Point, Second Lieutenant Custer rode out to join G Company, Second Cavalry, at Bull Run. In his only action of the battle, he was cited for bravery when he turned an every-man-for-himself retreat, which had blocked a bridge across Cub Run, into an orderly formation.

Due to his West Point education Custer was subsequently assigned to the staffs of several minor generals while new army commander Major General George B. McClellan attempted to mold raw recruits into a capable fighting force. Although serving as an aide-de-camp, Custer constantly sought out opportunities to see action.

In early May 1862, during the Siege of Yorktown, Custer served as a military observer from a hot-air balloon. He would ascend with field glasses, map, and notebook and count enemy campfires while sketching the locations of gun emplacements and tent positions.

On May 5, he was serving on the staff of General Winfield Scott Hancock, whose troops were engaged with Confederate soldiers at Williamsburg. The Union soldiers had been formed on a skirmisher line, and when the Rebels came within striking distance a bayonet charge was ordered. Hancock's troops hesitated—until Custer spurred his horse and burst from their midst. The Union soldiers obediently followed this gallant one-man charge, which resulted in routing the Confederates into retreat. Custer returned to friendly lines after single-handedly capturing an enemy officer, five enlisted men, and—the real trophy—the first Confederate battle flag taken in the war by the Army of the Potomac.

Armstrong Custer maintained unswerving loyalty to the Union but at times during the war demonstrated great compassion and generosity toward Southerners—especially his former West Point classmates who had chosen to join the Army of Northern Virginia.

In one instance, one of the Confederate prisoners taken at Williamsburg in May 1862 was Armstrong Custer's former classmate and friend Captain John "Gimlet" Lea, who had been badly wounded in the leg. Upon seeing Custer, Lea cried and hugged him. The two young men then exchanged information about classmates on both sides of the conflict. Custer received permission to remain with Lea and care for him for two days. Upon leaving, Custer gave Gimlet much-needed stockings and some money. Lea reciprocated by writing in Custer's notebook that, if captured, Armstrong should be afforded good treatment by the Southerners.

Later that month, Custer participated in a daring daylight reconnaissance along the Chickahominy River by guiding a raiding party to its objective. According to the official report "he was the first to cross the stream, the first to open fire, and one of the last to leave the field."

His heroic actions came to the attention of General McClellan, who requested Custer's presence. At that time, Custer accepted a prestigious position on McClellan's staff as aide-de-camp with the brevet rank of captain effective June 5.

McClellan would come to greatly depend on the adventurous nature of Custer, who was already a McClellan admirer, and their relationship flourished. "His head was always clear in danger," McClellan later wrote, "and he always brought me clear and intelligible reports."

When Custer arrived in Williamsburg in August 1862 with McClellan's staff, he learned that his Confederate friend Gimlet Lea was on parole and recuperating in that town. Lea was about to marry a young woman who had nursed him back to health in her family's home. Custer, dressed in his blue uniform, served as groomsman during the ceremony and proudly stood beside his gray-clad friend.

Soon after, McClellan, a known critic of the policies established by the Lincoln administration, was removed from his role as army commander on November 7, 1862.

Custer, who was devastated by the move, returned to Monroe, Michigan, to await further orders. This respite from the war, however, provided him the opportunity to become acquainted with Monroe resident Elizabeth Clift "Libbie" Bacon, with whom he would fall in love.

If first impressions were lasting impressions, Libbie Bacon, the beautiful and intelligent daughter of Judge Daniel Bacon, a leading citizen of Monroe, Michigan, certainly would never have become involved with George Armstrong Custer. She and her father had witnessed an episode in October 1861 when Custer and an army companion, both drunk and boisterous, had staggered past their house. And although Custer and Miss Bacon had not been acquainted at that time, "that awful day," as she called it, would indeed affect their future relationship.

Armstrong had been on leave, staying at the Reed home. He was greeted as a local war hero and enthusiastically immersed himself in the social scene. The popular officer could be found on most nights romancing an adoring young lady or carousing with friends and other soldiers on furlough at any one of the establishments that served alcohol and the merriment of music.

On one particular occasion Custer had imbibed to excess at a local tavern. He and an army companion staggered through the streets of Monroe on their merry way to Armstrong's half sister's house. The soldiers created quite a ruckus as they loudly laughed and sang without regard for the delicate ears of those within listening distance of the boisterous serenade.

The two revelers happened to pass the Bacon residence, where they were observed by Judge Daniel Bacon and his nineteen-year-old daughter, Libbie. Custer was unaware of it at the time, but Libbie Bacon would later in the year become the object of his affections and this drunken episode would not be forgotten by Libbie *or her father.*

Ann Reed, a woman of deep religious convictions, was appalled by her half brother's condition. Once home, Ann—with her Bible in hand—took Armstrong into her bedroom and delivered what must have been a temperance lecture for the ages. She made him promise before God that he would never touch another drop of intoxicating beverage. Her efforts were successful. From that day forth, Custer never again touched alcohol, not even wine at formal dinner parties.

Elizabeth Clift "Libbie" Bacon was born in Monroe, Michigan, on April 8, 1842. Her father, Daniel Stanton Bacon, was a descendent of the Plymouth colony and at one time or another had been a farmer, a schoolteacher, a member of the Territorial Legislature, a losing candidate for Michigan lieutenant governor in 1837, a probate judge, and a director of a bank and railroad. In September 1837, at the age of thirty-eight, Judge Bacon married twenty-three-year-old Eleanor Sophia Page of Grand Rapids by way of Rutland, Vermont, the daughter of a nursery owner who had been educated in one of the finest seminaries in the East.

Daniel and Sophia, as she was known, would have four children—two girls, Harriet and Sophia, died in infancy and a boy, Edward, died of a childhood disease at the age of eight. That left little Libbie to be doted upon. She was raised in an idyllic traditional American setting—living in an imposing white house with green shutters surrounded by a well-kept lawn, guarded by a white picket fence, and towered over by stately elm trees.

When Libbie was twelve, however, her mother passed away from a disease that, according to Judge Bacon, the "physicians were unacquainted with." The judge had promised his wife on her deathbed that he would properly care for their daughter. To that end, he enrolled Libbie in the Young Ladies' Seminary and Collegiate Institute—commonly known as "Boyd's Seminary" after its founder, Reverend Erasmus J. Boyd. Libbie graduated in the spring of 1862, the valedictorian of her class. At this time she was a willowy 5 feet 4 inches tall with chestnut-brown hair and light blue-gray eyes—and was regarded as the prettiest girl in Monroe, Michigan.

Armstrong Custer had been an occasional resident of Monroe, but due to their differing social levels the refined Miss Bacon and the son of the town smithy had not met as children. Their formal meeting came at an 1862 Thanksgiving party at Boyd's Seminary. Custer was instantly smitten with Libbie—claiming he dreamed about her that night and that it was love at first sight. He courted her relentlessly—like a frontal assault cavalry charge.

Libbie, however, was not too certain about him—after all, she was not exactly wanting for suitors. Judge Bacon noticed Custer's growing interest and decided to put an end to the relationship by making Libbie promise to not see Custer again or write to him after he returned to duty in the Civil War. He did not desire his daughter to marry a common military man, especially one who had demonstrated a drinking problem as evidenced by the display Bacon had witnessed in October 1861.

Custer, however, pledged his undying love for her. Libbie rebuffed him but later wrote in her diary: "He is noble, brave and generous and he loves, I believe, with an intensity that few know of or as few ever can love. . . . He tells me he would sacrifice every earthly hope to gain my love and I tell him if I could I would give it to him. . . . Oh, Love, love, how many are made miserable as well as happy by all the powerful influence."

On May 6, 1863, Custer was assigned as aide-de-camp to General Alfred Pleasonton, the commander of a cavalry division. The Custer–Pleasonton relationship developed into a mutual admiration society in which Custer claimed, "I do not believe a father could love his son more than Genl. Pleasonton loves me."

Of course, the one love that Custer desperately wanted, that of Libbie Bacon, waited back in Monroe. He vowed to set out to find some way to impress her father that he was worthy of her hand.

At this time Custer commenced an effort to gain a colonelcy of one of the regiments of the Michigan Cavalry Brigade. His application, although endorsed by various prominent generals, was denied by the Republican governor of Michigan, who considered that Custer was a Democrat and, worse yet, a "McClellan man." McClellan had continued to criticize the Lincoln administration and was rumored (rightfully so) to be the Democratic nominee in the 1864 presidential election.

At the June 9 Brandy Station battle—the first and largest true cavalry engagement of the war—Custer, as a personal representative of Pleasonton, rode in the spearhead of the surprise attack. Legend has it that he distinguished himself that day by assuming de facto command of three brigades after the death of Colonel Benjamin Davis. Union horsemen proved that day that they could compete with the legendary Confederate cavalry, and Custer was personally cited for bravery after having two horses shot out from under him and receiving a bullet in his boot while capturing artillery pieces.

Eight days later at Aldie, Custer was credited with a daring charge when his horse bolted and carried him through and around enemy lines, which required him to slay two Rebel cavalrymen in order to extricate himself. The press dismissed Custer's protestations that he was simply a rider on a runaway horse and embellished the tale, to the delight of the public.

On June 29, 1863, to the surprise of everyone including himself, twenty-three-year-old George Armstrong Custer—upon recommendation from Pleasonton—was unexpectedly promoted to brigadier general. Pleasonton wanted men "with the proper dash to command cavalry," and Custer fit that description perfectly. He had leapfrogged captain, major, lieutenant colonel, and colonel to gain this prestigious rank. In addition, he was assigned command of the Michigan Brigade, which was part of the First Division under Hugh Judson Kilpatrick, a man Custer would come to detest due to his recklessness. Custer had attempted to become colonel of one of the Michigan regiments; now he commanded them all. General Pleasonton silenced critics of the promotion by saying, "Custer is the best cavalry general in the world."

Upon seeing his new commander for the first time on June 30, 1863, Captain James M. Kidd wrote:

Looking at him closely, this is what I saw: An officer superbly mounted who sat his charger as if to manor born. Tall, lithe, active, muscular, straight as an Indian and as quick in his movements, he had the fair complexion of a school girl. He was clad in a suit of black velvet, elaborately trimmed with gold lace, which ran down the outer seams of his trousers, and almost covered the sleeves of his cavalry jacket. The wide collar of a blue navy shirt was turned down over the collar of his velvet jacket, and a necktie of brilliant crimson was tied in a graceful knot at the throat, the long ends falling carelessly in front. The double rows of buttons on his breast were arranged in groups of twos, indicating the rank of brigadier general. A soft, black hat with wide brim adorned with a gilt cord, and rosette encircling a silver star, was worn turned down on one side giving him a rakish air. His golden hair fell in graceful luxuriance nearly or quite to his shoulders, and his upper lip was garnished with a blonde mustache. A sword and belt, gilt spurs and top boots completed his unique outfit.

This would be the distinctive uniform that the dashing General Custer would be known by for the remainder of the war. His scarlet necktie became the defining element of the uniform, which made him known by sight to every news correspondent, Confederate soldier, and, more important to him, by his own men.

It should be noted that Custer has been singled out—and indeed mocked—for his ostentatious uniform. Many and most officers were known to design their own outlandish uniforms; Custer was no exception. Confederate cavalry commander Jeb Stuart, for example, favored an ostrich plume in his hat.

Brigadier General Custer made a memorable debut as a commander several days later at the Battle of Gettysburg. In fact, the argument can be made that Custer saved the day at Gettysburg on July 3, 1863, when he outgeneraled Jeb Stuart to change the course of that battle.

With the rallying cry of "C'mon, you Wolverines!" Custer twice led bold, bloody charges of his greatly outnumbered command that effectively denied Stuart access to the Union rear, which the Rebel legend had planned to attack simultaneously with General George Pickett's charge to the front. This one-two punch of Pickett and Stuart that had been devised by General Robert E. Lee would have placed the Union in a dire situation—if not for the heroic actions that day of George Armstrong Custer. Instead, Pickett's charge was a monumental failure and the Union held the day.

The significance of that battle east of Gettysburg has been all but ignored by modern-day historians, likely due to prejudices and controversies from the Boy General's later career and portrayals that have led to him being perceived as a symbol of defeat. Nonetheless, the bravery and leadership skills Custer demonstrated on that day are worthy of a prominent place in the history of the Gettysburg battle—perhaps even as the turning point—as well as in the history of the Civil War. But that was only the beginning for a young man destined for greatness.

Civil War officers were expected to motivate and inspire their troops under fire by example—bravery was thought to be contagious. George Armstrong Custer, however, had elevated that responsibility to a higher level. Custer had proven during the Gettysburg Campaign that, contrary to those who had questioned Pleasonton's judgment in promoting the twenty-three-year-old to brigadier general, he was quite capable of commanding a brigade. In addition to that, he had gained the admiration of his men with his propensity for leading charges rather than simply directing movements from a safe position in the rear. This one distinct trait had instilled within his troops a confidence that if Custer, a general, had the nerve to charge into the blazing guns of the enemy then there was no reason to believe that if they followed victory would not be within their grasp.

Edwin Havens of the Seventh Michigan described Custer in a letter dated July 9, 1863: "He is a glorious fellow, full of energy, quick to plan and bold to execute, and with us has never failed in any attempt he has yet made." Another proud Wolverine praised: "Our boy-general never says, 'Go in, men!' HE says, with that whoop and yell of his, 'Come on, boys!' and in we go, you bet." Captain S. H. Ballard of the Sixth Michigan said: "The command perfectly idolized Custer. When Custer made a charge, he was the first sabre that struck for he was always ahead." Another said that Custer "was not afraid to fight like a private soldier . . . and that he was ever in front and would never ask them to go where he would not lead." Lieutenant James Christiancy wrote: "Through all that sharp and heavy firing the General gave his orders as though conducting a parade or review, so cool and indifferent that he inspired us all with something of his coolness and courage."

The Michigan Brigade was so impressed that they had whipped Jeb Stuart at Gettysburg that they began to emulate their commander by adopting Custer's trademark scarlet neckties, which he wore to make himself conspicuous to his troops during a battle.

The young, dashing Boy General with the yellow curls and outlandish uniform certainly made for excellent copy. Newspaper and magazine correspondents saw a rising star, and the Custer legend was born.

Eleven days later, at Falling Waters, Custer's brigade nipped at Lee's retreating heels and captured fifteen hundred prisoners and three battle flags. An admiring private from the Fifth Michigan describing the hand-to-hand combat in that affair marveled when he saw Custer "plunge a saber into the belly of a rebel who was trying to kill him. You can guess how bravely soldiers fight for such a general." Custer continued to distinguish himself throughout 1863, particularly at Culpeper, where he received his lone war wound—shrapnel in the foot.

As Armstrong Custer was gaining national fame as a general and commander of the Michigan Brigade, Libbie Bacon had obeyed her father's wishes and refused to see or accept mail from Custer. That silence would be broken, however, when Annette "Nettie" Humphrey, a friend of Libbie's and the future wife of Custer's adjutant Jacob Greene, emerged as a go-between to pass information between the couple.

Libbie gradually fell in love with the gallant General Custer, and at a masquerade ball at the Humphrey house on September 28, 1863, she promised to marry him if he could gain her father's consent. Custer composed the most important letter of his life and asked that he simply be permitted to correspond with Libbie. The judge relented—no doubt partially due to Custer's growing fame—and granted Libbie permission to write. Her first letter began: "My more than friend—at last—Am I a little glad to write you some of the thoughts I cannot control?"

The romance escalated to the point that Custer wrote to Judge Bacon in late 1863 asking for Libbie's hand in marriage. The judge replied that he might ponder the matter for weeks or even months. Custer persisted with a frontal assault worthy of any cavalry charge and finally received the judge's blessing. He then persuaded Libbie to marry him at the soonest possible moment.

At 8:00 P.M. on February 9, 1864, George Armstrong Custer and Elizabeth Clift Bacon were united in marriage at the First Presbyterian Church, which still stands, in a storybook wedding with a standing-room-only congregation of witnesses. Reverend Erasmus J. Boyd, who served as principal at the seminary where Libbie had attended school, performed the ceremony, assisted by Reverend D. C. Mattoon.

Custer, with hair cut short and wearing his dress uniform, chose his adjutant Jacob Greene as best man. Libbie wore a traditional gown, described by her cousin, Rebecca Richmond, as "a rich white rep silk with deep points and extensive trail, bertha of point lace; veil floated back from a bunch of orange blossoms fixed above the brow." Libbie was given away by her father, who later boasted, "It was said to be the most splendid wedding ever seen in the State." The judge also said: "Elizabeth has married entirely to her own satisfaction and to mine. No man could wish for a son-in-law more highly thought of."

The wedding party was whisked away in sleighs with bells jingling for a reception in the Bacon parlor that was attended by more than three hundred guests. The judge provided a generous buffet of delicacies that featured tubs of ice cream.

The bridal party—four couples—boarded a train at midnight and arrived in Cleveland at nine the following morning. After an afternoon reception and an evening party hosted by friends, Armstrong and Libbie traveled to Buffalo, then on to Rochester, where they attended a performance of *Uncle Tom's Cabin*. The honeymoon continued with calling on Libbie's upstate New York relatives and a trip down the Hudson River to visit West Point, on to New York City, and finally to Washington, D.C., where the Custers dined with Michigan members of Congress and other dignitaries.

Custer then returned to duty to command a dangerous diversionary mission into enemy territory during the ill-fated Kilpatrick-Dahlgren Raid on Richmond. The plan called for a force commanded by Hugh Judson Kilpatrick to free prisoners held in Richmond as well as cause general mayhem. Meanwhile, Custer would draw Jeb Stuart's forces away from the Confederate capital, a mission he capably executed. The raid was a miserable failure, however, costing the Union 340 men killed, wounded, or captured. Papers found on Ulric Dahlgren, who was killed, instructed the raiders to burn the city and kill President Jefferson Davis. The Southerners were incensed by this plan, which inspired within them a renewed fighting spirit. Custer was commended for his actions, which was little consolation.

Major General Philip Sheridan assumed command of the cavalry and convinced Grant to change the mission of his force from support to active operations. Grant obliged, and Sheridan planned as his first mission the elimination of the legendary Jeb Stuart, whose cavalry had been such a thorn in the side of the Union.

May 1864 saw Custer victories in the Wilderness, at Beaver Dam Station, and on May 11 at Yellow Tavern he personally led the charge that resulted in the death of Jeb Stuart. An elated Sheridan, who would be Custer's mentor throughout his army career, was compelled to say, "Custer is the ablest man in the Cavalry Corps."

Custer's momentum was somewhat slowed the following month at Trevilian Station. Custer always exhibited an aggressive spirit of competition when facing any of them across the field of battle, his best friend, Tom Rosser, in particular. But it was Rosser who bested Custer at the June 11–12 battle of Trevilian Station. Custer's brigade became trapped between two Rebel divisions—"on the inside of a living triangle"—struck from behind by Rosser. Custer eventually fought his way out but left behind in Rosser's possession his adjutant and his cook, as well as the trappings of his headquarters—wagons, bedding, field desk, clothing, cooking outfit, spare horse, his commission to general, his letters from Libbie, and an ambrotype of her.

Custer was not demoralized by the loss, however. After this battle, Custer wrote to Nettie Humphrey, who would surely pass the information on to Libbie Bacon: "Oh, could you but have seen some of the charges that were made! While thinking of them I cannot but exclaim 'Glorious War!'"

In August, Sheridan was dispatched to the Shenandoah Valley to face Lieutenant General Jubal A. Early's Confederate army. Custer continued to reap glory and respect for his brilliantly executed charges and field generalship during this campaign—time and again exploiting the enemy's weaknesses with snap decisions—particularly at Winchester, where he brazenly led five hundred of his Michigan "Wolverines" against sixteen hundred entrenched Confederates and emerged with seven hundred prisoners.

On September 30, 1864, he was awarded his second star and command of the Third Cavalry Division.

At Tom's Brook on October 9, Custer exacted revenge on his friend Tom Rosser. Custer with twenty-five hundred horsemen faced Rosser's thirty-five hundred troops, who were entrenched on the high ground. When all was ready for battle, Custer—in an act of bravado of which legends are made—rode out in front of his command where he could be observed by both sides. He removed his broad-brimmed hat and swept it across himself in a salute as if to say, "May the best man win."

Custer charged with eight regiments to the front and three in a surprise attack on Rosser's left flank. Rosser's men could not withstand the pressure and were forced into a disorganized retreat. Custer's horsemen chased the fleeing Rebels for ten to twelve miles. Rosser had not simply been defeated; he had been humiliated.

To add insult to injury, Custer had captured Rosser's headquarters wagon. Custer got back the ambrotype of Libbie that had been captured at Trevilian Station and appropriated a pet squirrel that had belonged to Rosser. That night in camp, Custer adorned himself in Rosser's baggy, ill-fitting uniform and treated his men to a good laugh. He later added to Rosser's humiliation by writing and asking that his old friend advise his tailor to shorten the coattails for a better fit.

Custer's cavalrymen fought on with distinction. Ten days later at Cedar Creek they captured forty-five pieces of artillery, thirteen battle flags, and swarms of prisoners. One reporter wrote of that victory: "Custer, young as he is, displayed judgment worthy of Napoleon." In March 1865 at Waynesboro, he crushed the remnants of Jubal Early's forces, capturing sixteen hundred prisoners, eleven artillery pieces, over two hundred wagons laden with supplies, and seventeen battle flags.

Custer received his third star as a major general on March 29, 1864. He then led his division to decisive victories at Dinwiddie Court House, Five Forks, and Namozine Church.

The April 6, 1865, battle of Sayler's Creek, in which Custer played a major role, had been a smashing victory for the Union. Over nine thousand Confederates had been taken prisoner—more Americans than had ever before or after been captured at one time on this continent.

Custer formed his division the following morning for the march just as a long line of Confederate prisoners straggled past on their way to the rear. In a show of respect for his vanquished enemy, Custer ordered the band to play "Dixie" for these brave men, which evoked cheers from the Southern boys.

On the morning of April 9, 1865, Custer had pushed within sight of Appomattox Court House when a Confederate major arrived at his headquarters under a flag of truce with a request from Robert E. Lee to suspend hostilities. The Civil War had ended on Custer's doorstep.

That afternoon, General Lee presented himself to General Grant at the home of Wilmer McLean to surrender his army. Custer could be found either out in the yard or on the porch of McLean's house renewing acquaintances with his Confederate friends while the two commanders retired inside and signed the surrender document.

When the ceremony had concluded, the small oval-shaped pine table upon which Grant had written the terms of the surrender was purchased for twenty dollars in gold by General Phil Sheridan. The next day, the cavalry commander handed the table to Custer as a gift to Libbie Custer. Sheridan enclosed a note, which read: "My dear Madam, I respectfully present to you the small writing table on which the conditions for the surrender of the Army of Northern Virginia were written by Lt. General Grant—and permit me to say, Madam, that there is scarcely an individual in our service who has contributed more to bring about this desirable result than your gallant husband."

Libbie Custer cherished the table for the remainder of her life. After her death, the surrender table was added to the collection of the Smithsonian Institution.

But it was not solely on the sanguinary battlefields from Bull Run to Appomattox that Custer grew into manhood and developed the attributes necessary to be a leader of men. During this time, he also underwent several transformations in his personal life as he matured from a raw young man with ambition into an adult who worried about his responsibility toward the soldiers entrusted to his command. He had started out his post–West Point career with the reputation as a prankster, one who flaunted military discipline, but after that first shot had been fired he proved that he had not been sleeping through his classes. The lessons he had learned at the Point were combined with a natural compassion that he held for his comrades. He had always been a leader, albeit often on forays to the local tavern, but the fact that the stakes now were so high and lives were on the line each day added to the process of his personal growth.

Custer had earlier vowed to abstain from alcohol and had faithfully kept that promise. Ann Reed's other primary concern—along with wife Libbie—became saving the spiritual soul of George Armstrong. Ann had taken him to Sunday school at the Methodist church as a boy and attempted over the years to influence him to become a born-again Christian.

Custer was aware of the efforts of the two most important women in his life to convert him. Ann Reed continued her quest for Custer's salvation and wrote to him in August 1864: "O my dear brother I think of you every day. I do wish you were a good Christian. I have often thought that was the only thing you needed to make you a perfect man. I want to meet you in heaven."

The prayers of the two women were finally answered on Sunday evening, February 5, 1865, when Custer publicly professed his faith. The Custers had attended a service at the Monroe Presbyterian Church, and Armstrong at that time accepted Jesus Christ as his personal Savior.

Now, in the spring of 1876, Custer undoubtedly sat in that anteroom of the White House saying silent prayers to encourage President Grant to open the door to the Oval Office and welcome him inside. But the president remained adamant in his refusal to see Custer.

Certainly, he fretted about the task of outfitting his unit for the expedition against the Sioux. There were many aspects of training and logistics that he had developed over the years to ensure readiness and he needed to be there to make sure they were properly implemented. These lessons had not come without experience, and few army officers over the years had led the campaigns and expeditions that had been the learning ground that had brought George Armstrong Custer to this point in his career.

Three

Chasing Shadows
on the Plains

Following the war, in June 1865 Brevet General George Armstrong Custer had been assigned duty in Louisiana and Texas, once again under the command of General Phil Sheridan. More than fifty thousand troops had been dispatched along the Rio Grande as a show of force to the French, which had invaded Mexico. Custer would head a division of four thousand, organized in Alexandria, Louisiana, and later stationed in Texas.

Custer immediately encountered severe disciplinary problems with these veteran troops who had fought in the Civil War and wanted to return home. It was the first time that he had commanded troops who had not worshiped him, which compelled him to face a rumored assassination attempt and to squelch a near mutiny. The unit in August moved to Hempstead, Texas, and by November was headquartered at the Blind Asylum in Austin.

Although Custer and his troops remained at odds, he enjoyed his duty in Texas on a personal basis. He had been accompanied by Libbie, brother Tom, and his father, Emanuel—employed as a forage agent.

The local society was extremely cordial, and the Custer clan occupied their time riding, hunting, playing practical jokes on one another, and catching up on life after the wartime separation. This assignment ended in February 1866, when the Custers traveled to New York City—with one side trip to Monroe to attend the funeral of Libbie's father, Daniel Bacon, who had passed away on May 18 of cholera.

While in New York, due to his reputation from the Civil War, Custer was offered the position of adjutant general of the Mexican army, which was in a struggle with Emperor Maximilian, the French puppet. The position commanded a salary of sixteen thousand dollars in gold—twice Custer's major general pay. Although he was highly recommended by President Grant, Secretary of War Edwin Stanton, and Phil Sheridan, both Libbie and Sheridan counseled against Custer accepting the offer. The matter was settled, however, when Secretary of State William H. Seward, who thought France might be offended if an American officer directed soldiers against French troops, refused to allow Custer a leave of absence.

In September 1866, Custer and Libbie were members of an entourage that toured with President Andrew Johnson in an attempt to win support for the president's Southern policy. Johnson likened the Union to a circle that had been broken and required mending and therefore called his tour Swinging Round the Circle. Custer believed that he was engaging in a public service by pleading for leniency toward the vanquished Southerners. After all, many of his friends from West Point had been Confederate officers and he had always practiced decent treatment of them during the war.

Custer's participation was not well received by the Northern press, which attacked him vehemently for associating with traitor Southerners. Even in Custer country—Michigan, Ohio, and Indiana—the reception was unpleasant at best. This initial foray into politics had become a disaster. Custer soon decided he was better suited as a soldier and not a politician. Consequently, the Custers decided to leave the presidential party before the completion of the trip in order to escape the protesters and bad publicity.

On July 28, 1866, Congress authorized four new cavalry regiments—including the Seventh Cavalry, which would be formed at Fort Riley, Kansas. Custer would have preferred a colonelcy and command of one of the regiments but with the influence of Phil Sheridan was appointed a lieutenant colonel—second-in-command under Colonel Andrew Jackson ("A. J.") Smith—of the

Seventh Cavalry. He accepted the commission and made plans for him and Libbie to travel to their new duty station on the Great Plains, where he would resume his business of fighting, this time against hostile Indians.

Lieutenant Colonel George Armstrong Custer, wife Libbie, and their cook, Eliza Brown, reported for duty at Fort Riley, Kansas, on the evening of November 3, 1866. Custer, however, soon traveled to Washington to appear before an examining board and did not participate in the training of the unit until his return just before Christmas. In February 1867, commanding officer Colonel Smith departed to head the District of the Upper Arkansas and Custer assumed de facto command—a position he would hold until June 25, 1876. Enlisted recruits had arrived at the fort throughout the summer and fall, and by the end of the year the over eight hundred troops were joined by most of the officers.

The enlisted cavalryman of Custer's era was a volunteer who was paid thirteen dollars a month. Many young men had been attracted to military service by the prospect of romance and adventure, the shiny new uniforms they would wear, the pomp and circumstance of hearing the regimental band strike up a jaunty tune, and an escape from their mundane lives on the farm or apprenticeships in the city. There was romance and adventure to be found in the military, so they thought. Quite a number of them were emigrants from Ireland, Italy, Germany, and England—which often posed a language problem—and many were Civil War veterans.

These would-be soldiers reported to their duty station and found that their lives would be quite different than they had envisioned. They arrived at Fort Riley to discover a cluster of crude buildings in a remote location that was surrounded by a barren prairie covered with sagebrush that was scalded by the sun in summer and buried under snow and freezing temperatures in the winter. And they soon learned that upon signing up they had forfeited all rights as American citizens and were now under an alien jurisdiction that resembled a brutal dictatorship—and they were at the very bottom of this pecking order.

Recruits were schooled in the manual of the saber, manual of the pistol, manual of the carbine, and principles of target practice. They were taught how to ride and care for their mounts and learned how to fight on horseback or dismounted. In garrison, they endured months of isolation, monotony, and rigid discipline, interrupted only by the occasional brief action against their enemy, the Plains Indians.

Reveille typically blew at 5:30, with the first drill commencing at 6:15. That would be followed by stable call, guard mount, construction, woodcutting, and water details, inspections and dress reviews, and various forms of drill. Taps sounded at 8:15 and the men would retire to crude bunks fashioned with pole or board slats and a straw tick, or in some cases during warm weather they preferred to sleep outside.

The cavalryman wore a dark-blue blouse, sky-blue trousers, a gray shirt, black boots, and a wide-brimmed hat of either army-issue blue or white straw during the summer months. His uniform was crisscrossed with leather straps that held certain necessities, such as cartridge pouches and his three-pound seven-ounce light cavalry saber. He was initially issued a seven-shot 56/50-caliber Spencer repeating carbine and a .44-caliber Colt or Remington percussion revolver, and later a .45-caliber Springfield Model 1873 single-shot breech-loading carbine and a six-shot .45-caliber Colt single-action revolver.

The cavalryman's campaign outfit consisted of his weapons, a shelter half, haversack, poncho, canteen, mess kit, and blanket, extra clothing, extra ammunition, a feed bag, fifteen pounds of grain, a picket pin and lariat, personal items, and several days' rations—usually greasy salt pork or salt beef and hardtack washed down with bitter coffee. Occasionally soup made of hominy would be served at the mess hall in garrison, but vegetables and fruits were virtually nonexistent.

And then there was the discipline aspect of duty. Orders from all officers and enlisted men of a superior rank were to be regarded as sacrosanct and were to be obeyed instantly and without question. Failure to obey even minor military rituals, such as saluting an officer or calling him sir, could result in punishment. The penalties could range from walking for hours while carrying a log of wood on your shoulder for being dirty to carrying around a saddle all day for not being present at an inspection at first call. For more serious offenses, a court-martial would be ordered and if found guilty the soldier could be sentenced to confinement and loss of his pay. And then there was the lure of the gold fields in California or Colorado. Needless to say, desertions were commonplace.

The primary mission of this newly formed regiment was to protect work crews on the Kansas Pacific Railway from hostile Plains Indian tribes, which had been incessantly raiding. Regimental headquarters remained at Fort Riley with four companies, while the other companies were assigned to garrison various posts along the Santa Fe and Smoky Hill Trails.

Custer and his cavalry experienced Indian fighting for the first time during the spring and summer of 1867 on what would be called the Hancock Expedition. While the troops had been back east fighting the Civil War and Western forts were for all intents and purposes abandoned, the Indians had been taking control of huge chunks of land. One of the most active areas was western Kansas. Cheyenne, Sioux, Kiowa, Comanche, and Arapaho warriors had been roaming the territory, incessantly menacing homesteaders and workers on the Kansas Pacific Railway.

By early spring of 1866, the line—known as the Union Pacific Railroad, Eastern Division (UPED)—stretched for some 115 miles from Kansas City to Manhattan but had been delayed by frequent attacks from marauding Plains Indians, whose number of warriors was estimated at six thousand. The task of protecting surveyors and work crews from these hostiles was heartily embraced by General Sheridan, whose responsibility as commander of the Department of the Missouri included William Jackson Palmer's railroad, the UPED, which traced the route of the Smoky Hill Trail.

It was determined that a military force commanded by Major General Winfield Scott Hancock would be sent into the field to demonstrate the might of the United States Army and punish these Great Plains marauders for their crimes.

"Hancock the Superb," as he had been hailed by Civil War era newspapers, was born near Norristown, Pennsylvania, on February 14, 1824. He had graduated from the U.S. Military Academy at West Point in 1844 and distinguished himself in the Mexican War, had served in the Third Seminole War in the 1850s and the 1857 Utah Expedition, and was appointed brigadier general in the Union army in 1861.

Second Lieutenant George Armstrong Custer had served as a volunteer aide to corps commander General Hancock on May 5, 1862, in an engagement near Williamsburg when, as mentioned before, the first battle flag taken by the Union army was captured.

Hancock had become a bona fide hero at Gettysburg when, although he was badly wounded, his men held the Union center against Pickett's charge—unknowingly with help from Custer three miles to the east. He was formally thanked by Congress for his bravery but never fully recovered from his wounds received in that battle and accepted recruiting duty in Washington. Hancock was appointed commander of the Department of the Missouri in 1867 and was anxious to return to field duty in Kansas to show that he had not lost his fighting ability.

Construction of a transcontinental railroad had become a national obsession that had unified the post–Civil War country with purpose. The Union Pacific and Central Pacific were rushing to rendezvous from the west and east respectively when in 1865 a young railroad entrepreneur named William Jackson Palmer convinced investors that they could turn worthless land into expensive real estate by building a separate railroad line from Kansas City through the Great Plains to California.

Palmer, the future founder of Colorado Springs and better known for his Denver & Rio Grande Railroad, had traveled to Europe at age nineteen to study how coal burned in locomotives and then had worked as secretary to the president of the Pennsylvania Railroad. He had commanded one of Phil Sheridan's brigades in the Civil War—for which he achieved the rank of brigadier general and later received the Medal of Honor. With such credentials, Palmer had little trouble raising the necessary cash for his new railroad.

In late March, more than fourteen hundred soldiers—including eight companies of Custer's Seventh Cavalry—marched down the Santa Fe Trail to the Arkansas River.

The country through which they passed was mainly prairie with a thin cover of pale-green and rusty grass above sandy soil beneath. The air was fresh and carried breezy fragrances of native grasses—sandbur, wheatgrass, bluestem, and prairie sand reed, to name a few. Various species of songbirds—lark buntings, meadowlarks, and goldfinches being the most prevalent—darted and dived in flight around the formation, calling out shrill warnings and gobbling up insects disturbed by the horses' hooves. Every now and then a family of quail scooted away with heads lowered or a small rodent or lizard would scurry from one hole to another. Above, red-tailed hawks glided majestically about in wide, swooping circles in search of prey. A herd of pronghorn antelope could occasionally be observed in the distance, the buck standing guard.

Along the way, the troopers were kept busy staging aggressive battle exercises that were intended to intimidate and impress the unseen Indian observers. This show of force convinced Custer that the Indians would "accept terms and abandon the war-path."

Two notable members of the expedition were famed Civil War illustrator Theodore R. Davis representing *Harper's Weekly* and newspaperman Henry M. Stanley, who would later gain fame as the discoverer of the lost Livingstone in Africa. Davis and Stanley were the first correspondents to accompany an army campaign against the Plains Indians.

Earlier in the year, Davis had been traveling on a stagecoach bound for Denver when it was attacked by Indians. Davis and the other passengers held off the hostiles until rescued by the army. On February 17, 1866, *Harper's Weekly* published Davis' full-page depiction of this incident, which became the prototype of an Indian stage attack later shown on modern motion picture and television screens.

Stanley wrote about the prospects of engaging the Indians: "Custer is precisely the man for that job. A certain impetuosity and undoubted courage are his principal characteristics."

On April 12 Edward W. Wynkoop, the former Fort Lyon commander who now served as an Indian agent for the Cheyenne and Arapaho, invited several Cheyenne and Sioux chiefs—including Tall Bull and Pawnee Killer—to Fort Larned for a parley with General Hancock. Hancock professed his desire for peace but made it clear that the chiefs must live up to the provisions of their treaties and cease hostilities. The general then decided to march his men twenty-one miles up the Pawnee Fork to the village of the Indians and resume talks at that location. The apprehensive chiefs, as well as Wynkoop, requested that Hancock keep his distance from the village. Their protestations, however, fell on deaf ears, and Hancock commenced his march.

The Indians responded by painting themselves for war and riding back and forth in front of the army column to indicate their intention to defend their village. Hancock countered by ordering his men into battle formation.

Halfway to the Indian encampment, Hancock, Wynkoop, and a handful of officers rode forward to meet with the chiefs. Both sides agreed to avoid a battle, if possible. As a show of good faith, Hancock promised that his men would not enter the village or in any way molest the inhabitants. The Indians retired to their village with Hancock's column following and eventually halting to camp three hundred yards away.

That pledge by Hancock to avoid the village apparently held little credence with the Indians. When the command arrived at its destination, scouts informed Hancock that while the chiefs had been delaying the troops the women and children had fled the village. Hancock believed that he had been tricked. In a counsel with the chiefs, he demanded that the women and children be returned. Instead, scouts later observed the warriors also preparing for flight.

Hancock awakened Custer at about midnight and ordered that his cavalrymen surround the village. Custer arrived to discover that the nearly three hundred lodges had been abandoned. The inhabitants had departed in such haste that they had left behind most of their personal belongings. They did not trust the white man and had thought it best to place their women and children out of harm's way until judging Hancock's intentions. To Hancock's inexperienced and arrogant way of thinking that his word had been ignored, this insulting action signified war. At dawn on April 15, Custer and his eight companies were dispatched to pursue these hostiles.

Custer chased his prey for some thirty-five miles but discovered that the escaping Sioux and Cheyenne had split into numerous smaller groups and had simply vanished into the rugged landscape.

At the same time, Hancock was contemplating whether or not to employ Civil War standards of warfare and destroy the Indian village on Pawnee Fork. His men already had been disobeying orders by ransacking the lodges and looting for souvenirs. Hancock's mind was made up when a courier from Custer arrived to report that the Indians had been attacking stagecoaches and stations along the Smoky Hill Trail. On the morning of April 19—against the advice of Agent Wynkoop and Colonel A. J. Smith—the village and its contents were burned to the ground, which served as a declaration of war to the Indians.

In the meantime, Custer continued down the Smoky Hill Trail to camp near Fort Hays, where he had expected to find forage and supplies. Instead, the supply trains had been delayed and he would be forced to endure an undetermined period of waiting.

The weather had turned cold and rainy, disgruntled troopers were deserting in great numbers, and Custer, a man of action, became deeply concerned by his inability to resume his march and punish the hostiles. His only solace was the presence of wife Libbie, who visited for two weeks. Also during this respite from the march, Custer had the opportunity to continue his ongoing discussions about the culture and customs of the local tribes with James Butler "Wild Bill" Hickok, who had gathered valuable knowledge from years of experience on the Plains.

Throughout the last week of April, Hancock, now at Fort Dodge, met with various tribal chiefs, including Kicking Bird, Little Raven, and Satanta. Hancock was impressed by the unanimous declarations of peace, but his talks failed to produce positive results. The tribes had imposed their will on the territory for so long that they had no intention of seeking peace now. Promises made to white negotiators were never meant to be kept. Whites were the enemy, and nothing Hancock had said could change that fact. The raiding increased during the month of May. Stagecoach service along the Smoky Hill Trail at times was suspended, and no mail station or white traveler was safe.

On June 1, Custer and six companies—about 350 men guided by William "Medicine Bill" Comstock and Moses "California Joe" Milner—finally marched. The raiding had by then shifted from the Smoky Hill Trail to the Platte Road in Nebraska, the principal route to Colorado and California. Custer headed northward toward Fort McPherson with orders to clear out the hostiles in the area between the Republican and Platte rivers. The 215-mile march, however, was uneventful, other than the death of Major Wickliffe Cooper, who was said to have committed suicide—but it was later determined that he may have been the victim of murder.

Near Fort McPherson on about June 16, Custer held a parley with Pawnee Killer, who pledged peace and accepted gifts of coffee, sugar, and other goods.

Custer believed that the chief was sincere, but later was chastised for his position by General William T. Sherman, who arrived the following day. Sherman was of the opinion that Pawnee Killer should have been detained and sent Custer out on the improbable mission of locating and convincing the chief to move his village closer to the fort, where his actions could be monitored.

Custer's orders called for him to scout south to the forks of the Republican River, turn northward toward Fort Sedgwick, which had access to the Union Pacific Railroad, where he could replenish supplies and perhaps receive orders from Sherman, then sweep the plains along the Republican to the South Platte. Four days later, Custer went into camp along the forks of the Republican without finding any sign of Pawnee Killer.

Sherman had made vague mention about Libbie Custer perhaps joining her husband at some point at Fort McPherson. Custer, however, wrote to his wife and requested that she travel to Fort Wallace, the westernmost post in Kansas, and he would send an escort. Presumably for that reason, Custer chose not to report to Fort Sedgwick. Instead, on June 23 under the cloak of darkness Major Joel Elliott and a small detail were dispatched to Fort Sedgwick to check for orders.

At the same time, First Lieutenant William W. Cooke led a forty-eight-man wagon train south to Fort Wallace to requisition supplies—and possibly escort Libbie Custer back to her husband.

Custer's trusted adjutant, William Cooke, was born into a prominent family on May 29, 1846, in the hamlet of Mount Pleasant, a few miles south of present-day Brantford, Ontario, Canada, where his ancestors—British loyalists—had fled after the American Revolution. At the age of fourteen, he moved to Buffalo, New York, to live with relatives. He had lied about his age in 1863 to join the Twenty-fourth New York Cavalry in Niagara Falls as a recruiter and was commissioned a second lieutenant on January 26, 1864. Cooke was wounded on June 17, 1864, at Petersburg, and returned to duty a month later as unit quartermaster. He was promoted to first lieutenant on December 14, 1864, and in March 1865 assumed command of Company A and participated in battles at Five Forks, Dinwiddie Court House, and Sayler's Creek. He received brevets of captain, major, and lieutenant colonel for his service and returned home to Canada when honorably discharged on June 25, 1865.

Cooke's father encouraged his son to form a cavalry unit in Canada, but he instead chose the United States Army. He was commissioned a second lieutenant in Company D in the newly formed Seventh Cavalry and reported for duty on November 16, 1866. (His name at times has been listed as "Cook" due to an administrative error.) He became known by the nickname "The Queen's Own" and had the reputation as one of the best shots and fastest runners in the regiment. His appearance was also quite distinctive. He wore long "dundreary" side-whiskers, named after Lord Dundreary, a character in the play *Our American Cousin,* which was playing at Ford's Theatre the night President Lincoln attended and was assassinated.

Now Cooke was involved in a particularly perilous resupply mission to Fort Wallace.

At dawn on June 23, an Indian raiding party attempted to stampede Custer's horses but was driven off with only the sentry being wounded. The Indians formed on a nearby hill, and Custer requested a council. To his surprise, the raiders were led by Sioux chief Pawnee Killer. Custer refused to issue supplies and the parley ended without resolution.

Meanwhile, a small Indian decoy party invited pursuit and Custer obliged by sending Captain Louis Hamilton and two companies after them. The sturdy Indian ponies easily outdistanced the heavier army mounts, and the Sioux attempted to lure the cavalrymen into an ambush. Disaster was averted when Hamilton recognized the potential danger and dismounted his men to drive off the warriors.

On June 26, Lieutenant Cooke's fifty-man resupply detachment was attacked by an estimated six to seven hundred Sioux warriors on its return trip from Fort Wallace. Cooke formed the wagon train into two parallel columns, and a running battle ensued. The Indians, after being fought off on a direct assault, commenced circling the steadily moving wagons. The warriors exhibited great horsemanship skills by racing at full speed, leaning low to hide and fire from behind their ponies while the cavalrymen expended most of their ammunition.

This tedious battle lasted for more than three hours until, surprisingly, the Sioux abruptly withdrew. Custer had, without being aware of the circumstances, prudently ordered two companies—Captains Edward Myers and

Robert W. West—to ride out and reinforce the detail. The approach of this column was sighted by Indian scouts, and, just like in the movies, it had arrived in the nick of time to rescue Cooke's beleaguered command.

To Custer's relief, his letter to Libbie had never reached its destination or her life would have been in peril riding with the wagon train. Standing orders had been issued for officers to shoot any white women to save them from capture should an Indian attack appear overwhelming. There had been a number of female captives taken by the Indians, and the consensus opinion in the military—and the country at large—was that the husbands or fathers would rather have their wives or daughters killed than returned after being defiled and mistreated by a warrior.

Cooke reached camp on June 27, and Major Elliott returned the following day, without carrying any new orders. Those orders had actually arrived the day after Elliott had departed and likely would have been available had Custer reported to Fort Sedgwick as ordered. The dispatches were then placed in the care of Second Lieutenant Lyman S. Kidder and a ten-man detail.

While Kidder scoured the area, attempting to locate Custer, he was discovered by Pawnee Killer on July 2. The mutilated bodies of Kidder and his men were subsequently discovered by scout William Comstock strewn across the Plains near Beaver Creek where each had fallen in a desperate running battle with the Sioux.

Custer, complying with his original orders, resumed his sweep of the headwaters of the Republican, his route curiously leading away from locations where the Indians were known to be operating. The march into Colorado across a desolate, waterless terrain spotted with only cactus and rife with bothersome ravines under the scorching July sun proved torturous for both the troopers and the horses. Relief from this demanding march—as well as the prospects of riches in Colorado's mines—became a temptation that many of the troopers could not resist. The column was victimized by a mass desertion.

According to regimental records, over 120 cavalrymen since April 19 had already deserted. Then, on the morning of July 7, 34 more men disappeared. Theodore Davis noted, "This out of a force of less than three hundred was a serious misfortune." The readiness of the command in the event of an Indian attack had been severely compromised.

Shortly after noon on that same day thirteen troopers—seven on horseback—brazenly deserted in full view of the command. Custer ordered several officers—Elliott, Tom Custer, and Cooke—to give chase and stop the fleeing cavalrymen by whatever means necessary. Six of the deserters were subsequently returned to camp. Three of them had been shot and wounded, one of whom, Private Charles Johnson, would later die. Custer loudly ordered that the wounded not be given medical attention but quietly directed Dr. Isaac Coates to care for them.

The Hancock Expedition had for all intents and purposes fizzled to an end when on July 13 the exhausted command—without any additional desertions—headed into camp near Fort Wallace. Both men and mounts were in poor condition and could not return to the field until rested and resupplied. Custer had led his command to the fort, which was presently under the command of Captain Myles Keogh and Company I.

The handsome, mustachioed Keogh was one of the more colorful officers on the Seventh Cavalry muster roles. He was born at Orchard House, Leighlinbridge, County Carlow, Ireland, on May 25, 1840. Keogh later stated on his application for a commission in the United States Army that he had attended Carlow College until the age of sixteen, when he quit for a six-month tour of Europe. During that time, he claimed to have joined the French Foreign Legion and participated in the closing stages of the Algerian Campaign.

In August 1860, Keogh was appointed second lieutenant in the Battalion of St. Patrick, a volunteer unit that went to Italy to fight for Pope Pius IX when the Papal States were being threatened by Napoléon II and the Piedmontese. About one month later Keogh distinguished himself at the Adriatic port of Ancona when his outgunned battalion was attacked by a superior force of Piedmontese supported by artillery. Keogh's unit repulsed several bayonet charges and drove back their enemy. For his extraordinary gallantry during this battle, Keogh was awarded the coveted Pro Petri Sede medal and the Ordine di San Gregorio (Cross of the Order of St. Gregory the Great). After the flag of the Papal States was lowered in defeat the following month, Keogh remained to serve for two years in the Papal Guard.

This routine duty, however, was contrary to Keogh's adventurous nature, and in March 1862 he resigned his commission and sailed for the United States.

On April 1, he arrived in New York City and offered his services to the Union army. Keogh was commissioned a captain on April 9 and assigned as acting aide-de-camp to Brigadier General James Shields, another Irish emigrant.

Keogh's soldierly qualities soon came to the attention of General George B. McClellan, and he was assigned to the staff of the army commander. He subsequently served as an aide-de-camp to various generals and participated in such engagements as Cedar Mountain, Second Bull Run, South Mountain, Antietam, Brandy Station, Aldie, Gettysburg, and Mine Run.

Keogh was promoted to major in April 1864. Three months later he was on the staff of General George Stoneman during a raid to liberate Anderson-ville Prison when his seven-hundred-man unit was captured at Sunshine Church, near Macon, Georgia. His confinement, however, was brief. He was exchanged for Confederate prisoners two months later. Keogh went on to distinguish himself in operations in southwestern Virginia, North Carolina, and Georgia and was brevetted lieutenant colonel in March 1865. He was mustered out of the service on September 1, 1865, after having participated in over thirty engagements. With recommendations from several generals, Keogh joined the Seventh Cavalry on July 28, 1866, as a captain and commander of Company I.

Most accounts relate that Keogh was a favorite of George Armstrong Custer, but, contrary to his commander, he was known to habitually drink to excess and during those times his mood became dark and combative. Alcoholism was an epidemic at isolated posts that existed without any form of nearby entertainment, and the officers and men had a habit of retiring to the officers' club or sutler's wagon each day after work. There is no evidence, however, that Keogh's drinking affected his abilities as an officer.

Keogh also has been credited as the person who introduced Custer to the Seventh Cavalry's traditional regimental marching and battle song, "Garry Owen." Gaelic for "Owen's Garden," this distinctive, jaunty, Irish quick-step tune became synonymous with Custer's Seventh Cavalry, although when and by whom it was introduced to the unit has been the subject of much conjecture. Several Irish regiments, including the Fifth Irish Lancers, had embraced it as a rowdy drinking song. Keogh's father may or may not have been a member of the Fifth Irish Lancers.

Some researchers have disputed much of Keogh's heretofore-accepted bi-ography, which casts doubts about whether or not his father in fact ever served in that particular unit. Libbie Custer, however, was under the impression that Keogh had made her husband aware of "Garry Owen" shortly after the formation of the Seventh Cavalry at Fort Riley. The tune apparently dates back to Revolutionary War days and might have been known to Custer as early as his schooling at West Point. Regardless of its origins, "Garry Owen" became the regimental battle song of the Seventh Cavalry and was played during expeditions, campaigns, battles, and ceremonies to the delight of its members and onlookers alike.

Fort Wallace, the westernmost post in Kansas, had miserable, primitive living conditions and was under constant siege by hostile Plains Indians. Custer learned that mail and dispatches had not been able to get through on the Butterfield Overland stagecoach line due to the Indian presence along the Smoky Hill Trail.

General Hancock had recently passed through from Denver on his way east to the comforts of Fort Leavenworth but had not left behind any orders for Custer. Custer was also informed that Captain Albert Barnitz and his Company G, which had ridden to Pond Creek Station, had been attacked on June 26 by Roman Nose's Cheyenne and sustained six killed and six wounded.

On July 15, Custer, in an act that defied explanation, impulsively assembled three officers—Hamilton, brother Tom, and Cooke—along with illustrator Theodore Davis and seventy-two men with the best stock available. After assigning Major Joel Elliott the command, Custer headed east with his detail on the Smoky Hill Trail toward Fort Hays, a distance of about 150 miles.

Along the way, the detail met a wagon train containing forage commanded by Captain Frederick William Benteen, which unknowingly carried cholera germs that would infect Fort Wallace. Later, two mail stages were stopped by Custer in a futile effort to find a letter from Libbie. Just east of Downer's Station, a trooper disappeared, and Custer ordered Sergeant James Connelly and six men to chase after this deserter. The missing man was captured, but the party was attacked by Indians on the way back, suffering one man killed and another wounded, and took refuge at the station. Connelly reported the incident to Custer, who—even at the urging of Captain Hamilton—refused to delay his march to rescue the beleaguered men, who were only about three miles away. Custer reasoned that there was an infantry detachment guarding the station and that time was of the essence in their march east. An infantry detail later found the victims, and the wounded man survived.

Custer and the exhausted cavalrymen arrived at Fort Hays on the morning of July 18, having covered the 150-mile distance in an extraordinarily fast time of fifty-five hours. Custer, his brother Tom, Cooke, and Davis immediately departed from Fort Hays with four government mules and an army ambulance and proceeded sixty miles to Fort Harker, where Custer expected to find his wife, and arrived at 2:00 A.M. Libbie, however, had returned to Fort Riley. After informing Colonel A. J. Smith of his presence, Custer boarded a train headed to Fort Riley. The next morning, Smith sent a telegram to Custer ordering him back to Fort Harker to be placed under arrest for deserting his post at Fort Wallace.

Exactly why did Custer act like a man possessed and leave his post in such a manner to make a mad dash across Kansas—surely aware that he risked a court-martial?

Stories have circulated that Custer embarked upon his mad dash in a fit of jealous rage after hearing that his wife and Lieutenant Thomas Weir were becoming an item.

Twenty-eight-year-old Ohioan Thomas Benton Weir had moved to Michigan and enrolled at the University of Michigan but departed during his junior year at the outbreak of the Civil War to enlist in Company B, Third Michigan Cavalry. Weir served as an enlisted man until being appointed a second lieutenant on October 13, 1861, while serving in campaigns and expeditions, including New Madrid, the Siege of Corinth, and battles at Farmington, Iuka, Coffeeville, and Second Corinth. He was promoted to first lieutenant on June 19, 1862—seven days before being taken prisoner. He was released on January 8, 1863. While held prisoner, Weir was appointed captain on November 1, 1862, and eventually received brevets up to lieutenant colonel for his Civil War service. His regiment was assigned to reconstruction duty in Texas in 1865, and as a regular army brevet of major he served on the staffs of Generals Custer and Gibbs.

Weir was appointed a first lieutenant in the newly formed Seventh Cavalry on July 28, 1866, and promoted to captain on July 31, 1867. During the Hancock Expedition, he had remained back at Fort Hays, Kansas. At the time, Weir may have served as Libbie's escort in Custer's absence—as well as other ladies'—which was a normal occurrence for officers at frontier posts.

The accusation that Tom Weir and Libbie were becoming an item may have been more credible had it not been brought to light by Captain Frederick Benteen, who would become known as a serial Custer critic. No verifiable supporting evidence exists to indicate that Libbie Custer engaged in anything more than a flirtatious passing interest in Weir—if even that—again, a common event on frontier posts where women were few and far between.

The answer for Custer's actions may lie in the words of his wife. Libbie was later inspired to recall her husband's surprise visit to Fort Riley by writing: "There was in the summer of 1867 one long, perfect day. It was mine, and—blessed be the memory, which preserves to us the joys as well as the sadness of life!—it is still mine, for time and eternity."

Libbie also wrote about the incident to her cousin when explaining the reasons for the court-martial: "He took a leave himself, knowing none would be granted him. When he ran the risk of a court-martial in leaving Wallace he did it expecting the consequences . . . and we are quite determined not to live apart again."

Why then did Custer race across Kansas? Only he knows for certain. But it would not be too far-fetched, not too much of a romantic notion, given the evidence and the character of the man, to consider that Custer jeopardized his career simply because he desperately desired to see the woman he loved. The courtship and marriage of Armstrong and Libbie was one of the great romances of all time, one that transcends poetic thought and could cause a man to make rash decisions. Custer had likely become so disenchanted with Hancock and that wild-goose chase that he sought solace in the arms of the only person who understood him—in spite of the consequences.

The inability of Hancock to carry out his mission had allowed the Indians to remain free to terrorize settlements and travelers along the Smoky Hill, Platte, and Arkansas, which compelled Western governors to resume their appeals to Washington for relief. That disappointing result would without question require a scapegoat to blame for the failure.

Upon reporting to Fort Riley, Custer learned that he would stand a court-martial for his recent actions. It was perhaps a fitting conclusion to an expedition that had become a series of miscalculations and breakdowns of military discipline.

The court-martial of George Armstrong Custer convened at Fort Leavenworth at 11:00 A.M. on September 15, 1867.

Colonel A. J. Smith—at the urging of General Hancock—had charged Custer with "absence without leave from his command" for traveling from Fort Wallace to Fort Hays at a time when his command was expected to be engaged with hostile Indians, and "conduct to the prejudice of good order and military discipline" by completing a long and exhausting march when the horses were in unfit condition, neglecting to recover or bury the bodies of two troopers at Downer's Station, and procuring two ambulances and four mules belonging to the United States without proper authority.

An additional charge was preferred by Captain Robert W. West, who accused Custer of "conduct prejudicial to good order and military discipline" for ordering that the deserters from the column be shot down without a trial and denying the wounded proper medical attention.

Custer pleaded not guilty to all charges and had prepared his defense with the assistance of his counsel, Captain Charles C. Parsons, a former West Point classmate. His defense offered questionable reasons about seeking new orders, securing supplies at Fort Harker (although Fort Wallace was well stocked), and obtaining medical supplies to treat cholera victims (the cholera epidemic had not as yet reached Fort Wallace).

The trial lasted until October 11, concluding with Parsons reading a lengthy rebuttal written by Custer that answered each charge and specification.

The court, however, was not swayed by Custer's explanations or plea for acquittal. He was found guilty on all counts but cleared of any criminality regarding the ambulances and the treatment of the wounded deserters. His sentence was that he be suspended from rank and command for one year and forfeit his pay for that period.

Custer hoped that the reviewing officer might overturn the verdict, but on November 18 General Sherman issued a statement that the "proceedings, findings and sentence . . . are approved by President Grant."

Custer and Libbie were of the opinion that he had been the scapegoat for the failure of the Hancock Expedition. Some vindication came when Phil Sheridan, who sided with Custer, graciously offered the Custers the use of his quarters at Fort Leavenworth. Sheridan's offer was accepted, and the couple enjoyed the winter social season at that post before leaving for Monroe, Michigan, in the spring.

There were, however, two episodes of nasty business stemming from the court-martial. Custer charged Captain West with drunkenness on duty, for which West was found guilty and suspended for two months. West retaliated by preferring charges of murder in a civil court against Custer and Lieutenant William W. Cooke for the death of trooper Charles Johnson. On January 18, 1868, a civilian judge cited a lack of evidence and dismissed that case.

Further vindication for Custer would come two months short of the end of his suspension when he would be summoned back to duty for Sheridan's Winter Campaign of 1868–69. Custer would be participating in an expedition that would establish his reputation as the country's premier Indian fighter but would also initiate a controversy within the Seventh Cavalry as well as with the public at large. As with any great man or those who strive for greatness, there are always those whose envy or resentment compels them to spread rumors meant to cast doubts about the great man's character. In addition, much of the country was under the impression that the policy of treating the Indians with peaceful intentions would be reciprocated and the result of the upcoming campaign would be a real shock.

And George Armstrong Custer would be at the center of both of these controversies.

Four

Death Along the Washita

In the summer and fall of 1868, the Southern Plains were being terrorized by incessant attacks from Cheyenne, Kiowa, and Arapaho Indians. Raids by marauding hostiles against white settlements, soldiers, the railroad, and stage lines were so prevalent that the government was forced to seek a solution.

During George Armstrong Custer's absence from duty, government policy with respect to the "Indian problem" had been the subject of fierce contention between two diverse factions. The Eastern humanitarian groups combined with the Indian Bureau to favor a policy of tolerance, generosity, and fair treatment for the Indian, which they believed would encourage the Indians to respond in kind. Westerners allied with the army to scoff at this idealistic and impractical notion. The only manner in which to deal with the Indian, according to Westerners, was by a demonstration of military might—punishment and supervision.

Both sides, however, agreed that all Plains Indians should be removed from the pathway of westward expansion between the Platte and Arkansas rivers and resettled onto reservations north of Nebraska and south of Kansas. To that end, a peace commission was created by Congress and the Medicine Lodge and Fort Laramie treaties were negotiated. Due to cultural differences and miscommunication, peace was elusive and before long renegade warriors were raiding across Kansas, attacking settlements as well as detachments of the army that had been dispatched to subdue the hostiles.

Finally, in a victory for the army, Generals William T. Sherman and Phil Sheridan were called upon in the fall of 1868 to embark on a major winter campaign designed to restore peace on the plains. The army was directed to take whatever measures were necessary to force the hostiles onto reservations and punish those responsible for the atrocities. The two men had decided that a new ruthless measure was required to punish the Indians and implemented the concept of "total war," which both had pioneered in the Civil War— Sherman burning his way through Georgia on his March to the Sea and Sheridan trashing the breadbasket of the Shenandoah Valley.

Total war meant subjecting the civilian populace, not just the enemy fighting force, to a reign of terror. By invading the enemy's homeland and mercilessly destroying property—lodges, food stores, and ponies—the army would break their will to fight. Rarely could these nomadic Indians be caught in the summer, but a winter campaign would find them vulnerable. They would be camped along some waterway, ponies weakened from lack of forage and caches of food barely sufficient to last until spring. Sherman and Sheridan held the view that the torch was as effective a weapon as the sword and that poverty would bring about peace more quickly than the loss of human life. And if noncombatant lives happened to be lost, that would simply be a regrettable but excusable tragedy of war.

The campaign had an inauspicious beginning. In August, General Phil Sheridan had created an elite force of fifty-one seasoned scouts under trusted aide Major George A. "Sandy" Forsyth with orders to guard the railroad up the Smoky Hill Trail. On September 16, the command, which had been following the Arikaree Fork of the Republican River, camped for the night. At dawn, they mounted to resume their patrol when without warning hundreds of Indians attacked from the nearby hills.

Forsyth led his men to refuge on a timbered island about two hundred feet long by forty feet wide. The scouts frantically dug entrenchments as best as possible in the soft sand as the Indians raked the position with deadly rifle fire—inflicting numerous casualties, including Forsyth, who was wounded, and killing all the horses.

This siege, led by Chief Roman Nose, who was killed, would continue for nine days. Forsyth's couriers, however, had reached Fort Wallace, and on September 25 a detachment of the Tenth Cavalry—black "Buffalo Soldiers"—arrived to rescue Forsyth and his beleaguered men and escort them to Fort Wallace for treatment of their wounds, thus ending what could be considered one of the most heroic episodes in Western history. The tiny speck of land situated in the Arikaree would become known as Beecher Island in honor of Frederick H. Beecher, who had been killed on the first day of the battle.

Sheridan's next move was to dispatch Colonel Alfred Sully and his Third Infantry, bolstered by eight companies of the Seventh Cavalry under Major Joel Elliott, to hunt down the Cheyenne who had been raiding south of the Arkansas River. Sully, who had distinguished himself fighting Sioux in the Dakotas, had apparently grown timid and, much to the disgust of Sheridan, returned empty-handed after just one week in the field.

Sheridan, however, was well acquainted with an officer who had the tenacity to implement his strategy of total war. A telegram was sent to summon Lieutenant Colonel George Armstrong Custer, who was serving out his one-year suspension in Monroe, Michigan. An elated Custer was on the train the following morning and reported to Fort Hays on September 30 to prepare for a winter campaign.

Before firm plans had been developed, a debate ensued over the practicality of a cold-weather operation that could pose potential health dangers for the troops and present difficulty in keeping open a supply line. No less of an authority than the legendary trapper and mountain man Jim Bridger, a noted Indian expert, arrived from St. Louis to argue against the campaign. But Sheridan was won over by the argument that their only chance for success was to locate and engage the Indians at the time of the year when they were relatively immobile and therefore vulnerable.

On November 12, Custer and eleven companies of his Seventh Cavalry under the command of Colonel Sully, with his five infantry companies, marched south from Cavalry Creek to a supply base on the North Canadian River appropriately named Camp Supply. On the way to Camp Supply, Custer discovered the trail of an Indian war party estimated at seventy-five warriors. Custer was anxious to follow, but Sully refused permission until reinforced by the Nineteenth Kansas Volunteer Cavalry, commanded by Kansas governor Samuel J. Crawford, which was en route to Camp Supply.

Custer was furious. When Sheridan arrived on November 21, he complained about Sully's typical passivity. Sheridan resolved the tug-of-war over command by sending Sully back to Fort Harker. Custer now had the freedom to pursue the hostiles.

Two days later, Custer and the Seventh Cavalry—eight hundred men—marched south toward the Washita River Valley, where it was believed that large bands of Indians, perhaps as many as six thousand, were camped for the winter.

On November 26, Major Elliott and the Osage Indian scouts came across a fresh trail near Antelope Hills made by warriors returning from a raid on homesteaders in Kansas. Custer dispatched Elliott to follow the trail while he marched the main column forward through the deep snow.

Cheyenne chief Black Kettle and several subchiefs had returned to their camp on the Washita that night after a meeting at Fort Cobb with Colonel William Hazen, who had the unenviable task of determining which Indians were hostile and which were friendly. Hazen was convinced that Black Kettle was indeed peaceful, but advised the chief to personally make peace with Sheridan in the field to ensure his safety. The general could not easily be located, and Black Kettle simply went home. Although the chief's wife warned him that he should move the village that night, Black Kettle was convinced that the soldiers would wait for more favorable conditions and not brave the freezing temperatures and blizzard conditions to attack.

That opinion by the chief was probably true of most commanders in the field—but not this particular commander. George Armstrong Custer was undeterred by fatigue, weather conditions, or any other obstacle in his way to carrying out his orders. He was determined to aggressively follow orders and protect the lives and property of those innocent homesteaders.

Custer led his troops through the bone-chilling cold and dense morning fog until eventually halting on a ridge overlooking the Washita River. Below was situated a village of fifty-one lodges under Chief Black Kettle.

Custer sounded officer's call to detail his plan of attack. The regiment would be separated into four detachments. Major Joel Elliott would attack from the northeast with companies G, H, and M; Captain William Thompson would lead companies B and F from the south; Captain Edward Myers with companies E and I from the west; and Custer with two squadrons commanded by Captain Louis Hamilton and Captain Robert West, along with Cooke's sharpshooters, would strike from the north. Eighty men under quartermaster First Lieutenant James M. Bell would remain with the wagon train.

At dawn on November 27, 1868—as a shot rang out from within the village—the buglers sounded the charge and the Seventh Cavalry swept into the unsuspecting village. Bullets peppered the air, and most of the Indians fled their lodges to take refuge in the nearby timber or ravines or raced for the river. Chief Black Kettle and his wife tried to flee on his pony but were shot dead at the river.

In the opening moments, Captain Hamilton was shot through the heart and Captain Albert Barnitz was critically wounded. Thompson was late in arriving on the field, creating a gap between his command and that of Elliott, which permitted a number of Indians to escape.

While the battle along the Washita River raged, Major Elliott, without informing Custer, had rallied a group of volunteers to follow him downstream to chase Indians escaping from Black Kettle's village. As Elliott and his men galloped past Lieutenant Owen Hale, the major called out, "Here goes for a brevet or a coffin!"

Custer's cavalry controlled the village within ten minutes of the charge. They spent the remainder of the morning eliminating small pockets of resistance—103 Indians were killed, according to Custer's report. At one point, the overzealous command of Captain Myers, contrary to explicit orders issued by Custer, was observed firing into a group of women and children. Custer dispatched scout Ben Clark to order Myers to stop shooting and instead capture all noncombatants.

Meanwhile, Custer ordered that the entire Cheyenne village be destroyed. Bonfires soon blazed, and every possession belonging to the tribe was thrown onto the flames. While sorting through the contents of the village, Custer's men found mail, daguerreotypes, clothing, and other items taken from white settlements by raiding parties.

Custer had implemented total war to perfection on Black Kettle's village.

In addition to 103 killed and 53 women and children taken prisoner, the property loss was devastating. The pony herd estimated at 875 was destroyed, and the entire village—every lodge, buffalo robes, weapons, blankets, large quantities of dried meat and food stores, tobacco, and clothing—was either confiscated or burned to ashes.

At about noon, swarms of warriors from the villages downstream began massing to fire from the surrounding bluffs, which placed Custer in a precarious position. Fortunately, Lieutenant Bell bravely fought his way through the Indians with a critical resupply of ammunition. Custer formed his men into a defensive perimeter while the burning of the village was completed.

Additional warriors continued to arrive—perhaps as many as fifteen hundred now rimmed the bluffs—and the cavalrymen were for all intents and purposes surrounded by this superior force. It was approaching dusk, and Custer realized that he must withdraw.

Major Elliott and his men, however, had not returned. Custer dispatched Captain Edward Myers to scout downstream for any sign of the missing men. Myers reported that he ventured about two miles without success.

By this time, Custer's outnumbered Seventh Cavalry was under attack by bands of warriors from the villages downstream and it was imperative that they withdraw without delay. It was assumed that Elliott had simply become lost and would eventually find his own way back to the supply train.

Custer could not risk sacrificing his command by waiting any longer for Elliott, who had disobeyed orders and ridden away of his own accord. He mounted his troops and, in a bold tactical move, ordered the band to play "Ain't I Glad to Get Out of the Wilderness" while marching down the valley toward the downstream villages. When the surprised warriors hurriedly fell back to defend their families, Custer, with darkness as an ally, countermarched his command and escaped to the supply train.

Two days later, the Seventh Cavalry arrived triumphantly at Camp Supply—without Major Joel Elliott and his missing troopers.

Fifty-three women and children had been taken prisoner at Washita, including a girl named Mo-nah-se-tah, who would act as an interpreter throughout the remainder of the campaign and become a subject of controversy in Custer's personal life.

One of the most enduring and debated rumors about Custer concerns the nature of his relationship with Mo-nah-se-tah, the Cheyenne Indian girl. The question under debate has been whether or not this teenage daughter of Chief Little Rock, who was killed in the battle, also served as Custer's mistress and perhaps bore him a son.

The truth at times does not matter—there has always been a certain percentage of the public who would believe anything, resulting in a person's reputation being tarnished forever. And that was what has happened to George Armstrong Custer.

The female subject of the scurrilous accusations, Mo-nah-se-tah, also known as Me-o-tzi, which translated means "Young Grass That Shoots in Spring," was strikingly beautiful. Custer described her in the most glowing of terms. She was about seven months pregnant at the time of the Washita battle and gave birth to a son on January 14, 1869, who assuredly could not have been Custer's child. Cheyenne oral tradition, however, contends that Mo-nah-se-tah gave birth to another child in the fall of 1869, a boy named either Yellow Tail or Yellow Swallow—common names among the Cheyenne—and that Custer was the father. No documentation of this birth exists in reservation records at Fort Cobb, where she resided.

The accusations of Custer's infidelity have been based solely on the assertions of the notorious Custer critic Captain Frederick W. Benteen and Ben Clark, who blamed Custer for his dismissal as an army scout, in addition to Cheyenne Indian oral tradition. Oddly enough, apparently no other written source at that point in time bothered to document what would appear to be an exceedingly titillating and noteworthy allegation.

Benteen's hatred and resentment of Custer would make any accusation he made, which was for the most part merely a repeating of camp gossip, highly suspect. Benteen had hated Custer from their initial meeting, with the captain who was five years older barely masking his resentment for the younger and famous Custer whom he dismissed as a creation of the press. Benteen possibly disliked Custer due to the captain's loyalty and respect for his former Civil War commanding officer General James H. Wilson, who had been a Custer rival. Benteen apparently interpreted a statement made by Custer during their introduction as an insult toward Wilson. However, Custer and Benteen were very much like each other—brave under fire, attuned to military discipline, and possessing a strong character—and that in itself could have caused Benteen's bitterness.

Frederick William Benteen was born in Petersburg, Virginia, on August 24, 1834, and moved at age seven to St. Louis, where he attended a private academy and began working alongside his father painting houses and signs. Surprisingly for a young man with Virginia roots, Frederick turned his back on the South and entered the Civil War in September 1861 as a first lieutenant in Bowen's Battalion, which later became the Tenth Missouri Cavalry. His slave-owning father, Theodore C. Benteen, was furious at this betrayal by his son and, in addition to disowning Fred, was alleged to have said, "I hope the first bullet gets you!"

Benteen, who was promoted to captain on October 1, 1861, distinguished himself in eighteen major engagements, including Wilson's Creek and Pea Ridge, the Siege of Vicksburg, and the fight with Confederate Nathan Bedford Forrest at Tupelo. Most of Benteen's action took place in the Western Theater and in the deep South.

Benteen's "defection" to the North was probably not entirely due to philosophical reasons, rather encouraged by a young Unionist lady from Philadelphia named Catherine Norman, whom he would marry on January 7, 1862. Perhaps part of his bitterness could be traced to the fact that the Benteens would lose four children to spinal meningitis and raise one son, Fred, who would become a major in the army.

While his side fought for the Union cause, the elder Benteen was employed as chief engineer on a Mississippi steamboat named the *Fair Play,* which supplied the Confederacy. On August 18, 1862, Captain Benteen's company was part of a Union flotilla that captured his father's boat. The civilian crew members were soon released—except for T. C. Benteen, who was imprisoned for the duration of the war.

Benteen was appointed major in December 1862 and the following year fought in skirmishes at Florence and Cane Creek, at the Siege of Vicksburg, at Iuka and Brandon Station, and at the capture of Jackson. He was appointed lieutenant colonel in February 1864 and placed in command of the Fourth (Winslow's) Brigade of General Pleasonton's Cavalry Division. Benteen led his brigade in actions at Bolivar and Pleasant Hill, engagements on the Big Blue and Little Osage Crossing in Missouri, and in the assault and capture of Selma and the raid on Columbus. During the October 1864 Federal Pursuit of Confederate general Sterling Price, who had invaded Missouri, Benteen's brigade spearheaded the decisive charge at the Battle of Mine Creek that shattered the Rebel lines. On June 6, 1865, he was recommended for the brevet rank of brigadier general, but the recommendation was not accepted. Benteen was mustered out in Chattanooga on June 30, 1865.

After the war, Benteen was appointed colonel of the 138th United States Colored Volunteers and served in that unit from July 1865 to January 1866. He received his regular army commission as a captain in July 1866 and was assigned to the Seventh Cavalry.

Frederick Benteen was known as a solder's soldier, one who could be singled out as a role model for younger officers. He was a stocky man, with gray hair, blue eyes that can appear cold in photographs, and a smooth-shaven, round face. He quickly transformed H troop from a group of ragged civilians into the finest outfit in the Seventh Cavalry. But Benteen, like most other officers at frontier posts, had an affection for the bottle.

Along with Benteen's accusation about Mo-nah-se-tah were the questionable memories of Ben Clark, who did not refer to the girl by name and whose memories can be dismissed for the same reason—resentment of Custer. Therefore, it would seem that the credibility of the story hinges on Cheyenne oral tradition.

Plains Indian oral tradition has provided many valid details about nineteenth-century events but must be viewed under the same scrutiny as the writings of whites, which were often tainted by prejudices, failing memories, or other human factors such as camp gossip—boastful, malicious, or otherwise. Indian testimony was also often misinterpreted by accident or on purpose and occasionally swayed by a willingness to say what someone would want to hear or by a biased translation. And, in the case of Custer and Mo-nah-se-tah, there are known discrepancies in the Cheyenne stories.

Most Custer scholars deem the Cheyenne account nonsense. Common sense would point to the fact that a man of Custer's stature and prominence as a national hero would not be foolish enough to flaunt such behavior where any number of soldiers, much less correspondents—such as De B. Randolph Keim, who mentioned nothing about it in his book about the campaign—would have knowledge of it. In addition, Custer was said to have been sterile, which was likely the reason he and Libbie were childless.

Most important, however, given Custer's known moral discipline in other areas, was that his marriage to Libbie—based on their letters and testimony from those who knew them—was one of the great romances of all time. It would have taken more than a comely Indian girl to cause him to compromise his wedding vows.

Sadly, Captain Frederick Benteen was a good soldier whose deep resentment of Custer would contribute to the downfall of the Seventh Cavalry in the future and would sully his own legacy. Benteen would go down in history as Custer's most outspoken critic, making any information he provided about events or battles come under scrutiny and skepticism.

In early December, Sheridan and Custer, reinforced by the Nineteenth Kansas Volunteer Cavalry, returned to the Washita battlefield. On December 10, downstream from the site of Black Kettle's village, they found the mutilated bodies of Major Joel Elliott and his detachment.

Although Custer clearly had acted prudently at the November battle by withdrawing his command after making an attempt to locate the missing troopers, the tragic death of the popular Major Elliott provided his friend and former Civil War superior Captain Frederick Benteen with fuel to fan the flames of another controversy.

Benteen wrote a letter to a friend in St. Louis that made the accusation that Custer had "abandoned" Elliott, and included an evaluation of Custer's conduct at Washita that could only be called slanderous. This letter was published, anonymously and apparently without Benteen's permission, in the *St. Louis Democrat* newspaper and reprinted by *The New York Times* on February 14, 1869.

A copy of the newspaper found its way to Custer, who had officer's call sounded and allegedly threatened to horsewhip the author of the letter. When Benteen readily admitted that he had written the letter, Custer was surprised and somewhat befuddled. He reportedly dismissed his officers without another word.

Benteen related a different version of the incident in Custer's tent. The captain allegedly shifted his revolver to a ready position on his belt, and "at a pause in the talk I said, 'Gen. Custer, while I cannot father all the blame you have asserted, I guess I am the man you are after, and I am ready for the whipping promised.' He stammered and said, 'Col. Benteen, I'll see you again, sir!'"

Benteen claimed that he later returned to Custer's tent with newspaperman and author DeB. Randolph Keim as a witness and that Custer "wilted like a whipped cur."

Whatever the circumstances, some scholars have reasoned that Custer backed off his threat for the good of the outfit; others have questioned Custer's fortitude, which was absurd.

There is a good possibility that Benteen's accusation of abandonment, if there even was any abandonment, was misdirected. No evidence exists, but there is a distinct possibility that Captain Edward Myers could have provided the information necessary to answer the question at the time of the battle about the disposition of Elliott and his men.

Myers was dispatched by Custer to search for Joel Elliott and the missing troopers. The report by Myers that he rode about two miles without observing any sign of them has been taken for granted. At that time, Elliott was possibly within two miles of the battlefield—pinned down or already dead and remaining the subject of Indian interest. It is suspect that Myers could have ridden two miles without noticing anything suspicious—no heavy firing, no assemblage of aroused Indians nearby or up ahead.

Captain Myers had been known to disobey orders in the past and had in fact been convicted a year earlier at a court-martial and sentenced to be dismissed from the service but was later restored to duty. Could Myers have, in the face of an overwhelming number of Indians advancing from that direction, failed to ride those two miles or adequately search for Elliott and simply reported that he had? The immediate area was teeming with warriors, and human nature may have played a part in Myers being overly cautious and less than zealous in carrying out his orders. His patrol would certainly have kept their mouths shut about any deviation from Custer's orders.

Consequently, was it actually Myers and not Custer who had abandoned Elliott? Benteen should have questioned Myers—and the troopers in his patrol—with respect to how far they had ventured downstream looking for Elliott and why they had not kept searching until they had found the major and his men.

If the possibility exists that Myers could have been derelict in his duty, why then would Benteen choose to bypass Myers to place the blame on Custer?

Perhaps Benteen chose his commander as his target for practical reasons. Myers was known to be a hot-tempered man who had once pulled his pistol on a fellow officer. To add to the intrigue, Myers had been the officer who rushed into Custer's tent on June 8, 1867, during the Hancock Expedition to report that Major Wickliffe Cooper had just taken his own life. That ruling of suicide was years later changed to "died by hand of person or persons unknown." Myers was the last man known to be present with Cooper in that tent.

Could it be that Benteen wanted no part of the dangerous Captain Edward Myers and instead thought he had found an easier mark in Custer, whom he already hated and who it could be presumed—in the name of proper military order—would not publicly confront Benteen?

Regardless, Benteen's accusations that Custer had abandoned Elliott created dissension for years to come among the officers of the regiment who chose sides along loyalty lines.

And, strangely enough, the real blame in the matter has been completely overlooked as people chose sides—it was Elliott's own fault for riding off on his own, without orders from Custer. Elliott placed himself and his men in a dangerous situation, and when orders are disobeyed in combat soldiers often pay for it with their lives.

This controversy brewed within the Seventh Cavalry while Sheridan and Custer resumed their December march toward the remnants of the various Indian villages. Farther downstream from Black Kettle's village, Sheridan and Custer found a most disconcerting sight in an abandoned village reportedly belonging to Kiowa chief Satanta.

While preparing for this Winter Campaign of 1868–69 Phil Sheridan was nagged by the number of settlers, especially white women, who had fallen into the hands of the hostile Indians raiding across Kansas. One instance that particularly haunted Sheridan and later George Armstrong Custer was the fate of a young woman named Clara Blinn.

Richard and Clara Blinn and their infant son, Willie, had been traveling by wagon train to Franklin County, Kansas, when they were attacked on the Colorado plains by Arapaho or Cheyenne warriors. During the ensuing skirmish, Clara and Willie were somehow taken captive. The circumstances surrounding the abduction are unknown, although the wagon train was said to have been carrying eleven armed men, only one of whom was wounded, and no other members were killed or captured—including Blinn's husband. Clara soon managed to smuggle a heartrending letter out of an Indian camp beseeching someone, anyone, to help save her and her little boy.

Sheridan had been informed of Clara Blinn's captivity when he received a letter from her father, W. T. Harrington, who pleaded with Sheridan to rescue his daughter and grandson. The ultimate mission of Sheridan's Winter Campaign had now taken on a more personal chivalrous purpose—if not rescuing Clara Blinn, then protecting others from suffering the same fate.

Now Sheridan and Custer had returned to examine the battlefield. Downstream, at the site of a village determined to be Kiowa under Satanta, they encountered a grisly discovery—the bodies of Clara Blinn and her son, Willie. Mrs. Blinn had been shot twice in the forehead from point-blank range, her skull crushed, and her scalp taken. Willie, who had been reduced to skin and bones, had likely been picked up by the feet and bashed against a tree. It was speculated that the two captives had been killed at about the same time that Custer had charged into Black Kettle's village, perhaps because the Indians, as Custer reported, feared "she might be recaptured by us and her testimony used against them."

Sheridan and his seven-hundred-man force continued to follow the Indian trail for another seventy-five miles until happening upon a large band of Indians. The chief of these Kiowa, none other than Satanta, rode out to display a message from Colonel Hazen—who had the unenviable task of determining the status of Indians—that indicated that he and the other chief present, Lone Wolf, were friendly and should not be disturbed. Sheridan challenged Satanta to demonstrate his tribe's friendliness by accompanying him to the reservation at Fort Cobb. When Satanta hesitated, Sheridan seized the two chiefs and threatened to hang them if the tribe did not submit to the reservation. Most of the Kiowa grudgingly complied to save the lives of their chiefs.

In January 1869, Custer swept through the Wichita Mountains with only a detail of forty sharpshooters and convinced an Arapaho village of sixty-five lodges under Chief Little Raven to surrender. Another tribe had been subdued, which it was hoped would make a difference with bringing peace and tranquility to the plains.

On March 15, 1869, while campaigning with elements of the Seventh Cavalry reinforced by the Nineteenth Kansas Volunteer Cavalry, Custer was notified by his scouts that they had located two Cheyenne villages consisting of a combined 260 lodges under Chiefs Medicine Arrow and Little Robe at Sweetwater Creek, Texas.

The Kansans were certain that these were the Indians who held two white women, Mrs. Anna Belle Morgan and Miss Sarah C. White, whose rescue was a major reason the unit had mobilized the previous fall. Mrs. Morgan, a bride of one month, had been taken from James Morgan's homestead on the Solomon River near Delphos. Her brother, Daniel Brewster, had accompanied the expedition to search for her. Eighteen-year-old Sarah White had been seized at her family homestead on Granny Creek near Concordia at the same time that her father was killed.

In advance of his weary command, Custer, in the company of only First Lieutenant William W. Cooke, brazenly entered the Cheyenne village unannounced and was escorted to the lodge of Chief Little Robe. Custer shared the pipe ritual with the chief and was the subject of incantations and ceremonies by a holy man that, unknown to Custer, were intended to signify that if he acted treacherously toward the Indians he and his command would be killed. In spite of this attempted intimidation, which ended with ashes from the pipe bowl being dropped on Custer's boot, he confirmed that the two white women in question were indeed captives in the village.

Custer returned to announce the news to his command. The Kansas cavalrymen were elated, and demanded that an immediate attack be launched. The fate of Clara Blinn and her son, however, was foremost on Custer's mind. He had agonized over those deaths and feared that these captives would also be killed if he initiated an attack.

Much to the outrage of the Kansans—many of whom branded Custer a coward and a traitor—he decided that they would attempt to parley for the release of Mrs. Morgan and Miss White before taking any military action. It was all Custer could do to restrain the irate volunteers from taking matters into their own hands.

Opportunity arose, however, when Chief Little Robe and a delegation visited the cavalry bivouac under a flag of truce. Custer ignored the flag, seized three minor chiefs as hostages, and threatened to hang them if the white women were not released.

Three days later, when intense negotiation failed to break the stalemate and a battle loomed, Custer looped three ropes over the limb of a large willow tree and paraded his hostages beneath. At that point, the Cheyenne relented and released their white captives.

Custer also demanded that the Indians report to Camp Supply, but the chiefs argued that their ponies were too weak and could not travel. Instead, the Indians would report when their ponies grew stronger. Custer reluctantly agreed and offered as an incentive for compliance the release of the women and children captured at Washita.

The incident serves as an example of Custer's growing maturity as an Indian fighter, that bloodshed was not always the correct course when dealing with the enemy.

The participation of the Seventh Cavalry in the Winter Campaign quietly concluded on March 28, 1869. At that point in time, however, not all Cheyenne had submitted to the reservation.

On July 11, the Fifth Cavalry under Major Eugene Carr—about 250 troopers and 50 Pawnee scouts—swept down on an unsuspecting encampment at Summit Springs. The surprised Cheyenne dashed from their lodges, many running to reach the cover of nearby ravines, while others were cut down in the initial charge. When the smoke of burning lodges had lifted, fifty-two Indians had been killed, among them Chief Tall Bull.

Seventeen women and children were taken prisoner, including Tall Bull's wife. A pony and mule herd estimated at four hundred was confiscated, and then the entire village—weapons, food, and clothing—had been destroyed. The village also revealed the presence of two white women who had been captured on May 30 on the Saline River—one of them was killed when Carr charged; the other was severely wounded but survived.

The Battle of Summit Springs broke the will of the Indians and finally accomplished General Sheridan's mission of clearing all hostiles from between the Platte and Arkansas rivers.

But the conflict that had gained the most publicity and criticism was the Battle of the Washita. This conflict was considered a great victory in the estimation of the military establishment. Eastern humanitarians, however, called the action a massacre.

Newspaper editorials and a deluge of letters criticized the army and condemned George Armstrong Custer—unfairly comparing him to militia colonel John M. Chivington, who had attacked a Cheyenne village on November 27, 1864.

The Sand Creek affair had been a deliberate and indiscriminate slaughter. The undisciplined militia, with the blessing of their commander, killed, mutilated, and scalped at least 150 Cheyenne—two-thirds of them women and children—who had been promised safety at that location. The triumphant militiamen were hailed as heroes in Denver when they later displayed Indian scalps and other trophies during a parade and to an appreciative audience between acts at a theatrical performance.

Sand Creek had been motivated by the political ambitions of John Chivington and Colorado governor John Evans and could not remotely be called a battle or anything but a massacre based on three separate government investigations, each of which condemned this rogue attack. There was simply no comparison between Sand Creek and Washita.

Interested parties decried in particular the death of Black Kettle, whom they called a fine example of a peace-loving Indian. Indian agent Edward W. Wynkoop resigned his post in protest over the killing of the Cheyenne chief. Peace commission member Major General W. S. Harney and member Samuel F. Tappan, along with Superintendent of Indian Affairs Thomas Murphy, attested to the fact that Black Kettle was truly friendly and his death was an outrage.

Division commander General William T. Sherman summed up the army's sentiments in a letter to General Sheridan dated December 3, 1868: "This you know is a free country, and people have the lawful right to misrepresent as much as they please—and to print them—but the great mass of our people cannot be humbugged into the belief that Black Kettle's camp was friendly with its captive women and children, its herds of stolen horses and its stolen mail, arms, powder, etc.—trophies of war."

Sheridan went on the offensive to refute the assertion that Black Kettle was on a reservation at the time of the attack, and blamed the wanton raiding of the Indians for the army's retaliation. He listed as evidence items found in the village, such as mail—including a military dispatch carried by one of Sheridan's couriers who had been killed—daguerreotypes, bedding, and other domestic goods taken from settlers' cabins.

The contention that Black Kettle was a proponent of peace was true. He made a mistake, however, by harboring members of his band who had participated in recent raiding parties. The peace chief paid for it with his life.

The Battle of the Washita was without question a one-sided affair but does not by any means fit the definition of a massacre. Black Kettle had been warned prior to the attack by Hazen that his safety could not be guaranteed unless he surrendered to Sheridan, which he failed to do. The village contained captives and items taken by resident armed warriors who had recently skirmished with the soldiers and had been on raiding parties against white settlers, which was evidenced by the fact that Custer's Osage scouts tracked them to Black Kettle's doorstep.

Furthermore, Custer did not order a slaughter, rather issued specific orders to spare noncombatants. In fact, Custer followed his orders from Sheridan to the letter: "To proceed south, in the direction of the Antelope hills, thence towards the Washita river, the supposed winter seat of the hostile tribes; to destroy their villages and ponies; to kill all warriors, and bring back all women and children." Custer was a soldier following the orders of his superiors.

Incidentally, although the battle at Summit Springs was similar in most respects to Custer's victory at Washita, there was no public outcry condemning the destruction of this Cheyenne village or employing the term "massacre" to describe the battle.

The inability of the army to catch the Indians on the open plains and the failure of the government to clearly state specific hunting grounds in the provisions of the peace treaty at Medicine Lodge made necessary the implementation of "Total War," and the Battle of the Washita was the tragic result.

George Armstrong Custer may have borne the brunt of criticism from minority voices, but he understood that war was an unpleasant business and there were bound to be detractors in any conflict. However, he could take pride in the knowledge that the campaign had established him as the premier Indian fighter in the land.

Five

Battling Sioux in Yellowstone Country

Armstrong and Libbie settled in for the summer of 1869 at the Seventh Cavalry regimental campsite at Big Bend, two miles east of Fort Hays, Kansas. Much of the time was whiled away enjoyably entertaining a succession of guests—including P. T. Barnum, who wanted to meet Custer and accompany him on a buffalo hunt. Detachments of the Seventh Cavalry were stationed at various posts along the Kansas Pacific Railway. Custer would occasionally accompany patrols, but for the most part his summer was leisurely, with evenings spent enjoying horseback rides with Libbie.

One famous neighbor of the fort was the notorious gambler and gunslinger James Butler "Wild Bill" Hickok. Wild Bill has been the subject of so many tall tales and dime-novel exaggerations that it is often difficult to separate fact from fiction. One of those colorful stories at issue concerns Tom Custer, Armstrong's younger brother, while the Seventh Cavalry was stationed at Fort Hays, Kansas, in 1869 and Hickok was the marshal of nearby Hays City.

Tom Custer was a wild and reckless young man, who frequently drank to excess. On one of those inebriated occasions, Tom was said to have ridden through Hays City shooting out lights and windows, then urging his horse into a crowded saloon, which caused considerable damage. This apparently had not been the first time Tom had sent the patrons of a saloon scrambling with his horse. Although Wild Bill was a friend of the elder Custer, enough was enough. Tom was promptly dragged off his mount by Wild Bill, hauled before a justice of the peace, and fined for his rash act. Tom was incensed with Hickok over the arrest and vowed revenge.

On New Years's Eve, Tom returned to Hays City with three burly soldiers and hung around the saloon to wait for Hickok. When Wild Bill strolled into the establishment, the soldiers cornered and disarmed him and it appeared that physical revenge for Tom's arrest was about to be exacted. A friendly bartender, however, tossed a loaded pistol (or shotgun) to Wild Bill and he commenced firing. When the smoke had cleared, the three soldiers lay sprawled on the barroom floor, wounded but from all accounts still very much alive. Tom Custer lit out for Fort Hays to seek the assistance of his brother.

George Armstrong Custer, however, had departed for Fort Leavenworth to spend the holiday. Tom then sought out General Phil Sheridan, who ordered the arrest of Hickok.

Word of the impending arrest reached Wild Bill before the soldiers whom Sheridan had dispatched. Hickok thought it prudent to vanish for the time being and hopped a freight train headed for Ellsworth and Abilene until cooler heads prevailed.

The impetuous Thomas Ward Custer was born on March 15, 1845, in New Rumley, Ohio, to Emanuel and Maria Custer, the third of five children. At the outbreak of the Civil War he attempted to enlist in the army from his home in Monroe, Michigan, but was thwarted when Emanuel notified the recruiter that his son was only sixteen and therefore too young for service. Tom, however, would not be denied. He crossed the border to the town of his birth, New Rumley, Ohio, and on September 2, 1861, was sworn in as a private in Company H of the Twenty-first Ohio Infantry. He fought as a common foot soldier for the next three years, participating in such battles as Shiloh, Stones River, Chickamauga, Missionary Ridge, Chattanooga, and the Atlanta Campaign. His distinguished service gained him duty as escort for various generals, and he was promoted to corporal on January 1, 1864.

Tom, however, craved the excitement and notoriety that the cavalry had provided for his famous brother. On October 23, 1864, Tom accepted an appointment as second lieutenant, Company B, Sixth Michigan Cavalry, and he was soon detailed as an aide-de-camp to his older brother. Armstrong showed Tom no favoritism and often chose him for extra assignments—which evoked grumbling from the sibling, who swore it was not fair. Nevertheless, the hardened veterans of the unit were skeptical of their commanding officer's sibling—until early April 1865. Tom, in the tradition of his brother, was about to make some history of his own.

On April 3, 1865, General Robert E. Lee, with eighty thousand men, was retreating west through the Appomattox River Valley and happened to pass just north of General Custer's campsite. Custer followed until reaching Namozine Creek, where the bridge had been destroyed. Rebel fortifications could be observed across the river, and Custer, not knowing he was greatly outnumbered, ordered one detachment to outflank the position while men with axes were detailed to remove fallen trees from the creek in order to permit the remainder of his troops to charge across.

Tom Custer, however, became impatient, and spurred his horse to brazenly streak across the creek toward the enemy position. His action inspired the other troops to follow, and the Rebels quickly broke under the surprise pressure. Tom chased the retreating enemy and unhesitatingly charged directly into a skirmish line near Namozine Church. In the end, Tom presented his brother with a Confederate battle flag, which at that time was considered quite a prize, and fourteen prisoners, including three officers. Major General Philip Sheridan recommended that Tom be brevetted to major and awarded the Medal of Honor for his bravery.

Three days later when Lee's exhausted army inadvertently split into two columns, General Custer's opportunistic cavalrymen plunged into them at a place called Sayler's Creek. Tom Custer was at the front of the Third Brigade when it led the charge against enemy fortifications. The Rebels once again broke but continued to fight as they withdrew. Tom spotted an enemy standard-bearer and was about to capture another prized flag when the Confederate soldier fired point-blank at the charging Custer's head. The bullet struck Tom in the cheek and exited behind his ear, knocking him backward against his horse's rump. Tom's face was blackened with powder and blood poured from the severe wound. Tom righted himself, coolly drew his pistol, shot the standard-bearer, and grabbed the coveted banner.

Colonel (later General) Henry Capehart had witnessed the scene and later said that "for intrepidity I never saw this incident surpassed." Tom wheeled his horse and raced to show his trophy to his brother. The general took one look at Tom's face and ordered him to the rear for medical attention. Tom, however, refused, stating that he would not leave the field until the battle was over. Armstrong Custer placed his younger brother under arrest and had him escorted to the surgeon who had set up a hospital at a nearby plantation. For this demonstration of courage, Tom was brevetted lieutenant colonel and awarded his second Medal of Honor.

Thomas Ward Custer became the first person in history to be distinguished with two awards of our nation's highest military medal and was the only double honoree during the Civil War.

Tom served with his brother in Texas until being officially mustered out on April 24, 1866. After a brief appointment as second lieutenant, First Cavalry, he accepted an appointment to first lieutenant, Seventh Cavalry, effective July 28, 1866.

During the 1867 Hancock Expedition, Tom was involved in the shooting of deserters and his brother's mad dash across Kansas, which led to the elder Custer facing a court-martial. The following year he participated in the Battle of the Washita, where he was slightly wounded in the right hand and assumed command of Company C when Captain Louis Hamilton was killed.

Tom, who worshiped his older brother, endeared himself to Libbie Custer and was a prominent member of the Custer "royal family" at the various frontier posts where the Seventh Cavalry was garrisoned. He did, however, have an affinity for playing cards and was known to habitually drink to excess. It has been rumored that he had fathered several children in Ohio. He apparently was prepared at some point to marry a New Jersey woman named Lulie Burgess, but she died before the union took place and Tom remained a bachelor for the remainder of his life.

After wintering at Fort Leavenworth, George Armstrong Custer returned to the field. The summer of 1870 was bloody in Kansas, and he was kept busy chasing marauding bands of Indians who terrorized the homesteaders and railroad.

The monotony of military life and frontier duty, however, gnawed at him, and he had begun to question his future in the army. The Seventh Cavalry was scheduled to be dispatched in small units on Reconstruction duty to various areas of the South, and Custer desired to test the civilian waters before that assignment. In fact, Armstrong and Libbie discussed the prospect of his retirement from the service.

Rather than make a hasty decision, Custer decided to obtain a leave of absence in order to investigate opportunities in New York, where he was a well-known and popular figure. On January 11, 1871, he sent Libbie to Monroe by way of Topeka and traveled east on a leave that would extend until September of that year.

Custer quickly cultivated his friendships with wealthy investors such as John Jacob Astor, August Belmont, and Jay Gould. He traveled comfortably in this circle of high financial and influential political society and had soon developed an idea that would interest these men—and, he hoped, make himself rich.

The lure of silver and gold from rich strikes in Western mines had been the reason for many of the desertions that had plagued the Seventh Cavalry from its inception. For Custer, these mines held the prospect of an investment that could reap great rewards. He had at one point taken the time to investigate the potential of one such silver mine, the Stevens Lode, which was located about ten miles from Georgetown, Colorado.

Custer, whose famous name gained him entrée to the most reclusive tycoon, pitched his confidence in the Stevens Lode to potential investors with the fervor of one of his cavalry charges. Two thousand shares of stock were issued at fifty dollars a share with a valuation of one hundred dollars each. Astor handed over ten thousand dollars, Belmont was in for fifteen thousand dollars, others chipped in thousands more, and Custer subscribed to thirty-five thousand dollars, although likely not in cash but rather a promoter's share.

While in New York promoting his silver mine, Custer dressed in Brooks Brothers suits and was a welcome guest at fashionable dinner parties and other events reserved for the social elite. He mingled with celebrities and dignitaries at Delmonico's and other fine restaurants, attended gala affairs at local mansions, frequented the opera and theatrical performances (Custer loved the theater throughout his life), sailed on private yachts, and traveled to Saratoga for the horse races.

When September rolled around, however, Custer had failed to find his fortune in the big city and chose the army over civilian life. He returned with wife Libbie to duty with a two-company detachment of the Seventh Cavalry that was stationed in Elizabethtown, Kentucky.

In time, Custer sold his shares in the Stevens Lode and sent the money to his brother Nevin to use as a down payment on a farm near his parents—a most prudent decision. His investors never realized a profit from the silver mine. The enterprise collapsed after several years of assaying and mining.

This quiet community not far from Louisville was known as E-Town or Betseytown by the locals. Custer's duties included assisting federal marshals in keeping track of the activities of the Ku Klux Klan and moonshiners and purchasing horses for the army. Otherwise, his days were marked with boredom, except perhaps for a stimulating game of chess with a local judge, an afternoon at the racetrack, discussing horses at a local farm, or hunting to the hounds—his leash of hounds totaled about eighty. Custer also owned a number of thoroughbreds that he raced, the best being Don Juan and Frogtown.

Custer's loyal orderly, or striker, at the time was thirty-year-old John W. Burkman from Allegheny County, Pennsylvania. His autobiography states that he was an emigrant from Germany, but his death certificate lists Missouri as his birthplace. He worked as a teamster for trader William Bent before enlisting in the Fifth Missouri Volunteer Mounted Infantry and fighting in the August 1861 Civil War battle of Wilson's Creek. At some point, Burkman joined Brigadier General Henry H. Sibley's troops in Minnesota and campaigned against the Sioux in the early 1860s.

Burkman enlisted in Company A, Seventh Cavalry, in August 1870 but was soon detailed as an orderly to George Armstrong Custer. Both men shared a common love of animals, and Burkman over the years would lovingly care for Custer's horses and dogs.

John Burkman, who was bestowed with the nickname Old Nutriment for his insatiable appetite, was illiterate and slow of speech and movement but became indispensable to the Custers. Libbie Custer wrote: "My husband and I were so attached to him, and appreciated so deeply his fidelity, we could not thank the good fortune enough that gave us one so loyal to our interests."

In January 1872, George Armstrong Custer enjoyed a pleasant respite from duty in Kentucky when he was summoned to Nebraska by General Phil Sheridan to be part of an escort for Russian Grand Duke Alexis Romanov.

The visiting nineteen-year-old third son of Russian czar Alexander II, who spoke excellent English, had been receiving royal treatment from the government and the military in the form of lavish banquets, flowery speeches, and rifle salutes. Russia had been a trusted and valuable ally to the Union during the Civil War. The presence of a Russian squadron in the ports of San Francisco and New York had served as a warning to France and England not to interfere in the conflict. The young man enjoyed his excursion through the various cities—even handing out gold coins to the impoverished—but the highlight of his trip would be a buffalo hunt, the most famous sport in the United States at that time.

In addition to Custer, Sheridan, Russian admirals, various other dignitaries, and a flock of reporters, the Nebraska hunting entourage would include William F. "Buffalo Bill" Cody and about one hundred Lakota Sioux Indians led by Chief Spotted Tail. The chief brought along his comely, flirtatious sixteen-year-old niece, the first cousin of Crazy Horse, who was nicknamed Miss Spotted Tail by the infatuated soldiers.

Another invited guest, a questionable choice to say the least, was Lakota Sioux war chief Pawnee Killer, Custer's nemesis from the 1867 Hancock Expedition who had murdered Lieutenant Kidder's detachment and later was an enemy participant in the Beecher Island and Summit Springs battles. But Pawnee Killer was a guest of the government and therefore received a sort of temporary amnesty—certainly to the ire of Custer and other army officers who wanted to see the warrior pay for his treachery.

The hunting party established a base camp on Red Willow Creek—dubbed Camp Alexis—which had been furnished with plush accouterments featuring forty of the army's best wall tents, two elegantly carpeted hospital tents, Chinese lanterns hanging from trees, and meals served with caviar, champagne, and other delicacies. The guests were entertained with singing and dancing and by exhibitions of tribal war dances, horse races, and prowess with bow and arrow.

On January 14, Custer, who had been appointed to lead the hunt, and Cody, accompanied by Spotted Tail and eight warriors, led the Grand Duke through snow that rose to eighteen inches deep in search of their prey. Cody located a small herd, and Custer and Alexis charged. The Grand Duke twice emptied his six-shot revolver without success. Finally, Alexis brought down his first buffalo with a well-placed pistol shot to the head. A courier was immediately dispatched to North Platte—fifty miles away—to cable the czar in Russia with the triumphant news.

When camp broke up two days later, the Grand Duke, who had taken quite a fancy to Custer, received permission from Sheridan allowing his newfound friend to accompany him on the remainder of his tour. Custer and Alexis boarded the Union Pacific to visit Denver and engaged in another buffalo hunt before heading east.

Libbie joined them at Louisville and marveled at the royal treatment at each stop. The Custers enjoyed grand balls, elegant restaurants, receptions, shopping, and even coffee and rolls served in bed in a suite adjacent to that of the Grand Duke. The entourage traveled by steamboat down the Ohio to the Mississippi and on to New Orleans, where Alexis boarded a Russian warship for a trip to Havana before heading home.

In a decidedly less lavish style, Armstrong and Libbie traveled to Monroe, Michigan, to attend the wedding of Custer's sister Margaret Emma, "Maggie," to First Lieutenant James Calhoun.

James (Jimmy or Jimmi) Calhoun was born on August 24, 1845, in Cincinnati, Ohio. He graduated from Mt. Pleasant Academy in Ossining, New York, in June 1860 and spent the initial years of the Civil War traveling through Europe. Calhoun enlisted as a private in the Fourteenth Infantry in January 1864 and was promoted to first sergeant in February 1865. He applied for a commission in May 1865 but was found unqualified by an examining board. Calhoun remained a first sergeant until July 1867, when he was appointed second lieutenant, Thirty-second Infantry, at Camp Warner, Oregon. He served with his unit in Arizona and at Camp Grant for two years before being transferred to the Twenty-first Infantry in July 1869.

When the army was reorganized in 1870, Calhoun was unassigned and awaiting orders. At this time he was apparently present at Fort Leavenworth, Kansas, where he met the visiting Maggie, with whom he became romantically involved. Custer must have taken to Calhoun as well—Calhoun, along with First Lieutenant W. W. Cooke, witnessed Custer's April 1870 last will and testament.

In January 1871, with assistance from Custer, Calhoun was appointed first lieutenant and assigned to the Seventh Cavalry. He reported for Reconstruction duty at Bagdad, Kentucky, as commander of Company L. Calhoun expressed his appreciation of Custer's help in a letter dated April 23, 1871: "I have just received my commission as 1st Lt. in the 7th Cavalry, and it reminds me more vividly than ever how many, many times I am under obligations to you for your very great kindness to me in my troubles. I shall do my best to prove my gratitude. If the time comes you will not find me wanting."

This man who was relentlessly teased because of his seriousness and nicknamed Adonis due to his good looks, blond hair, and six-one height married Maggie Custer on March 7, 1872, in the Methodist church in Monroe. The couple would not have children.

Finally, mercifully, in February 1873, Custer's dreaded duty in Kentucky came to an end. The War Department had agreed to continue providing protection to engineering parties of the Northern Pacific Railroad that were exploring and mapping the Yellowstone region in Montana and Wyoming. The Seventh Cavalry would be reunited, and George Armstrong Custer would be a part of that summer's expedition.

In 1870, the Northern Pacific Railroad had commenced laying tracks and was moving steadily westward from its eastern terminus in Duluth, Minnesota. In order to continue plotting the route of the line west of the Missouri River into Montana, however, the survey crews would be venturing into the home of hostile Indians. Fortunately for the railroad, the army regarded the completion of rails across this relatively unexplored region as having great national strategic importance and was enthusiastic about offering protection for the engineering work.

The first Yellowstone Expedition, designed to determine the Northern Pacific's route between Bismarck and Bozeman, Montana, was undertaken in

1871 and lasted only one month. In 1872, Colonel David S. Stanley provided escort for a survey by the Northern Pacific, which was soon terminated due to frequent skirmishes with superior forces of hostile Sioux led by Hunkpapa chief Gall. To remedy that threat, horsemen—George Armstrong Custer's Seventh Cavalry regiment—would support Stanley's infantry on the 1873 expedition.

The forty-five-year-old Ohioan David Stanley had graduated from West Point in 1852, ninth in a class that would include fifteen future generals. Stanley's classmate Phil Sheridan had been set back a year due to a suspension. Stanley had served on duty fighting Cheyenne on the Solomon River; married Anna Maria Wright in 1857—the couple would have seven children—and during the Civil War was wounded by a bullet in the neck while leading the decisive assault at the November 1864 Battle of Franklin, for which he would be awarded the Medal of Honor for his bravery. Now Colonel Stanley had been chosen to command this expedition with the mission of protecting surveyors and scientists with the Northern Pacific Railroad.

The Seventh Cavalry regiment had been spread out around the South on Reconstruction duty and assembled as a unit in Memphis, Tennessee, during the last week of March 1873. From Sioux City, Iowa, Custer led ten companies up the Missouri toward Dakota Territory to prepare for the expedition.

Meanwhile, Major Marcus Reno with Captain Thomas B. Weir's Company D and Captain Myles W. Keogh's Company I would continue by rail to Fort Snelling, Minnesota, where they would participate in the Northern Boundary Survey, a joint British-American operation organized to map the border between the United States and Canada. An accurate survey of the boundary line was required in order to determine responsibility for raids by Indians and crimes by outlaws, as well as a manner in which to inform settlers whether they were settling in the United States or Canada.

Colonel David Stanley's expedition marched from Fort Rice on June 20. The column was comprised of nineteen infantry companies, two cannon, ten companies of the Seventh Cavalry—over fifteen hundred soldiers—and about 350 civilians, which included the engineering and scientific party and the teamsters, a detachment of white and Indian scouts, a herd of nearly 450 cattle, and a train of 275 wagons. Two steamboats—the *Far West* and the *Josephine*—had been chartered to haul supplies on the Yellowstone River.

Custer had endured three years of inactivity and was thrilled to be out in the field once again. He joyously roamed ahead of the column acting as scout and led daily hunting parties, which kept the messes stocked with fresh meat. Custer also collected fossils and embraced taxidermy, working late into the night preparing game for mounting.

In spite of traveling through hail, rain, and windstorms, the initial portion of the trek heading west across Dakota toward Montana could be described as an extended party, with the regimental band furnishing musical accompaniment. Custer occupied his time with outdoor-related activities and writing letters to Libbie—including one that was forty-two pages long—that described the remarkable terrain and detailed his hunting exploits. A number of other men, however, let their vices get the best of them.

For instance, Captain George W. Yates, Custer's good friend, fretting over the poor health of his wife, who had endured a difficult pregnancy, went on a binge and remained intoxicated for days while losing hundreds of dollars playing cards.

The father of thirty-two-year-old George Yates was a Princeton graduate, and other ancestors included a mayor of Albany, New York, and a governor of New York State. Yates' father died in 1855, and at that time his mother relocated to Lansing, Michigan, with three of her four sons—George was left behind to live with an uncle in Ontario County, New York. In 1860, at age seventeen—with five hundred dollars from his uncle—George traveled to Texas and became involved in horse trading.

At the outbreak of the Civil War, Yates enlisted in Company A, Fourth Michigan Volunteer Infantry, and participated in the First Battle of Bull Run. He was wounded at Fredericksburg when a shell exploded beneath his horse. While recuperating in Michigan, Yates struck up a friendship with George Armstrong Custer. In May 1863, Custer convinced his superior, General Alfred Pleasonton, to add Yates to the general's staff.

In March 1864, when Pleasonton was removed from his cavalry command, Yates accompanied the general to the Department of the Missouri in St. Louis. In June 1864 he was mustered out of the Fourth Michigan, and two months later he obtained a commission as first lieutenant, Forty-fifth Missouri Infantry, while remaining on Pleasonton's staff. On January 5, 1865, Yates married nineteen-year-old Lucretia "Lily" Beaumont Irwin, who was from a prominent St. Louis family. In November 1866, Yates filed for divorce on the grounds that Lily had abandoned him. Rumors circulated, however, that it was Yates' interest in other women that doomed the marriage.

In May 1866, Yates was appointed second lieutenant, Second Cavalry, and reported to Fort McPherson, Nebraska. One year later—with assistance from his friend Custer—Yates was appointed captain, Seventh Cavalry, and joined the regiment in November 1867 at Fort Leavenworth as commander of Company F, which became known as the "Band Box" troop for its smart appearance. Yates led this company at the November 1868 Battle of the Washita.

In February 1872 he married Annie Gibson Roberts, a refined and well-educated young lady whose grandfather had served as chief justice of the Pennsylvania Supreme Court and whose father was chief engineer of the Northern Pacific Railroad. The couple would have three children.

Yates was not the only loser at cards. First Lieutenant Jimmy Calhoun, Custer's brother-in-law, lost all of his money playing poker and could not find anyone who would trust him with a loan. Lieutenant Colonel Frederick Grant, the president's son, who was attached as an observer for General Phil Sheridan, also drank to excess—although Custer found Grant to be a fine companion most of the time. Tom Custer had a streak of losing card hands and had been borrowing money in order to continue playing.

One member of the expedition whose company Custer particularly enjoyed was West Point best friend and former Confederate general Thomas L. Rosser, who was in charge of the surveying crews as chief engineer of the Northern Pacific Railroad's Dakota Division.

Rosser had been born into a farming family on October 15, 1836, in Campbell County, Virginia, and moved thirteen years later to Panola County, Texas, from whence Rosser entered the U.S. Military Academy at West Point in 1856. Custer roomed next door and the two young men became intimate friends— Rosser tall and swarthy with jet-black hair and piercing black eyes; Custer slender with wavy blond hair, blue eyes, and fair complexion. This close relationship sadly ended in late April 1861—two weeks before graduation—when Rosser resigned from the Academy to join the Confederate army.

Rosser was commissioned a lieutenant and assigned duty as an instructional officer with the Washington Artillery. He was in command of a company of that unit three months later at the First Battle of Bull Run and was promoted to captain two months later. Rosser distinguished himself while commanding the battery during the Peninsula Campaign and the Seven Days' battles and was wounded in May 1862 at Mechanicsville—the first of nine wounds he would suffer during the war.

He was promoted to lieutenant colonel of artillery while he recovered from his wound and when he returned to duty was promoted by Major General Jeb Stuart to colonel of the Fifth Virginia Cavalry. On September 28, 1863, he was promoted to brigadier general and assumed command of the Laurel Brigade. His brigade was in constant action, including the May 11, 1864, battle at Yellow Tavern, where General Stuart was killed. Rosser faced his friend Custer as an opposing general on the field of battle on several occasions, with Custer generally—with one exception at Trevilian Station—gaining the upper hand.

Throughout the war, Rosser proved himself an excellent field commander, but eventually his depleted ranks presented little challenge to the Union horsemen. In spite of the lack of success, he was promoted to major general on November 1, 1864, and remained in the Valley until March 1865, when he joined the main army.

After the war, Rosser and his wife moved to Baltimore, where he briefly studied law and became superintendent of the National Express Company. He soon accepted the position as an assistant engineer in the construction of the Pittsburgh and Connellsville Railroad. Rosser left that position in the spring of 1870 to join the Northern Pacific Railroad. In February 1871, he was appointed chief engineer of the Dakota Division at Fargo.

Custer later wrote about their relationship on the Yellowstone Expedition:

Scarcely a day passed, during the progress of the expedition from the Missouri to the Yellowstone, that General Rosser and I were not in each other's company a portion of the time as we rode in our saddles, boot to boot, climbed together unvisited cliffs, picked our way through trackless canyons, or sat at the same mess table or about the same campfire. During the strolling visits we frequently questioned and enlightened each other as to the unexplained or but partially understood battles and movements in which each had played a part against the other.

Although the expedition moved along at its normal pace, it was inevitable that the headstrong Custer and Colonel Stanley, who has been described as "a squat, humorless, peevish alcoholic . . . the antithesis of Custer," would come to loggerheads. Neither man had much respect for the other.

Shortly after the expedition was under way, a drunken Stanley, who had invited another sutler along for his infantry, ordered that Augustus Baliran, a sutler attached to the cavalry, return to Fort Rice by that evening or face death by hanging. The incident was reported to Custer, who reminded Stanley that permission had been given to Baliran to accompany the Seventh Cavalry. Stanley relented but ordered Colonel Frederick Grant to destroy Baliran's stock of whisky. Instead of carrying out the order, the kindhearted Grant advised the sutler to temporarily distribute his stores to various Seventh Cavalry officers for safekeeping. Stanley rescinded the order when he sobered up.

Another matter of contention concerned the presence of Custer's black cook, Mary Adams, and the cast-iron stove that he had brought along. Mary's preparation of wild game made Custer's mess extremely popular, and this apparently did not sit well with Stanley. The colonel ordered that Custer rid himself of the stove, which was nonmilitary equipment, but it survived several attempts to have it abandoned.

The column halted on July 1 at Muddy Creek, which was overflowing and would require the infantrymen to construct a makeshift bridge in order to cross. Custer, whose troops Stanley had expected to assist with the crossing, had, under his own initiative, marched a detachment of his cavalry some distance ahead of the main body. He then dispatched a messenger requesting that Stanley send him forage and rations. An angry Stanley ordered that Custer return at once and consider himself under arrest.

The Seventh Cavalry with its insolent commander was exiled to march at the rear of the column. Tom Rosser reasoned with Stanley, advising that common sense dictated that the cavalry lead the way. A sober Stanley agreed and not only lifted the arrest but also apologized to Custer, asked his forgiveness, and vowed to quit drinking. Regardless of promises, Stanley remained in an intoxicated state, which for all intents and purposes permitted Custer to assume leadership of the expedition.

In mid-July, Custer led two companies on a treacherous march through the Badlands to reach the Yellowstone River where the steamer *Far West* waited with provisions and mail. They constructed a supply depot on the south bank of the Yellowstone about eight miles above the mouth of Glendive Creek and left Captain Frederick W. Benteen and two companies behind to guard "Stanley's Stockade."

The party atmosphere ended when the expedition moved into the Yellowstone River Valley, an area known to be populated by the Lakota Sioux tribe. The order of march was Custer's cavalry, followed by the surveyors with their transits and maps, and the infantry brought up the rear.

Custer, his favorite scout, Bloody Knife, and a small detachment would normally ride in advance of the column. Bloody Knife became concerned by the frequency of fresh Indian sign and warned Custer to be prepared for an attack.

Custer generally heeded the advice or information provided by Bloody Knife without question. There was no doubt that a bond of trust had developed between the two men, although their time together had been brief.

Bloody Knife (Arikara name: Nee si Ra Pat; Sioux name: Tamina WeWe) was born sometime between 1837 and 1840 in Dakota Territory to a Hunkpapa Sioux father and Arikara (Ree) mother. He lived with the Sioux, who were traditional enemies of the Arikara, and was discriminated against due to his mixed blood and treated as an outcast. This resulted in a deep hatred for that tribe and in particular one of his peers, Gall, with whom Bloody Knife developed a feud that endured for years. Sitting Bull, who had adopted Gall as a younger brother, also subjected the mixed-blood boy to abuse.

When Bloody Knife was about fifteen years of age, his mother left her husband and returned to her people at Fort Clark, an American Fur Company trading post on the upper Missouri near present-day Stanton, North Dakota. He was able to make good use of his multicultural background in the early

1860s when he carried mail between Fort Totten and other Missouri forts. Many mail carriers were killed by Sioux on this route, which made it difficult to employ riders, but Bloody Knife almost always got the mail through on time. He also occasionally worked as an army scout and a runner and hunter for the American Fur Company.

The animosity between Bloody Knife and Gall nearly resulted in Gall's death during the winter of 1865–66. Bloody Knife was serving as a scout with a detachment of soldiers who went to arrest Gall, who was visiting a Sioux camp south of Fort Berthold. Gall attempted to escape, and was bayoneted. Bloody Knife stepped forward with intentions of shooting his enemy in the head but was stopped by an officer who believed that Gall was already dead. Gall miraculously survived and became a war chief with whom to be reckoned.

In 1866, Bloody Knife married an Arikara woman named either She Owl or Young Owl Woman, who would give birth to at least one daughter and one son. The daughter, however, evidently died young, according to a grave marker at Fort Buford that bears the inscription: "Daughter of Bloody Knife, December 28, 1870, Disease."

Bloody Knife enlisted as a corporal in the army's Indian scouts at Fort Stevenson in May 1868 and soon acquired a serious problem with alcohol, which may have contributed to his desertion that September. He was, however, promoted to lance corporal in 1872.

When Fort Abraham Lincoln was established in June 1872, Bloody Knife was a leader of the Arikara scouts attached to it. Bloody Knife was hired for the Yellowstone Expedition of 1873, which was where he met George Armstrong Custer for the first time. He quickly became Custer's favorite scout by proving himself a faithful companion and invaluable at reading sign.

By early August, the expedition was deep into hostile territory, camped on the Yellowstone several miles downstream from the Tongue River. At noon on August 4—with the temperature hovering around 110 degrees—Custer, Captain Myles Moylan, First Lieutenants Tom Custer and James Calhoun, and Second Lieutenant Charles A. Varnum, with about ninety cavalrymen from companies A and B, had taken a break from a scout to halt in a grove of cottonwood trees near the mouth of the Tongue River (the site of present-day Miles City, Montana). The horses had been turned out to graze, the men were lazing around, and Custer was taking a nap when pickets shouted, "Indians!" The cavalrymen began firing at the small group of warriors who were attempting to scatter the horses.

Custer, with his brother and Jimmy Calhoun, mounted twenty men and gave chase. Moylan was ordered to advance more slowly with the main body. After riding about two miles up the valley, Custer became suspicious and halted his squadron. Custer, accompanied by two orderlies, cautiously continued after the Sioux, in his words, "to develop their intentions." Those intentions quickly became known when three hundred mounted warriors burst from a stand of timber and charged. It had been a trap.

Custer wheeled his thoroughbred, Dandy, and easily outdistanced the Indians to arrive back where he had left his small detachment. Moylan brought up the remainder of the squadron, and the troopers were formed into a skirmish line in the cottonwoods behind the bank of a dry streambed. The men would rise up to fire point-blank into the onrushing warriors with effective volleys that discouraged each advance. The Sioux pulled back, dismounted, and began to creep through the tall grass toward the position of the cavalrymen.

Custer and his troopers spent the long, hot afternoon defending their position against repeated assaults. The Sioux eventually set fire to the grass and advanced behind the smoke but were repulsed each time.

By late in the afternoon, ammunition was running low when—just like the script of a Western movie—the rest of the cavalry could be observed riding to the rescue. A confident Custer mounted his men and surprised the Sioux by executing a counterattack. The Indians broke and ran, and the cavalrymen chased them several miles down the valley. Custer lost only one man and two horses in the skirmish.

While Custer had been pinned down, about thirty Sioux had happened upon veterinarian Dr. John Honsinger and sutler Augustus Baliran as the two men, unaware of danger, rode ahead of the main body to join Custer. Honsinger and Baliran were brutally murdered. Most accounts relate that Private John H. Ball was also killed, although evidence does exist to suggest that he had deserted.

The command pushed up the Yellowstone until—on August 8—scout

Bloody Knife, riding with Custer in the advance, discovered the site of a recently abandoned Indian village. The scout estimated that it consisted of five hundred lodges, which would indicate the presence of perhaps as many as one thousand warriors.

Custer received permission from Stanley to follow this hot trail found by Bloody Knife and immediately dashed off with eight companies and the Arikara scouts.

After a thirty-six hour march, the trail led to the banks of the Yellowstone near the mouth of the Bighorn River. Bloody Knife swam across to determine that the tracks continued on the south side, but the river at this point was too deep and swift for the cavalry to cross. Custer decided to camp for the night and would resume attempts to cross the following morning, August 11.

At daybreak, however, the Sioux made their presence known. Hundreds of warriors hidden in the cottonwoods on the opposite bank opened up with withering rifle fire and a torrent of arrows. While the women and children gathered on the bluffs to watch, hundreds more warriors began swimming the river above and below Custer's position.

Custer reacted quickly and deployed sharpshooters to engage and, he hoped, pin down the entrenched warriors. To counter the threat from the flanks, he dispatched two companies commanded by Captain Thomas H. French down the valley and two companies under Captain Verlin Hart up the valley. Hart posted twenty men under Second Lieutenant Charles Braden in a forward position on a benchland rising from the valley.

Braden's detachment bore the brunt of the initial assault. His small unit bravely repelled four concerted efforts by the superior force to breach their line. During the battle, Braden's left thigh was shattered by a bullet and he fell critically wounded.

Custer was seemingly everywhere, handling his command with the calm deliberation and battlefield instincts that he had developed in the Civil War. He rode along his line shifting companies to meet each attack or to flush out groups of warriors from nearby ravines, all the while exposing himself to a vicious onslaught of bullets and arrows.

Finally, Stanley arrived on the field and began lobbing artillery shells into the timber across the river. Custer decided to seize the initiative. He mounted his entire 450-man command, signaled for the band to strike up "Garry Owen," and ordered a charge. He once again had surprised his enemy with this bold tactic. The Sioux responded by scattering and racing away as fast as their ponies could run. The cavalrymen chased the fleeing Indians for nine miles before losing the trail.

The Seventh Cavalry had suffered three men killed, four wounded, and eight horses lost during the engagement. Custer estimated that about forty Indians had been killed in both August battles. The identity of the Indians who attacked the Seventh Cavalry has been a matter of speculation—although Frank Grouard, a future army scout who was known to have been adopted by Sitting Bull, claimed to have participated.

Following this skirmish, the survey moved up the Yellowstone another thirty miles before halting on August 15 at Pompey's Pillar, a solitary sandstone landmark some 380 miles west of Fort Rice that had been named by Lewis and Clark. The column had settled in to rest for the day when a group of Sioux warriors opened fire on some swimming soldiers, who were scared and scattered but were otherwise unharmed. Custer chose not to pursue the hostiles.

Had the Sioux known that the cheap transportation provided by new railroads would eventually lead to the extermination of the buffalo, they might have offered more resistance to the Yellowstone Expedition. By this time the southern herds were steadily being decimated, and the northern herds were soon to follow. By 1883, all but a few small herds had vanished, and with them the fortunes of the Plains Indian tribes, who were dependent on this beast for life itself.

The Plains Indians not only regarded the buffalo as sacred, but these nomadic hunters also viewed a herd of these shaggy animals with the same prospects that modern consumers might contemplate a spacious shopping mall or grocery supercenter. There in one centralized location was nearly every item required not solely for basic survival but also as a dependable source for those luxuries that provided a comfortable standard of living.

Best of all, this shaggy beast had covered the plains in abundance. During the early nineteenth century, buffalo herds were estimated to total upwards of 75 to 100 million, an impressive figure considering that each animal weighed around a ton, with most bulls tipping the scale at a ton and a half. Nowhere else in the annals of food resources can such an infinite provider of sustenance be documented.

There has been a continuing debate about whether or not the by-products derived from the buffalo were indeed vital to the health and welfare of the average Plains Indian. Granted, there was an abundance of other wild game and those animals were assuredly a part of the menu and wardrobe. But these nomadic people sustained a thriving self-sufficiency by ingeniously utilizing every portion of the buffalo but the bellow.

The most obvious, and important, benefit was food. Buffalo were truly a four-legged commissary. The muscle was high in protein, and other parts supplied more than the daily requirements of vitamins and minerals. What was not readily consumed could be preserved for the long winter months. One manner was by drying the meat under the sun, another by pounding berries and fruit into that dried meat to create pemmican—a treat that provided every element necessary for a balanced diet.

Within the village proper, the first thing to catch the eye would be the structures, the lodges or tepees, which were constructed mainly from buffalo hides. Inside those lodges were warm coats and sleeping robes also fashioned from those same hairy hides and summer blankets made soft by scraping off the hair and tanning both sides. These dressed hides were also sewn into shirts, leggings, moccasins, and women's dresses.

Green skins made serviceable kettles for drinking and cooking. Buffalo hair was braided into ropes, lariats, and reins for ponies. Horns were used for ladles, cups, and other containers. Bull boats to traverse the rivers were made watertight with stretched hides. Hooves were boiled down to make glue for many applications. Bones could be carved into arrowheads, spear tips, or needles. Sinew for bowstrings. Skin for battle shields. Axes and hoes from shoulder blades. Sledge runners from ribs. Paint from blood. Hair to stuff pillows. Fly swatters and whisk brooms from the tail. The black beard an ornament to adorn clothing. Fuel for campfires from buffalo chips, the dried droppings. Primitive toys, including baby rattles, were constructed from various parts. And the list goes on and on.

Another advantage was that the buffalo was relatively easy to kill in whatever numbers desired. As white hunters quickly discovered when one fell, the others simply continued grazing and if the herd should happen to stampede it could be directed toward a cliff and chased over to die at the bottom.

Other game may have collectively provided the bulk of the aforementioned products, but the buffalo offered everything. It was the difference between a shopping trip to the mall compared to one to the corner convenience store.

Thus, the destruction of the great buffalo herds led to the demise of this major aspect of traditional Plains Indian lifestyle. And the railroads, which brought the hunters and made it easy to ship millions of hides to Eastern tanners, were largely responsible for those huge piles of weathered bones that were scattered about the plains as a tragic reminder of man's greed and disregard for other cultures—or for the buffalo. Railroads advertised that passengers could actually shoot buffalo while the train moved along the tracks, and the thousands of carcasses that littered the nearby landscape attested to that fact. The expanding trail of railroad tracks also chased the great herds of buffalo away from traditional ranges, which caused the various nomadic Indian tribes to follow where they came into conflict with white settlements and wagons moving west.

On August 16, Custer's column headed east on a difficult yet uneventful return march overland to the Musselshell River and down the Missouri, finally reaching Fort Abraham Lincoln on September 21—several days before Stanley's plodding foot soldiers and wagon train made their appearance. Stanley estimated that the expedition had covered 935 miles in ninety-five days.

Ironically, on the day that Custer reached Fort Lincoln, Jay Cooke & Company, the sponsor of bonds for the Northern Pacific Railroad, collapsed, bankrupting the railroad. The demise of that firm was followed by those of numerous banks and even caused the temporary closure of the New York Stock Exchange in what became known as the Panic of 1873. The end of track would be stalled at Bismarck for six years until the Northern Pacific could raise the resources to resume operations westward.

But the expedition into the Yellowstone had afforded George Armstrong Custer his first taste of battling the Sioux. It would not be his last.

Six

---◆◆◆---

Black Hills, Red Spirits

G eorge Armstrong Custer was showered with further accolades as the country's foremost Indian fighter for his actions during the Yellowstone Expedition—not to mention strengthening his relationship with the Northern Pacific Railroad. His official report of the campaign, which was published by *The New York Times* and the *Army and Navy Journal,* was well received by an adoring public.

Upon his return, he was issued orders from the War Department assigning him the command of the newly established Fort Abraham Lincoln—five miles south of Bismarck, Dakota Territory, on the Missouri River—which was still under construction when the Seventh Cavalry arrived. Six companies of the Seventh and three infantry companies would be posted at the fort, while the four additional cavalry companies, under the command of Major Joseph G. Tilford, would be stationed at Fort Rice, twenty-five miles downstream. Major Marcus A. Reno and companies I and D were wintering at Fort Totten, where they would resume escort duty for the Northern Boundary Survey in the spring.

Almost immediately, Custer departed for Monroe, Michigan, and returned with Libbie to their new duty station in November. The regimental band struck up "Home Sweet Home" and then "Garry Owen" as the officers and wives warmly welcomed the first couple.

The Custers settled into their quarters and presided over the busy winter social season at the isolated fort. There were drama performances to participate in and they would enjoy hunts, sleigh rides, monthly company balls, and nightly gatherings for conversation and playing charades and card games. On many occasions guests would assemble around the piano that had been rented in St. Paul to sing all the favorites. Custer spent much time reading and writing and, with no school at the fort, volunteered to tutor several children.

From all accounts, the atmosphere that winter at Fort Lincoln was quite congenial, which was rare at military posts where petty jealousies were known to disrupt harmony. One visitor to the Custer home said: "One was permitted to receive the courtesies of the happiest home I ever saw, where perfect love and confidence reigned. The whole regiment with one or two exceptions seemed imbued with the spirit of its commander, and in fact so close was he to his officers, that when off duty one would be led to think that all were brothers, and happy brothers at that."

Perhaps that cordiality could be attributed to the fact that notorious Custer critic Captain Frederick W. Benteen as well as Major Marcus Reno, with whom Custer shared cool relations, were stationed elsewhere.

Unfortunately, that happy home suffered tragedy on the night of February 6, 1974, when the Custer residence burned to the ground. The attic had been insulated with "warm paper," a petroleum-based product, which caught fire, and it consumed the entire house. Carpenters began work on a new two-story house that would meet Libbie's request for a bay window in the parlor.

Fort Abraham Lincoln was located on the fringes of Sioux country and therefore was rarely threatened. An Indian raiding party in April stampeded a herd of civilian mules, which Custer and all six companies recovered after a chase. Again in May, Custer rode out in an effort to prevent a rumored Sioux attack against the Arikara and Mandan but was unable to make contact. Otherwise, duty settled into the typical monotonous routine of an isolated frontier post that was known to provoke troopers into desertion, bad behavior, or drowning themselves with whisky.

Winter in Dakota Territory, however, meant blizzards dropping huge piles of snow and barbed-wire winds that tore through the countryside. It was a difficult time for man or beast, especially the Indians, whose ponies would become weak from lack of forage, and their own supplies would quickly dwindle. This was the season when patrols from the fort were limited and the officers and men settled in, waiting for spring.

While Fort Lincoln shivered in the arctic blasts, General Phil Sheridan was in Chicago making plans. He had set his sights on establishing a post that would be strategically located near the Red Cloud and Spotted Tail agencies for the purpose of discouraging the Sioux from raiding into Nebraska and the travel routes to the south. Ideally, this fort would be located somewhere in the western portion of the Great Sioux Reservation—in the vicinity of the Black Hills—territory that had been given to the Indians by provisions of the Fort Laramie Treaty of 1868 and had been deemed sacred by that tribe.

The Revolutionary War patriots had been engaged in fighting to gain independence from England when a small band of Sioux Indians led by warrior Standing Bear—prompted by their nomadic instinct—had walked from their homeland in Minnesota to visit for the first time a wilderness region along the South Dakota–Wyoming border that runs roughly one hundred miles north to south and sixty miles east to west and was known as the Black Hills.

This group of adventurers were members of the Teton or Lakota Nation of Sioux who, along with their brethren the Dakota and Nakota Sioux, had migrated from the South in the sixteenth century to settle near the headwaters of the Mississippi in northern Minnesota. The three groups over time had split into distinct nations, each speaking a different dialect and occupying their own territory, and collectively were known as "Sioux." That title, however, a French interpretation of the Chippewa word *nadoue-is-iw* meaning "little snake" or "enemy," served only as a genetic name for the three separate nations.

Standing Bear's Lakota Sioux hunting party were not by any means the first American Indians to view the Black Hills, for its dominion had been the matter of contention between a number of tribes for centuries. These particular explorers, however, regarded the discovery as if it had been preordained by their Creator. There was apparently an awakening within their souls that spoke to tell them that the innate spirits that dwelled within the Black Hills had reserved that place for them—as if some mystical magnet was calling home those who had wandered for so long. Although other tribes may have discovered this place before them, the Lakota were the first to recognize that it was sacred land.

Standing Bear returned home from his trek and spoke in glowing terms about his wondrous discovery. His assessment of the Black Hills affected his people with such a seductive force that they abandoned the north and journeyed en masse to that unknown territory to establish a homeland for the Lakota Sioux Nation. The Dakota and Nakota remained in Minnesota.

The seven principal Lakota Sioux bands that comprised the tribe— Blackfeet, Brulé, Hunkpapa, Miniconjou, Oglala, Sans Arc, Two Kettle— became the final group of Native Americans to arrive in that part of the country.

The emigrating Lakota declined to settle permanently inside the boundaries of the Black Hills, for it was considered sacred land. For three-quarters of a century they would rarely make camp out of sight of this place they now called Paha Sapa, "Hills That Are Black," and would enter only to hunt, cut lodge poles, hide out after raiding parties, or to perform ceremonies.

Each autonomous band established its own territory throughout Montana, Wyoming, Kansas, Nebraska, and the Dakota Territory but enjoyed greater numbers than their rivals due to a supportive alliance and thereby became the strongest tribe on the Great Plains. They acquired proprietorship of the area by force from the Cheyenne, who years earlier had pushed aside the Comanche, who years earlier had pushed aside the Crow. Land was taken, controlled, and protected by violence, and no tribe was better at gaining and holding territory than the Lakota Sioux.

And the Lakota would not simply fight against the encroachment of other American Indian tribes but were also bold enough to test the might of the United States of America. While George Armstrong Custer had been chasing Indians around the Kansas plains in 1867, another conflict was being waged to the north.

In 1862–63, explorer John Bozeman had pioneered a route to the Montana gold fields that passed directly through prime Lakota Sioux buffalo hunting grounds. In 1865, the government built a road from Fort Laramie, Wyoming, to Montana along this Bozeman Trail to protect white travelers.

Oglala Sioux chief Red Cloud and other bands retaliated by attacking miners, army patrols, and wagon trains that trespassed onto this land that had been promised them under the terms of the Fort Laramie Treaty of 1851. In 1866, the army attempted to negotiate a nonaggression treaty but balked at Red Cloud's demand that no forts be built along the Bozeman Trail. In fact, the army commenced construction on two new forts—Phil Kearny in Wyoming and C. F. Smith in Montana—and reinforced Fort Reno in Wyoming.

Chief Red Cloud responded by intensifying hostilities. He masterminded hit-and-run tactics to harass the soldiers with his two thousand warriors—including ambitious young braves Crazy Horse, Gall, and Rain-in-the-Face—which kept Fort Phil Kearny under constant siege.

On December 21, 1866, Captain William J. Fetterman, who had once boasted that he "could ride through the entire hostile nation with eighty good men," commanded a detachment of eighty men from Fort Kearny as escort for a woodcutting wagon train. Crazy Horse and a band of Sioux appeared and pretended to flee from the soldiers. When Fetterman took the bait and chased after this decoy, he and his men were ambushed and annihilated.

On August 1, 1867, Crazy Horse and a group of warriors estimated at five to eight hundred strong attacked a detachment of nineteen soldiers and six civilians who were guarding a hay-cutting detail near Fort C. F. Smith. In the ensuing three- to four-hour battle—known as the Hayfield Fight—two soldiers and one civilian were killed and two soldiers were wounded before troops from the fort arrived and the Sioux broke contact.

The following day, Company C of the Twenty-seventh Infantry was guarding a woodcutting detail about six miles from Fort Kearny when attacked by warriors under Crazy Horse. In what became known as the Wagon Box Fight, the soldiers took refuge in a corral crudely constructed from wagon beds. The Indians alternated sniping and charging for a period of about four hours before reinforcements arrived from the fort to drive them away. The soldiers lost 6 killed and 2 wounded; Indian losses were 6 killed and 6 wounded, although the army estimated 60 killed and 120 wounded.

Red Cloud's constant harassment made the soldiers virtual prisoners in their forts, and safe travel along the Bozeman Trail was impossible. The United States government finally yielded to Red Cloud's demands, and the Fort Laramie Treaty of 1868 was drawn up to end hostilities.

Provisions of this treaty called for the United States Army to abandon forts

Phil Kearny, Reno, and C. F. Smith and establish a Sioux reservation, which would encompass nearly all of present-day South Dakota west of the Missouri River, including the region known as the Black Hills, as well as other concessions. Whites were expressly forbidden to trespass on this land. In return, the Sioux agreed to withdraw all opposition to the construction of railroads not passing through their reservation and to cease attacks against white travelers and settlers.

More than two hundred chiefs and subchiefs signed the treaty at Fort Rice on July 2, 1868. Red Cloud, however, waited until November 6 to sign—after the three forts had been abandoned and burned to the ground.

And thus, in what became known as "Red Cloud's War," the Oglala chief became the only Native American in history to ever force the United States government to grant treaty demands due to acts of violence.

The treaty represented a victory for the Sioux, and a majority of the tribe—about fifteen thousand members—settled on the reservation where they would gradually become dependent on government rations.

Sioux leaders Sitting Bull, Crazy Horse, and Gall—none of whom had "touched the pen" to the treaty—refused to report to the reservation. Instead, they found a haven in the unceded territory, which they considered traditional buffalo hunting grounds, designated in the treaty. This area, which was roughly east of the Bighorn Mountains and north of the North Platte River (known as the Powder River Basin), had been reserved for Indians only. In summer months, countless other Indians would leave the reservation to join bands of their "free" kinsmen in the unceded territory to live the old way of life. This land separate from the reservation would later pose a problem with respect to exact boundaries—and by the presence of Indians who were hostile to whites.

The Panic of 1873, however, compelled the United States government to view the Black Hills in terms of its valuable resources. Now, in 1874, the military had decided to trespass into the Black Hills with soldiers. There was vocal public and political opposition when an expedition into the region was proposed by the military. According to the Fort Laramie Treaty, it was argued, the Sioux reservation was strictly off-limits to whites. Therefore, a reconnaissance through this area would constitute a violation.

The army position on the legality of the Black Hills Expedition was summed up by General Alfred Howe Terry, a member of the 1868 treaty commission, who wrote in a letter to General Phil Sheridan: "I am unable to see that any just offense is given to the Indians by the expedition to the Black Hills. From the earliest times the government has exercised the right of sending exploring parties of a military character into unceded territory, and this expedition is nothing more." Terry backed up his interpretation by stating his belief that provisions in the treaty never intended to exclude military forces, and he was certain that the Indians understood that as well.

General William T. Sherman concurred and wrote in his endorsement of Terry's statement: "I also was one of the commissioners to the treaty of 1868, and agree with General Terry, that it was not intended to exclude the United States from exploring the Reservation for Roads, or for any other national purpose."

In June 1874, Lieutenant Colonel George Armstrong Custer was advised that he would be leading an army expedition into the Black Hills region of Dakota Territory. The published purpose of this controversial reconnaissance was to identify likely locations for military posts. It was a poorly kept secret, however, that Custer was also interested in verifying claims of valuable mineral deposits—gold in particular—within the Black Hills.

Custer marched out of Fort Abraham Lincoln on July 2, 1874, at the head of a column comprised of ten companies of the Seventh Cavalry, two infantry companies, a train of 110 wagons, three Gatling guns, scouts, interpreters, a scientific corps, two professional miners, and numerous journalists—more than one thousand participants.

After a march of about three hundred miles, Custer and his column entered the northwestern edge of the Black Hills on July 20 by traveling along a well-worn Indian trail. Two days later at Inyan Kara, an extinct volcano, some of his Arikara and Santee scouts warned him that if he did not turn back there would be severe retaliation from the Sioux. Custer ignored their protests and, perhaps because these scouts had never been to the region before and would have little to offer with respect to information, released them. Those few Indians who did remain with the column included Bloody Knife, Custer's favorite scout.

Before leaving Inyan Kara, Custer, accompanied by chief engineer William

Ludlow, who, by the way, was one of the cadets involved in the fight that nearly caused Custer's dismissal from West Point years earlier, botanist A. B. Donaldson, and several others, climbed to the sixty-five-hundred-foot summit of this mountain. Ludlow created a monument of sorts when he chipped an inscription with hammer and chisel into a rock that read: "74 CUSTER."

Without capable scouts who were familiar with the territory to guide them, Custer personally rode ahead of his column and blazed the trail, which eventually gained him the reputation of always being able to locate a passage through even the most difficult terrain. He would assume this responsibility throughout the remainder of the expedition.

On July 24, Custer entered a resplendent valley surrounded by pines that overwhelmed everyone with its beauty and provided the botanists a virtual field day. Correspondent Samuel Barrows of the *New-York Tribune* said it was "an Eden in the clouds—how shall I describe it! As well try to paint the flavor of a peach or the odor of a rose." A. B. Donaldson, who collected fifty-two varieties of flowers in bloom, raved: "It is hardly possible to exaggerate in describing this flowery richness. Some said they would give a hundred dollars just to have their wives see the floral richness for even one hour."

Neither did Custer exaggerate when he chose the name Floral Valley for the area he described: "In no private or public park have I ever seen such a profuse display of flowers." Nearly every diary, letter home, or report contained a glowing description of this wondrous valley that teemed with wildflowers and offered a mystical serenity. Hard-bitten troopers decorated mule harnesses and hats with flowers and preserved blossoms as gifts for wives, girlfriends, or other family members. Custer noted that while seated at the mess table they could pick up "seven beautiful varieties" of flowers within reach. The column camped in Floral Valley for two days before moving on.

George Armstrong Custer, as had been his habit on previous expeditions, spent much of his free time along the way enjoying outdoor activities and indulging his curiosity of nature by exploring. He would frequently ride off with a detachment to hunt game, climb hills, or explore caves or other intriguing terrain. One notable cave shown him by a scout named Goose extended for four hundred feet, with provocative carvings and drawings on the walls and eerie shrieks and howls of unknown origin emanating from within its depths.

Custer also accumulated his customary menagerie of wildlife. This one consisted of a jackrabbit, an eagle, two prairie owls, several toads, rattlesnakes, and a number of birds among other species. Unfortunately, two badgers had been accidentally smothered to death in the overloaded wagon. These live specimens as well as generous samples of flora and fossils, including a petrified tree trunk, required an ambulance detail of twelve men under Fred "Antelope" Snow for transport.

Custer was quite the sportsman and had never let his military duties get in the way of a good hunt—whether for capture, trophy, or the table.

Popular culture has created an image that frontier military posts were a hub of exciting activity as the cavalrymen mounted up and bravely rode off to the sound of the bugle to engage in one thrilling skirmish after another with hostile Indians. Nothing could be further from the truth. For the most part, these isolated posts—and even campaigns and expeditions—were a constant routine of boredom and monotony. The officers and men, therefore, were compelled to find diversions to entertain themselves. Many turned to the bottle—alcoholism was rampant. Others, however, took advantage of the plentiful wildlife on the plains and hunted for pleasure—and for a change of menu.

It could be said that the most enthusiastic hunter in the West was George Armstrong Custer. His passionate outdoor interests, however, went beyond simply killing animals. He was like a child in a playground of nature. His correspondence never failed to mention the beauty of his surroundings and his fascination with the flora, fauna, fossils, or natural wonders that he had happened upon. On numerous occasions he captured live game and donated it to zoos. And no one was fonder of good horseflesh or a well-bred leash of hounds than Custer. At one point, his leash of Russian wolfhounds and English staghounds were said to number more than eighty under the care of orderly John Burkman. Custer was much in demand by dignitaries—including political leaders, Eastern industrialists, and English noblemen—and over the years, he had gained the reputation as the finest sportsman in the army.

Custer's first buffalo hunt, however, had proven to be somewhat embarrassing, although he related the episode with good humor. He was out hunting on the open prairie accompanied only by several English greyhounds during the Hancock Expedition of 1867 when he sighted a buffalo—the first he had ever observed up close. He had chased the beast with his horse and brought up his pistol to shoot. At that moment, the buffalo wheeled around and charged. Custer's horse reared as he pulled the trigger. The bullet went into the horse's brain, killing the animal and sending Custer toppling head over bootheels. He was stranded on foot in hostile Indian country—until fortunately for him a detail of the Seventh Cavalry happened upon him.

The Black Hills expedition afforded Custer an opportunity to hunt in new territory. He led hunting parties nearly every day, and bagged deer, elk, pronghorn antelope, buffalo, geese, ducks, prairie chickens, and sage hens, which kept the messes in fresh meat. He also shot two white wolves and a red fox. He wrote Libbie on June 26: "Such hunting I have never seen." Other wildlife was captured, including rattlesnakes, a badger, a wildcat, two marsh hawks, a jackrabbit, and a porcupine, which were later donated to the Central Park Zoo. During this trip, his study of animals led him to taxidermy—perhaps to preserve the moment as much as the mount. He would work in his tent late into the night under the tutelage of C. W. Bennett, a taxidermist who had accompanied the column. Custer learned to mount many species, including a complete elk, which he donated to the Detroit Audubon Club.

On August 7, Custer attained what he considered his greatest feat as a hunter. He killed a grizzly bear—although bullets from the rifles of Ludlow and Bloody Knife had contributed to the demise of the beast. Not only that, but this particular griz' was said to be less than fearsome, being an old male with teeth reduced to mere stumps, many incisors missing, and claws severely worn down. The photograph of Custer posing with the bear, however, became quite popular in Eastern stationery shops.

Custer also quite often served as a host, inviting guests to his large hospital tent, perhaps with the regimental band supplying entertainment. His brothers Tom and Boston were always present, along with favorites Fred Grant, the president's son who was Sheridan's personal observer, and Major "Sandy" Forsyth of Beecher Island fame, who maintained a log that was later published in the *Chicago Tribune,* as well as scout Charles (Charley) Reynolds.

One of the more interesting members of the expedition who dined with Custer was George Bird Grinnell, a young naturalist and paleontologist, who would be assisted by scout Luther North. Grinnell would later become an environmental activist and a prolific author who would write about the customs and history of the Cheyenne and other Western tribes.

Grinnell was presently serving on the staff of the Peabody Museum of Natural History at Yale and his expenses were paid by that school. Although hurried across the plains by Custer's steady itinerary, Grinnell began collecting numerous specimens and compiled lists of indigenous birds and mammals, including jackrabbits, prairie dogs, mule deer, elk, mountain lion, grizzly bears, bighorn sheep, and 110 species of birds. He saw no live buffalo but did find the skull of an old bull.

Grinnell was amazed to observe a pronghorn antelope with two broken legs outdistance Charley Reynolds on horseback for more than two miles. The leg bone of an animal that Grinnell speculated to be a dinosaur was found at Castle Butte, about six miles north of Prospect Valley. Most of the fossils, however, consisted of marine specimens, mainly shells.

Although Custer, the noted teetotaler, assured his wife in a letter that there were no incidences of intoxication on the march, just the opposite was true. The sutler's wagon carried an ample supply of liquor, which was freely consumed by those who so desired. It has been reported that Fred Grant "was drunk nearly all the time," which sounds like an exaggeration—except that Custer did at one point place Grant under arrest for drunkenness to send a message to the rest of the officers and men.

Another incident that points to frequent alcohol abuse by those in authority concerns the entire medical staff. An ill trooper, Private John Cunningham, apparently died when the three doctors who had accompanied the column were all too drunk to adequately care for the man and prescribe proper medicine. Cunningham had been feeling poorly for a week and complained of diarrhea, but the medical staff had returned him to duty. Finally, he fell off his horse and was transported in the ambulance. The medical staff was in a state of intoxication and neglected the trooper. Custer eventually intervened, but by that time it was too late. Cunningham died of unknown causes near midnight on July 21.

In spite of these moments of indiscretion, there can be no doubt that the march through the Black Hills was as pleasant as any ever experienced by the participants—especially for the officers, if not enlisted, who were often assigned undesirable duty. Lieutenant Jimmy Calhoun perhaps summed up the senti-ments of his peers when he wrote: "The air is serene and the sun is shining in all its glory. The birds are singing sweetly, warbling their sweet notes as they soar aloft. Nature seems to smile on our movement. Everything seems to en-courage us onward."

This was the first trip west for Boston Custer, and he quickly became the victim of his older brothers' good-natured teasing and practical jokes. Tom Custer had presented Bos with a rock that he claimed was a "sponge-rock" and if placed underwater would transform into a sponge. Bos soaked the rock for a few nights, much to the delight of his brothers, until realizing that he had been taken in by his brother. Another more alarming prank had been played on Bos when he paused on the march to pick a rock from one of his horse's shoes. Armstrong and Tom galloped ahead and hid and then fired shots over Bos' head when he appeared, which sent the young man racing to spread the word of an Indian attack.

The Sioux had thus far chosen not to interfere with this—to them—insulting invasion of troops but indicated with smoke signals that they were aware that there had been an intrusion upon their land. The tribe had not been prepared for a response to this sudden appearance by the soldiers. The various bands had been scattered across the plains and were likely taken by surprise. No doubt certain warriors, such as Crazy Horse or Gall, would have commenced gath-ering warriors. If they were able to mount an offensive against the troopers, the Black Hills would become a battlefield that favored the Indians.

On July 28, the column happened upon a small hunting party of five lodges and twenty-seven occupants under Oglala chief One Stab (or Stabber) in Cas-tle Creek Valley. According to one account, the wife of One Stab was the daugh-ter of Red Cloud. These particular Indians from the Red Cloud and Spotted Tail Agencies apparently had not noticed the smoke signals and were quite surprised to encounter the soldiers. Custer, under a flag of truce, smoked the peace pipe with One Stab and graciously invited the chief and several of his people to visit the army camp for coffee, sugar, and bacon, a courtesy that was gratefully accepted.

The Indian scouts who had remained with the column were not as gra-cious as their commander and wanted to kill their traditional enemy. Due to the threat of hostilities, Custer assigned a detail of fifteen troopers to escort his Sioux guests back to their lodges and protect them through the night. In spite of that precaution, the wary Sioux abruptly galloped away with the soldiers and scouts in hot pursuit. During the chase—although Custer had ordered no violence—one of the Sioux was shot by one of the Santee scouts. The troops arrived at the Indian camp to find that it had been abandoned.

Custer, however, had detained Chief One Stab, as either a hostage or a guest. Custer wrote, perhaps with tongue in cheek: "I have effected arrangements by which the Chief One Stab remains with us as a guide." Whatever the circumstances, the chief, who was understandably greatly distressed by his captivity, guided the expedition for several days into the southern hills. During this time, rumors had spread throughout the reservations that One Stab had been killed. His eventual safe release prevented any possible retaliation by the Sioux.

On July 30, about one hundred miles into their reconnaissance, the column camped in a glade that Custer modestly named Custer Park, which was near the site of present-day Custer City, South Dakota. While the troops passed the time playing cards, writing letters, catching up on their sleep, or exploring their new surroundings, miners Horatio Ross and William McKay discovered some "color" along the upper part of French Creek.

Which one of the miners actually was the first to recognize gold has been a matter of speculation. Ross generally receives credit for the discovery. McKay, however, noted in an undated journal entry: "In the evening I took a pan, pick and shovel, and went out prospecting. The first panful was taken from the gravel and sand obtained in the bed of the creek; and on washing was found to contain from one and a half to two cents, which was the first gold found in the Black Hills."

Regardless of who struck color first, the two miners wrapped the few specks of gold in a piece of paper and together presented their findings to Custer that night. Ross and McKay were skeptical about the prospects of a big strike but vowed to continue panning in the morning.

At dawn, the miners returned to French Creek, while Custer and an escort commanded by Lieutenant Charles Varnum rode to seventy-two-hundred-foot Harney's Peak, the highest point in the Black Hills. Custer, along with

Forsyth, Ludlow, Donaldson, geologist Newton Winchell, and topographer W. W. Wood, climbed the summit and pointed out two other distinctive peaks that he named for General Terry and himself. The climbing party wrote their names and the date on a piece of paper that was rolled up, inserted into a copper cartridge casing, and slipped into a crevice. The casing was found sixty years later, but the message was missing.

On August 1, Custer moved the camp three miles away to a better grazing area and named the site Agnes Park after Agnes Bates, a friend of his wife. The miners tested the loose soil around the creek and were impressed with the results. They speculated that under the right conditions a miner could expect to reap perhaps as much as $150 a day. French Creek was soon lined with ambitious soldiers who sought their fortunes digging with shovels, picks, knives, pothooks, plates, cups, and any other implement that could penetrate dirt. Twenty troopers later staked a claim under the name Custer Park Mining Company.

On August 2, George Armstrong Custer was sufficiently assured that the deposits held prospects of gold in payable quantities. At that time, he wrote a dispatch to Phil Sheridan about the find that would forever change history in the Black Hills region. "Gold has been found in several places," Custer wrote, "and it is the belief of those who are giving their attention to this subject that it will be found in paying quantities."

He turned to his trusted scout Charley Reynolds, who by prearrangement had been engaged to carry this important message to the outside world.

"Lonesome Charley" Reynolds was likely born on a farm near Stephensburg, Hardin County, Kentucky, on March 20, 1842, although some accounts question that date and note the place of his birth as Warren County, Illinois. His father, a farmer and physician, moved the family at some point to Abington, Illinois—where Reynolds attended Abington College—and in 1859 to Pardee, Atchison County, Kansas.

In 1860, Reynolds heeded the call "Pike's Peak or Bust" and headed west on a wagon train to the Colorado gold fields. The emigrant train, however, was attacked and looted by a Cheyenne war party. The survivors fled to Fort Kearny, where Reynolds joined a mountain man to run a trap line along the Platte.

In July 1861, Reynolds returned home and enlisted in Company E, Tenth Kansas Infantry. He served primarily on border duty in Missouri and Kansas, participating in the Battle of Prairie Grove, then on escort duty along the Santa Fe Trail to Fort Union, Mexico. One account states that Reynolds scouted against Confederate general Sterling Price on what became known as Price's Missouri Raid in the fall of 1864. If so, Reynolds would have been a civilian—he was mustered out of the service in August 1864 at Fort Leavenworth, prior to Price's October raid.

In 1865, Reynolds decided to establish a trading venture in New Mexico, but the enterprise ended when his partner was killed by Cheyenne on Rabbit Ears Creek in southwestern Kansas. Reynolds wintered in Santa Fe—reportedly having a failed romance with a Mexican girl—and then embarked on several years as a buffalo hunter on the Republican River furnishing game for military posts. During the winter of 1866–67 he shot and wounded a drunk and abusive army officer from Fort McPherson at Jack Morrow's ranch on the Platte.

Reynolds then traveled to Dakota Territory on the upper Missouri to hunt and trap and became known to the local Indians around Fort Rice as "White Hunter Who Never Goes Out for Nothing." His initial work as a scout for the army came when he hired on for Colonel David Stanley's Yellowstone Expedition of 1872.

By this time, Reynolds not only was familiar with the territory but also understood the Sioux tongue and Indian sign language. Personally, he was said to be quite reticent of speech and by nature reserved, hence the nickname Lonesome Charley. He was never heard to brag about his exploits, although his skill as a hunter—his courage, endurance, and resourcefulness—was highly regarded by both Indians and whites. He preferred spending his free time hunting alone or in a small party rather than frequenting bars or playing cards. These traits and extraordinary talents elevated him to a position on the highest level of Western scouts.

Reynolds first became acquainted with George Armstrong Custer when he was engaged as a scout for Stanley's Yellowstone Expedition of 1873. The well-educated Reynolds shared a lot in common with Custer, including interest in geology, zoology, and reading—not to mention hunting and wildlife—and neither man drank or smoked.

Libbie Custer would write: "My husband had such genuine admiration for him that I soon learned to listen to everything pertaining to his life with marked interest. He was so shy that he hardly raised his eyes when I extended my hand at the General's introduction. He did not assume the picturesque dress, long hair, belt full of weapons that are characteristic of the scout. His manner was perfectly simple and straightforward, and he would not be induced to talk of himself. He had large, dark blue eyes, and a frank face."

Reynolds would now travel alone about ninety miles through hostile country to reach Fort Laramie. Custer provided Reynolds with a canvas mailbag that had been inscribed: "Black Hills Express. Charley Reynolds, Manager. Connecting with All points East, West, North, South. Cheap rates; Quick Transit; Safe Passage. We are protected by the Seventh Cavalry." Reynolds galloped away from the column with the awareness that his route would intersect several Indian trails and there was a distinct possibility that he would be discovered by hostiles.

The most stirring account of this daring ride was provided by Libbie Custer in her *Boots and Saddles or, Life in Dakota with General Custer.* Although embellishing somewhat, Libbie wrote in part: "During the day he hid as well as he could in the underbrush, and lay down in the long grass. In spite of these precautions he was sometimes so exposed that he could hear voices of Indians passing near. The last nights of his march he was compelled to walk, as his horse was exhausted and he found no water for hours. His lips became so parched and his throat so swollen that he could not close his mouth. In this condition he reached Fort Laramie and delivered his dispatches."

Charley Reynolds fulfilled his mission by reaching Fort Laramie in four days of hard riding and then moved on to Sioux City, where his swollen throat apparently healed. While in that fair city he gave an interview to the editor of the *Sioux City Journal,* which was published on August 19. Although Reynolds said that he personally had not found any gold, he admitted to having seen specks of the mineral washed from surface dirt that would likely yield two or three cents a pan. He then set out for Bismarck and Fort Lincoln, leaving behind the spark that helped ignite a gold rush in the Black Hills.

The expedition moved onward, following its old trail in a northerly direction. On August 14, Custer chose Bear Butte, an isolated granite laccolithic formation rising twelve hundred feet above the prairie on the northern fringe of the Black Hills, as the location to halt his column and prepare his official report. Ironically, Bear Butte held a special place in the Sioux Nation, where they had for a century gathered to trade, share news, and participate in religious ceremonies.

The column marched east from Bear Butte through the hot, dusty plains, with Custer pushing the troopers hard. With the band striking up "Garry Owen," the Seventh Cavalry triumphantly paraded into Fort Abraham Lincoln on August 30, after a march of sixty days and 883 miles.

Public outcry for admittance to this forbidden territory became overwhelming following Custer's expedition. The nation was gripped in a deep economic depression, and the news about gold aroused the imagination of the poverty-stricken public. Adventurers immediately made plans to journey to the Black Hills to prospect for gold. It was reasoned that the Sioux were not settled within the Hills and they should therefore be opened to settlers, miners, and loggers and for any other practical purpose.

Naturally, word of this potential intrusion into Lakota Sioux land in violation of the treaty infuriated many tribal leaders. The Lakota called Custer's route through the Black Hills the Thieves' Road and prepared for war. This tribe of fierce warriors was not about to give up Paha Sapa without a fight. They had taken the Black Hills by force and would defend it with force, if necessary.

Seven

Prelude to War

While the Sioux and their allies held meetings to discuss this grievous intrusion into the Black Hills, George Armstrong Custer and Libbie visited Monroe, Michigan, for six weeks before settling in for another winter at Fort Abraham Lincoln. The social season was once again quite agreeable to the Custers as the post maintained its normal routine of drills and monotony. In addition, Armstrong put his free time to good use by writing about his remarkable career.

One of Custer's classmates at West Point, J. M. Wright, wrote that the "greatest surprise in Custer's whole career in life was that he should turn out to be a literary man. If any one had said in the four years before the Civil War that Cadet Custer would in fifteen years be a scholar of artistic tastes and writer of graphic contributions to the magazines, the prediction would have been derided."

To consider that this devil-may-care cavalier could gain fame as an author may have seemed preposterous given his lack of attention to academics, but Custer did indeed turn out to be a literary man, and an accomplished one at that.

Custer's initial foray into the publishing world was with a New York–based weekly sportsman's journal called *Turf, Field and Farm*, which suited his taste for horses, hounds, and hunting. His first article or "letter," which he wrote under the pseudonym Nomad, was submitted on September 9, 1867—just six days before his court-martial convened at Fort Leavenworth. In spite of the pseudonym, readers knew that Nomad was actually the famous General Custer. He would write a total of fifteen letters describing his adventures to this publication between September 1867 and August 1875.

Custer, convicted by court-martial, served out much of his one-year suspension with Libbie while residing in Phil Sheridan's quarters at Fort Leavenworth. It was during this period of time that Custer began work on his Civil War memoirs, and six years later at Fort Lincoln he was still working on this subject. Unfortunately, he never finished these memoirs, completing only the period from his reporting for duty at Bull Run in July 1861—three days out of West Point—to the May 5, 1862, Battle of Williamsburg where he was said to have captured the first battle flag taken by the Union army.

In 1872, while stationed at Elizabethtown, Kentucky, Custer began writing a series of articles for a magazine called *Galaxy*. In 1874, Sheldon & Company, the owners of the magazine, published selected articles in book form titled *My Life on the Plains or, Personal Experiences with Indians,* which remains in print today. The book, which detailed his activities on the Great Plains from 1867 to 1869, established Custer as a bestselling and respected author.

Also in 1874, Custer became embroiled in a literary feud of sorts with Colonel William Hazen over the merits of the land that the Northern Pacific Railroad was attempting to sell along its route. The sale of this property was vital to the future of the railroad, but Hazen responded in a letter to the *New-York Tribune* on February 7, 1874, with a pessimistic view, claiming that the land in that region was not worth "a penny an acre."

Custer received a request from friend Tom Rosser to aid the cause. Custer obliged with an April 17 letter published in the *Minneapolis Tribune* that refuted Hazen's assertions and presented a glowing picture of the future of the railroad and the agricultural opportunities along its route. He added that "the beneficial influence which the Northern Pacific Railroad, if completed, would exercise in the final and peaceable solution of the Indian question, and which in this very region assumes its most serious aspect, might well warrant the general Government in considering this enterprise one of National importance, and in giving to it, at least, its hearty encouragement."

Custer's letter was reprinted in a booklet published by the railroad and widely circulated. He wisely ignored Hazen's rebuttal and declined to engage in a full-scale literary duel. Instead, Custer relied on the public to determine whose opinion was more credible—and Custer was a respected and famous man whose word was golden.

Predictably, Custer was treated like a VIP by the railroad and richly rewarded for his loyalty. He was presented with a spacious wall tent, which had been stenciled with "NPRR." Custer and Libbie traveled on the Northern Pacific compliments of free passes, occasionally in a private coach, and were once provided a special train.

He also was known to write speculative political pieces without a byline for leading Democratic papers such as the *New York World* and for his friend James Gordon Bennett, publisher of the *New York Herald*. In the summer of 1876, Bennett expected to receive anonymous articles from Custer about the Little Bighorn Campaign.

Perhaps the most entertaining and revealing, if not informative, writing by Custer, however, is his letters to Libbie and others and her letters to him. This correspondence, which was edited into a book by Marguerite Merington, one of Libbie's closest friends, reveals the intrigue of their courtship, the terror of the Civil War, the adventures and dangers of frontier life, and an inside story of the politics that ruled the day. The subject of each letter could range from the most mundane to an outburst of personal intimacy but most of all showed the devotion that these two lovers shared throughout the years.

The only other excitement at that time was the arrest, capture, and escape of Sioux warrior Rain-in-the-Face, who had boasted about killing sutler Augustus Baliran and veterinarian Dr. John Honsinger during the Yellowstone Expedition of 1873.

The killing by the Sioux of Baliran and Honsinger, which occurred on August 4, 1873, during the Yellowstone Expedition, was not on anyone's mind until scout Charley Reynolds visited Standing Rock Agency during the winter of 1874. While observing a scalp dance, Reynolds overheard Sioux warrior Rain-in-the-Face brag to a large audience of his peers that he had killed the two men. Reynolds immediately relayed that information to George Armstrong Custer at Fort Abraham Lincoln.

Custer summoned his friend Captain George Yates and ordered him to assemble fifty men for an unspecified detail. This detachment from companies F and L, along with First Lieutenant Tom Custer, proceeded to Fort Rice, where it was joined by another fifty-man detachment from the Seventh Cavalry commanded by trusted Seventh Cavalry captain Thomas H. French.

"Tucker" French was born on March 5, 1843, in Baltimore. His father passed away from a fever when Tucker was fifteen. In January 1864, French enlisted in the Tenth Infantry, and he fought in the Petersburg siege and the Battle of Weldon Railroad and was wounded at Chappell House, Virginia. In 1868, he accepted a captaincy in the Nineteenth Infantry on March 26, 1868. When the army was reorganized he was assigned to the Seventh Cavalry on January 1, 1871, and gained a reputation as a crack shot with the .50-caliber "Long Tom" Springfield infantry rifle that he carried. French had distinguished himself on August 11 during the Yellowstone Expedition of 1873 while commanding two companies dispatched by Custer to thwart an attempt by the Sioux to cross the Yellowstone River. His detachment successfully prevented the Indians from crossing and closing with the main body. French had also commanded Company M during that summer's Black Hills Expedition of 1874.

Now, on December 13, 1874, the temperature was fifty-four degrees below zero as the column moved along the frozen Missouri River. After traveling twenty miles as instructed, Yates opened the sealed envelope that contained Custer's orders. Yates was directed to Standing Rock Agency to arrest Rain-in-the-Face for the murders of Baliran and Honsinger. Total secrecy was to be maintained; Custer feared that if the Indian agent learned of the mission he would warn the Sioux warrior. Charley Reynolds would travel ahead of the column to ascertain the whereabouts of the fugitive.

After arriving at Standing Rock that evening and spending a freezing night in an unheated warehouse, Yates learned that Rain-in-the-Face was located in a Hunkpapa Sioux camp some three miles away. It was ration day, and all the Indians would be visiting the Hatch Trading Store at the agency to draw provisions. As a diversion, a forty-man detachment was dispatched to another Indian camp ten miles away to inquire about some other Sioux who were wanted for depredations on the Red River. Yates and the remaining men then rode to the traders' store.

Tom Custer, Charley Reynolds, and several others entered the store while the remaining troopers waited outside the entrance. Reynolds pointed out Rain-in-the-Face to Custer, who grabbed the surprised warrior and threw him to the floor. Rain-in-the-Face's hands were bound, and he was escorted outside and strapped on a waiting horse.

Due to the lateness of the hour, the cavalrymen and their captive remained at the agency that night. They departed on the morning of December 15 and struggled through eighteen-inch-deep snow to arrive at Fort Lincoln the next day.

Rain-in-the-Face was confined in the wooden guardhouse in the company of a civilian caught stealing grain from the government. Custer, through an interpreter, patiently interrogated his prisoner for hours. Finally, Rain-in-the-Face confessed to the murders in the presence of all the officers, his account matching the conclusions of the military.

Rain-in-the-Face and the white thief remained chained together in the guardhouse for several months until friends of the thief tore through the wall one night and freed them both. Rain-in-the-Face later said that he had been released by a sympathetic "old soldier," who had waited until he was safely away before firing his weapon to sound the alarm. Whatever the circumstances, the Sioux warrior fled to Sitting Bull's camp, where Rain-in-the-Face vowed revenge for his arrest—promising to someday cut out Tom Custer's heart and eat it. As fate would have it, both Tom and Rain-in-the-Face would meet one day in the future.

The interminable winter on the Northern Plains finally turned into springtime and afforded an opportunity for its inhabitants to move about the territory. In spite of government warnings to the contrary, by the summer of 1875 more than eight hundred prospectors had invaded the Black Hills to seek their fortune. This provoked the Sioux, led by Sitting Bull and Crazy Horse, to retaliate by attacking these invaders and raiding wagon trains, mail routes, and settlements in the unceded territory. Soon the miners were demanding that the government protect them from Indian attacks.

Brigadier General George Crook was dispatched to uphold the provisions of the Fort Laramie Treaty of 1868 and chase off the miners. And if anything could be done to pacify the miners, Crook was the man who could do it.

George Crook was born on a farm near Dayton, Ohio, on September 8, 1828. He had graduated from the U.S. Military Academy at West Point in 1852, near the bottom of his class, and was assigned to an infantry regiment in the Pacific Northwest. In addition to escort duty and building military posts, Crook was involved in the Yakima War of 1855–56 in eastern Washington Territory, as well as the simultaneous Rogue River War in southern Oregon. He received a poisoned arrow in the hip during one engagement with the Pitt Indians.

At the outbreak of the Civil War, Crook was made colonel of the Thirty-sixth Ohio Infantry, which was assigned to western Virginia, and by applying lessons learned on the frontier successfully fought guerilla actions against Confederate interests. He was wounded at Lewisburg in May 1862 and promoted to brigadier general three months later. Crook commanded the Kanawha Division at South Mountain and the September 1862 Battle of Antietam. He was then placed in command of the Second Cavalry Division and participated in the heavy fighting of the August–September 1863 Chickamauga Campaign. In February 1864, Crook assumed command of the Kanawha District and led a series of raids between Lynchburg, Virginia, and eastern Tennessee. He was given command of the Department of Western Virginia in the summer of 1864 and was part of Major General Phil Sheridan's Shenandoah Valley Campaign, where Crook distinguished himself on numerous occasions and became known as Uncle George.

Crook was promoted to major general in October 1864 and was at his headquarters at Cumberland, Maryland, on February 21, 1865, when he and Brigadier General Benjamin F. Kelly were captured by Southern partisans. He was released one month later, just prior to the end of hostilities.

George Crook returned to the regular rank of lieutenant colonel after the war and commanded the Twenty-third Infantry in Idaho Territory, where he fought against Northern Paiutes during the Snake River War of 1866–68 in the deserts of southern Idaho and eastern Oregon—eventually forcing a surrender. In 1871, at the request of President Ulysses S. Grant, Crook was placed in command of the Department of Arizona to contend with Chiricahua Apache. Crook won great acclaim by developing a successful strategy of using small, mobile detachments and recruiting surrendered Apache to track renegade Apache. By 1873 the Apache had been relatively subdued, and the following year Crook was rewarded with a brigadier general's star.

Now, in 1875, he was given command of the Department of the Platte and assigned the dubious task of removing the miners who had been trespassing in the Black Hills to prospect for gold.

Late in July, Crook called a meeting with the miners and issued an ultimatum, which diplomatically suggested that the miners would have an opportunity to prospect the area once it had been opened in the near future, but for the present they must depart. The miners were quite impressed with Crook's forthrightness, and most agreed to comply. They even drew up a proclamation that thanked the general for "the kind and gentlemanly manner with which his command have executed his (the President's) order."

Crook's ability to reason with the miners can be attributed in part to his folksy, if not somewhat eccentric, personality. He was an imposing man, standing well over six feet, braided his parted blond whiskers, wore canvas coveralls rather than a uniform, and preferred riding a mule instead of a horse.

Nevertheless, newspapers, especially those from nearby Dakota towns, ignored the ban on mining and jumped on the golden bandwagon and promoted these towns as the ideal places from which to outfit and enter the Black Hills.

There remained skepticism in some circles, however, over the validity of Custer's discovery, which was partially due to high-profile people such as geologist Newton Winchell and Fred Grant, the president's son, claiming not to have personally observed any gold. The government therefore authorized another expedition into the Black Hills in the summer of 1875 to confirm Custer's conclusions.

This expedition was headed by New York School of Mines geologist Walter P. Jenny, with escort provided by six cavalry and two infantry companies under Lieutenant Colonel Richard I. Dodge. Although Jenny reported that it would be difficult for individual miners to extract enough gold with primitive pan and rocker to make it worth their while, he confirmed that the Black Hills did indeed hold rich mineral deposits that could be profitable if sophisticated mining equipment was utilized.

Jenny's guarded opinion meant little to the public. Gold had been confirmed, and the rush to strike it rich commenced in earnest.

Red Cloud, Spotted Tail, and other Lakota Sioux chiefs were invited to Washington, D.C., in that summer of 1875, believing that the meeting would pertain to agency business. To their surprise, the government requested that they sign over the title to the Black Hills. The chiefs refused, saying they lacked authority to make such an important decision.

The government, however, promised to reward the Lakota well should they sell the Black Hills. Spotted Tail was asked to estimate the worth of the region, which he subsequently set at between $7 and $40 million and enough provisions to provide for seven generations of Sioux.

The tribe was split over that proposal to sell the Black Hills to the United States government. Those members who resided on the reservation approved of the idea, thinking only of the rewards that they would receive. Another faction, led by medicine man Sitting Bull and warrior Crazy Horse, vowed that this sacred land would be sold only over their dead bodies.

The Allison Commission, named for its chairman, Iowa senator William B. Allison, convened near Red Cloud Agency in September 1875 to discuss the sale. The commission members were greeted with a show of hostility from the younger warriors, who disrupted the proceedings and threatened severe reprisals against any chief who dared sign a treaty giving away the Black Hills.

Senator Allison proposed that the Sioux accept $400,000 a year for mining rights or the United States would buy the Black Hills for $6 million. The offer was declined.

The commission returned to Washington empty-handed and recommended that Congress simply offer whatever value they judged was fair. If the Lakota refused to sell at that price, rations and other provisions should be terminated.

Prior to the Civil War, the government had established an Indian policy that called for removing offending tribes to the Great Plains, where they could live on one big reservation in a region where the whites had no interest. After the war, however, whites became interested in the Plains—both for crossing to points to the west and for settling—and Indian resistance was dealt with by military force. At that point, the government had two choices when setting policy with respect to the Indian—annihilation or assimilation. On the one hand, the military, including George Armstrong Custer, were predictably proponents for war, which did not sit well with President Grant. On the other hand, Grant was becoming frustrated with his failing peace policy.

The Lakota Sioux did not make it easy for the proponents of assimilation to maintain their stance. Warfare was fundamental to the way of life for young males in the tribe. Warriors gained status by brave deeds performed in battle with their enemies. Warfare was both a sport and ceremony and closely related to the supernatural.

Young men would journey alone to a mountaintop and meditate without food or rest until a vision appeared to them. This image would become an important part of a warrior's protection and preparation for battle for the remainder of his life. Crazy Horse, for example, would never enter battle without painting his body with white hail spots, a streak of lightning on one cheek, and a brown pebble tied behind his ear.

Horses were the Sioux medium of exchange. An individual's wealth was measured by the number of horses he possessed. Therefore, stealing horses from rival tribes became the primary target of raids. All-out war was generally waged only to defend their village or hunting ground. Counting coup was the act that brought the most glory upon a warrior. This meant closing with an enemy and, with a sacred stick or hand-to-hand, striking the first blow or wound. A coup could also be awarded for saving a life or stealing a horse. The reward for each coup was an eagle feather that could be worn in the warrior's war bonnet on future raids.

Consequently, the Lakota Sioux would be required to abandon traditional warring rituals and ceremonies and promise to live in peace to even consider assimilation. Those military officers who had experienced the fighting abilities of the fierce Sioux warriors could not imagine these men laying down their weapons and living in peace alongside enemy tribes, much less white people.

One factor in favor of the Sioux, however, was that the public believed that enough Blue and Gray blood had been shed on the continent and for that reason they favored trying a peaceful approach to the Indian problem. By the time Ulysses S. Grant won the election of 1868, major treaties had been negotiated and reservations for the various tribes set aside. Grant made an admirable effort to treat the Indian with fairness. In his 1869 inauguration speech, he had stated: "The proper treatment of the original occupants of this land—the

Indians—is one deserving of careful study. I will favor any course towards them which tends to their civilization and ultimate citizenship."

Shortly thereafter, he announced his federal Indian policy, which endorsed his goal of acculturating the Indians and eventually inviting them to become United States citizens. His plan of action became known as the "peace policy," due to its intended mission, which was "the hitherto untried policy in connection with Indians, of endeavoring to conquer by kindness."

Grant affirmed his intentions by appointing Ely Parker, a full-blooded Seneca Indian who had become his friend in Illinois, commissioner of Indian affairs, the first Indian to hold that post. Incidentally, Parker had been Grant's aide at Appomattox when he and Robert E. Lee signed the surrender papers.

The president had initially assigned mainly army officers for duty as Indian agents, but in 1870 Congress banned military personnel from serving in civil service positions. At that time Grant refused to make patronage appointments and instead chose Indian agents from Christian denominations, which then set to work implementing the process of peacefully relocating tribes to reservations where they could be protected by the army.

Grant believed that his "Quaker policy," as it was called, would pacify the Indians and encourage them to accept his policies. The churchmen had final authority on the reservation, but Grant warned that "a sharp and severe war policy" would face those tribes that would not submit to the reservation.

The president personally assisted in the effort by entertaining many tribal leaders in the White House over the years—including Lakota Sioux chiefs Red Cloud and Spotted Tail. Many of the chiefs toured various cities, and the United States Indian Commission organized Indian lectures in New York and Boston.

Grant also helped to raise funds—both public and private—for the assimilation of Indians into white society. "Friends of the Indian" reform groups also were established and raised a considerable amount of money for education and other expenses necessary to bridge the cultural gap.

Politics, however, played a major role in Grant's Indian policy. The Interior Department and the army, which claimed that they could police Indian agencies better than government bureaucrats, waged a behind-the-scenes battle over the direction of Indian affairs. Even Grant's old military colleagues were surprised and angered over the president's decision to favor civilian control over that of the military.

Unfortunately for all concerned, Grant's compassionate approach toward the Indian failed to bring an end to Indian hostilities on the Plains. By late 1875, the economy was still adversely affected by the Panic of 1873. The public was clamoring for the government to acquire the Black Hills and its gold deposits. The Sioux and Cheyenne were abandoning the reservations to roam free and once again sought to display their dominance over the Plains with acts of violence that endangered the traveling public and denied the possibility of settling Western territories.

The frustration over the Black Hills and Indian raids in the unceded territory finally came to a head. Grant lost patience with the peace policy and was persuaded by Generals William T. Sherman and Philip Sheridan to permit the military to find a solution.

President Grant issued an order on December 6, 1875, stating that all Indians must report to the reservation by January 31, 1876. Otherwise, the Interior Department would assign disposition of the hostiles to the War Department.

This ultimatum was carried by runners to those Sioux and Cheyenne who were known to be camped along the Yellowstone River and vicinity. In all fairness, it should be noted that it would have been extremely difficult for the Indians to move at that time of year even if they had wanted to comply with the order—ponies were weak from lack of forage and winter travel could be hazardous to families.

It was evident, however, that Sitting Bull and his kinsmen never intended to obey the order. They regarded themselves as free to roam as they pleased and vowed to protect their culture and traditions—even if it meant an armed confrontation with the mighty United States of America.

On February 1, 1876, as stated in the order, those Indians were deemed hostile, and General Phil Sheridan set in motion plans for an immediate campaign designed to catch the Indians.

But there was missing one man who was the most experienced and trusted Indian fighter in the country. He had been the victim of the president's retaliation for his testimony at the Belknap hearings and cooled his bootheels in

Washington when he should have been in Dakota Territory. There had been one attempt at returning to his duty station, but he had been met on the way in Chicago and ordered to return to Washington to get his clearance papers in order and pay customary visits to General Sherman and the president.

Finally, on May 6, a desperate Custer sent the following telegram to President Grant:

> I have seen your order transmitted through the General of the Army directing that I not be permitted to accompany the expedition to move against hostile Indians. As my entire regiment forms a part of the expedition and I am the senior officer of the regiment on duty in this department I respectfully but most earnestly request that while not allowed to go in command of the expedition I may be permitted to serve with my regiment in the field. I appeal to you as a soldier to spare me the humiliation of seeing my regiment march to meet the enemy and I not share its dangers.

Generals Sherman, Sheridan, and especially Terry, who realized the need for Custer's experience, interceded on Custer's behalf.

On May 8, the president grudgingly relented and gave permission for Custer to join the march for the Little Bighorn Campaign. But the Dakota column would be commanded by General Alfred Terry—another slight to Custer's prestige. Terry's best days were behind him, and he was by no means a capable field officer any longer or, perhaps more important, a man of action in the same vein as Custer.

Regardless, that same day, Custer, thrilled by the decision, rushed to Fort Abraham Lincoln to lead the Seventh Cavalry on what would be his final campaign.

Eight

---◆◉◆---

First Blood

The strategy for the Little Bighorn Campaign was designed primarily by Generals Alfred H. Terry and George Crook. Crook had experience in the Black Hills and had subdued the Apache in Arizona. Terry was an administrator who had sat on various commissions and had experience and knowledge of dealing with the Lakota. He was for all intents and purposes retired from active participation in battle but brought to the table the lessons he had learned from past events.

The forty-eight-year-old Connecticut native Alfred Howe Terry had briefly attended Yale Law School but withdrew after a year. He had, however, become fluent in French and German and decided to travel in Europe on an inheritance. In 1858, he became clerk of the New Haven County Superior Court, a position he held until the outbreak of the Civil War.

At that time, Terry became colonel of the Second Connecticut, a ninety-day militia regiment, which he commanded at the First Battle of Bull Run. He then recruited the Seventh Connecticut and led this regiment to share the capture of the important naval base at Port Royal, South Carolina, in November 1861. In April of the following year, Terry's regiment helped take Fort Pulaski, Georgia, which led to his promotion that month to brigadier general. In the fall of 1863, he assumed command of X Corps in the Army of the James, which operated against Petersburg and Richmond.

Terry participated in Major General Benjamin F. Butler's ill-fated attempt to capture Fort Fisher, North Carolina, in December 1864. When Butler was recalled, Terry replaced him and personally led the storming and capture of Fort Fisher in January 1865, which sealed off Wilmington, the last Confederate port on the East Coast.

For this accomplishment, he received the rarely awarded "Thanks of Congress," a coveted citation published in the *Congressional Record,* and was promoted to major general of volunteers and brigadier in the regular army, as of January 15, 1865. He ended the war in the Carolinas as part of the Army of the Ohio under Major General William T. Sherman.

After the war, Terry remained in the army as a brigadier general and was given command of the Department of Dakota, which included Minnesota and parts of the Dakota and Montana Territories. He served on the commission that condemned the Sand Creek Massacre and was a member of the presidential Peace Commission, which negotiated the Medicine Lodge Treaties in 1867. He was transferred to the Department of the South to contend with Reconstruction in 1869 and returned to Dakota as department commander in 1872.

The general was somewhat of a walking contradiction. He was a strong advocate of Indian rights and a proponent of arming Indians with weapons for hunting purposes, which was a controversial position within the army. He opposed any intrusion by whites into the Black Hills region but nonetheless served as supervisor for Custer's Black Hills Expedition of 1874 and the subsequent Jenny Expedition of 1875. In an apparent conflict with Terry's personal beliefs, he was a member of the Allison Commission, which met with the Sioux at Red Cloud Agency in June 1875 and was unsuccessful in negotiating the sale of the Black Hills.

The Terry-Crook strategy called for three columns to converge on the Indians—whose exact location was unknown—and crush them within this three-pronged movement. General George Crook would command one column, which would march north from Fort Fetterman, Wyoming. The Montana Column would be led by Colonel John Gibbon and would march east down the Yellowstone River from Fort Ellis.

Gibbon was born on April 20, 1827, near Holmesburg, Pennsylvania, and during his childhood the family moved to Charlotte, North Carolina. He graduated—with future generals Ambrose E. Burnside and Ambrose P. Hill—from the U.S. Military Academy at West Point in 1847, ranking twentieth in his class. Gibbon was commissioned a second lieutenant in the Fourth U.S. Artillery and assigned to duty in Mexico after hostilities had ceased. He took part in operations against the Seminole Indians in Florida two years later and was promoted to first lieutenant in 1850.

From May 1853 to August 1854 he assisted in the removal of the Seminole from Florida to Indian Territory. His next assignment was as an artillery instructor at West Point, where he spent five years. While at West Point, Gibbon wrote the basic *Artillerist's Manual,* which was published by the War Department. Gibbon then served briefly in Utah and as captain of the Fourth U.S. Artillery at Fort Leavenworth until the outbreak of the Civil War.

Although three of his brothers chose to serve in the Confederate army, Gibbon remained with the North. He had been severely wounded at Gettysburg and thereafter walked with a decided limp. Gibbon was promoted to major general in June 1864 and assumed command of the XXIV Corps in January 1865.

After the war, Gibbon became colonel of the Thirty-sixth Infantry in July 1866 and colonel of the Seventh Infantry at Fort Ellis, Montana, in March 1869. Known to the Plains Indians as No Hip Bone or One Who Limps, he then commanded the District of Montana from Fort Shaw.

John Gibbon assumed command of the Montana Column on March 21, 1876, and marched from Fort Ellis on April 3, east down the Yellowstone River, with six companies of his own regiment and the Second Cavalry under Major James Brisbin.

The third column, commanded by Brigadier General Alfred Terry, included Lieutenant Colonel George Armstrong Custer and the Seventh Cavalry and would march west from Fort Abraham Lincoln.

The first column to take to the field was one with eight hundred men commanded by George Crook, which set off in early March from Fort Fetterman, Wyoming Territory. They immediately encountered a savage adversary in the Wyoming winter but pushed north toward known hostile country.

On March 16, his scouts located a Sioux-Cheyenne village on the Powder River that consisted of about a hundred lodges, with perhaps as many as 250 warriors. Colonel Joseph Reynolds with six companies of the Third Cavalry—about three hundred men—was issued orders to attack the unsuspecting village the following morning.

At dawn, Reynolds' men charged into the unsuspecting village. They were met without much opposition and quickly routed the surprised warriors—losing four soldiers killed and six wounded in the process. The cavalrymen took control of the village and commenced destroying everything of value, including a large quantity of beef that the poorly supplied army could have used for themselves. This loss of provisions and lodges, however, was far greater to the Sioux people than the reported one killed and one wounded during the brief fight.

In early afternoon during a raging snowstorm, Sioux warrior Crazy Horse, who had been camped downstream, rallied the warriors and initiated a counterattack from the nearby bluffs.

Reynolds, perhaps panicking, ordered an immediate withdrawal, abandoning several dead soldiers and at least one wounded man. The soldiers also left behind the Indian pony herd, which was easily recaptured by Crazy Horse.

Crazy Horse (Tashunka Witco, Tashunca-Uitco, "His horse is crazy") was born about 1842 on the eastern edge of the Black Hills near the site of present-day Rapid City, Sioux Dakota. His mother was a member of the Brulé band, reportedly the sister of Spotted Tail, and his father an Oglala medicine man. Crazy Horse's mother died when he was quite young, and his father took her sister as a wife and raised the child in both Brulé and Oglala camps.

Curly, as he was then called due to his light, curly hair and fair complexion, killed a buffalo when he was twelve and received a horse for his accomplishment. At about that time while residing in Conquering Bear's camp, he witnessed the 1854 Gratten affair—where an army lieutenant named John L. Gratten and his twenty-nine men were slaughtered after a Sioux warrior had killed a stray Mormon ox and Gratten went to arrest him for the alleged crime. Curly also had viewed the destruction of the Indian village at Ash Hollow caused by General William Harney's punitive expedition in response. Those experiences made an indelible impression on Curly and helped shape his militancy toward the white man.

Not long after the Gratten massacre, Curly sought guidance and underwent a Vision Quest by meditating on a mountaintop. He experienced a vivid dream depicting a mounted warrior in a storm who became invulnerable by following certain rituals, such as wearing long, unbraided hair, painting his body with white hail spots, tying a small stone behind each ear, and decorating his cheek with a zigzag lightning bolt. Curly's father interpreted the dream as a sign of his son's future greatness in combat.

The following year, Curly was said to have killed his first human. Curly was in the company of a small band of Sioux warriors who were attempting to steal Pawnee horses when they happened upon some Osage buffalo hunters. In the midst of a fight, he spotted an Osage in the bushes and killed this person, who, to his surprise, turned out to be a woman. It was not shameful in Sioux culture to kill a woman, but he was so upset that he refused to take her scalp and left it for someone else.

Curly proved his worth as a warrior when he was sixteen years old during a battle with Arapaho. Decorated like the warrior in his dream, he was in the thick of the fighting, scoring coup after coup, taking many scalps, but, to his dismay, was struck by an arrow in the leg. Curly wondered why he had been wounded when the rituals he had imitated from the warrior on his Vision Quest promised protection. He finally realized that his dream warrior had taken no scalps and he had. From that day forward, Curly would never again scalp an enemy.

He received a great tribute after that battle. His father sang a song that he had composed for his son and announced that the boy would now be known by a new name—Crazy Horse. Incidentally, that name was nothing special, rather an old, common name among the Sioux tribes.

Throughout the ensuing years, Crazy Horse had built a reputation among his people as a crafty, fearless warrior. He participated in many successful raids against traditional Indian enemies and the occasional small party of whites traveling through Sioux country but had not yet faced the might of the United States Army. In 1865, that would dramatically change when an endless stream of whites—gold seekers headed for Montana—flooded the Bozeman Trail and the army garrisoned several forts to protect them.

In 1866–67 during what became known as Red Cloud's War, Crazy Horse was instrumental in rallying his fellow warriors and displaying an almost mythical courage and tactical craftiness. Due to Red Cloud's leadership and the efforts of Crazy Horse, Hump, Gall, and Rain-in-the-Face the army finally admitted defeat and negotiated a treaty to end hostilities.

Crazy Horse, however, refused to "touch the pen" to the Fort Laramie Treaty of 1868, disdained the reservation, and chose instead to freely roam traditional Sioux hunting grounds and wage war against the Crow and Shoshoni. It was said that during this time of wandering he married a Northern Cheyenne woman, which gained him friends and followers from that tribe. His interest in a certain Lakota Sioux woman, however, would nearly cost him his life.

Crazy Horse, who had gained the reputation of being introverted and eccentric, had ten years earlier vigorously courted Black Buffalo Woman, Red Cloud's niece. At that time, however, she had spurned Crazy Horse in favor of a warrior named No Water. Gossip spread that Crazy Horse had continued to visit Black Buffalo Woman when her husband was away. In 1871, Crazy Horse convinced her to run away with him. No Water was incensed and set out on the trail, finally finding the couple together in a tepee. He shot Crazy Horse, the bullet entering at the nostril, fracturing his jaw, and nearly killing him. Crazy Horse gradually recovered from this serious wound. Black Buffalo Woman returned to No Water but some months later gave birth to a sandy-haired child who suspiciously resembled Crazy Horse. The Sioux warrior licked his romantic wounds and in the summer of 1872 married Black Shawl, who would bear him a daughter, They-Are-Afraid-of-Her.

The military had been encroaching on Sioux buffalo-hunting grounds for some time, and when George Armstrong Custer's Yellowstone Expedition of 1873 served as escort for the Northern Pacific Railroad survey crews it has been said that Crazy Horse may have participated in the violent opposition.

The discovery of gold during Custer's Black Hills Expedition the following year brought hordes of miners into that sacred Sioux region that had been promised them by the provisions of the 1868 Fort Laramie Treaty. Negotiations by the United States government to buy the land angered Crazy Horse and other free-roaming Sioux. The bodies of many miners—not scalped, which was Crazy Horse's custom—began turning up in the Black Hills. Although no direct evidence exists, it has been widely speculated, even by his own people, that Crazy Horse was the one behind these brutal acts.

Another incident occurred about this time that had a profound effect on Crazy Horse. He was out fighting Crow Indians when his daughter died of cholera. The village had moved about seventy miles from the location of the burial scaffold on which lay They-Are-Afraid-of-Her. Crazy Horse tracked down the site and lay for three days beside his daughter's body.

The United States government had issued the edict that all Indians in the vicinity of the Yellowstone River Valley report to the reservation by January 31, 1876, or face severe military reprisals. Crazy Horse, Sitting Bull, and others, however, ignored the demand and remained free.

Now, in the middle of the night and in the midst of a raging snowstorm Crazy Horse had come to the rescue of his people on the Powder River, recapturing the pony herd and salvaging whatever he could of the village.

General George Crook was furious with Colonel Reynolds for not holding the village. When the command returned to Fort Fetterman on March 26, Crook filed court-martial charges against Reynolds, who was subsequently found guilty of neglect of duty. Reynolds was punished with a one-year suspension from duty, which was eventually commuted by his former West Point classmate, President U. S. Grant. Reynolds, however, would be quietly retired on disability the following year.

On May 29, Crook, with a column consisting of fifteen companies of cavalry and five of infantry—more than one thousand men—once again departed from Fort Fetterman as a part of General Alfred H. Terry's three-pronged approach designed to close in around the hostile Indians. Crook reached the head of the Tongue River near the Wyoming-Montana border on June 9 and established a base camp on Goose Creek while waiting for about 260 Shoshoni and Crow who wanted to take part in the campaign against their traditional enemies.

At about this time, the Sioux held a Sun Dance on the Rosebud. The highlight of this gathering was the revelation that revered medicine man Sitting Bull had experienced a sacred vision that would change history for the Lakota Sioux tribe and their allies.

Sitting Bull (Tatanka Yotanka, "a Large Bull Buffalo at Rest") was born about 1830 at a supply site called Many Caches along the Grand River, near present-day Bullhead, South Dakota. He was the son of a chief named either Four Horn or Sitting Bull, and his boyhood name was "Slow" or "Jumping Badger." At age ten he killed his first buffalo, and four years later he counted coup on an enemy Crow, an act that prompted his father to change the boy's name to Sitting Bull. Also at about that time, he went on a Vision Quest and was accepted into the Strong Hearts warrior society. Sitting Bull proved himself a fierce warrior, gaining the utmost respect of his peers for his daring exploits, especially after he sustained a wound in battle with the Crow that forced him to limp for the rest of his life. He assumed leadership of the Strong Hearts at age twenty-two.

Sitting Bull subsequently led raiding parties of his warriors against traditional Sioux enemies, such as the Crow, Blackfeet, Shoshoni, and Arapaho. He eventually became known as someone special, a warrior whose medicine was good, and became a *Wichasha Wakan*—a man of mystery, or medicine man. He also became legendary for practicing the Sash Dance, where in the face of the enemy he pinned himself to the ground to indicate that he would never retreat.

Sitting Bull, who did not "touch the pen" to the Fort Laramie Treaty of 1851, avoided any confrontation with the United States Army until the early 1860s when General Alfred Sully encroached on Hunkpapa territory in the Dakotas while pursuing Santee Sioux fugitives. He carried out hit-and-run raids on small army detachments and led his Strong Hearts at the July 28, 1864, Battle of Killdeer Mountain.

During Red Cloud's War, Sitting Bull's band roamed farther north, where he led attacks in northern Montana and Dakota Territory, particularly in the vicinity of newly constructed Fort Buford at the confluence of the Missouri and Yellowstone rivers. Many Sioux gave up their freedom and moved onto the reservation when Red Cloud negotiated the Fort Laramie Treaty of 1868.

Sitting Bull refused to submit and continued to follow the traditional nomadic lifestyle of his people. He and his band, however, would occasionally visit the reservation to obtain supplies and spread discontent among their brethren. His warriors were said to have been the Sioux who aggressively protested the presence of the army during Custer's Yellowstone Expedition of 1873.

When Custer marched through the Black Hills the following year, Sitting Bull considered this intrusion and that of the prospectors who later came to dig for gold to be tantamount to a declaration of war. He assumed the position as head of the war council and gathered around him allies from the Northern Cheyenne and a few other tribes.

In his mind, war had been declared by the United States government when an edict was issued requiring all Indians in the Yellowstone Valley to report to the reservation by January 31, 1876, or face the consequences. This defiant spiritual leader had no intention of obeying the order.

It was during early June 1876 while camped in the Rosebud River Valley that Sitting Bull's people held a Sun Dance. Sitting Bull did not personally participate in this ritual where warriors would have strips of rawhide attached to a stick and inserted into their chests, then dangle in the air from a center pole. Instead, he directed his adopted brother to slice strips of flesh from his arms and then commenced dancing until he passed out. When Sitting Bull was revived, he told of a vision that he had experienced: dead soldiers falling from the sky into their camp. This vision was interpreted to mean that they would be victorious in battle against their enemy.

The first opportunity to verify this vision came in mid-June when General George Crook's troops were observed approaching on a route that would take them directly into a Sioux village.

Unknown to Crook, his presence was being closely monitored by Cheyenne scouts led by Wooden Leg. When Crook broke camp on June 16, those scouts determined that the army was following a trail that would lead them directly to Sitting Bull's village, located a few miles north of present-day Busby, Montana. The Indians, concerned about the well-being of their families, held a council and decided that they would not wait for the army—Crazy Horse with as many as one thousand Sioux and Cheyenne warriors would attack Crook's column.

On June 17, Crook called a halt at midmorning for coffee and to graze the horses in a valley of the Rosebud short of Big Bend. This cul-de-sac-shaped valley with steep walls was made up of broken terrain dotted with trees, bushes, ridges, and rock formations. It was sometime between 8:00 and 10:00 A.M. when Crow scouts raced into this camp from the north to spread the alarm that they had spotted a large body of hostile Indians.

Crook, however, would not be afforded the opportunity to assemble his troops in a battle formation or employ effective military tactics. Crazy Horse had departed from his customary tactic of circling around his prey from a distance and instead immediately followed the Crow scouts over the hills to lead his warriors on a charge into the surprised cavalrymen.

Due to the terrain, the fighting was reduced to small, hastily organized units engaging the determined warriors—at times hand-to-hand—at various locations around the three-mile-long field of battle. The Indians would hit-and-run, riding in and out among the troops, who would attempt to hold their positions against each onslaught.

As the battle ensued, Crook decided that the best defense was an offense. In an effort to divert the warriors, he ordered that a detachment led by Captain Anson Mills ride downstream and attack the Indian village that he incorrectly presumed was just a few miles away. Mills, with the promise that Crook would be following with the main column, rode down the valley, which as he progressed became narrower. He correctly assumed that Crazy Horse, the master of the decoy, had deployed warriors in ambush, and proceeded with caution. Mills eventually turned back from his harrowing ride, either of his own accord or perhaps with recall orders from Crook, and thereby escaped disaster.

The fierce battle had raged for perhaps as long as six hours or until midafternoon when the Indians began massing for one final concentrated attack. Crook, however, recognized the strategy and ordered Mills to maneuver his cavalry behind the Indians. Crook's tactic was successful—his enemy broke contact and left the field to the cavalrymen, effectively ending the battle. The Indians later claimed that the reason they had fled at that point in time was because they were low on ammunition and their horses were worn out.

Crook proclaimed victory because his troops held the field at the end, but he had in truth fought to a stalemate at best. His fate might have been even worse had not the Shoshoni and Crow saved the day on more than one occasion with bold feats of bravery.

The army's casualty figures have become a matter of controversy. Crook's official report stated that he suffered ten killed and twenty-one wounded. Scout Frank Grouard's estimate of twenty-eight killed and fifty-six wounded would probably be closer to the truth. Crazy Horse later acknowledged that he had lost thirty-six killed and sixty-three wounded.

Rather than resume his pursuit of the hostiles, Crook chose to countermarch and return to his camp on Goose Creek to lick his wounds. Without notifying the other columns with whom he was expected to rendezvous in the Valley of the Little Bighorn, Crook had of his own accord taken his command out of action. Had he aggressively followed the fresh Indian trail, Crook would have likely arrived at Sitting Bull's village on the Little Bighorn either before Custer's Seventh Cavalry or in coordination with the other two columns, which had been the intention of General Terry's plan.

Crook's battalion would have the distinction of letting and shedding the first blood of the Little Bighorn Campaign. It would not be the only cavalry blood that would stain the ground in Powder River country.

Nine

————◦◉◦————

The March of the
Seventh Cavalry

On April 3, Colonel John Gibbon marched from Fort Ellis with six companies of his own regiment and the Second Cavalry under Major James Brisbin—about 450 troops. The Terry-Custer Dakota Column—nearly one thousand men—which had been delayed by poor weather that prevented the receipt of supplies, finally marched on May 17 from Fort Abraham Lincoln.

The various Indian bands in the vicinity—primarily Sioux and Northern Cheyenne—were aware that the army was on their trail and began to assemble under Sitting Bull's command. Perhaps as many as four hundred lodges— some three thousand people—moved steadily toward a gathering point in the Rosebud River Valley.

Scouts under Colonel Gibbon had noticed this activity as early as May 16. But for reasons known only to himself, Gibbon had failed to inform General Terry until his column arrived on June 9 at the mouth of the Powder River where the steamer *Far West* had been docked. This steamship, along with the *Josephine*, both owned by the Coulson Line, was awarded the contract to haul supplies for the Little Bighorn Campaign.

The *Far West*, built in 1870, was 190 feet in length with a beam of 33 feet

6 inches and could accommodate more than two hundred tons of cargo. She had been designed to operate in the shallow and hazard-filled Western rivers and had power to spare—two 15-inch-diameter engines of 5-foot piston stroke and a steam capstan on each side of her bow to pull her through the strongest of rapids.

The captain of the *Far West* was forty-two-year-old Grant Marsh, who began his career at age twelve as a cabin boy on a Pittsburgh steamer. He had begun navigating the Missouri River in 1864 and quickly became known as the premier navigator on that river—so expert that it was said that he could "navigate a steamer on a light dew." Marsh and his steamship had transported supplies for the Yellowstone Expedition of 1873. On June 7, 1875, Marsh, piloting the *Josephine,* had gained fame by ascending from the mouth of the Yellowstone River to the highest point ever reached by a steamship, near present-day Billings, surpassing the previous best by 250 miles.

The column under General Alfred H. Terry that had marched from Fort Abraham Lincoln had depended on the *Far West* for the two hundred tons of cargo that she carried—including forage, ammunition, medicine, and general supplies. The quartermaster department had established a supply depot on the Yellowstone River near the mouth of Glendive Creek. When Terry had reached that point, Captain Marsh and his *Far West* began shuttling supplies and troops upstream to the mouth of the Powder River. Terry wanted to keep the steamship as close to the troops as possible and directed Marsh to reach the juncture of the Bighorn and Little Bighorn rivers.

Terry, who established his headquarters aboard the steamship, decided that a reconnaissance would be in order to verify Gibbon's assertion of Indians moving toward the Rosebud. Custer was opposed to the scout of an area with no evidence of the enemy. He argued that such a plan was a waste of time and believed that the entire force should move forward to locate and engage the enemy before they could flee. Although voicing his disapproval of the scout, Custer halfheartedly volunteered to lead the operation.

Terry instead chose Major Marcus A. Reno for the command. The general evidently was certain that Reno would not encounter hostile Indians on his scout and simply wanted to make sure that the area was free of Indians; otherwise Terry assuredly would have chosen Custer as the commander.

Marcus Albert Reno had been born on November 15, 1834, in Carrollton, Illinois. He entered the U.S. Military Academy at West Point in 1851 and was scheduled to graduate with the class of 1855. Due to excessive demerits (he allegedly set the record with 1,031—Custer had accumulated only 726 in his four years), however, Reno finally graduated in 1857 ranked twentieth in a class of thirty-eight. He was commissioned a brevet second lieutenant in the First Dragoons in July 1857, and second lieutenant in June 1858. Reno served with his unit on frontier duty at Forts Dalles, Oregon, and Walla Walla, Washington Territory, until the outbreak of the Civil War.

Reno was appointed first lieutenant, First Dragoons, in April 1861 and captain, First Cavalry, in November. In March 1863, at Kelley's Ford, he was cited for bravery and brevetted major for his actions when he led a charge against the Rebels and his horse fell, pinning him beneath with an injury.

On July 1, 1863, Reno married Mary Hannah Ross, the daughter of a Pennsylvania banker and industrialist, in Harrisburg. The couple would have one son.

At the October 1864 Cedar Creek battle Reno once again distinguished himself and was brevetted lieutenant colonel. He also fought at Gaines' Mill, Beverly Ford, and Upperville and on the Peninsula. Reno was appointed colonel of the Twelfth Pennsylvania Cavalry from January until July 1865, when he was mustered out. On March 13, 1865, he was brevetted colonel, USA, and brigadier general, USV, in recognition of his exemplary record.

After the war, Reno served briefly as an infantry tactics instructor at West Point and then was assigned as provost marshal in New Orleans. He requested frontier duty, which took him to Fort Vancouver, Washington, as acting assistant inspector general of the Department of the Columbia. He was appointed major, Seventh Cavalry, in December 1868 but did not report for duty until late the following year. Reno was stationed at Fort Hays, Kansas, from December 1869 to July 1871, when he was assigned to New York City as a member of the Small Arms Board for two years.

Reno returned to the Seventh Cavalry in 1873 but did not participate in the Yellowstone Expedition that year or the Black Hills Expedition the following year. Instead, he was in command of a two-company detachment that provided an escort for the Northern Boundary Survey.

His wife unexpectedly passed away on July 10, 1874. Reno requested permission from headquarters to attend her funeral and received the reply: "While fully sympathizing with your affliction, the Department Commander feels it is imperative to decline to grant you leave." To add insult to injury, his wife's family denied him a share of the family fortune.

In November 1875, Reno returned from leave in Europe to become temporary commander of the Seventh Cavalry while Custer was embroiled in Washington politics. Reno requested that the position be permanent, but General Alfred H. Terry delayed making a decision until Custer's fate had been determined.

When Custer returned in time to assume command for the Little Bighorn Campaign, Reno was without question quite resentful—an attitude that had festered from the day Reno had been assigned to the Seventh Cavalry. This resentment, not unlike that of Captain Frederick W. Benteen, stemmed from professional jealousy over the fact that the younger Custer had reaped glory during the Civil War and was a national hero. Although Reno was not outwardly antagonistic toward Custer, his opinion of his superior officer was decidedly less than complimentary. This opinion was said to be mutual, which had made Reno's lengthy absences beneficial to Custer and the morale of the regiment.

Reno was not without his vocal detractors. It has been said that he was not liked and was even despised by many of his contemporaries. Hugh Scott, then a young second lieutenant who was later to become a general, "disliked him intensely." Lieutenant Francis M. Gibson was "wary of Reno and considered him to be arrogant and vicious." Another future general, then First Lieutenant Edward S. Godfrey, wrote in his journal, "Reno's self important rudeness makes him unbearable." Even Captain Benteen, who shared a common dislike of Custer, once slapped Reno in public, called him an "S.O.B.," and challenged him to a fight. Reno prudently declined the invitation.

Reno, who had never been in even a skirmish with Indians, along with six troops of the Seventh Cavalry, moved out on the afternoon of June 10 with a definite route provided by Terry to scout the Powder and Tongue valleys.

Terry meanwhile had decided to move his supply depot from Stanley's old stockade on Glendive Creek to the mouth of the Powder River. On June 11,

Custer arrived at that location with his left wing. He was disappointed that wife Libbie was not aboard the *Far West* and perhaps more disappointed that the steamer had brought a sutler who spent the afternoon serving whisky to the regiment over a makeshift bar of planks and barrels.

By June 13, Reno was camped on the upper Mizpah Creek, a waterway that was part of his assigned scout. Rather than inspect that creek, however, Reno determined that he could see far enough in that direction from a promontory on the western divide and decided that a scout was unnecessary.

On June 16, Reno came upon an abandoned Indian village estimated at four hundred lodges that would include perhaps one thousand warriors. In direct disobedience of Terry's orders, Reno chose to follow the trail of this village down the Rosebud. Unknown to him, on June 17 he came within forty miles of General George Crook, who was engaged in the battle of the Rosebud.

On June 19, Reno camped at the mouth of the Rosebud, upriver from Colonel John Gibbon, and notified Terry by courier of his present position. Reno informed Terry that he had not only scouted the Powder and Tongue river valleys but also entered the Rosebud Valley while following the fresh Indian trail. He had traversed more than 240 miles of an itinerary that had been set by Terry at about 175 miles.

Terry as well as Custer was furious with Reno for differing reasons. Terry had explicitly warned Reno not to go to the Rosebud for fear that the action would alert the Indians to the presence of soldiers and jeopardize the movement of the three columns. The commanding general would have certainly preferred charges against Reno had he not been the only major in Custer's command. Custer, however, believed that Reno should have pursued and attacked the hostiles he had trailed.

But Reno, to his dubious credit, had provided vital information by identifying that the Indians were not on the lower section of Rosebud Creek. General Terry could now assume that the hostiles were moving toward the Valley of the Little Bighorn and formulate his plans accordingly.

Sitting Bull had indeed moved his village to that location, and their numbers had grown. Bolstered by those brethren who had left the reservations for a summer of freedom, the village had swelled to about one thousand lodges—

some seven thousand people, including perhaps two thousand or more warriors.

On June 21 aboard the *Far West,* which was moored on the Yellowstone at the mouth of the Rosebud, General Alfred Terry, who would not accompany the march, issued orders for Lieutenant Colonel George Armstrong Custer and his Seventh Cavalry. These orders would later create a controversy when some—including Terry and of course Frederick Benteen—would contend that Custer had disobeyed them.

Perhaps Custer had a premonition that Terry's orders would have a historic value. Captain Grant Marsh placed the final words Armstrong wrote to his beloved wife, Libbie, in the mail sack at the junction of the Yellowstone and Rosebud rivers, Montana Territory, on the morning of June 22. The letter read in part:

> *My Darling—I have but a few moments to write as we start at twelve, and I have my hands full of preparations for the scout. Do not be anxious about me. You would be surprised how closely I obey your instructions about keeping with the column. I hope to have a good report to send you by the next mail. A success will start us all toward Lincoln.*
>
> *I send you an extract from Gen'l Terry's official order, knowing how keenly you appreciate words of commendation and confidence in your dear Bo: "It is impossible to give you any definite instructions in regard to this movement, and, were it not impossible to do so, the Department Commander places too much confidence in your zeal, energy and ability to impose on you precise orders which might hamper your action when nearly in contact with the enemy."*
>
> *Your devoted boy Autie*

Incidentally, Major Marcus Reno, Captain Myles Keogh, Captain Tom Custer, First Lieutenant James Calhoun, and Marsh stayed up all night that night before the regiment marched playing cards on board the docked *Far West.* Perhaps this was their way of relieving tension before life became deadly serious the following morning.

As the officers and men of the Seventh Cavalry prepared for this campaign, they were confident in their ability to meet the challenge of their enemy. They were well armed and trained and anxious to relieve garrison boredom with action.

In the early 1870s, the army's Ordnance Department staged field trials of prospective rifles and carbines for use by the troops. The army was seeking a weapon that could take a beating yet remain reliable and one that used a single-shot system rather than a repeating system because of its lower manufacturing cost. The rifles were tested for every factor from defective cartridges to the effects of rust and dust. In the end, about ninety entries by such makers as Elliot, Freeman, Mauser, Peabody, and Spencer were winnowed down to four finalists: the Remington Rolling Block; the vertically sliding breechblock Sharps; the trapdoor Springfield; and the Ward-Burton bolt-action. The final selection was made in 1872 by a board of officers, which was presided over by General Alfred Terry and included Major Marcus Reno as a member.

On May 5, 1873, the winner of the rifle competition was announced in the board's final report to the secretary of war. The Model 1873 Springfield .45/55-caliber, single-shot, breech-loading carbine had emerged on top. The Springfield weighed about 6.9 pounds and was 41.3 inches long. It fired a .45-caliber copper-cased cartridge with fifty-five grains of black powder, with an effective range of about 250 to 300 yards, although it could shoot as far as 1,000 yards. A properly trained rifleman could fire his weapon up to a maximum of seventeen times per minute with accuracy. The Seventh Cavalry had been issued the Springfield just prior to the Black Hills Expedition of 1874 but had not encountered circumstances that had put the rifle to a real test as yet.

Each trooper would be carrying one hundred cartridges for his Springfield carbine—fifty in his cartridge belt and fifty in his saddlebags. This would afford Custer's detachment more than twenty thousand available rounds of ammunition. The cavalrymen also would carry a Model "P" 1872 Colt Single Action revolver, which had been chosen over the Smith & Wesson Schofield due to its simpler operation, stronger parts, and dependability. The army had placed an initial order of thirteen thousand in 1873–74 and then bought about one thousand a year thereafter until 1891. Called a thumb-buster by the troops, this .45-caliber revolver, with a seven-and-a-half-inch barrel, fired six metallic cartridges with twenty-eight grains of black powder and had an effective range of about sixty yards. Each man would have twenty-four rounds for his Colt. This popular revolver, which came to be known as the "Peacemaker" to frontier lawmen, was manufactured by the Colt company into the 1980s.

Some of the officers and men, however, would carry personal weapons. George Armstrong Custer would go into battle with his .50-caliber Remington sporting rifle with an octagonal barrel and two self-cocking white-handled British Webley Bulldog double-action revolvers. Captain Thomas A. French was widely known for his marksmanship with his .50-caliber Springfield rifle known as "Long Tom." Sergeant John Ryan took along a specially made .45-caliber Sharps rifle with a telescopic sight that weighed fifteen pounds.

Contrary to depictions by some artists, the Seventh Cavalry—with perhaps the exception of European first lieutenants Charles DeRudio and Edward Mathey—would not carry their sabers into the battle. These heavy, cumbersome, and noisy weapons, which were for the most part merely ornaments for inspection and parade, would be left behind at the Powder River base camp.

At noon on June 22, George Armstrong Custer, wearing a wide-brimmed hat, light-colored buckskin suit, and his distinctive Civil War red tie, shook hands one final time with General Alfred Terry. The regimental band was positioned on a knoll overlooking the Powder River and performed the marching song "Garry Owen" to a chorus of hearty cheers from the troops. It would be the final tune heard by Custer and his cavalry before marching into the Valley of the Little Bighorn.

Custer then led his column of troops on the march toward their objective. The command would cover over seventy miles in the next three days—locating and following the Indian trail on the second day out.

Accompanying Custer was a member of the press—newspaperman Marcus H. "Mark" Kellogg, who was being paid to send back dispatches to an interested reading public. The forty-three-year-old Kellogg had been a reporter for newspapers throughout the Midwest during his career. His wife had died in 1867 and his daughters were being raised by an aunt, so Kellogg was free to pursue his career. He had worked at various papers, including one in Brainard, Minnesota, in 1872 until May 1873, when he assumed a position as an editorial assistant for *The Bismarck Tribune*. Kellogg apparently worked only part-time for the newspaper—in the summer of 1974 he ran a hay camp north of Bismarck while studying law. He then went east and returned to Bismarck in early 1876 aboard the same train as the Custers. The train became snow-bound, and Kellogg was said to have fashioned a telegraph key that summoned Tom Custer to come to the rescue with a sleigh.

Kellogg had not been scheduled to accompany Custer's Seventh Cavalry on this campaign but at the last moment had replaced his *Tribune* employer, Clement A. Lounsberry, whose wife suddenly became ill. During the march, Kellogg had thus far submitted three dispatches, dated May 31, June 12, and the final one from the mouth of the Rosebud on June 21.

On the morning of June 24, Custer had passed the limits of Reno's scout and happened upon a large abandoned village where the Indians had recently held a Sun Dance. The column followed this fresh trail from the village and camped at dusk on Mud Creek, after a march of about twenty-eight miles.

Scouts under Second Lieutenant Charles Varnum who had been dispatched earlier to gather information returned to report that the Indians were likely on the lower Little Bighorn River.

Varnum had just celebrated his twenty-seventh birthday three days earlier. The New York native was a West Point graduate who had reported for duty with the Seventh Cavalry in time to participate in the Yellowstone Expedition. Now he had been chosen to command the Crow and Arikara scouts for this campaign and led the advance up the Rosebud following the Indian trail toward the Valley of the Little Bighorn.

Custer marched his command at 11:00 P.M. and paused three hours later in the wee hours of June 25 for a brief rest before resuming the march. The column eventually went into bivouac just before dawn. The men heated cof-fee over sagebrush and buffalo chip fires to drink with their hardtack, those unsalted, cracker-like biscuits that were issued for field duty.

The officers and men were exhausted but perhaps not in as bad a shape as the horses. Cavalry horses were accustomed to at least fourteen pounds of hay a day along with twelve or so pounds of grain. These horses had been eating only about three pounds of grain a day and whatever they could forage from the sparse valley grass.

George Armstrong Custer, contrary to common belief, was not immune to weariness and took this opportunity to curl up under a bush and fall asleep.

During the night, Lieutenant Varnum and his scouts had camped on a promontory—a traditional Plains Indian lookout—that afforded a fair view of the Valley of the Little Bighorn. Varnum had named this terrain feature Crow's Nest after a similarly shaped mountaintop back at West Point that bore that name.

In the clear light of dawn, Varnum's scouts—Charley Reynolds, Minton "Mitch" Bouyer, and a number of Arikara and Crow—observed smoke some fifteen miles distant as well as what they believed to be a sizable pony herd grazing in the valley, although neither the river nor the bordering trees were visible. Varnum himself, even with spyglasses, could not observe anything but dismissed that failure as a symptom of lack of sleep. Nonetheless, Varnum trusted his scouts and sent a message to Custer at 8:00 A.M. that a huge village had been located on the Little Bighorn River.

By the time Custer arrived at about 9:00 A.M., a haze had settled over the hilly terrain that made it impossible for him to recognize anything that far away. He did, however, accept the assessment of his scouts that a large Indian village along the river lay ahead.

Custer returned to camp and was informed by his brother Tom that Captain Myles Keogh, whose battalion had been detailed with the pack train, reported that a troubling incident had occurred. Troopers with Company F had been sent back to retrieve a box of hardtack that had fallen off a mule during the night march. When the detail located the box it was surrounded by several Indians, who had been sampling the contents and raced away as the soldiers approached.

That information convinced Custer that the presence and location of his command was certainly now known by the hostiles. This would necessitate immediate action or—as was the custom of the Indians when discovered by the army—the village would vanish into the hills. Time was now of the essence.

Custer assembled his officers and informed them of the situation. Every one of them was concerned that the Indians would escape and understood that they must move quickly to prevent that. The column, Custer told them, would march at once in the direction of the presumed location of the village. Each company would detail one noncommissioned officer and six troopers to escort the pack train. Captain Frederick Benteen's Company H would have the advance.

Custer informed his orderly, John Burkman, that his horse Dandy was weary from his trip to Crow's Nest. Burkman was asked to saddle Vic, a chestnut thoroughbred with three white fetlocks that Custer had obtained in Kentucky. Burkman was told to remain with the pack train and make sure that Custer's hounds did not follow him.

George Armstrong Custer was ready for a fight, and would formulate his battle plan as events warranted—just as he had done during the Civil War with great success. He had no reason to believe that the Sioux and Cheyenne would provide much of a contest, especially since he believed they were running away and he would likely be chasing down small bands throughout the territory.

If everything went as planned, the Seventh Cavalry would be attaining further glory by sundown that day. But that wasn't to be the case.

Ten

———◆◈◆———

Into the Valley

There has been a concerted effort over the years by historians to demonize Custer and place guilt and disgrace by association on the members
of the Seventh Cavalry who rode under his command to wage battle in the
Valley of the Little Bighorn. In fact, there are those Americans who shamefully regard these soldiers as the enemy in this engagement, believing that
they were less than honorable for fighting against the hostile Sioux and Cheyenne.

Any implied dishonor toward these brave men who rode under the colors
of the United States of America has been misdirected and should be considered a grievous insult to anyone who has ever served in the military—as well
as any true American.

Custer was not a loose cannon or some sort of rogue commander who was
free to pillage, plunder, and kill his way through the West. Neither he nor his
men had the power to formulate national policy or to choose their enemies—
that falls into the category of politics and the national interest. The soldiers
were simply doing their duty and following orders under the United States
Constitution, the document that they had sworn to uphold when they had volunteered for the army.

If there was to be an argument about the right or wrong of this mission,
then that argument should be with the politics, policies, and principles of the

president, his cabinet, the Congress, and the War Department, which, in this case, overwhelmingly supported this military mission.

These soldiers marched off under orders from their government with the blessing and admiration of the country's population, which, along with their elected leaders had determined that the Sioux and Cheyenne, were a threat that must be dealt with harshly. Any blame for fighting a particular enemy should never be directed at those citizens who stepped forward to proudly wear the uniform representing their country and sacrificed so much to protect the national interests—including at times the ultimate sacrifice, their lives.

Make no mistake about it, at that point in time in America Custer and the soldiers of the Seventh Cavalry were every bit as much heroes for doing their duty in Montana as were those forthcoming soldiers who fought in the bloody trenches at Belleau Wood in World War I, or the courageous men who stormed the deadly beaches at Normandy or Iwo Jima, or those fighting servicemen who braved the freezing season at the frozen Chosin Reservoir in Korea, or the men who risked their lives battling brutal communist insurgents in South Vietnam, or those Marines who cleared the dangerous streets of Fallujah in Iraq, or servicemen who came under siege at an outpost in Nuristan Province, Afghanistan.

The men of the Seventh Cavalry—as they rode into that dangerous valley—deserve the respect of the public now just as they did back then for their service. They were indeed the military heroes of their time.

Before too many miles on the march, George Armstrong Custer decided to relieve Benteen and take the advance himself, as was his customary position. He always wanted to personally be the first to know what was ahead and the first to engage in a fight.

At about noon, without any sign of the enemy, the Seventh Cavalry paused at the head of Reno Creek. They were now in full attack mode, and a battle was imminent. Custer conferred briefly with his adjutant, William Cooke, before issuing orders for the regiment to separate into three battalions.

Captain Frederick W. Benteen was assigned companies D, H, and K—about 125 men. Benteen's battalion was detailed on a reconnaissance to the west along a series of ridges that overlooked the Little Bighorn River for the purpose of thwarting an Indian escape in that direction. Benteen was also told to pitch into any Indians he might happen upon. Custer was worried that the Indians from the village would try to run in that direction to escape when the troopers appeared on the scene. Benteen was told to catch up later with the main column farther down Reno Creek.

Major Marcus A. Reno would command a battalion consisting of companies A, G, and M—about 140 men. Reno led his column of men in a southerly direction toward the supposed location of the village while he awaited further orders.

The third battalion would consist of two detachments that would remain under Custer's direct control. The Irish soldier of fortune Captain Myles W. Keogh would command companies C, I, and L and Custer's friend from Monroe, Michigan, captain George Yates, would lead E and F—about 225 total men.

Captain Thomas M. McDougall was placed in charge of security for the pack train, which consisted of his Company B, the escort of troopers from various companies, and the civilian packers—about 85 men. Frenchman First Lieutenant Edward G. Mathey, Company B's second-in-command, would command the pack train.

Benteen and his battalion veered off to the left as the remainder of the regiment—with McDougall's pack train quickly falling behind—marched toward the suspected location of the village.

The sun-baked terrain that spread out before Custer and his men was a frustrating and deceptive landscape of ravines and crevices that cut through grassy rolling hills that sharply plunged into deep valleys. The tree-lined Little Bighorn River lay somewhere down below, but just when they thought they would lay eyes on it another bluff would rise up before them to obscure the view. Custer desperately wanted to observe the village and its position along the river with his own eyes in order to have a better idea of formulating a plan of attack. But even Lieutenant Varnum and the Indian scouts who rode ahead of the column were unable to distinguish their objective.

The column rode eight miles more before halting when they came upon an abandoned village site. This village they called Lone Tepee had signs of fresh occupancy, but only one tepee with the body of a dead warrior from the Rosebud battle lying inside was still standing.

The Arikara scouts were setting fire to the tepee as scout Frederic Girard (aka Gerard, the Canadian spelling of his name), who had a Canadian father and an American mother, galloped up on his black stallion waving his hat. He had been scouting from a nearby knoll when he observed billows of dust that signified to him an enemy that was retreating in the face of the approaching soldiers. "Here are your Indians, General!" Girard shouted. "Running like devils."

Indeed, great plumes of dust could be observed rising from beyond the distant hills. Custer understood that he must act immediately or his enemy would vanish into the landscape. The regiment was quickly moved another two miles before halting on a fork of Reno Creek.

It was here that First Lieutenant William W. Cooke, Custer's trusted adjutant, carried orders from George Armstrong Custer to Major Marcus Reno for an action that would open hostilities in the June 25, 1876, Battle of the Little Bighorn.

Reno was directed to move rapidly forward down the valley toward the village "and charge afterward, and you will be supported by the whole outfit," or words to that effect. Numerous bystanders—including Reno's subordinate officers such as Myles Moylan and Thomas French—claimed to have heard Cooke relay the orders, and each version was basically the same other than the specific verbiage. Reno had his orders—charge into the village with his battalion.

Major Reno's three companies immediately trotted away and crossed the creek a short distance upstream from where it flowed into the Little Bighorn River. Cooke and Captain Myles Keogh rode along with Reno until the battalion paused to water the horses and adjust their gear. The two officers then returned to their duties with the main column. At that point, saddles were tightly cinched and equipment tied down and the men made sure their Colt .45s and Springfield carbines were fully loaded and operational.

Custer, watching Reno ride off, met briefly with Lieutenant Varnum, who remarked that apparently the whole valley was full of Indians. Custer suggested that Varnum, if he so desired, could take his scouts and accompany Reno. Varnum was agreeable to that idea and called to his friend First Lieutenant George "Nick" Wallace, the regimental topographical engineer, to join him with Bloody

Knife and the other scouts. These men raced to catch up with Reno's battalion.

It was just after 3:00 P.M. on that brutally hot Sunday afternoon when Major Reno and his three companies of cavalrymen advanced on the western side of the Little Bighorn River steadily toward their objective, the huge village, which lay about two miles directly to their front.

By this time, Custer was maneuvering his battalion onto the high ridge on the eastern side of the Little Bighorn River. From this vantage point he and his troopers could view for the first time a large portion of the Indian village. This maze of white tepees that contrasted with the blue of the river and the sky was certainly breathtaking. No doubt this was the largest village any of these men had ever seen—a full one and a half miles long and a quarter of a mile wide—along with a pony herd above the village that likely numbered twenty thousand animals.

Custer did not know how many warriors he would be fighting, but that number would not have deterred him. He had faced an overwhelming enemy many times during the Civil War with quick and aggressive strategies designed on the spur of the moment to exploit weaknesses and had generally prevailed. He would have been aroused by the prospect of a battle but not fazed by this magnificent sight stretching out before him.

Now that he could view the better part of the valley, he was secure in the knowledge that he had been correct with his initial plan of attack. They were certainly in for a big fight, but that was why they had come. With that in mind, he dispatched Sergeant Daniel Kanipe with orders to tell Captain McDougall to hurry the pack train, which was laden with ammunition.

Custer turned back to the task at hand and keenly assessed the terrain ahead on the ridgeline. He intended to send the men of his battalion down the various ravines at intervals toward the river and into the village on the other side. These natural approaches to the river and the village across it were ideal routes for his purpose. Each detachment could ride down the coulee and strike at a different location along the length of the complex of tepees to wreak havoc among the Sioux and Cheyenne. It would be the knockout blow of the perfect one-two punch after Reno had struck the village with his men.

A number of the coulees were impassable or channeled into nearby ravines that resulted in dead ends, however, so it was imperative that he choose each one wisely. Meanwhile, he would watch events unfold in the valley so as to coordinate his efforts with Reno's charge into the south end of the village.

Sergeant Kanipe rode off to carry Custer's message just as Major Marcus Reno's men thundered down the widening valley on a collision course with Sitting Bull's village. The ground was flat and without obstacles but torn up and reduced to loose dirt by the hooves and overgrazing of the massive Indian pony herd.

No doubt hearts and adrenaline were pumping as every man said his silent prayers as this large village rose up larger and larger as they drew closer. Reno's cavalrymen had the field to themselves; the Indians had not as yet made an appearance. The excited troopers, fueled by the prospect of a fight, could not contain themselves and spontaneously began to wildly cheer—until Reno ordered them to be quiet.

Every advantage was with Reno and his cavalrymen. Custer's plan was working to perfection. The village had been taken completely by surprise. There was no opposition in sight. Reno could sail into the village and have his way with the unwitting occupants.

Now, as Reno was about halfway across the open prairie to his objective his presence was noticed by the stunned occupants. The village became the scene of bedlam as this danger approached its southern end. The women had been tending to their domestic chores, while some men were sleeping, fishing, or repairing weapons and equipment when word spread that soldiers were attacking. Many of the warriors had gone out hunting and others were with the pony herd at the far northern end, and it would take some time for them to react with any effectiveness.

According to Lakota chief Gall, whose Hunkpapa band was camped in their traditional place to guard the vulnerable edge facing Reno's approach, orders were given to quickly strike the village and flee when they observed the troops charging. Gall and a handful of other warriors mounted their ponies and rode back and forth just outside the village to give the animals their second wind while firing wildly to try to cover the withdrawal.

Incidentally, the presence of Custer's command on the high ridge to the east remained unknown to Gall or the village at this time. The second part of the trap could be sprung as soon as Reno entered the chaotic village, where Custer's men would find the vulnerable inhabitants easy targets as they ran to and fro to escape this surprise onslaught from the south.

The cavalrymen under Major Reno steadily advanced, prepared to sweep through the village and shoot down the warriors and round up women and children prisoners. A baffling occurrence, however, was about to change the complexion of the entire battle.

About a quarter of a mile away from the village—just a couple of minutes from its doorstep—Major Marcus Reno inexplicably aborted his charge and halted the battalion. Reno had not suffered any casualties and had faced little opposition, yet, in his first meaningful encounter with hostile Plains Indians the major had countermanded Custer's orders and abruptly called for a halt short of his objective.

Perhaps the dust swirls that obscured vision, or his uncertainty about Custer's whereabouts, or simply the fear of the unknown had caused this rash decision by Reno. He must have known that he was disobeying orders, but the consequences of that act became secondary to his impetuous need for self-preservation.

Admittedly, there were more than one thousand lodges within that village and perhaps as many as two thousand warriors in the area, but Reno wouldn't have had any knowledge of that fact. He had not lost a man up to that point, nor had he encountered any direct contact with the enemy, and he should have known from his training that the panicked village was packing to leave.

The question of how many warriors were present in Sitting Bull's village was bandied about even before the smoke on the battlefield had cleared. No definitive answer has been agreed upon to this day. There has been, however, no lack of those who have speculated about the figure.

It is known that the village had grown considerably in size from earlier in the year. Families had departed from the reservation to join their brethren for a summer enjoying the old ways—just how many would be a matter of speculation. The Indian agent would have underreported these defections in order to receive supplies for a higher number, and then dispose of the surplus with the profits going into his own pocket. An article in the *Army and Navy Journal*, dated October 21, 1876, states that at Standing Rock Agency "Out of

7,000 [Indians]—the basis upon which supplies have sent out by the Bureau for the last year or two—only 2,300 are now present."

A year after the battle, Lieutenant H. L. Scott visited the site of the village and quit counting lodge circles when he arrived at fifteen hundred. His effort proved little inasmuch as families were known to move as many as several times and each occasion left an empty circle remaining. In addition, the village also contained hundreds of wickiups—brush shelters—that would have blown away without leaving a trace.

Estimates of the number of warriors by army personnel who either participated in the battle or examined the site ranged from twenty-five hundred to nine thousand. It might be thought that the Indians themselves could have provided an exact number of warriors, but that was not the case. Gall was unable to offer any estimate. Other Indian participants claimed between one and eight thousand. Crazy Horse said at least seven thousand were there. Nonparticipant Red Cloud set the figure at two thousand. Allegedly, Indians believed that the number was inconsequential and that anyone who counted higher than one thousand must be dishonest.

The total number of lodges has been estimated at about one thousand, not including the small number of Arapaho, who were known to have members of their tribe in the village. It has been said that each lodge would be home to two warriors, perhaps more if the older boys were involved. Add to that the wickiups on the north end of the village that housed young warriors who did not live with their families; subtract those men who had reached "retirement" age, which was said to be sometime around their fortieth birthday.

Whatever the exact number of warriors, it would be safe to say that their number far exceeded Custer's troops that day by perhaps as much as five to one—odds not much different than Custer had faced in his first Civil War encounter as a general against Jeb Stuart at Gettysburg in which he had emerged victorious, as well as subsequent battles, such as Falling Waters, the Wilderness, Winchester, and Tom's Brook.

Gall stated that the soldiers had come so quickly that he could rally only a handful of warriors to fight to cover the hasty retreat of the village—until Reno unexpectedly stopped his charge.

Chief Gall was no stranger to conflict with the white man. He was a physically imposing man—standing more than six feet tall and weighing over two hundred pounds—and had a reputation as a fierce warrior. He was born about 1840 along the Moreau River in present-day South Dakota. His unusual name was said to have been given him by his mother when he ate the gallbladder of an animal. He was orphaned as a child and, after proving his worthiness as a warrior, was adopted by Sitting Bull as a younger brother.

His earliest recorded relations with the white man occurred when he was visiting friends near Fort Berthold during the winter of 1865–66. Some unknown crime had been committed, and authorities presumed that Gall was responsible—which probably was not the case. Nevertheless, a reward was placed on him, dead or alive. Soldiers from Fort Stevenson came to arrest Gall at Fort Berthold, and he attempted to escape by slashing his way through the back of his tepee. Unfortunately for him, this move had been anticipated and soldiers were stationed on the other side. Gall was said to have been bayoneted, perhaps so severely that the bayonet passed through him and a soldier had to place one foot on Gall's chest to remove it. Some accounts claim that he was shot and stabbed numerous times. Custer scout Bloody Knife had been prepared to shoot the severely wounded Gall with a shotgun but was thwarted by an officer who believed that the Sioux warrior was already dead. Regardless of the specific circumstances, Gall was not dead when the soldiers departed. He crawled away—perhaps twenty miles through the snow—to the cabin of a friend, who nursed him back to health.

In 1866, Gall and other Sioux warriors had joined Red Cloud when war was waged with the United States Army over the intrusion of the Bozeman Trail. Gall claimed to have not signed the Fort Laramie Treaty of 1868, which ended those hostilities. He was possibly involved in the Sioux attacks on Custer's Seventh Cavalry during the Yellowstone Expedition of 1873, although no confirming evidence exists.

Now Gall would play a major role as a field commander as he rode out to delay or discourage Major Marcus Reno and his troops from entering the village while it was being packed for flight. No doubt Gall was both surprised and energized when Reno aborted his charge. That pause in the action permitted the Indians time to assemble a defense and subsequently to mount a counterattack on Reno. Word spread throughout the village that the soldiers were no longer charging and that the warriors should mount their ponies and ride out to protect the village.

This sudden factor had not been included in Custer's battle plan and the present was no time to try to amend tactics. Reno would soon find himself in a tight spot, one that he should not have had to face had he simply obeyed orders. He could only hope that the Indians would not take advantage of his misdeed or that Custer had noticed and would ride to his rescue. But Custer and his battalion were far away, high atop the hillside to the east. They would have been deployed by Custer and it would not have been an easy task or timely to assemble the command and ride to the rescue of Reno.

Major Marcus Reno must now depend on his own devices to remove himself and his men from harm's way or carry out his orders and head for the village. Another mistake could be fatal to the entire command.

Eleven

The Crimson Trail

Those Sioux and Cheyenne warriors who rode out to meet Major Reno and his battalion were armed with weapons that ranged from primitive clubs, bows and arrows, lances, knives, and hatchets to an array of new and old firearms. They had obtained their firearms, which the Lakota Sioux called *maza wakan* or "holy iron," through trade, gunrunning, or capture from enemies or from the United States government for hunting purposes in fulfillment of annuities.

Archaeological excavations of the battlefield that began in 1983 recovered cartridge casings from at least forty-five different makes of firearms. That evidence indicated that the Indians were in possession of Spencers, Sharpses, Smith & Wessons, Evanses, Forehand & Wadsworths, Remingtons, Henrys, Stars, Winchesters, Maynards, Enfields, and, of course, many Springfields and Colt revolvers that would be taken that day from dead cavalrymen.

The weapon most frequently observed and mentioned by the soldiers was the Winchester repeating rifle. This was the rifle of choice for the Indians, when they could get their hands on it. The Model 1866 Winchester fired a .44-caliber rimfire cartridge, used a two-hundred-grain bullet with twenty-eight grains of powder, had a capacity of seventeen cartridges, and was deadly accurate at a hundred yards but fell off dramatically at longer distances. The Winchester was similar to the 1860 Henry, which fired the same

.44-caliber rimfire cartridge, with a 216-grain bullet and twenty-five grains of powder. The Winchester had a spring cover on the right side of the receiver, while cartridges were inserted into the front of the Henry magazine.

By the time the small defense party was organized by Gall in the village, Reno had dismounted his troopers and formed a skirmish line a few hundred yards in length across the prairie. Some of the men happened upon a convenient prairie dog colony that served as breastworks. Other than those small dirt mounds, the prairie was not an ideal location for the exposed troopers. They lay on their bellies, their rifles tucked tightly into their shoulders, and awaited orders. The horse holders, every fourth man, led the mounts away from direct harm to the protection of the underbrush by the riverbank fifty yards to the east. Reno had lost only two men whose horses had bolted and carried them into the village.

Custer, from his vantage point—which could have been down a coulee and shielded from a view of the valley by the terrain—may or may not have been aware of Reno's reckless actions. He could also have possibly noticed that the village was no longer being disassembled, which meant that the Indians, for some reason, intended to stand and fight. He likely headed north and west at a trot, halting his command a short distance down Cedar Coulee.

Custer, now able to gauge the size of the village from a closer perspective, dispatched orderly Private John Martin with a hastily scribbled order written by adjutant William Cooke to locate Captain Benteen and urge the captain to hurry his troops and bring the ammunition packs with him.

At about this point in time, Reno's men may have thought they observed Custer on the ridge watching them and then waving his hat before moving on, or it could have been a straggler or a messenger. This soldier could have been Sergeant Daniel Kanipe or Private John Martin, both of whom would eventually have been heading south, *away* from the battlefield to carry their messages from Custer. If it had been Custer waving his broad-brimmed hat, he assuredly was waving it toward the village to encourage Reno to carry out his orders and charge.

Back on the prairie, the ninety or so vulnerable men on Reno's skirmisher line could observe the Indians gathering, growing in numbers, and in spite of being out of range commenced firing in earnest at the village. No attempt was made by Major Reno to moderate this heavy rate of fire and ammunition, which was quickly becoming exhausted. Troopers took turns dashing to the river where the horses were tethered to grab ammo from their saddlebags and return to the line.

During this initial assault, Chief Gall claimed that two of his wives and three of his children were killed by Reno's men firing blindly into the tepees.

A group of Indians made one concerted charge toward the skirmisher line, but several volleys from the Springfield carbines discouraged them. These warriors veered off toward the river, a number of them maneuvering down the gulley toward the cavalry horses. Company G was ordered to the river to ward off this threat, which left the skirmisher line spread out much too thinly to be effective. The longer Reno's men remained exposed on the prairie the more time warriors would have to join their comrades. There would have to be some relief soon or they would be overwhelmed.

Reno was now flustered and uncertain about what course of action to undertake. Custer's battalion could not be observed anywhere in the vicinity, so the chance of reinforcements arriving was not imminent. Scout Fred Girard claimed that at this point the major drank lustily from a bottle of whisky while contemplating his next act.

Reno noticed a stand of trees some fifty yards away near a cut bank formed by the river's changing course. Either he weakly ordered a retreat to that location or the battalion simply executed one of its own accord. The men ran for their horses—and their lives—certainly thankful to be away from that exposed position on the prairie.

Contrary to military standard operating procedure, no tactical covering fire was employed for this impulsive movement that led the battalion to a crescent-shaped stand of timber—some twenty-five yards wide—near the river. Firing by the soldiers had almost ceased during this mad dash, and the Indians took advantage of that by rushing out of the village in numbers and surrounding this new wooded position.

Apparently no officer—not Reno, his adjutant Second Lieutenant Benjamin H. Hodgson, or Captain Thomas French, along with Lieutenants DeRudio, Donald "Tosh" McIntosh, Wallace, and Varnum, who was in charge of the scouts—took over the responsibility for organizing a formation with covering fire or setting up a perimeter as basic military tactics would dictate. No doubt these officers attempted to encourage their men to maintain intervals and fire discipline, but it would have been of no consequence. If Major Reno, their commander, had run away helter-skelter there was little the men could do but follow in the same disorderly fashion.

When finally straggling inside this arboreal refuge, the troopers began to return fire. They lay on the grassy floor with a canopy of trees above, ignoring the steady pelting of seed pods, leaves, twigs, and other debris that were ripped by bullets and arrows from the cottonwoods, willows, elders, and assorted shrubs.

Their military training had taught them to take it upon themselves to instinctively deploy into a defensive position, and they were successful at keeping the Indians at bay. Small groups of warriors would charge up close, empty their weapons, and then gallop away, soon to be replaced by another group. The volleys were loud and dramatic but caused few casualties among the troopers who hugged the ground.

It was now about 3:30 P.M. Reno's command had lost only several killed and wounded up to this point. The position inside the stand of timber was an excellent site to defend due to its density and thick underbrush. In addition, it posed no direct threat to the village because it was lower in elevation, which made direct fire difficult. The Indians could now pack up and depart if they so desired. Reno could simply hunker down in this defensive position and await the arrival of Custer and Benteen. Both battalions could not be far away, and the enemy would surely flee when reinforcements approached.

But Major Marcus Reno, who had lost his straw hat in the fray and had wrapped a red bandana around his sweaty head, evidently assessed his situation without taking into consideration military strategy, much less common sense. For reasons known only to him, he was not satisfied with his relative safety or ability to hold the timber until it became absolutely necessary to move.

It was apparent that at this point Marcus Reno had lost control of his senses and perceptions, which would not be expected of a competent army officer at such a crucial time. The major was in the midst of a major emotional breakdown. He was no longer rational, not knowing whether to stand his ground or change his position. But one thing was clear: Major Marcus Reno wanted no part of that enemy village to his north. The thought of what sort of doom could be waiting for him inside that village prompted him to want to get as far away from it as quickly as possible.

Without asking for counsel from his fellow officers, Reno greatly miscalculated his circumstances, perhaps fearing that enough Indians would soon creep up close and overwhelm his command. He impulsively determined that his men—or at least he—should move to the high bluffs across the Little Bighorn River.

Rather than executing a bugle call that could have been heard above the din, he issued a verbal command ordering his men to mount and prepare to move out. The troopers near Reno who could distinguish the order mounted, but most of the men were too distant to hear anything above the firing. Those cavalrymen planning to retreat with Reno had problems controlling or catching their excited mounts, which caused mass confusion. Few of the soldiers understood what was happening—until they noticed their comrades preparing for flight.

In their haste to assemble, once again the soldiers' firing had almost completely ceased. This lull allowed a party of Indians to approach the bunched-up troops and fire their weapons at close range. The deadly volley dropped a number of troopers.

One particularly gruesome casualty was Bloody Knife, Custer's favorite scout, who had been standing beside Reno. The bullet struck the scout in the head to send a gory burst of blood and brains splattering onto the face of Major Reno. Could it be that Gall, the boyhood adversary of Bloody Knife, had spotted the scout and fired that mortal bullet to settle a long-standing grudge?

Regardless of the identity of Bloody Knife's assassin, that gruesome act was all that the major could endure and shattered any resoluteness he might have been able to summon. The shocked Marcus Reno panicked and surrendered to his fear. He ordered the troops to dismount and then ordered them to remount. Sergeant John Ryan said he then heard Reno shout, "Any of you men wish to make your escape, follow me!" Those men within hearing, including Ryan, must have thought it odd that Reno was offering an invitation rather than issuing an order.

Then, without regard for the welfare of his men in the timber, Major

Marcus Reno mounted and put the spurs to the flanks of his own horse, racing for the river to try to save himself.

The troopers must have been quite disturbed and confused as they watched their leader run away in the face of the enemy. If bravery was contagious, so, too, was fright. They must have wondered what Reno had observed to cause him to react in such a manner—after all, the soldiers were holding the perimeter. Enlisted men were trained to look to their officers for guidance to direct them in combat. Reno was the commander of this battalion, and his word and deeds were sacrosanct and final. The command had no choice but to catch up with their shaken leader.

Once again, it appears that no subordinate officer stepped forward to assume de facto command. Several officers, such as Thomas French, would later relate their disgust with Reno at this point in time, but apparently none of them took it upon themselves to organize this out-of-control mob that raced haphazardly for the river.

Military discipline had completely broken down and it was now every man for himself. The cavalrymen were accustomed to receiving distinct orders, not depending on their own devices for survival. Uncertainty of what course of action to undertake on the battlefield was rarely a situation that favored trained soldiers, especially mounted men with terrified horses. They were a unit and had been schooled in tactics executed in coordination with their comrades. Now they were expected to discern for themselves the whims of a commander who could no longer make proper decisions.

The Indians would have been empowered by this unexpected, disorganized retreat from the timber to the open plains and were closing on the hapless soldiers. The Indian horses were fresh from lazily grazing all day, whereas the cavalry horses had been underfed for days and then ridden for miles and were on the verge of exhaustion. These expert Indian horsemen riding on their sturdy ponies tore across the terrain to head off the fleeing cavalrymen.

But not all the troopers were able to escape the warriors from the timber on horseback. Facing an alarming fate were a number of soldiers and scouts who found themselves stranded in the timber during this unruly retreat—First Lieutenant Charles DeRudio, Private Thomas O'Neill, and scouts William "Billy" Jackson, George B. Herendeen, and Fred Girard among them.

The Sioux and Cheyenne war party had now for the most part situated itself between the timber and the river, and there was no possible escape for these men. The soldiers were trapped in that wooded area while the remainder of the command rode for the river. These unfortunates would be compelled to hunker down for now and hope to conceal themselves well enough to survive detection by the gathering swarms of Indians.

The crossing point at the Little Bighorn River was approximately one-half to one mile of open terrain away. No effort had been made to cover the movement of the battalion with a base of fire and the soldiers on horseback could offer little resistance. The result was disastrous for the cavalrymen.

The Sioux and Cheyenne were well educated in warfare—it was a basic component of their culture—and they understood exactly what was happening. These soldiers were not attempting to fight them. They were running away.

The invigorated warriors seized the opportunity and at first rode to within fifty feet on the flanks of the loose formation and opened fire. They easily picked off the exposed troopers one by one and then closed in to kill the wounded and those whose horses had faltered. This wanton slaughter could be likened to a buffalo hunt, with the Sioux and Cheyenne finally riding into the midst of the frantic troopers and shooting them at close range. Other soldiers were knocked from their horses with stone hammers, clubs, and lances or were riddled with arrows.

The soldiers in blue made a feeble attempt to defend themselves by firing their pistols, but the Indians simply slipped behind the necks of their horses for protection. In addition, there was no easy way to reload in the saddle as the wild-eyed horses galloped across the dusty plain. The soldiers' six-shooters were soon empty and useless.

Custer's favorite white scout, Charley Reynolds, who was suffering from an infected hand, had a premonition that he was going to die that day and had given away all of his possessions. He was the last man to leave the timber and now rode for the river—until his horse was shot out from underneath him. Reynolds made a gallant stand either pinned under his mount or using the animal for breastworks before eventually being killed. One report—likely an exaggeration—stated that fifty-eight spent cartridge shells were found near his body.

Interpreter Isaiah Dorman, who was likely a runaway slave, had lived with the Sioux and at that time befriended Sitting Bull. This friendship did not help Dorman today, however, as he dashed for the river. Sioux chief Runs-the-Enemy described the death of Dorman: "We passed a black man in a soldier's uniform and we had him. He turned on his horse and shot an Indian right through the heart. Then the Indians fired at this one man and riddled his horse with bullets. His horse fell over his back and the black man could not get up. I saw him as I rode by. I afterward saw him lying there dead."

Canadian first lieutenant Donald "Tosh" McIntosh, whose father had been an agent with the Hudson's Bay Company and his mother a direct descendent of Red Jacket, a chief of the Six Nations, had made an effort to lead his men out of the timber. McIntosh, however, couldn't find his horse and finally "borrowed" one as the dismayed enlisted owner watched. The lieutenant, who had a reputation for being a slowpoke, was shot off that horse and went down in a mass of twenty to thirty warriors. McIntosh—in addition to numerous other wounds—was struck with a tomahawk, his scalp torn from the forehead to the neck.

The Little Bighorn River at this makeshift ford offered additional obstacles for Reno's panicked command. The swift-flowing water itself was a hindrance, but on the far side awaited a steep and slippery eight- to twelve-foot-high riverbank. Numerous cavalry horses balked and lost their footing, and when the command bunched up the warriors waded into the water and clubbed the soldiers off their mounts.

At this point, Captain Thomas French, to his credit, made a heroic attempt to establish a one-man covering base of fire. He remained at the ford while his men tried to cross, firing his pistol—killing at least eight warriors single-handedly. But it would not be enough to save everyone. Eventually, French would be forced to flee to save his own life.

West Point graduate Second Lieutenant Benjamin H. Hodgson was serving as adjutant to his friend Major Marcus Reno. At the riverbank, Hodgson's horse was killed and he had been shot in both legs while attempting to cross. Private James Darcy (aka James Wilber) stated: "Right at the Little Big Horn a trooper was shot down in front of me and Lieutenant Hodgson got his first wound. . . . Hodgson hung on to the stirrup of Bugler [Frank] Myers and got over the river and part way up the hill, but received another wound and was killed."

Civil War veteran and acting assistant surgeon Dr. James Madison DeWolf and his orderly had chosen the wrong ravine to climb up from the river. They were halfway to the top when DeWolf stopped to assist a wounded soldier. DeWolf and his orderly were cut down by the warriors.

Those troopers who managed to reach the eastern shore and scramble up the bluff provided no assistance to their comrades. They were intent on reaching the top of the hill, as far away from the warriors as possible. Consequently, there was no organized covering fire to assist the vulnerable soldiers, who then became easy prey for Indians firing from both banks. Once again, neither Reno nor his officers had the presence of mind to set up a covering fire to protect the retreat.

Major Marcus Reno was among the first to arrive safely at the top of the bluff across the river. The remnants of his command had by necessity straggled up the cliff behind him, dodging withering fire, and began hastily forming a defensive position.

Reno had lost about forty killed and thirteen wounded in the action thus far. The trail of blood and dead bodies of both man and horse marked the route Reno had taken in his chaotic retreat from the timber to the river.

The Indians set fire to the grass in the valley. Smoke billowed up and combined with bodies floating in the Little Bighorn River and distant voices of wounded soldiers crying out for help to create a macabre hellish effect. The survivors of Reno's battalion watched with horror from their high perch onto the field below to observe warriors, along with women and children, killing the wounded and mutilating the dead in plain sight. One such victim was Dr. James DeWolf, who was scalped within view of the soldiers on the bluffs. The troops were frantically digging into the porous soil and attempting to maintain military discipline once again following the harrowing experience of the disorganized retreat. No doubt they each had one eye trained on their task at hand and the other scanning the surrounding landscape. The hilltop was a precarious position at best, and the Indians were very much in evidence.

It was suggested to Reno by a soldier that they should go back and try to save the wounded—to which Reno reportedly replied that the soldier could rescue the wounded himself if he wanted. In other words, there would be no attempt to save the lives or retrieve the bodies of the fallen on the valley floor—or the men stranded in the timber, where they had taken refuge and remained very much alive and waiting for rescue.

Dr. Henry R. Porter, the acting assistant surgeon, approached Reno and stated that the troops were quite demoralized by the disorganized retreat.

Major Marcus Reno replied with indignation, "That was a cavalry charge, sir!"

Twelve

———◦◉◦———

Battle Ridge

While Reno's command had been running for their lives from the hostiles, the 125-man battalion led by Captain Frederick Benteen had reconnoitered ten grueling miles along ridges and ravines of broken terrain without observing anything of interest. Benteen considered his mission a wild-goose chase and finally decided to return to the main trail and follow the Custer and Reno battalions. He maintained a leisurely pace, watching the dust kicked up by Captain McDougall and the pack train to their right.

Benteen called a halt of perhaps twenty minutes to let the horses drink from a muddy water hole when his command first heard the faint sound of firing—Reno's men engaged in the valley fight. Benteen's officers wanted to move out immediately, especially Captain Tom Weir, Custer's friend, who even started down the trail. But the captain ignored these requests for some time, until the pack train reached them and the thirsty mules dashed for the water. Only then did Benteen mount the battalion and ride away at a slow trot.

Three miles later they encountered Sergeant Daniel Kanipe, who carried orders from Custer to Captain McDougall, which read in part to "bring the pack train straight across to high ground—if packs get loose don't stop to fix them, cut them off. Come quick. Big Indian camp." Kanipe said he had heard Custer order the men to hold their horses, that "there are plenty of them down there for us all."

Kanipe hollered, "We've got them, boys," as he rode past Benteen's command.

Most of the battalion took that to mean that Custer had engaged the hostiles and the fight was on. Still, Benteen refused to hurry. About a mile farther, unwittingly within a mile or so of where Reno's men had taken refuge on the hilltop, Benteen again halted to water the horses.

It was there that Private John Martin, Custer's orderly, who was riding a wounded horse, arrived from the north. Martin presented Benteen a message that had been hastily scribbled by adjutant William W. Cooke. This note would be Custer's last known order.

The message read: "Benteen. Come on. Big village. be Quick. bring packs. W. W. Cooke. P. bring pacs."

Martin told Benteen that Custer had exclaimed: "Hurrah, boys, we've got them!" Martin could have been confused by the unfamiliar English language, or Custer may have believed that victory was at hand. Martin also told Benteen that the village was the largest he had ever seen and that Reno's troops had charged and were killing everybody, which was not true.

Frederick Benteen discussed the message with his subordinate officers, wondering if there was any need to hurry when Martin had indicated that the Indians were probably fleeing. And, Benteen disdained, how did Custer expect him to hurry if he was ordered to bring along the lumbering pack train?

The positive statements by Martin, however, may have contributed to Benteen's subsequent inaction when he dawdled along the trail instead of obeying orders to "be Quick." Incidentally, Benteen later referred to Martin as a "thick-headed, dull-witted Italian, just as much cut out for a cavalryman as he was for a king."

It was not as if a lack of courage on Benteen's part could be blamed for his inaction. He had distinguished himself in fierce combat during the Civil War and bravely fought at Washita against the Cheyenne.

In fact, at Washita Benteen became the subject of a story written by George Armstrong Custer in his book, *My Life on the Plains or, Personal Experiences with Indians*. Custer related the story of an unavoidable duel between Benteen and an Indian boy. The incident cast considerable favor upon the humanitarian aspects of the captain.

Before the Battle of the Washita, Custer had issued orders for his troops to avoid killing anyone but warriors. When the charge had been sounded, Captain Benteen rode with the lead squadron. Upon entering Black Kettle's village, Benteen was boldly confronted by a mounted Indian whom Custer described as "scarcely fourteen years of age." The youngster, armed with a pistol, appeared to invite Benteen to engage in a personal duel. Benteen admirably resisted the boy's entreaties and instead made "peace signs" in an attempt to encourage the boy to surrender.

This youthful warrior, however, refused to obey those gestures and spurred his horse toward Benteen while discharging his revolver. The bullet whistled past the captain's head. The boy closed the distance, again firing with the same result. Benteen maintained his discipline as a third round was fired at him, this one passing through the neck of his horse and dumping Benteen onto the snowy ground.

Still, Benteen made one final appeal for his antagonist to surrender. The determined boy answered by leveling his revolver for another shot. Regretfully, Benteen had no other choice but to shoot and kill this brave young warrior.

Later, a trooper retrieved from the boy's saddle a small pair of moccasins, elaborately ornamented with beads, and presented the trophy to Benteen. Custer wrote: "These (the moccasins) furnished the link of evidence by which we subsequently ascertained who the young chieftain was—a title which was justly his, both by blood and bearing." George Bent, the half-white, half-Indian son of trader William Bent, who had married Black Kettle's niece, identified this young duelist as a twenty-one-year-old named Blue Horse, a nephew of Chief Black Kettle.

Tribute must be paid to the courage and discipline of Captain Benteen, whose restraint could have cost him his life—as well as to his respect for the courage of the warrior who may have looked younger than he actually was when he bravely rode out to defend his village.

But now Frederick Benteen demonstrated too much restraint. He and his men heard firing in the distance and had confirmation from the messengers that Custer and Reno were engaged in battle. Orders had arrived for Benteen to "come on" and to "be Quick." Yet he saw no urgency and continued to lollygag along the trail.

Boston Custer, who had been with the pack train, came riding up, leaving plumes of dust behind him. He waved to the men in Benteen's battalion as he rode past, hurrying to catch up with his brothers at the front. Bos, as he was called, had been hired as a citizen guide at one hundred dollars a month for the Little Bighorn Campaign—regardless of the fact that he could not recognize one trail from another. He was well known to the members of the Seventh Cavalry, having accompanied his brother as a forage master for the Black Hills Expedition of 1874.

Bos had written to his mother on June 21, 1876, from camp at the confluence of the Yellowstone and Rosebud: "My Darling Mother—The mail leaves to-morrow. I have no news to write. I am feeling first-rate. Armstrong takes the whole command, and starts up the Sweet Briar on an Indian trail with the full hope and belief of overhauling them—which I think he will, with a little hard riding. . . . I hope to catch one or two Indian ponies with a buffalo robe for [brother] Nev, but he must not be disappointed if I don't. . . . Now don't give yourself any trouble at all as all will be well. . . . Goodbye my darling Mother."

Bos would try to catch up to not only his two brothers but also his brother-in-law Jimmy Calhoun and his eighteen-year-old nephew, Harry Armstrong "Autie" Reed. Autie, the son of David and Ann Reed—Custer's sister, who was his trusted confidante and surrogate mother—had been named after his famous uncle and had come out west to spend the summer. He had initially been hired as a cattle herder for the campaign but was presently without an assignment and had attached himself to the headquarters group.

It was a little after 4:00 P.M. and remarkably to Reno's men on the hilltop the Indians broke contact with them and could be noticed excitedly whooping and hollering as they rode away toward the north. The troopers miraculously had been afforded an unexpected respite from the constant barrage of bullets and arrows, other than a handful of Indians who had remained to harass them. The soldiers had been under the impression that the Indians would press the issue and attempt to overrun their flimsy position.

The troops were too involved in their own preservation, however, to consider the reason for this sudden departure. They were not aware that another force of Sioux and Cheyenne who had assembled from the village and pony herd had encountered Custer's command at the riverbank some four miles away and that their tormentors were hurrying to join that fray.

Perhaps Custer had noticed only Reno's initial skirmisher line, not the retreat, and believed that Reno would be fighting his way toward the village as ordered. The terrain did not afford a clear view of the entire valley. Regardless, instead of retreating, George Armstrong Custer had chosen to approach the village with his battalion from the east.

Earlier, Custer had moved his command down Cedar Coulee to upper Medicine Tail Coulee, pausing for an undetermined amount of time to adjust equipment as well as to allow Benteen and the pack train additional time to arrive. This coulee sloped from the northern ridge about three hundred yards to the river at the southern end of the Indian village, which was on the opposite bank.

Orderly John Martin, who had looked back as he rode off, claimed that his last sight of Custer's command was Company E, the Gray Horse Troop, named for the color of their mounts, commanded by Lieutenant Algernon E. "Fresh" Smith, galloping down Medicine Tail Coulee, heading toward the center of the village. This detachment was undoubtedly personally led by Custer along with battalion commander Captain George Yates. Custer had a propensity for leading the charge or, possibly in this case, gaining important reconnaissance information by approaching the village to observe with his own eyes the probability of attacking or checking on Reno's progress.

Even if Custer was aware of the fate of Reno's battalion, he may have believed that he could attack the village with only his battalion and prevail. After all, the Sioux and Cheyenne were no more ferocious, skillful, or cunning than the Confederate officers and men with whom he had engaged and more often than not defeated even when greatly outnumbered. He had faced overwhelming numbers of warriors at Washita and had completed his mission and escaped with minimal casualties. His experience against the Plains tribes had given him respect for his adversary, but he was not in the least bit intimidated.

Then again, it could be that Custer understood that Reno's retreat had placed him in a precarious position and instead of charging he should prudently seek a place to fall back and regroup. He had never hesitated to lead his men away from the battlefield to spare them, if necessary. He had broken contact with Jeb Stuart at Gettysburg after driving the Confederates back into their original position—and understood that to press the issue would have been costly in casualties.

Captain Myles Keogh with companies C, I, and L would have by this time ascended the slope to higher ground, with orders to ride toward the northern end of the village and cut off retreat in that direction or attack down convenient coulees at that end. Custer's action of heading down the Medicine Tail Coulee also may have been intended as merely a feint or decoy to distract the attention of the enemy from Keogh's battalion or even to allow Reno's men a better chance to save themselves.

Custer must have been frustrated that he had not received any word from Reno. The major should have reported his progress, position, and intentions by that time. No matter, Custer would have expected Reno's battalion to somehow make it into the village. Orders were orders, and Custer could not imagine that Reno would simply disregard his mission and flee.

The Indians who had routed Major Reno's troops and chased them to the hilltop could now concentrate on this new threat posed by Custer's battalion—joined by their brethren who had been tending the pony herd or been out hunting. The troopers under Custer and Yates were met with fierce resistance from warriors hidden in the bushes along the river as they approached the village, certainly more opposition than they had expected.

It would be possible that small war parties of warriors rode to elevated positions along neighboring ravines, firing their weapons and trying their best to discourage the cavalrymen from entering the village. The women and children were packing up to leave, and their lives and well-being would have been a priority to protect before mounting any full-scale assault.

In a very short time, Custer and the Medicine Tail Coulee detachment were receiving enough fire to force them to initiate a pullback and head for higher ground until reinforcements arrived. Custer would have ordered these troops to cover the movements of each unit with measured rifle fire as they executed a disciplined retreat.

There has been speculation that Custer had been struck down on this assault down Medicine Tail Coulee. Although no definitive evidence exists to prove or disprove this theory, dead or alive Custer would have been transported by his troopers to the high bluffs. Had he been killed, Captain Keogh as senior officer would have assumed command and adjutant Cooke would have moved to Keogh's side. Cooke's body, however, was found with Custer on Custer Hill—the northern edge of the ridge—while Keogh was quite some distance away to the southeast. So there was a good chance that Custer remained alive and in charge throughout this forced withdrawal and subsequent actions.

In spite of such speculation, this was not the way that the battle was supposed to unfold according to Custer's well-designed battle plan. Custer had expected to face little resistance from a village in turmoil as his men approached in a surprise attack down the various convenient ravines.

What had become of Reno? It was now clearly evident to Custer, if it had not been before, that the major and his battalion had not struck the village as ordered.

At this moment, Reno's men should have been causing general mayhem by slicing through the tepees and shooting down fleeing warriors. The unexpected attack from Custer's command from the eastern hills would have added firepower to the heavy assault and finished the task. It would then have been a matter of chasing down the warriors trying to escape to the north and west, rounding up the women and children as prisoners, and beginning the task of burning the village. But Reno was nowhere to be seen. Where was Reno?

Now, with the appearance of such a vast number of warriors, Custer decided that he must postpone his plans to attack, withdraw and re-form his battalion, and wait for Benteen and Reno and the pack train of ammunition to arrive.

And the best tactical position to fight off the enemy in a delaying action, although there were few natural terrain features to use as breastworks, was on the ridge above. Whoever commanded the high ground in a battle usually had the upper hand. His troopers scrambled up the coulees to avoid the withering fire and halted at what would become the last-stand position to form a perimeter. This place would not have been the ideal location chosen by Custer for a defensive position, but by then he had no choice in the matter. The warriors who were gathering in strength all around him were now dictating his actions.

Captain Keogh had either observed Custer's movement or received a message or signal and aborted his own ride to the north to instead rendezvous with his commander. Keogh's battalion was then dispatched to a position on the high ridge south of Custer—known as Battle Ridge—between Medicine Tail and Deep Ravine and formed a skirmisher line. Company L under First Lieutenant Jimmy Calhoun assumed the position farthest south on what would be known as Calhoun Hill—acting as rear guard waiting for the expected arrival of Reno and Benteen.

Custer must have been furious at the failure of Reno to charge the village and the fact that neither of his two other battalions—Reno nor Benteen—could be seen riding to the rescue. He had ordered Benteen to come quickly, yet there was no sight of any soldiers within the craggy ravines and spotted vegetation to the south. Nor had there been any messengers dispatched to inform Custer of the position and disposition of the two missing battalions.

Could they not have heard the firing? This battle was far from lost. Additional firepower from the rifles of the 250-plus men from the other battalions could save the day. The thought that he had been betrayed by his subordinates who had disobeyed orders and abandoned him must have crossed his mind.

Perhaps Custer entertained another more chilling reason for the absence of Reno and Benteen. Had the other two battalions suffered the unthinkable and were at that moment lying slaughtered on the valley floor to the south? Was that the reason they had not ridden to rendezvous with Custer? He could not recognize any blue-clad bodies lying in the vicinity where Reno had executed his charge. So there must have been some other explanation for the mysterious disappearance of more than half of his command.

Army officers and men in the field would never ignore the heavy firing that could be heard from miles away—unless they were dead. They would rush at all costs to reinforce their comrades. It was well known from his Civil War days that Custer agonized over every casualty and took his responsibility as a commander seriously knowing men's lives were in the balance. And he had observed the swarms of warriors approaching from the south, where he assumed was the location of his other battalions. It would not have been out of the question to speculate that Reno's command had been overrun and killed to a man. There were an overwhelming number of Sioux and Cheyenne warriors out there.

Possibly Custer observed smoke from the burning prairie several miles to the south and believed that the other battalions were engaged in battle. But . . . what were they doing several miles to the south? The village, their objective, was right there directly across the river. The officers who had served in Custer's Civil War commands were always eager to sail into the enemy at any cost. Where were Reno and Benteen?

The Custer battlefield was by now the scene of intense fighting, with dust and smoke and fear filling the air. But there was no panic. These men were trained soldiers, and many of them had fought with Custer in the Yellowstone or at Washita and a number were Civil War veterans. Their commander was known for his coolness under fire and his uncanny ability to succeed against any enemy. There was no reason to suspect that this encounter would be any different.

The attitude of these cavalrymen toward their Sioux and Cheyenne counterparts initially had been one of an impersonal, dispassionate hate for a people that their government had chosen to fight. Soldiers were indoctrinated in that manner and expected to hate someone they may have to kill, which was supposed to make killing easier. They had been informally conditioned to dismiss any respect they might have had for their enemy as human beings and consider them simply savages who deserved to die. That was and will be the mind-set of American soldiers toward their enemy in every war, past and future.

In this case, the powers that be did not have to work too hard to demonize the Sioux and Cheyenne in the eyes of the average cavalryman. Stories of atrocities by these tribes toward innocent whites—killing, raping, kidnapping, stealing livestock, and burning homes—were well documented. It was not difficult—perhaps it was human nature—for a soldier to hate a group of nameless, faceless people of an alien race who had terrorized and killed their fellow countrymen. As far as they were concerned, these Indians had been given their chance to live in peace as civilized human beings and had answered that entreaty with violence.

All things considered, it was the soldiers' job to protect the interests of America, which was why they wore the uniform. They were paid to kill, if necessary. But now, as bullets and arrows filled the air, they were not fighting out of a hate for their enemy.

The soldiers of the Seventh Cavalry were fighting to preserve and protect the lives of their comrades as much as their own lives. It became a quest for group survival. Triumph over the enemy became secondary—only as a means to end the battle. The men on each side had shared one another's intimate joys and sorrows and knew everyone's life story almost as well as they knew their own. There had been an unspoken bonding as they had trained and played together in a unique atmosphere that only the military provides. They expected to be able to depend on their comrades, and that engendered a sense of security.

Each one of them would do whatever was called for to protect his fellow cavalryman with his own life, if necessary. Nothing brought out a comradeship—even a kinship—in men like experiencing combat. In addition, they were fighting to return to see once more their mothers and fathers, or wives and girlfriends, or simply to experience that familiar, peaceful routine in their lives that they had foolishly called boredom and monotony. The thought of the broken hearts at home should they fail to return was too sad to even consider.

This brotherhood under fire explains why men throughout history have performed uncommon individual acts of heroism on the battlefield worthy of high commendation. A man would impulsively smother a live grenade with his own body to save the lives of comrades while losing his own, or brazenly rush into an expanse of intense enemy fire to carry the wounded back to safety, or execute a suicidal charge into a gun emplacement to relieve the rate of fire that was devastating his company's position. No one ever ordered these acts of valor and they were not planned—they came naturally in combat. A soldier does not consciously think about becoming a hero—he simply reacts to the situation.

Anxiety increased as casualties mounted around the cavalrymen. This engagement above the Little Bighorn River had now become a life-or-death struggle, and the outcome was in question. Seeing close companions beside them die and the thought of themselves dying was a powerful motivator to make a man fight with a will and determination he never knew he had within him. The unnaturalness of looking death in the eye was a time of indescribable controlled terror, when a man depended on his instincts and military training. With ammunition running low and more and more Indians appearing around them, the peril of their predicament quickly became evident. They would be firing and reloading their rifles and pistols at will, praying that the seemingly endless stream of warriors who confronted them would end before their ammunition ran out.

It was not only the stress of combat that plagued the cavalrymen but natural and man-made elements as well. The fiery sun had transformed the barren prairie into a sweltering wasteland of heat that dried mouths, cooked heads to the point of dizziness, and even in the dry air produced a drenching sweat that caused them to itch with the bites of a million insects. The acrid odor from plumes of gunpowder mixed with swirling dust to torture the nostrils and stab the eyes to blur vision, not to mention the constant firing of weapons around them that caused temporary deafness.

The Little Bighorn River below with its tree-lined shady banks must have looked like paradise from up on that hillside. But the pathway to the river was blocked by hundreds, if not thousands, of well-armed enemy warriors intent on killing. It was entirely possible, however, that a few soldiers were tempted to break ranks and make a dash for that narrow ribbon of a waterway. They would have been quickly cut down.

By now, word had spread through the ranks that ammunition and reinforcements had been summoned. Help was surely on the way. No doubt these brave men fighting for their lives along Battle Ridge would often glance with anticipation toward the south for any sign of cavalrymen and a pack train approaching at double time.

Just as Custer wondered about the disposition of Reno and Benteen, the common trooper along Battle Ridge understood that his fate was now in the hands of his missing brothers in blue. It was evident the troopers could not prevail alone, but they had a chance to survive if more men would arrive with the firepower and ammunition to relieve the pressure of the mounting number of warriors.

The Indians had effectively surrounded Custer's beleaguered battalion that had hastily formed along Battle Ridge and on Custer Hill, but even with a huge advantage in numbers they did not immediately charge the soldiers. Most warriors remained at a safe distance—hidden in the tall buffalo grass, sagebrush, or bushes, using the rugged terrain for cover—and fired an endless stream of arcing arrows and rifle fire at their pinned-down adversaries. Some warriors would sneak up close to wave blankets and pick off horse holders in an attempt to run off the cavalry mounts that carried precious ammunition in their saddlebags. Small herds of captured horses would then be stampeded through the various positions in an attempt to roust the men from their cover.

The frantic, outnumbered cavalrymen shot their few remaining horses for breastworks, trying to conceal themselves while returning fire—like little dogs barking as loud as possible to keep the big dogs away—until ammunition ran out.

Eventually, as the defenses along Battle Ridge became more vulnerable and no more bullets remained, incidences of hand-to-hand combat became commonplace. The Sioux and Cheyenne came forward in overwhelming numbers with hatchets, clubs, and coup sticks—with others shooting their rifles and firing arrows point-blank at the unarmed and exposed soldiers.

By then, the cavalrymen were reduced to fighting by swinging their empty rifles and slashing with their knives and whatever else they could use as a weapon. One by one, agonizing cries of pain and horror filled the air and soldiers fell dead and severely wounded as each pocket of resistance became weakened by the loss of manpower and the overpowering number of enemy rushed in for the kill. The ground became littered with bloody bodies of soldiers who would never fight again.

The ammunition and reinforcements that could have saved them never arrived. And there were too many attackers to fend off. According to testimony by various warriors, the bravery of the troopers was admirable as they fought for their lives—a trait earning them great respect in the eyes of the Sioux and Cheyenne.

The timetable of events during this battle is difficult to piece together accurately due to the tactics employed by the warriors on the battlefield. The Indians, unlike the United States Army, did not fight as a unit under specific orders.

Certain respected warriors, such as Crazy Horse and Gall, may rally a group of men to follow them, but when the battle was under way each individual warrior was free to do whatever he pleased. He could close with the enemy or hide behind a shrub and launch arrows or fire bullets. No chief would think of tell-

ing any warrior specifically how to fight. Therefore, individuals generally had
no idea about time frames or an overall perspective of a battle. Occasionally
testimony may appear contradictory when in truth it was merely a view of one
particular warrior who had no knowledge of the movements of his brethren
on the field.

George Armstrong Custer was no stranger to being surrounded by his enemy. He had punched his way through the Confederate ring of fire more than
once during the Civil War when surrounded. At some point, however, Custer,
who had fought and survived so many murderous battles throughout his young
adult life, must have become aware that the end was near for himself and all
of the men around him.

There would be no last-minute bugle calls signaling the distant sound of
thundering cavalry horses approaching. It was too late for that anyway—the
enemy was closing in too quickly. Instead, the sounds in his ears were of a
growing number of war whoops that ventured closer and closer combined with
cries of the wounded and dying and the whinnies of terrified horses.

For unknown reasons, Reno and Benteen would not be coming to save them.
And where was "Custer's Luck" to save him? Apparently he had used up his
nine lives.

The picture that could be painted of Custer in those final moments was
one of a soldier who would fight until the last drop of his blood was spilled.
There was a likelihood that he had watched his two brothers fall, and his
nephew, and others who were dear to him—and he himself was on the thresh-
old of the worst that could happen in battle.

In his career, he had witnessed countless men die and he had sent countless men to their graves. It was perhaps only fitting that he would fall under
such circumstances—as a warrior fighting against other worthy warriors. He
had chosen the course of his life and had been the embodiment of a soldier—
and he was prepared to die like a soldier.

In May 1864, while on the trail of Confederate general Jeb Stuart, Custer
had written to Libbie from Virginia:

On the eve of every battle in which I have been engaged I have never omitted to pray inwardly, devoutly. Never have I failed to commend myself to

God's keeping, asking Him to forgive my past sins, and to watch over me while in danger . . . and to receive me if I fell, while caring for those near and dear to me. After having done so all anxiety for myself, here or hereafter, is dispelled. I feel that my destiny is in the hands of the Almighty. This belief, more than any other fact or reason, makes me brave and fearless as I am.

Today, June 25, 1876, thirty-six-year-old George Armstrong Custer would embark on that most mysterious journey of all to the hereafter and into the hands of the Almighty. Custer's name would be added to that elite list of soldiers who had courageously made the ultimate sacrifice for their country.

The romantic view would be that Custer's last thoughts as he surveyed the tumultuous landscape from that smoke-filled grassy slope would have been of Libbie. He would have been nagged by shame and despair for his inability to prevail in this fight and return to her. His greatest regret would be that he would be leaving behind his beloved wife, his soul mate, to face the future alone so early in her life. What would become of her without him? The guilt he would have experienced in those final moments must have been unbearable.

Perhaps in his mind he saw her lovely face, gazed one final time into her luminous blue-gray eyes, and heard the words that she had written to him during the Civil War: "Don't expose yourself so much in battle. Just do your duty, and don't rush out so daringly. Oh, Autie, we must die together." It was not to be.

The end of Lieutenant Colonel George Armstrong Custer and his battalion on the ridge came within an hour's time of their retreat up the hillside or according to Gall, "about as long as it takes a hungry man to eat dinner." The troopers had run out of ammunition and additional warriors had entered the field—too many of them to count. And there was still no sign of Reno and Benteen riding to the rescue.

According to Gall, the fatal blow was administered by Crazy Horse and Two Moon, who led a large force of warriors down the valley above the village, crossed the river, and attacked those few left alive on Custer Hill. One can only imagine the fearsome sight of Crazy Horse as he waded through the small group of soldiers, his body painted with white hail spots and a streak of lightning adorning one cheek, swinging his club or coup stick to gain even more respect from his fellow warriors for his bravery.

After dispatching Custer's command post, Crazy Horse and his war party continued south. These warriors swept down the eastern slope, crushing the remnants of Keogh and Calhoun's troops against Gall's warriors who were attacking from the direction of the village. Before long, there were no more cavalrymen left to kill. Bodies in blue uniforms that were drenched in crimson dotted the hillsides and the ridge.

It should be mentioned that there have been theories based on random Indian testimony that Crazy Horse actually attacked from the south, starting at Calhoun Hill and working his way north along Battle Ridge. If this was true there would indeed have been a traditional "Custer's Last Stand," as that position would have been the final spot of resistance to meet the enemy and fall.

Immediately following the battle, the warriors left the field to the women, old men, and children. These noncombatants waded into the gore to loot and mutilate the bodies.

Sitting Bull did not actively participate in this battle against the cavalry; that was the responsibility of the young warriors. His place as an older medicine man and counselor was to remain in the village to protect the women and children from harm. He did at one point ride onto the field to encourage his braves for a short time before returning to his duties across the river.

By late afternoon, however, Sitting Bull could take satisfaction in the fact that his vision of soldiers falling into camp had come true. His medicine was indeed powerful.

The Battle of the Greasy Grass, as the Sioux called the nearby river, had been a victory of unforeseen proportion. Still, their battle wasn't entirely complete. The warriors now rode four miles to the north where the remnants of Major Marcus Reno's command had taken refuge on that high bluff above the river.

For the Indians, this was a good day to kill every soldier who had ridden earlier into the Valley of the Little Bighorn.

Thirteen

━━◉━━

The Siege of the Hilltop

Captain Frederick Benteen eventually could no longer ignore the unmistakable sound of firing. The battalion moved out at a gallop and topped a ridge to view the valley below where Reno's men were in the process of crossing the river and scrambling up the bluffs on the other side. Benteen estimated that at least fifteen hundred warriors were in the river bottom and farther upstream. He turned his troops and rode for the bluffs on the eastern side of the Little Bighorn River to rendezvous with Reno.

The Benteen battalion was within two hundred yards of Reno's position when the major galloped out to meet them. "For God's sake, Benteen," Reno implored, "halt your command and help me! I've lost half my men!"

Benteen produced Custer's order to "Come on," which according to the military chain of command and protocol was now Reno's to obey. Reno, however, ignored that order and requested that Benteen join his command on the hilltop. When Benteen asked about Custer's whereabouts, he was informed that Custer had started downstream with five companies and had not been heard from since earlier in the day.

The distinct clamor of a battle in progress could be heard from that direction. Several officers suggested to Reno that they should ride to Custer's support—that in the absence of direct orders they should march to the sound of firing. Although there had been direct orders, those delivered to Benteen,

Reno replied that they could not leave due to the low supply of ammunition, which was not true—plenty of ammo was available on the pack train.

Captain Thomas Weir, commander of Company D, lost patience with Reno's timidity and requested that Reno at least permit a detail to scout downstream. Permission was denied, and a heated exchange ensued.

Weir then blatantly disobeyed orders and rode off to the north on his own initiative. Weir's second-in-command, Second Lieutenant Winfield S. Edgerly, was under the impression that Weir had obtained permission to move and began following him with Company D. Weir rode forward about a mile or so to a promontory now known as Weir Point. His vision was obscured by dust and smoke, but he nonetheless could recognize what he believed to be Indians riding around in the distance shooting at objects in an area that later would become known as Custer Hill. Weir then observed another group of warriors advancing toward Edgerly and his company, who were moving along a ravine, and ordered them back to high ground.

By then, Major Reno apparently had a change of heart and dispatched a courier to inform Weir that the rest of the command would soon follow. He directed the captain to attempt to open communications with Custer.

It was too late. The firing downstream had for the most part ceased, and a huge force of Indians was presently riding rapidly toward Weir Point.

Weir's company had been followed by most of the remainder of Reno's disorganized command. Those troops had halted at Weir Point when they became aware of the large force of onrushing hostiles. An impromptu retreat ensued as the troops hastened back to the more defensible position where they had first arrived on the bluffs and began to dig in for cover.

It was nearing 7:00 P.M. on that hot summer day when the defensive perimeter consisting of seven companies, including Captain McDougall's pack train, had firmly established itself on the hilltop. This defensive position above the Little Bighorn River was formed by two parallel ridges running east and west with a depression between that resembled a horseshoe. The troops ringed the crests of the ridges, and the horses, mules, and a field hospital for the wounded were placed in the low-lying portion.

The Sioux and Cheyenne, fresh from the severe beating of Reno and the annihilation of Custer, unleashed a furious barrage of arrows and rifle fire from the surrounding bluffs and ravines. The cavalrymen were pinned down in their vulnerable makeshift rifle pits.

George B. Herendeen, the Civil War veteran who had worked as a cowboy and prospector before becoming a scout, had earlier been stranded in the timber during Reno's mad dash for the river. Herendeen had hidden in a willow thicket until before dark and now found his way back to the command—with tales to tell about his harrowing experience.

The Indians broke contact with the advent of darkness and returned to their village to prepare for a night of feasting, dancing, and recounting their individual exploits of killing and counting coup from the day's victory. They would leave behind a sufficient number of snipers placed in strategic positions to keep the soldiers pinned down.

Meanwhile, the exhausted and desperate cavalrymen took this opportunity to attempt to fortify their positions. The soil was maddeningly porous and there were few shovels with which to dig, so they resorted to fashioning breastworks with packs, saddles, hardtack boxes, and a picket line of dead horses and mules. The stench of the decaying animal carcasses was overpowering but could be endured when considering that they were vital protection between the cavalrymen and about two thousand warriors.

Before long, the night became a nightmare for the troopers. Sitting Bull's village erupted in clamorous celebration. The darkness reverberated with pounding war drums, the exultant war cries by dancing warriors, and the terrifying wails of the women who mourned their dead—all illuminated by the flames of a huge bonfire that could be observed for miles.

The dancing began with a line of a dozen or so seated men serving as drummers who pounded out in unison a monotonous beat on primitive stretched-skin drums. Around these drummers stood a circle of Sioux warriors who had painted their faces and bodies with colorful streaks and symbols and had adorned themselves in their finest costumes and ornaments. Each warrior would step forward in turn and in a loud voice recount his bravery from earlier that day on the battlefield. While speaking, he would whirl and dance to the rhythm of the musicians' drumming. These bodies cast intimidating shadows across the circle of spectators and beyond as more fuel was added and the bonfire leaped to send sparks and cinders rocketing high into the darkness above.

At the conclusion of each recitation the women of the tribe would signify their approval by uttering shrill, earsplitting cries. When a warrior had completed his own bragfest he would remain inside the circle, stomping his feet and waving his arms in dance, occasionally releasing a bloodcurdling whoop or war cry while listening to his brethren relate their own triumphs.

The chiefs and many of the war leaders, such as Sitting Bull, Crazy Horse, and Gall, would not have participated in this ceremony—the bravery and accomplishments of these great warriors against their enemies was well known. The self-glorification was reserved for the less celebrated men who one day would rise to leadership roles based on their personal exploits.

In the civilized world it would have been quite bizarre to hear people taking turns boasting about brazen deeds of violence—killing, taking scalps, mutilating bodies, and counting coups on other human beings. Onlookers would regard these treacherous crimes as worthy of a prison sentence or execution. In this native society, however, the confessors were revered rather than condemned for their actions. The tribe had not ruled the Plains by compromise or peaceful means—they had controlled their domain by dealing ruthlessly with any intruders.

It can only be imagined the effect this morbidly spectacular war dance performed around an immense fire in the middle of the wilderness had in chilling the blood of even the bravest cavalryman. The terrain surrounding the hilltop defense site had been transformed into a flaming, smoking, boisterous hell on earth for them as they listened to the warriors and women screaming in a foreign tongue and as they caught glimpses of misshapen bouncing, reaching shadows of warriors gyrating around the fire. None of the troopers had ever experienced such a display of mixing raw malevolence with rejoicing, which was happening within sight of the dead bodies of their fellow soldiers lying on the valley floor and, unknown to the hilltop, those bodies lying along Battle Ridge.

The exhibition would have certainly conjured up in the soldiers' minds those stories they had heard about the various tortures the Indians would perform on captive white men, especially soldiers. Their greatest fear was that the purpose of this Sioux ritual was a call to arms and rally to reenergize spirits. When it was over, an endless stream of warriors would come rushing up the hilltop en masse and ride over to the other side, leaving not even a blade of grass alive in their wake—and God help those who might be captured alive.

It was thought at one point that columns of cavalry could be recognized in the distance, which caused the trumpeters to alert those soldiers to the presence of Reno's hilltop position. It was soon determined, however, that this "cavalry" was likely Indians wearing army uniforms and riding cavalry mounts.

There was one effort during the night to make contact with Custer or General Alfred H. Terry, who was accompanying Colonel John Gibbon's Montana Column, by sending several Indian scouts outside the lines. These men were fired upon and hurried back to safety.

Much speculation ensued that night regarding the whereabouts of Custer's command. One faction, led by Captain Frederick Benteen, was of the opinion that Custer had abandoned them. Another group objected to that notion and stated that Custer would be there if it were humanly possible. That same division within the regiment that had pervaded from years earlier at Washita was once again played out. Apparently no one seriously considered that Custer and his command had been wiped out by the Indians.

At the same time, back in the timber on the valley floor, First Lieutenant Charles DeRudio, scouts Fred Girard and Billy Jackson, and Private Thomas O'Neil had been trapped while the remainder of the command had scrambled for safety. After dark, the four men caught two stray horses and were riding cautiously upstream when they were challenged by an Indian. The two scouts galloped away while DeRudio and O'Neil dropped to the ground and concealed themselves on a small island. Apparently the Indian lost interest in them and wandered off.

The forty-three-year-old Lieutenant DeRudio already had a colorful résumé and this escapade would only add to his legend as a swashbuckler—if he survived it.

He had been born Carlo Camillo di Rudio on August 26, 1832, in Belluno, Venetia Province, Austria, into a family with royal roots, making him a minor nobleman. He graduated from the Royal Austrian Military Academy and subsequently held a commission in Emperor Franz Josef's army. On December 9, 1855, DeRudio married Eliza Booth, reportedly an illiterate eighteen-year-old confectioner's assistant, at Parish Church, Godalming, Surrey, England. At some point, DeRudio decided to become a revolutionary activist. He was involved in a January 14, 1858, plot planned by Felice Orsini to assassinate Napoléon III and Empress Eugénie at the Paris Opera. Orsini held Napoléon responsible for the failure of the Italian revolutions of 1848–49. Napoléon and the empress arrived outside the opera house that evening as the orchestra inside struck up the William Tell Overture. Three bombs exploded nearby, killing several guards and a horse. Napoléon narrowly escaped injury when a piece of metal struck his hat, and Eugénie suffered a cut eyelid.

Orsini and his three accomplices were captured and convicted. One man received life imprisonment, and the others, including DeRudio, were sentenced to execution by guillotine. Orsini and another man met that fate. DeRudio received a last-minute reprieve when his wife appealed to Empress Eugénie. His sentence was commuted to life on the Devil's Island penal colony in French Guiana. In the fall of 1858, however, DeRudio and about a dozen other men hollowed out a log to fashion a canoe and sailed to freedom in British Guiana and then traveled by more conventional means to England.

In February 1864, DeRudio and his wife immigrated to the United States, where they had four children. He served in the Civil War from August 1864 and was mustered out at Key West, Florida, in January 1866.

On August 31, 1867, DeRudio received an appointment as second lieutenant, Second Infantry, but it was held up while the government investigated his European criminal background. The appointment was restored on October 25, 1867, and he had been unassigned until joining the Seventh Cavalry in July 1869. He remained with the unit from that day forth.

Ironically, the night before the battle Charles DeRudio and several other officers—Benteen, Keogh, and Porter—were swapping stories of thrilling escapades and escapes, and DeRudio's tale of his escape from Devil's Island certainly topped the list. Little did he know at that time that he would experience another impossible situation the following day.

The two others who had been stranded, scout William "Billy" Jackson, who was half-Blackfoot, and interpreter Fred Girard, found a convenient hiding place in a willow thicket and dug in to await rescue.

Incidentally, even though the battle was just hours old, word of Custer's defeat had already spread across Indian Country, but the only whites to hear about the disaster would not believe it. The reason for their skepticism could be attributed to the source of the information, a controversial frontier character named Frank Grouard, who happened to be an army scout.

Grouard had been born on the Polynesian island of Tubuai to a Mormon missionary and a native girl and soon moved to Utah Territory and later to California. At age fifteen Grouard was said to have killed a classmate and ran away to Montana Territory. He worked as a teamster and later a mail carrier before either stealing some mail horses and fleeing or being captured by Sioux Indians in 1869 or 1870.

Around 1870, Grouard was captured by the Sioux and adopted into the family of Hunkpapa medicine man Sitting Bull. Grouard at that time was given the name Standing Bear and became a trusted counselor to Sitting Bull. In 1873, Grouard participated in the Sioux attacks against George Armstrong Custer's Seventh Cavalry during the Yellowstone Expedition. Shortly afterward, he had a falling-out with Sitting Bull and joined Crazy Horse's band. Grouard became known as the Grabber and continued to fight against whites.

Perhaps due to in-law problems, he defected from the Sioux in 1875 and appeared at Camp Robinson. Grouard was known as a crack shot and skilled plainsman. General George Crook was impressed with Grouard's credentials and hired him as an army scout.

In March 1876, Grouard had led the advance party to the Sioux camp on the Powder River, which was attacked by Colonel Joseph Reynolds with disappointing results. Grouard then located Crazy Horse's village on Rosebud Creek, which led to the June 17 battle in which Crook claimed victory but had actually fought to a stalemate.

At the time of the Little Bighorn battle, Grouard was said to have read smoke signals and informed some officers about Custer's defeat, but he was not believed. He dressed like an Indian and rode off to investigate—likely passing near Reno's beleaguered troops on the hilltop without noticing them—and confirmed the story. Consequently, Crook's scouts were aware of Custer's fate before the general had been officially informed. He had likely heard rumors but dismissed them due to the source.

One fact remained—the remnants of the Seventh Cavalry remained pinned down on that hilltop. The conduct of Major Marcus Reno at this defensive position during that night has been the subject of controversy. A number of officers later recalled that Reno had hidden himself in a protected position and issued no orders from darkness until dawn. Other witnesses claimed that Reno gave the appearance of being under the influence of alcohol. The major later admitted that he had brought along a flask filled with whisky, but he was in no way inebriated or incapacitated that night.

Another matter of contention arose when Reno suggested to Benteen that they mount the command and make a forced march back to the base camp on the Powder River. The wounded who could travel would accompany them; the wounded who could not would be left behind. Benteen, to his credit, rejected the idea. Rumors of this insidious plan, however, spread to the wounded and caused predictable anxiety among them. One can only imagine the horror of men lying wounded and helpless with the war cries of a vicious enemy nearby and then being confronted with the thought that abandonment was being contemplated at the highest level. Tradition and common decency dictated that soldiers did not leave behind their wounded if it was humanly possible to save them.

It should be noted that Captain Benteen displayed great courage throughout the ordeal as he constantly exposed himself to enemy fire. Evidently, Reno was willing to relinquish de facto command of the unit to Benteen while the major made himself scarce.

The agonizingly long night finally melted into a predawn haze. The light revealed that thongs of warriors had crept alarmingly close to the lines during the night. This situation would require immediate action to prevent the position from being overrun. Benteen led a detail of troopers who leaped from behind their barricades to impudently counterattack and successfully pushed back the surprised hostiles.

After that bold act, lone warriors or a small group of warriors would from time to time charge on foot or horseback, only to be repulsed by volleys of rifle fire from the perimeter. It became clear to the men on the hilltop that it would have been possible for the Indians to mount one concerted attack and overwhelm the blue-clad defenders. Chief Gall later explained that the medicine men did not consider the medicine right for such an attack or they would have done so.

In any event, the troopers remained surrounded by as many as two thousand warriors who sustained a withering fire from nearby ridges, some of which were of a higher elevation than the defensive position. One particular Indian sharpshooter on a hilltop about five hundred yards to the north picked off a number of troopers with his accurate fire until either losing interest or being silenced by a bullet.

Also at daybreak, First Lieutenant Charles DeRudio, secreted with Private Thomas O'Neil on that small island, thought he observed soldiers approaching. DeRudio called out to one, thinking it was Tom Custer. But it was apparently an Indian riding Tom's horse, and the warriors fired at the two cavalrymen. DeRudio and O'Neil fired back and then scampered away into the brush, breathing a sigh of relief when the Indians broke contact. DeRudio and O'Neil would remain hidden, hoping for a rescue that would not come.

By that morning of June 26, the cavalrymen on the bluff had been without water for quite some time and were in desperate need—especially the wounded. The men had carried full canteens when the siege had begun, but much of that water had been depleted and most of them were now severely suffering under the hot sun on the barren hill. "Our throats were parched," wrote Private Edward H. Pickard of Company F, "the smoke stung our nostrils, it seemed as if our tongues had swollen so we couldn't close our mouths, and the heat of the sun seemed fairly to cook the blood in our veins."

Perhaps this condition was one reason that the Indians chose not to mount an attack on the hilltop. Not only would a frontal assault cost many Indian lives, but it also was apparent that sooner or later the troops would need water to survive. And in order to procure any water the cavalrymen would have to traverse a six-hundred-yard ravine that led to the river from the hilltop—and that ravine was presently occupied by armed warriors.

Captain Benteen realized that they could not remain in their defensive position much longer without water—and riding off into the mass of hostiles in an escape attempt was not an option. The cavalrymen must have water right now to survive.

Acting on his own without consulting Major Marcus Reno, Benteen decided that they must first try to drive the Indians from their positions in the ravine. He led a charge of troops toward the astonished Indians, killing several of them and chasing away the others. He had not lost a man until returning to the line, where one cavalryman was shot and killed.

This action, however, may have cleared the ravine itself, but anyone attempting to reach the river at the bottom would be required to cross areas of open space, with Indian sharpshooters firing point-blank from the opposite bank.

Benteen declined to order any of the troops to make the perilous journey down the steep ravine and, rather, asked for volunteers—and there were plenty of them. These brave volunteers collected every possible container that could hold water and were ready to depart on what could be called a suicide mission. Benteen deployed four of the best shots available—George H. Geiger, Henry Meckling, Otto Voit, and Charles Windolph—in a skirmisher line and ordered them to lay down a serious base of fire into the bushes across the river.

With fear and trepidation, the volunteers cautiously descended the treacherous ravine, stumbling on loose dirt and struggling to maintain their balance by grabbing bushes, all the while trying to keep a low profile to avoid the bullets and arrows directed at them. Each man was aware as he slid down that hillside what would happen if he would be wounded and fell into the hands of the hostiles. The sharpshooters furiously fired their Springfield carbines, shooting and reloading as quickly as possible, mindful that their sustained fusillade was the only chance their fellow soldiers had of staying alive.

This initial attempt at gathering water could be called successful—although one man was killed and six or seven wounded. Enough water was hauled back to the hilltop to temporarily quench the thirst of wounded and alive alike.

The intense fire from the Indians had decreased by about noon. Some soldiers thought it was a trick to lure them out of their positions to where they could be more easily picked off. Regardless, troops were dispatched to fill canteens and other receptacles with river water and made the trip without incident.

It has been theorized that it was at this point that the Terry-Gibbon Column had entered the valley and was noticed by the Indians, who commenced packing up their village. One pocket of Indian snipers, however, remained to devastate the position of Captain McDougall's Company B. Another detail was formed and executed a charge on foot to rout those hostiles.

In late afternoon, a column of Sioux and Cheyenne men, women, and children with all their possessions and horse herd could be viewed marching southwesterly toward the Bighorn Mountains. Benteen observed: "It started about sunset and was in sight till darkness came. It was in a straight line about three miles long, and I think a half mile wide, as densely packed as animals could be. They had an advance guard and platoons formed, and were in as regular order as a corps or division."

Major Marcus Reno was suspicious—a few snipers had remained behind to nag them—and, in keeping with his habitual timidity, decided to remain in position for the time being. Nevertheless, the men on the line relaxed and prepared meals, and details escorted the horses and mules to the river to drink and then put them out to graze.

DeRudio and O'Neil had remained hidden down below in the valley, watching as a long procession of Indians, mostly women and children, passed within fifty yards of their position on their way toward the Bighorn Mountains. That night, DeRudio contemplated walking to the Rosebud until he heard the braying of a mule and realized that soldiers must be nearby. He and O'Neil took the initiative to investigate and soon approached Reno's perimeter on the bluffs. They identified themselves and were saved. Scouts Jackson and Girard had presented themselves sometime earlier.

The night passed without incident, other than one act of bravery. Captain Thomas McDougall, who had been slightly wounded in the fighting, snuck away from the perimeter and retrieved the body of Second Lieutenant Benjamin H. Hodgson, which he buried on Reno Hill.

On the morning of June 27, a long, winding column of blue could be observed approaching from the south. The Terry-Gibbon Column, following rumors that Custer had engaged the Indians, was about to make contact with the survivors of Reno's beleaguered command.

The Battle of the Little Bighorn had come to an inglorious end—but was far from concluded in the minds of the public or future historians.

Fourteen

———◆◆◆———

Bodies on the Field

It had been at about 9:00 on the morning of June 27 while leading an advance guard of mounted infantry attached to the Montana Column with General Alfred Terry and Colonel John Gibbon that First Lieutenant James H. Bradley came upon a horrible sight. Bradley had the dubious distinction of being the man who discovered the more than two hundred bodies of Custer's command lying where they had fallen on the field. He dispatched a messenger to take word of this tragedy back to the main column.

Bradley then resumed his march looking for additional bodies and happened upon Reno's command on the hilltop. Those troops who had endured two days pinned down by hostile Indians were relieved and elated to be rescued. They also were informed at this time about the fate of Custer's command, a shock that certainly dampened their spirits.

The entire outfit moved from the hilltop four miles north to a more defensible position in the valley not far from the abandoned Indian village. They then visited the scene of Custer's defeat. By that time, the more than two hundred mutilated bodies—along with many horse carcasses—had been decomposing in the summer heat for two days.

First Lieutenant Edward S. Godfrey described the scene as they approached: "We saw a large number of objects that looked like white boulders scattered over the field . . . and it was announced that these objects were the dead bodies." He added that "many faces had a pained, almost terrified expression."

Captain Thomas Weir exclaimed: "Oh, how white they look! How white!"

First Lieutenant Francis M. Gibson sadly said, "It was the most horrible sight my eyes rested on."

Captain Frederick Benteen looked down at the body of George Armstrong Custer—the man he had enjoyed tormenting and slandering for so many years—and said with emotion: "There he is, God damn him; he will never fight anymore."

After all of the cavalrymen had been killed, their bodies had suffered further indignities. The Sioux and Cheyenne women, and perhaps a number of children and older men, had descended on the field to mutilate the bodies, quite a few beyond recognition. The extent of the mutilation has been a subject of debate, with many eyewitnesses claiming that there was very little and an equal number taking the opposite view that it was widespread. This disparity of opinion could be explained by the fact that each troop was assigned a different area of the field to bury the dead and certain portions may have received the brunt of the post-death violence.

The acts of mutilation that have been documented include dismemberment of arms, legs, hands, fingers, and penises; decapitation; scalping, lacerations, and slashes from butcher knives, tomahawks, and axes; crushing skulls with stone mallets; and multiple gunshots and arrows fired from close range. The field was said to have been littered with hands, heads, feet, and legs that had been severed.

Those men lying facedown were likely killed by Cheyenne, a tribe that may have believed that it was bad luck to leave an enemy facing the sky. The ones with a slashed thigh indicated the manner in which the Sioux traditionally marked a dead enemy. The Indians even went as far as to mutilate some of the dead horses. For unknown reasons, the names had been cut out of the few items of clothing, an undershirt or pair of socks, not stripped from the bodies and taken away. Everything of value—money, watches, rings, photographs, et cetera—had been stolen from the dead cavalrymen.

Captain Tom Custer had been singled out for perhaps the worst treatment and was identified only by tattoos on one arm. Godfrey wrote that Tom's body was:

> lying downward, all the scalp was removed, leaving only tufts of his fair hair on the nape of his neck. The skull was smashed in and a number of arrows had been shot into the back of the head and in the body . . . the features where they had touched the ground were pressed out of shape and were somewhat depressed. In turning the body, one arm which had been shot and broken, remained under the body; this was pulled out and on it we saw "T. W. C." and the goddess of liberty and the flag. His belly had been cut open and his entrails protruded.

The extent of Tom Custer's abuse has caused some to believe that Sioux warrior Rain-in-the-Face made good on his threat to cut out Custer's heart and eat it as revenge for the Indian's 1875 arrest.

Libbie Custer, Tom's sister-in-law, believed that the Sioux warrior had indeed made good on his promise. She wrote: "The vengeance of that incarnate fiend was concentrated on the man who had effected his capture. It was found on the battlefield that he had cut out the heart of that gallant, loyal, and lovable man, our brother Tom."

A drunken Rain-in-the-Face at one point admitted to killing and mutilating Tom Custer when he told reporters at Coney Island in 1894: "The long sword's blood and brains splashed in my face. . . . I leaped from my pony and cut out his heart and bit a piece out of it and spit it in his face." Rain-in-the-Face's startling confession was likely nothing more than a flippant response to the badgering of sensationalism-seeking reporters.

Captain Frederick Benteen, who examined Tom Custer's body on the field, swore that the heart had not been removed, and there exists no evidence to suggest that Rain-in-the-Face cut out, ate, or in any other way disturbed the heart or any other body part of Tom Custer. Mutilations were normally reserved for the boys, women, and old men. The warriors would have already left the field to celebrate by the time that took place. And with respect to cannibalism—it was just as repugnant to the Sioux as it was to the white man.

Another myth surrounding the revenge of Rain-in-the-Face has been debated for years—that he killed George Armstrong Custer. In fact, there was a good chance that Rain-in-the-Face had remained with the pony herd that day and did not even set foot on the field of battle. The warrior who killed Custer remains unknown, although many later bragged about being the one.

The naked body of George Armstrong Custer, from all accounts, had not been mutilated or at least not badly cut up. He was found in a seated position leaning against and between two troopers, his face said to be wearing the expression of a man who "had fallen asleep and enjoyed peaceful dreams."

Custer was found with two wounds—a bullet hole in front of the left temple and another in the left breast. Sioux chief Gall said in 1886 that Custer was not scalped "because he was the big chief and we respected him," which seems ludicrous. Gall and the others had no idea until long afterward that they had been fighting Custer, thinking instead that it had been General George Crook, whose troops had attacked a week earlier on the Rosebud.

Cheyenne Kate Bighead also fabricated a popular story. She later stated that Custer had not been mutilated out of respect for their tribal sister Mo-nah-se-tah, who they believed had gained Custer's affection while working as his translator following the 1868 Battle of the Washita. Kate contradicted herself in saying that the women thrust a sewing awl into each of Custer's ears to "improve his hearing," because he had not heard when he had smoked the pipe with them in 1867.

Some scholars have speculated that Custer's body had indeed been mutilated, and the truth was deliberately withheld out of respect for the feelings of Libbie Custer. This certainly could be true, but there can be no doubt that his body was not mutilated beyond recognition. He was easily recognized by a number of the men, as were other bodies. Perhaps the mutilation was a selective process rather than widespread. There were those troopers who swore that some bodies on various parts of the field had barely been touched. In addition, if he had been mutilated, some witness, especially Captain Frederick Benteen, would have considered it his duty to report it later.

There were about forty bodies lying in the grass in the vicinity of their commander. In addition to Tom, family members included nephew Arthur "Autie" Reed and brother Boston. Brother-in-law Jimmy Calhoun was farther south along the ridge at a location that would become known as Calhoun Hill. His body was identified by a distinctive dental filling.

The man who had written Custer's last message and was considered a close family friend, First Lieutenant William W. Cooke, also died alongside Custer. Cheyenne warrior Wooden Leg claimed that he scalped the whiskers from one side of Cooke's face and presented the unusual scalp to his wary grandmother, who discarded it two nights later at a dance. The body of another dear friend of the Custers, George Yates, was found downslope from that of Custer. Twenty-two-year-old Second Lieutenant William Van Wyck Reily, a graduate of the Naval Academy whose father had been lost in the China Sea while Reily was an infant, had been assigned temporary duty from Company E as second-in-command of Captain George Yates' Company F. Reily's body was found near that of Yates on Custer Hill.

First Lieutenant Algernon E. "Fresh" Smith had assumed temporary command of the Gray Horse Troop when the Seventh Cavalry marched out of Fort Lincoln. Smith had been severely wounded in the shoulder during the Civil War while leading a charge in the January 1865 assault on Fort Fisher, North Carolina. He had been hospitalized for two months at that time and had limited use of his arm for the remainder of his life. Smith could not even put on his own coat without assistance.

It has been theorized that during the opening stages of the Little Bighorn battle Smith's troop had been deployed down Medicine Tail Coulee to probe the Indian village. The company was apparently forced to retreat and subsequently annihilated, the bodies later buried in Deep Ravine, where they have thus far eluded detection. Smith's body, however, was the only one of his company found on Custer Hill, which has led to speculation that he, along with several other officers, had been wounded and taken to that location for medical treatment or had been responding to officer's call by whoever was in command at that time.

Also found on Custer Hill were the remains of assistant surgeon Dr. George E. Lord. The doctor had become ill on the march up the Rosebud on the Seventh Cavalry's approach to the Little Bighorn valley and halted some distance behind the column to rest. He straggled to Custer's camp the night of June 24 and was too weary and sick to eat. At that time Custer advised Lord to remain behind with the pack train but the doctor refused. It has been speculated that Lord had been brought to that location on the ridge to tend to the wounded, perhaps even George Armstrong Custer. Dr. Lord's surgical case was discovered in the abandoned Indian village.

Twenty-two-year-old Lieutenant John J. Crittenden came from a well-known family. His namesake grandfather was governor of Kentucky, a three-term United States senator, and United States attorney general. John's father, Thomas, was a lawyer who served as an aide to General Zachary Taylor at the Mexican War battle of Buena Vista and rose to the rank of Union major general in the Civil War. An uncle, George B., became a major general in the Confederate army.

With his father's influence, John Crittenden was assigned service with the Seventh Cavalry in May 1876. He was second-in-command of Calhoun's Company L and his mutilated body was found at the southern end of Battle Ridge. His father requested that his son be interred where he fell, which made him the only officer buried in a marked grave on the field. On September 11, 1931, however, his remains were exhumed and reinterred with full military honors in the nearby Custer Battlefield National Cemetery.

Most estimates of Indian losses that day make the case that only thirty or forty were killed. As Custer once pointed out, the Indians invariably endeavored to conceal their exact losses. The only Indian casualties that were found after the battle consisted of eight bodies located in two lodges—five in one, three in the other—within the abandoned village. These dead warriors were dressed in their finest clothing and were lying on scaffolds.

Few Indian participants offered an opinion with respect to casualties. Red Horse did later say that "the soldiers killed 136 and wounded 160 Sioux." It would stand to reason that the allied Indians likely lost that many and perhaps more.

On June 28, 1876, while the remnants of Major Marcus Reno's command were occupied with the unenviable task of burying the dead from Custer's command, Colonel John Gibbon stood on the battlefield and scribbled a message in his notebook. "General Custer's command met with terrible disaster here on the 25th," he wrote. "Custer, with five companies, were so far as we can ascertain, completely annihilated. . . . Roughly stated the loss of Custer's command is about one-half, say 250 men."

The dispatch most likely would have been written above the signature of General Alfred H. Terry, the highest-ranking officer present. Gibbon tore the pages from his notebook and ordered scout H. M. "Muggins" Taylor to carry the message without delay to Captain D. W. Benham at Fort Ellis, near Bozeman, Montana, which was the closest telegraph station.

Taylor, who has been described as a gambler and professional hunter, embarked upon a circuitous route to the fort and on the evening of July 2 arrived in Stillwater, Montana, now present-day Columbus, too exhausted to continue his mission. He presented himself at the general store, owned by William H. Norton and Horace Countryman, and related the news of Custer's fate. Norton, apparently a stringer for the Helena *Herald,* interviewed Taylor and quickly wrote a story that his partner, Horace Countryman, would deliver to Helena.

On the morning of July 3, Taylor and Countryman departed from Stillwater and arrived at Fort Ellis by midafternoon. Taylor delivered Gibbon's dispatch to Captain Benham, who immediately turned it over to the telegraph office for transmission. Inexplicably, the message was set aside and would not be sent out over the wire until after the July 4 celebration.

Horace Countryman resumed his ride toward Helena. Taylor, however, left Fort Ellis and chose as his first stop the offices of the Bozeman *Times.* He told his story to the editor, E. S. Wilkinson, who hurriedly assembled a crew to set type and prepare the presses. By 7:00 that evening Wilkinson had scooped the world by publishing an "extra" that recounted Taylor's slightly embellished tale, which, among a few other altered details, had changed the number of dead to 315. Unfortunately, no copies of this edition are known to presently exist.

On July 4, Horace Countryman delivered a copy of the extra from the *Times* along with Norton's story to coeditor J. A. Fisk at the Helena *Herald.* Fisk immediately published a special edition that made its debut at 6:30 P.M. At that time, Fisk sent the story across the wire to the Associated Press in Salt Lake City. He also informed the governor, who confirmed the news with Captain Benham at Fort Ellis, then telegraphed Commander of the Army General

William T. Sherman. Sherman and others at the War Department were said to have been skeptical about the validity of the tragic news.

Additional Montana newspapers picked up the story from the *Herald* and from independent sources and published their own special editions—the Deer Lodge *New North-West* released an extra on the evening of July 4, with many other newspapers following suit during the next several days.

Several Eastern newspapers received the Associated Press wire story and included the news in their late editions on July 5. The prestigious *New York Herald* ran the story on July 6—eleven days after Custer's defeat. This story, which was also published in the *Army and Navy Journal* on July 8, cited sources from Salt Lake City (the Associated Press), Stillwater, Montana (William H. Norton), and a special correspondent from the Helena *Herald*. The *New York Herald* then set up telegraph communications with Bismarck, Dakota Territory, and spent upward of three thousand dollars receiving information that included additional details of the battle and interviews with members of Reno's command.

The gruesome task of burying the dead began soon after the rescue of Reno's command on the hilltop and continued until at least the evening of June 28 when the regiment marched away with the wounded on litters toward the mouth of the Little Bighorn River.

The soldiers on the burial detail—many of whom were quickly overcome with nausea and vomiting—did not possess proper digging implements for the task. Only a dozen or so spades, shovels, and picks were available that had been found in the rubble of the Indian village. Therefore, anything that could scoop away the dirt to hasten the job was utilized. The soil was dry and porous, described as resembling sugar—just like they had encountered on their hilltop defense position—and proper burial was simply a token gesture. The bodies were basically left lying where they fell and covered as best as possible with sagebrush and dirt or rolled into shallow trenches. Officers were identified by their names written on a slip of paper that was stuffed into a cartridge case and then hammered into a crude cedar stake placed near the gravesite.

The bodies at the various locations were counted: 42 on Custer Hill, 208 or 210 on the Custer portion of the field, and a total of 263 when all the officers, enlisted, civilians, and scouts had been tallied. One group of 28 or 29 bodies from Company E was reportedly found in Deep Ravine but have disappeared.

Newspaperman Mark Kellogg's body apparently had been found in the ravine with those of Company E. Colonel John Gibbon stated that he happened upon a body at that location that was missing an ear and had been scalped but was not stripped: "The clothing was not that of a soldier, and, with the idea of identifying the remains, I caused one of the boots to be cut off and the stockings and drawers examined for a name." No name was found, but the boots were later identified as belonging to Kellogg.

Myles Keogh was killed along with his troops on the eastern slope of Battle Ridge within half a mile of Custer Hill, which was where his remains were found. The body of West Pointer First Lieutenant James E. Porter, second-in-command of Keogh's Company I, either was too mutilated to be recognized or was not on the field, for it was never found. His bloody coat, containing two bullet holes, was discovered at the abandoned Indian village site.

Another body that was not found that day was that of guide and interpreter Minton "Mitch" Bouyer. The son of a Frenchman and a full Santee woman, Bouyer had access to both white and Indian cultures and could speak English, Sioux, and Crow. This protégé of Jim Bridger had accompanied Lieutenant Charles Varnum to the observation point known as Crow's Nest on the morning of June 25 and warned George Armstrong Custer that they would find more Indians than they could handle in the distant camp. Custer reputedly told Bouyer that he could stay behind if he was afraid. Bouyer replied that he would go wherever Custer went and thus became the only army scout killed with Custer's detachment.

The steamship *Far West* had been moored about a half mile above the mouth of the Little Bighorn River on June 27 when the first word arrived about the fate of Custer's command. Captain Grant Marsh hurriedly converted the area between the stern and the boilers into a hospital, covering the planks with fresh grass, then spreading tarpaulins on top to create a soft mattress for the wounded.

On June 30, about thirty (or as many as fifty-two, as Terry had stated in a note to Marsh) wounded cavalrymen were transported from the battlefield on crude litters to the *Far West*. Marsh was cleared to leave shortly after 5:00 P.M. on July 3.

The *Far West,* her colors at half-mast and decks draped in black mourning cloth, made the 710-mile trip to Bismarck, with only two brief stops, in a record-setting time of fifty-four hours, arriving at 11:00 P.M. on July 5. This heroic feat made Marsh the most hailed and famous steamboat captain in the history of navigation on the Yellowstone.

On Sunday, June 25, 1876, while the Battle of the Little Bighorn raged, thirty-four-year-old Libbie Custer and other wives had gathered as usual at Fort Abraham Lincoln to sing hymns. The women had heard about General Crook engaging in the earlier unsuccessful fight on the Rosebud and naturally were worried about the fate of their loved ones. They had heard unconfirmed reports of an Indian battle affecting their husbands and had been offering daily moral support and companionship to one another as they waited for these rumors to be confirmed. No doubt a shroud of dread had descended over Fort Lincoln.

Finally, in the early morning hours of July 6—eleven days after the battle— Libbie was awakened by a knock on the back door. She slipped into her dressing gown, and entered the hallway to be greeted by Maria Adams, whose sister Mary had accompanied the expedition as Custer's personal cook. Libbie opened the door to three men, Captain William S. McCaskey, Lieutenant C. L. Gurley, and Dr. J. V. D. Middleton, the post surgeon.

McCaskey asked that Libbie rouse Margaret "Maggie" Custer Calhoun, the wife of Jimmy, from her bed and the two of them come to the parlor with him. Once there, the captain read a formal message announcing the tragedy at the Little Bighorn. There was no easy way to break the news—George Armstrong Custer, James Calhoun, and scores of other cavalrymen and civilians had died on June 25.

Libbie asked for her shawl and bravely joined the party of men to visit the two dozen or so women at the fort who would be read that same tragic statement that would change their lives forever. Although she was emotionally crushed, Libbie Custer, like her husband always had, would do her duty as the post "first lady" and help comfort the other new widows. Maggie Calhoun gradually digested the words of the statement and chased after Captain McCaskey and the others. She had lost three brothers, a nephew, and her husband. "Is there no message for me?" she cried.

No, there was no message. The five men in her life had all died fighting the Sioux and Cheyenne at the Little Bighorn River.

On June 25, 1877—one year to the day after the battle—Captain Henry J. Nowlan and the newly recruited Company I of the Seventh Cavalry arrived at the battlefield for the purpose of collecting the remains of the officers who had fallen. Nowlan was accompanied by Lieutenant (later major general) Hugh L. Scott, Colonel Michael V. Sheridan, brother of General Phil Sheridan, and all the Crow scouts who had gone with Custer the year before. Fortunately, there would be no need for guesswork to identify the dead. Nowlan had been provided a chart that designated where each officer was buried.

The bodies of the officers from both the Custer and Reno battlefields were gathered up and transferred into pine boxes for transport to cemeteries designated by the next of kin. Apparently at that time many of the enlisted men were reburied either individually where they were found or together in mass graves on the field. One group of the dead—twenty-eight or twenty-nine bodies from Company E—was not located.

George Armstrong Custer had told wife Libbie that when the time came for his passing he wanted to be buried at the U.S. Military Academy at West Point, and she was determined to honor his wishes. Libbie had fretted about the identification of her husband's remains when they were exhumed from the battlefield and shipped to West Point for burial. She was assured, however, by Major Joseph G. Tilford, who had been on a leave of absence during the Little Bighorn Campaign, that the remains being sent east were indeed those of her husband.

Tilford wrote to Libbie on July 28, 1877:

On yesterday I shipped by U.S. Express via Chicago, the remains of your heroic husband Genl. Custer to West Point, N.Y., care of the Commanding Officer at that post. Those were my instructions from Genl. Sheridan. I presume an officer will accompany the remains from Chicago on. It may be some consolation for you to know that I personally superintended the transfer of the remains from the box in which they came from the battlefield to the casket which conveys them to West Point. I enclose you a lock of hair taken from the remains which are so precious to you. I also kept a few hairs for myself as having been worn by a man who was my beau ideal of a soldier and honorable gentleman.

Due to the fact that West Point was relatively vacant during the summer, Libbie was advised to wait until fall to hold the funeral. Custer's remains were stored in a Poughkeepsie, New York, vault owned by Philip Hamilton, whose son Louis had fallen at the 1868 Battle of the Washita.

On October, 10, 1877, crowds lined the Hudson River as the bunting-draped *Mary Powell*, her flags flying at half-mast, brought the remains of George Armstrong Custer to the south dock of the Academy. The casket, which was adorned with an American flag that had belonged to Captain Hamilton, was escorted by a cavalry detachment to the chapel.

Shortly before 2:00 P.M., Major General John M. Schofield, commandant of the military academy, escorted Libbie into the chapel. Other close family members in attendance were Emanuel Custer and Margaret "Maggie" Custer Calhoun. Classes had been suspended, and the cadets crowded into the chapel to witness this event. The West Point chaplain, Dr. John Forsyth, presented an Episcopal service, concluding with the Nineteenth Psalm, a Psalm of David to the chief Musician, which begins: "The heavens declare the glory of God; and the firmament sheweth his handywork."

After the service, the casket was carried to a caisson by cadets and moved toward the cemetery. A lone horse displaying a pair of cavalry boots with spurs in which the toes had been turned to the rear followed the caisson. The procession halted at the cemetery, the chaplain spoke, three volleys were fired, and George Armstrong Custer was laid to rest.

Fifteen

---◆◆◆---

Custer's Avengers

The nation was understandably horrified and outraged by the Custer disaster at the hands of the Sioux and Cheyenne. The act served to unite the country with purpose as nothing ever had as they mourned their fallen heroes. Custer, a national hero, had been cut down in the prime of his life and the public wanted revenge.

Congress immediately voted to authorize two new forts—Custer and Keogh—on the Yellowstone and recruited an additional twenty-five hundred fresh cavalry troops for duty. Many recruits, calling themselves "Custer's Avengers," enlisted specifically to serve in the Seventh Cavalry. The hostile Sioux and Cheyenne, keenly aware that there would be some sort of retaliation for the battle on the Little Bighorn River, broke up into smaller bands and scattered across the plains.

The conflict that would become known as "The Great Sioux War of 1876–77" resumed in early July 1876 when eight hundred Cheyenne warriors fled Red Cloud Agency and headed for the Powder River country. The Fifth Cavalry, now under the command of Lieutenant Colonel Wesley Merritt, intercepted about thirty of the renegades on July 17 at War Bonnet, or Hat, Creek—twenty-five miles northwest of the agency.

Scout William F. "Buffalo Bill" Cody had accompanied the column and engaged in a "duel" with a Cheyenne subchief named Yellow Hair. Actually,

Cody was said to have shot the Indian off his pony, ridden him down, then killed and scalped him. The celebrated scout held up the bloody scalp for all to see and announced that this was the "first scalp for Custer." This "duel" became a featured attraction of Cody's Wild West Show and also a play, *The Red Right Hand, or Buffalo Bill's First Scalp for Custer.*

On August 5, General George Crook, along with Wesley Merritt's troops—nearly twenty-three hundred in total—marched from his base camp on Goose Creek down the Tongue River trailing the Indians. At the same time, General Alfred Terry, with Colonel John Gibbon and the Seventh Cavalry, took another seventeen-hundred-man detachment down the Yellowstone to the mouth of the Rosebud.

The columns—to their mutual surprise—happened upon each other on August 10 in the Rosebud Valley. The reinforced column then embarked on an arduous march through rain and mud, with many men succumbing to sickness and fatigue. They arrived on August 17 at the mouth of the Yellowstone River without having come within one hundred miles of the hostiles. By this time, Sitting Bull and his band had escaped to the lower Missouri, and Crazy Horse was leading his people toward the Black Hills.

On September 5, General Terry made the decision to disband his portion of the expedition. Gibbon returned to Fort Ellis, and the Seventh Cavalry rode for Fort Abraham Lincoln. Crook, however, decided on a forced march to the Black Hills in an effort to overtake those Indians who had earlier embarrassed him on the Rosebud.

Crook was under the impression that he could quickly catch up with the hostiles and ordered that all wagons, extra clothing, tents, and other nonnecessities be abandoned. His column, however, was soon plagued by bad weather and supply problems on what would become known as the "starvation march." Scores of exhausted animals died, and the men were reduced to eating mule and horse meat. Near the town of Deadwood, Crook dispatched Captain Anson Mills with a detail of 150 cavalrymen to buy rations.

On September 9, Mills happened upon a Sioux camp of thirty-seven lodges near Slim Buttes, a landmark rock formation. The cavalrymen charged and routed the enemy—killing Chief American Horse—and occupied the camp while withstanding heavy fire from warriors who took up a nearby defensive position.

At about noon, Crazy Horse and another two hundred warriors arrived and attacked. A fierce battle raged without a decision until Crook and rein-forcements reached the field and the Indians broke contact. The army lost three killed and twelve wounded; Indian casualties are unknown. A search of the camp revealed various items taken from Custer's command—clothing, horses and saddles, a guidon, and a gauntlet that had belonged to Captain Myles Keogh.

Crook's beleaguered column was finally rescued when wagons laden with supplies accompanied by a herd of cattle reached them on September 13. At that time, he made the decision to abandon his futile search for the hostiles.

The Little Bighorn Campaign had come to an inauspicious end, and the United States Congress vowed to make the Lakota Sioux tribe pay dearly for its treachery. It was decreed in the annual Indian appropriation act of August 15 that the Sioux would be denied subsistence until the tribe relinquished all claims to hunting rights outside the reservation and signed over ownership of the Black Hills to the government.

This ultimatum was delivered to the reservations in September and Oc-tober, and in order to save their people from starvation, a number of chiefs at the various agencies signed the new treaty—instead of the two-thirds of adult males as specified by the Fort Laramie Treaty of 1868. Regardless, Paha Sapa, formerly Lakota land, was now officially owned by the United States. Colo-nel Nelson A. Miles worked throughout the fall building winter quarters at his Tongue River Cantonment, which he used as a supply base from which to chase various Sioux tribes, including that of Sitting Bull, across half of Mon-tana. Skirmishes and negotiations between the two warring factions failed to produce agreeable results, although small bands did occasionally submit to the reservations.

Nelson Miles, a thirty-seven-year-old Massachusetts native, had helped or-ganize an infantry unit during the Civil War. He had been deemed too young to command at that time but proved himself in such battles as Seven Pines, Fredericksburg, Chancellorsville, and Petersburg—he was wounded in each of them. He had been awarded the Medal of Honor for his actions at Chancellorsville and promoted to brigadier general after Petersburg. After a stint as commander of a black regiment, he was placed in charge of Fort Monroe, Virginia, where former Confederate president, Jefferson Davis, was being held. Miles assumed command of the Fifth Infantry in 1869, commanded them in the so-called Red River War of 1874–75, and had now come north to pursue hostile Cheyenne and Sioux.

Meanwhile, General Crook, with a column of more than twenty-two hundred men, had marched on November 14 from Fort Fetterman up the old Bozeman Trail to a location near his earlier battle on the Rosebud. At that point, scouts reported finding a large Cheyenne village to the west in the Bighorn Mountains. Crook dispatched Colonel Ranald Mackenzie with ten cavalry troops—about eleven hundred men—to engage the hostiles.

At dawn on November 25, Mackenzie and his cavalrymen stormed into a canyon of the Red Fork of the Powder River and attacked a two-hundred-lodge village under chiefs Dull Knife and Little Wolf. The army horsemen quickly routed the surprised occupants.

About four hundred warriors, however, regrouped within the boulders on a nearby bluff and poured a deadly fire back into the village while others closed with the soldiers and Indian scouts, fighting hand to hand. Chief Little Wolf was said to have been wounded seven times but escaped and survived.

It was midafternoon before the cavalrymen had fought off the assault and maintained control of the village. They then set to work destroying everything of value—lodges, clothing, and food—and capturing the herd of seven hundred ponies. Once again items from Custer's command were found, including a guidon that had been made into a pillowcase. Also, a bloody photograph of Captain Thomas McDougall's sister that for some unknown reason had been carried by Captain Myles Keogh was also found in that Cheyenne village.

Mackenzie lost one officer and five enlisted killed and twenty-six wounded. The Indians suffered about forty dead—including the horrible loss of eleven babies who had frozen to death that night.

The Cheyenne fled in search of Crazy Horse on the upper Tongue River. Crook determinedly followed but after enduring low temperatures and blizzards ended his campaign in late December without another major engagement.

The military pressure, however, was taking its toll on the renegade Indians. Many of these people submitted to the reservation and others were prepared to surrender. To that end, communication was opened between the chiefs and Colonel Nelson Miles to discuss terms.

On December 16, a delegation of Cheyenne approached the Tongue River Cantonment to talk but was attacked by some of Miles' Crow scouts, who killed five of their enemy. The Cheyenne fled, and hostilities resumed.

In early January 1877, Miles and about 350 men set out to search for hostiles up the Tongue River Valley. On January 7, the Indians attempted to lure them into an ambush, but anxious warriors sprang the trap too soon, which enabled Miles to escape and in the process capture a number of Cheyenne women and children. At daybreak the following morning, January 8, Crazy Horse and about five hundred Sioux and Cheyenne warriors attacked Miles's command with intentions of freeing the captives.

The two sides fought fiercely throughout the morning on a battlefield covered with deep snow. Miles was well prepared for the attack and skillfully deployed his artillery and marksmen, which kept the Indians at bay. The Battle of Wolf Mountain, or Battle Butte, ended about noon when a blizzard obscured visibility and the Indians withdrew. Miles had intended to continue his campaign, but the difficulty in obtaining supplies forced him to return to Tongue River Cantonment.

The battle, although each side had sustained only light casualties, convinced many of the hostiles that they could never prevail against the army. Sitting Bull decided to take his band to Canada, while other small bands scattered across the Plains and mountains and still others chose to straggle onto the reservations.

After the Battle of the Little Bighorn, Crazy Horse and his followers, who probably numbered around six hundred, spent about a month celebrating their victory with feasts and dances. He then returned to the Black Hills to harass prospectors. While other Sioux bands split up and had apparently lost their lust for war, Crazy Horse waged what amounted at times to a one-man fight to regain the land promised to his people.

But Crazy Horse's defiance began to waver as time passed. His people were starving, and his wife had contracted tuberculosis. General George Crook had promised Crazy Horse a reservation of his own if he would submit. On May 5, 1877, the legendary warrior led eight to nine hundred of his brethren in a parade two miles long, guided by Red Cloud, into Fort (Camp) Robinson.

There were, however, a few bands that remained defiant and vowed to continue their resistance. One such group of Sioux under Lame Deer had chosen not to surrender with Crazy Horse. Colonel Miles, acting on information from Indians who had surrendered, marched up the Tongue to search for these hostiles.

A village of fifty-one lodges was located on Muddy Creek, a tributary of the Rosebud. At dawn on May 7, Miles, with four cavalry troops, charged into Lame Deer's village. The surprised Indians fled to the hillsides, while the army easily secured the village and commandeered the 450-head pony herd.

One of Miles' scouts convinced Chief Lame Deer and Iron Shirt, the head warrior, to surrender. Another scout, however, rode up and shot at the two men, who, in turn, retrieved their weapons and fled toward the high ground while firing—one bullet just missing Miles and striking a trooper to the rear. Both Indians were shot down by a barrage of fire from the troops.

Fourteen Indians had been killed in the assault, while the army lost four enlisted killed and one officer and six enlisted wounded. More than two hundred of Lame Deer's band had escaped, and Miles gave chase, without success, before returning to destroy the village. These Indians were followed throughout the summer by Miles—including eleven troops of the Seventh Cavalry under Colonel Samuel Sturgis—which resulted in most of them eventually surrendering.

Discontent and tension gripped the Lakota Sioux reservations throughout the summer of 1877. The presence of Crazy Horse at Red Cloud Agency had a great effect on young braves who worshiped him, the older chiefs who resented him, and the army, which distrusted him. The reservation that Crook had promised apparently had been simply a ruse to encourage Crazy Horse to surrender. He was asked by Crook to visit Washington but refused. Crook, through interpreter Frank Grouard, asked Crazy Horse if he would help the army fight against the Nez Percé. Grouard reportedly misinterpreted the re-

Cadet George Armstrong Custer, West Point, 1861. *(Author's Collection)*

Brevet Maj. Gen. Armstrong Custer, 1865. *(Author's Collection)*

Generals Sheridan, Merritt, Custer, Forsyth, and Deven, circa 1864. *(Author's Collection)*

Elizabeth "Libbie" Bacon Custer, 1874. *(Author's Collection)*

Fort Laramie Treaty of 1868 negotiations. Commissioner Gen. Alfred Terry, 2nd from right. Gen. William T. Sherman, 6th from right. *(Courtesy Little Bighorn Battlefield National Monument)*

George Armstrong Custer during the winter campaign of 1868. *(Author's Collection)*

George Armstrong Custer and Grand Duke Alexis, 1872. *(Courtesy Little Bighorn Battlefield National Monument)*

Custer with the first grizzly he killed, August 1874. From left: Scout Bloody Knife; Custer; Pvt. Noonan; Capt. William Ludlow. *(Courtesy Little Bighorn Battlefield National Monument)*

Outing at the Heart River, 1875. From left: 1st Lt. James
Calhoun; Mr. Leonard Swett; Capt. Stephen Baker;
Boston Custuer; 2nd Lt. Winfield S. Edgerly; Miss
Emily Watson; Capt. Myles W. Keogh; Mrs. Margaret
Custer Calhoun; Mrs. Elizabeth "Libbie" Custer;
Dr. Holmes O. Paulding; Lt. Col. George Armstrong
Custer; Mrs. Nettie Smith; Dr. George E. Lord; Capt.
Thomas B. Weir; 1st Lt. William W. Cooke; 2nd Lt.
Richard E. Thompson; Miss Nellie Wadsworth; Miss
Emma Wadsworth; 1st Lt. Thomas W. Custer; 1st Lt.
Algernon E. Smith. *(Courtesy Little Bighorn Battlefield
National Monument)*

Lt. Col. George Custer, Circa 1875.
*(Courtesy Little Bighorn Battlefield
National Monument)*

George and Elizabeth Custer in study at Fort Lincoln, Dakota Territory, 1874. *(Courtesy
Little Bighorn Battlefield National Monument)*

Boston Custer *(Courtesy Little Bighorn Battlefield National Monument)*

Capt. Myles W. Keogh, wearing his Army dress uniform in 1875, was an Irish soldier of fortune who fought in three wars on three continents and distinguished himself in our Civil War. He first acquired his appreciation for horses and horsemanship when exposed to the flashy Arabians in Northern Africa during the Algerian Conquest of 1859. *(Courtesy Little Bighorn Battlefield National Monument)*

Capt. Tom Custer, wearing his two Medals of Honor, 1870. *(Author's Collection)*

Sioux Sitting Bull, 1881. *(Courtesy Little Bighorn Battlefield National Monument)*

Cheyenne Two Moon(s). *(Courtesy Little Bighorn Battlefield National Monument)*

Maj. Marcus A. Reno, 1875. *(Courtesy Little Bighorn Battlefield National Monument)*

Sioux chief Gall. *(Courtesy Little Bighorn Battlefield National Monument)*

From left: Sioux Chief American Horse, William F. "Buffalo Bill" Cody, Sioux leader Red Cloud. *(Courtesy Little Bighorn Battlefield National Monument)*

Sioux Warrior Rain-in-the-Face. *(Courtesy Little Bighorn Battlefield National Monument)*

1st. Lt. William W. Cooke, 1875. *(Courtesy Little Bighorn Battlefield National Monument)*

Capt. Frederick W. Benteen, 1885. *(Courtesy Little Bighorn Battlefield National Monument)*

Scout "Lonesome Charley" Reynolds, 1874. *(Courtesy Little Bighorn Battlefield National Monument)*

Harry "Autie" Reed *(Courtesy Little Bighorn Battlefield National Monument)*

Capt. Tom Custer *(Courtesy Little Bighorn Battlefield National Monument)*

1st Lt. James Calhoun *(Courtesy Little Bighorn Battlefield National Monument)*

Painting *Custer's Last Fight* by Cassilly Adams, 1885. This painting was later recreated by Otto Becker for a famous advertisement by Anheuser-Busch that adorned saloon walls in the late nineteenth century. *(Courtesy Little Bighorn Battlefield National Monument)*

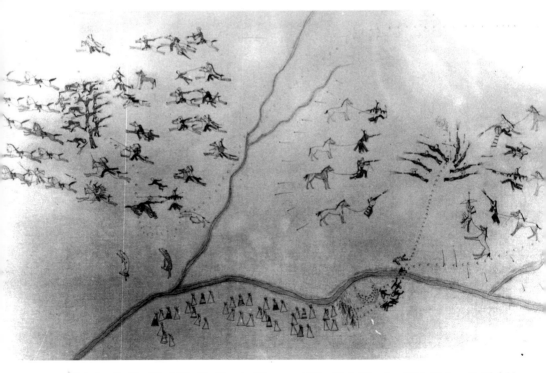

Painting *Battle of the Little Big Horn* by Cheyenne White Bird. *(Courtesy Little Bighorn Battlefield National Monument)*

sponse on purpose to indicate that Crazy Horse wanted to fight whites, which led Crook to believe that the Sioux warrior intended to lead his people in a rebellion.

Crazy Horse requested that he be allowed to take the ill Black Shawl to Spotted Tail Agency, but that was viewed as a threat and he was denied permission. He went anyway, chased by soldiers who failed to catch him. He did, however, agree to return and did so—to his surprise as a prisoner—on September 5.

Crazy Horse was being led to the stockade at Fort Robinson when he panicked at the thought of incarceration and tried to escape. Little Big Man and several other Indian guards grabbed him, and Private William Gentiles stepped forward to run his bayonet through Crazy Horse's body.

Crazy Horse said as he lay on his deathbed:

I was not hostile to the white man. . . . We had buffalo for food, and their hides for clothing and our tipis. We preferred hunting to a life of idleness on the reservations, where we were driven against our will. At times, we did not get enough to eat, and we were not allowed to leave the reservation to hunt. We preferred our own way of living. We were no expense to the government then. All we wanted was peace, to be left alone. . . . They tried to confine me, I tried to escape, and a soldier ran his bayonet through me. I have spoken.

The great warrior Crazy Horse died later that day. His father, also named Crazy Horse, buried the body of his son at some secret location in his homeland—legend has it near Wounded Knee Creek—which has yet to have been discovered by the white man.

The Northern Cheyenne—including chiefs Dull Knife and Little Wolf—unlike the Sioux, had been denied the right to live on a reservation located in their own part of the country and had been escorted in August to their new home at Fort Reno in Indian Territory.

Meanwhile, the Nez Percé, a tribe from Wallowa Valley, Washington, led by the legendary strategic genius Chief Joseph, had gone to war against the United States government. The tribe had been pressured to move onto a reservation in Idaho, which would have forced them to reduce the size of their prized herds of Appaloosa horses. Chief Joseph negotiated a peaceful settlement of the dispute and the tribe was prepared to move when a clash between settlers and young warriors over stock stolen by the settlers left eighteen whites dead. Joseph was compelled to head into the mountains with 650 of his people and was chased by the army.

The outnumbered Nez Percé were caught by surprise on three separate occasions—at White Bird Canyon and Clearwater, Idaho, and by Colonel John Gibbon at Big Hole Valley, Montana—but each time fought off the attack of the superior force and escaped. As skirmishes escalated, casualties on both sides mounted and Chief Joseph decided to make a mad dash to Canada in an attempt to join Sitting Bull's band of Sioux.

On September 13, Colonel Samuel D. Sturgis and 350 troopers of the Seventh Cavalry intercepted the Nez Percé at Canyon Creek, Montana, near present-day Billings. In a running battle, Sturgis, who was criticized for his timidity, failed to prevent the tribe from escaping.

Colonel Miles marched with reinforcements and on September 30 attacked Chief Joseph's camp on Snake Creek near the Bear Paw Mountains. In the ensuing bloody battle, the Seventh Cavalry bore the brunt of the casualties—Captain Owen Hale was killed, and Captain Myles Moylan and First Lieutenant Edward S. Godfrey were wounded.

Miles subsequently laid siege to the Indian camp with artillery until finally, on October 5, Chief Joseph, who had been captured and exchanged, eloquently surrendered the remainder of his people. The tribe had covered about twelve hundred miles on their "Long March" through Washington, Oregon, Idaho, and Montana—losing about 275 warriors and killing about 266 soldiers. The heroic struggle of the Nez Percé, who took no scalps, killed no prisoners, and harmed few noncombatants, gained the sympathy of the American public.

By September 1878, the Cheyenne who had been sent to Indian Territory were beset by hunger, homesickness, and disease. Chiefs Dull Knife and Little Wolf fled the reservation with three hundred of their tribe in an effort to return to their Tongue River homeland. More than ten thousand soldiers and civilians followed the renegades and engaged in several minor skirmishes. After crossing the North Platte River, however, the two chiefs argued, which divided the tribe. Dull Knife and his band eventually surrendered to a cavalry patrol near Fort (Camp) Robinson on October 23, while Little Wolf resumed his journey north to take refuge at Red Cloud Agency after a fifteen-hundred-mile journey.

Dull Knife's people were held in a barracks at the fort and refused requests to return peacefully to Indian Territory. The post commander attempted to persuade them by cutting off food, water, and fuel. On January 9, 1879, the Cheyenne, who had secreted weapons, were driven by the unbearable conditions to shoot the guards and flee the post. They were chased down, and almost half of them—men, women, and children—were shot down or froze to death. The survivors, who included Chief Dull Knife and his family, took refuge at Red Cloud Agency and were later settled on Pine Ridge Reservation.

Little Wolf and his band remained at large throughout the winter, finally surrendering on March 27 to a detachment of the Second Cavalry from Fort Keogh. In 1884, the Northern Cheyenne were awarded their own reservation at Tongue River—one year after Dull Knife had died.

During the ensuing years, the Sioux who had fled to Canada straggled into reservations. The Canadian government refused to provide supplies, and life became hard for Sitting Bull's band. He had married as many as nine wives and had fathered about the same number of children and was worried about their well-being.

On July 19, 1881, under a pledge of amnesty, he led two hundred of his people to Fort Buford. Sitting Bull was held a virtual prisoner for nearly two years at Fort Randall in present-day Gregory County, South Dakota, before being permitted in May 1883 to settle at the Standing Rock Indian Agency. The surrender of Sitting Bull, however, had for all intents and purposes ended Sioux resistance and opened the Plains to the army, the settlers, and the railroad.

In June 1885, Sitting Bull signed a four-month contract with Buffalo Bill's Wild West Show for $50 a week and a bonus of $125, along with the rights to sell his photograph and autograph. His reception by Eastern audiences, who frequently hissed when this Indian villain appeared, was quite disrespectful, which was a source of displeasure to the Sioux medicine man. During the tour, he also met President Grover Cleveland and a number of the army officers who had futilely chased him around the Northern Plains.

Relative peace was maintained on the Sioux reservations until 1890 when the Sioux became captivated by a new religion. In 1889, a Paiute Indian named Jack Wilson, who called himself Wovoka, claimed to have had a spiritual experience that prompted him to create a religion called the Ghost Dance movement, which was based on the premise that the white man would disappear and the buffalo would return. Most Western tribes accepted the peaceful doctrine of this Ghost Dance, but the Sioux converted the ceremony to conform to their hostility and began to defy authority. The army feared that there would be an outbreak of war and increased the number of troops at the two Sioux reservations, which included bringing in the Seventh Cavalry from Fort Riley.

Sitting Bull did not participate in this ritual but clearly enjoyed the turmoil it provoked among his people. Indian agent James McLaughlin, who had always regarded Sitting Bull as a threat to good order, believed that the Sioux leader was indeed inciting members of his tribe to defy the government. McLaughlin and General Nelson Miles ordered that Sitting Bull be arrested.

On December 15, Indian police went to serve the arrest warrant. A confrontation between more than forty Indian police and about 150 Ghost Dancers ensued outside Sitting Bull's cabin. In the resultant melee, the Sioux medicine man was shot and killed by Indian policemen Lieutenant Bullhead and Sergeant Red Tomahawk. Sitting Bull's seventeen-year-old son, Crow Foot, and six other Ghost Dancers were killed, along with six Indian policemen.

The death of Sitting Bull ended forever the domination of the ancient regime among the Sioux of the Standing Rock Reservation. And that was likely the true motivation for the murder of Sitting Bull.

The murderous act that took the life of Sitting Bull convinced Miniconjou chief Big Foot, who was also singled out for arrest, to flee the reservation with three hundred of his people and head for Pine Ridge. Miles dispatched the Seventh Cavalry, commanded by Colonel James W. Forsyth, to catch Big Foot and his band and escort them back. Forsyth overtook Big Foot twenty miles from Pine Ridge in the valley of Wounded Knee Creek, where the two factions camped for the night.

The Sioux awoke on the morning of December 29 to find themselves surrounded by five hundred troops and four cannon. Colonel Forsyth requested that the Indians hand over their firearms. When they refused, Forsyth ordered that a search be made. One Indian, perhaps Yellow Bird, called for the others to resist. A soldier and a warrior engaged in a scuffle, and a weapon was discharged.

The young men of the tribe immediately commenced firing into the nearest soldiers. That fire was returned, and in the close-range battle that followed, with the cavalry supported by artillery, the Indian camp was destroyed. Eighty-four Sioux men and boys—including Chief Big Foot—forty-four women, and eighteen children lay dead. In addition, fifty-one Indians were wounded, with seven later dying.

The Seventh Cavalry lost one officer, Captain George D. Wallace, along with eighteen enlisted killed and thirty-three wounded.

On New Year's Day, 1891, the Indian bodies were gathered up and buried in a mass grave on the hill from where the artillery had been fired. The Wounded Knee massacre was viewed by the army as a terrible blunder committed by Colonel Forsyth, who was relieved of command and the subject of a court of inquiry.

The event brought to an end the Ghost Dance ritual and with it any hope that the Plains Indians had for ever regaining the traditions, land, and culture that had been lost in decades of war against the United States.

The end of the Plains Indians was only the beginning of the controversy and debate about their fate as well as the particulars surrounding the most famous battle of the war—the Little Bighorn.

Sixteen

Mysteries, Myths, and Legends

Perhaps the most enduring mystery about the battle has been the whereabouts of Troop E. This was the company—the Gray Horse Troop commanded by First Lieutenant Algernon "Fresh" Smith—that had ventured down Medicine Tail Coulee with Custer to probe the village in the opening stages of the battle and likely had been forced back to the ridge.

According to accounts, the bodies of about twenty-eight troopers from Company E were located on June 27, 1876, at the bottom of a narrow gash in the land now known as Deep Ravine. This drainage, also known as North Medicine Tail Coulee, was located near the end of the slope that ran from Custer Hill about two thousand feet west to the Little Bighorn River.

When discovered, these bodies were said to have been too badly decomposed to be moved and therefore were not carted away for individual burial. The detail simply covered them with dirt where they lay.

By 1877 when the burial detail arrived on the field and searched for those bodies, they were nowhere to be found. Not only that, but these bodies have remained missing to this day. Modern-day excavations with heavy equipment, not to mention volunteers with metal detectors, have not unearthed a single clue. Twenty-eight bodies have apparently vanished.

One particular body from Company E that had not been found immediately after the battle when accounting for all of the officers was that of Second Lieutenant James Garland "Jack" Sturgis. This twenty-two-year-old West Point graduate was the son of Colonel Samuel D. Sturgis, who at that time commanded the Seventh Cavalry. Locating the body of their commanding officer's son would have been paramount for the soldiers, but nonetheless it could not be found anywhere on the field.

Sturgis had been the youngest and the final regular officer assigned to the regiment before it marched on the Little Bighorn Campaign. He had initially been assigned as third-in-command of Company M—where it was said that he was very popular with the troops—but was transferred to Company E as second-in-command just before the march.

The head of James Sturgis, as well as a blood-soaked undergarment belonging to him, was discovered in the abandoned Indian village site two days after the battle. In the archives of the United States Signal Corps there is a photograph taken on the battlefield depicting a primitive monument made of stones with a board lettered "Lt. STURGIS, 7th CAV JUNE, '76." That photo, however, was staged in an effort to mislead Sturgis' mother, who had not been informed that her son's remains had not been found.

If the bodies had indeed been observed in Deep Ravine, they could have fallen prey to nature by the following year. The shallow graves may have been eroded by rain and wind and blizzards. Predators might have robbed those shallow, hastily dug trenches and scavenger birds could have picked clean the bones, and then the skeletons could have been scattered to the four winds by animals and the elements.

One theory proposed that the mystery could be solved by simply searching in a neighboring ravine, that observers in 1876 had noted the wrong place. No evidence whatsoever exists for this theory. Taking into consideration military tactics, it would have been unlikely that Company E would have even been deployed anywhere within the vicinity of that location down Deep Ravine or nearby ravines, nor would the men have fallen back to that location during the fighting. And modern-day searchers would have surely observed remnants of twenty-eight bodies anywhere in the vicinity.

The body of Company E commander "Fresh" Smith had been found with

Custer and forty others on that hill far from the river. Smith would not have deserted his command at the river to save himself alone on high ground. It has been speculated that he was on Custer Hill seeking medical assistance for a wound. Smith was probably there for a reason—his troopers were deployed nearby. The missing bodies from Company E likely were not missing at all but were lying on the upper reaches of the slope leading to Deep Ravine not far from Custer Hill.

As far as the contention that the 1876 detail had plotted these bodies down Deep Ravine, human error could be to blame. There were Indians who testified that very few soldiers were seen down Deep Ravine during the battle. It was a stressful time for the burial detail, immediately after a horrendously bloody fight, confronted with decomposing, mutilated bodies of fellow soldiers, and both officers and enlisted wanted nothing more than to finish this gruesome job and return to Fort Abraham Lincoln as quickly as possible. People in that condition can make mistakes. Mystery solved?

Another body that was never found was that of Second Lieutenant Henry Moore Harrington, who was second-in-command of Tom Custer's Company C. It has been speculated that Tom Custer was serving as an aide-de-camp to his brother and that this twenty-seven-year-old West Pointer was actually in command of that company during the battle. Company C fell on Battle Ridge, but Harrington's body was not with them.

Sioux chief Gall told Walter Camp that four eyewitnesses told him about a soldier who rode through the Indians on a very swift horse, which they could not catch. After the Indians chased him for about a mile or two, the soldier drew his pistol and killed himself. The pursuers were puzzled by this act because the man's horse was faster than their horses and he was continually gaining ground away from them.

It has been reported that Harrington had a premonition before the battle and drew a sketch that he mailed to a friend that depicted himself tied to a tree surrounded by hostile Indians. The soldier on that horse certainly could have been Harrington, racing away from his evident fear of capture.

Stranger yet, however, is the legend of Harrington's wife, Grace of Highland Falls, New York. Grace was said to have mysteriously vanished at some point after the battle, leaving two children behind. She was found two years later in Texas suffering from amnesia. An attack of pneumonia restored her mind, but she recalled nothing about the missing two years. Her daughter stated that the Indians told about a woman dressed in black who had been seen several times on the Little Bighorn battlefield during that two-year period, and she believed this to be her mother.

There was one survivor of the battle who can be confirmed—Comanche, a claybank sorrel or buckskin gelding that has gone down in legend as being the only living thing found on the field following the Little Bighorn battle and has become one of the most famous horses in history.

Comanche's cavalry career began on April 3, 1868, when he was part of a herd of forty-one mustangs purchased by First Lieutenant Tom Custer for the army from a St. Louis trader. Upon arrival at Fort Leavenworth, Kansas, for processing, which included branding of the distinctive "US" on his shoulder, Comanche was listed as five years old, stood fifteen hands, weighed 925 pounds, and was described as being a cross, 75 percent American and 25 percent Spanish.

The horse quickly caught the attention of Captain Myles W. Keogh, commander of Company I, who was known to be an excellent judge of horseflesh. Although officers normally bought their horses from private traders rather than the army, Keogh decided that this particular horse would make an ideal second mount and purchased him for ninety dollars.

It has been said that Comanche received his name following a skirmish with the Cheyenne on September 13, 1868, near the Cimarron River in southwestern Kansas. Keogh noted that the horse had been somewhat skittish during the brief yet furious fight but continued to perform admirably. The captain discovered upon returning to camp that the animal had been struck in the right quarter by an arrow during the encounter. The arrow shaft had broken off, leaving the flint inside, which was removed by the farrier. A soldier volunteered the information that he had witnessed the horse being struck by the arrow and he had squalled as loud as a Comanche Indian. Fittingly, Keogh named his brave horse Comanche.

Comanche was wounded by an arrow once again in June 1870 and received an injury to his right shoulder in January 1871 while with Keogh on Reconstruction duty in Kentucky.

From all accounts Keogh was shot off Comanche's back during the Little Bighorn battle. The bullet was said to have passed through the forequarters of the horse and emerged to shatter Keogh's left leg. Keogh, although severely wounded, apparently declined to shoot his horse for breastworks and may have been found near death still clutching Comanche's reins in his hand.

On the morning of June 27, while the remnants of Reno's command and the Terry-Gibbon column examined the battlefield, several cavalry horses were found wandering about. Apparently First Lieutenant Henry Nowlan, who had been Keogh's best friend, recognized Comanche and decided to save the horse. Nowlan found that Comanche had been wounded perhaps as many as seven times and was in extremely poor condition. The other horses either were too badly wounded to rescue and were shot or were simply left behind.

Comanche, however, was transported by wagon fifteen miles to the steamship *Far West,* where a stall had been provided between the rudders and he was supported within by a sling. At Fort Abraham Lincoln, he was diligently nursed back to health by blacksmith Private Gustave Korn. At that time, the famous horse became a favorite for a young ladies' riding mount—so much so that his use caused a bitter rivalry among potential riders at the fort. This problem was solved by Colonel Samuel D. Sturgis, commanding officer of the Seventh Cavalry.

On April 10, 1878, Sturgis issued General Order No. 7, which read:

1. The horse known as "Comanche" being the only living representative of the bloody tragedy of the Little Big Horn, Montana, June 25, 1876, his kind treatment and comfort should be a matter of special pride and solicitude on the part of the 7th Cavalry, to the end that his life may be prolonged to the utmost limit. Though wounded and scarred, his very silence speaks in terms more eloquent than words of the desperate struggle against overwhelming odds, of the hopeless conflict, and heroic manner in which all went down that day.

2. The commanding officer of "I" troop will see that a special and comfortable stall is fitted up for Comanche. He will not be ridden by any person whatever under any circumstances, nor will he be put to any kind of work.

3. Hereafter upon all occasions of ceremony (of mounted regimental formation), Comanche, saddled, bridled, and led by a mounted trooper of Troop I, will be paraded with the regiment.

Thereafter, Comanche lived a life of privilege as the "2nd commanding officer" of the Seventh Cavalry. He roamed the post at will, rooting through garbage pails and begging for buckets of beer at the enlisted men's canteen. Comanche would follow Private Korn around like a puppy, once trailing the blacksmith into town and creating a jealous ruckus on the front lawn of a home Korn was visiting. When Korn was killed in 1890 at Wounded Knee, however, Comanche became quite despondent and his health began to fail. He passed away on November 6, 1891, at age twenty-eight.

Professor L. L. Dyke, a naturalist at the University of Kansas, volunteered to have Comanche mounted if the animal would be donated to the University Museum at Lawrence. His offer was accepted. Comanche was exhibited at the 1893 Chicago World's Fair and then went on display at the museum. He presently stands in a humidity-controlled glass case designed to discourage souvenir hunters—including students wishing for good luck on a test—from plucking hair from him.

There was at least one soldier singled out by the Indians for extraordinary bravery during the battle. Perhaps the most intriguing and difficult puzzle to solve with respect to the battle is the identity of this cavalryman who distinguished himself as the bravest man the Sioux ever fought.

The controversy was ignited by an interview on February 27, 1877, in which Sioux chief Red Horse said:

Among [the soldiers] . . . was an officer who rode a horse with four white feet. The Indians have fought a great many tribes of people, and very brave ones, too, but they all say that this man was the bravest man they have ever met. I don't know whether this man was Gen. Custer or not; some say he was. I saw this man in the fight several times, but did not see his body. It is said that he was killed by a Santee, who still holds his horse. This officer wore a large-brimmed hat and a buckskin coat. He alone saved his command a number of times by turning on his horse in the rear in the retreat.

In speaking of him, the Indians call him "The man who rode the horse with four white feet." There were two men of this description, looking very much alike, both having long yellowish hair.

From the context of Red Horse's statement, it would seem that this action occurred during Reno's retreat from the timber to the hilltop. Former battlefield superintendent Edward S. Luce claims that only four officers wore buckskin that day—both Custer brothers, W. W. Cooke, and Captain Myles Keogh. Author Edgar I. Stewart adds to that list Captain George Yates and First Lieutenants James Calhoun, Algernon Smith, and James E. Porter. None of those officers were members of Reno's battalion, but they were with Custer.

Oddly enough, in spite of the glaring discrepancies, many believe that the officer alluded to by Red Horse was Captain Thomas French, although he was one of the first officers to reach the bluffs and could not have covered his men, apparently was not wearing buckskin, did not have long yellowish hair, and was not killed.

It should be noted that tactics employed by Indians on the field of battle make it quite difficult to piece together one consistent story from various eyewitness accounts. Indians did not fight as an organized unit, rather once the battle commenced they were free to fight as individuals and for that reason generally had no idea regarding specific time frames, places, movements of their comrades, or an overall perspective of events.

Although Red Horse's statement would lead us to believe that the "bravest man" was with Reno, no one in that command comes close to fitting the description. Perhaps another officer, this one in Custer's battalion, was actually the subject of the Indian's admiration—as the last man to die.

A statement by Cheyenne chief Two Moon describes this bravest man, who would have been on the Custer battlefield while the Cheyenne rode up the ridge. "We circled all around him—swirling like water around a stone. We shoot, we ride fast, we shoot again. Soldiers drop, and horses fall on them. Soldiers in line drop, but one man rides up and down the line—all the time shouting. He rode a sorrel horse with white face and white forelegs. I don't know who he was. He was a brave man. . . . He wore a buckskin shirt, and had long black hair and mustache. . . . His men were all covered with white dust."

Cheyenne warrior Wooden Leg describes the last man killed: "It appeared that all of the white men were dead. But there was one of them who raised himself to a support on his left elbow." Wooden Leg described how this man was finally killed, then: "I think he must have been the last man killed in this great battle where not one of the enemy got away. This man had a big strong body. His cheeks were plump. All over his face was a stubby black beard. His mustache was much longer than his other beard, and it was curled up at the ends."

Similar statements by Indian eyewitnesses have led many historians, including two excellent researchers, Edward S. Luce and Charles Kuhlman, to conclude that this brave officer was Captain Myles W. Keogh. Author Bruce A. Rosenberg also suggests that Keogh was this man, quoting a Captain Will A. Logan, who was with Gibbon's column, as saying that an "Irish or Irish-American" officer was the last to die.

David H. Miller, who interviewed seventy-one Indian survivors of the battle, describes the bravest man—whose white metal bars, captain's bars, had little meaning to the Indians—in terms similar to Wooden Leg. Miller wrote: "He was the last man of Custer's command to be killed on the ridge. This brave man may well have been Captain Myles Keogh, gallant Irish soldier of fortune, former papal guardsman and Civil War hero."

Of the officers wearing buckskin, those on Custer Hill—the Custer brothers, Yates, Cooke, and Smith—must be ruled out, if not for other reasons, by the location where their bodies were found on the field. The body of Porter, who was Keogh's second-in-command, was never found. Calhoun was killed nearby, but, as was the case with Porter, he was a lieutenant, not a captain. In addition, most of the above do not fit the consensus description—the black hair and mustache in particular.

Every description, except for the white feet of his horse, Comanche, would seem to point to Keogh as the last man to die that day. More than one eyewitness described the dust on the field, which could have coated Comanche's sweaty forelegs and given the impression of white feet.

Perhaps Myles Keogh was not the celebrated "bravest man the Sioux ever fought" as described by Chief Red Horse and the identity of that man will remain unknown. There does exist, however, more than enough evidence to indicate that Keogh fought with a courage that distinguished him in the eyes of his enemies and that he was probably the last man killed at the Battle of the Little Bighorn.

Predictably, there were many people over the ensuing years who would claim to be the sole survivor of the Little Bighorn battle. Some who basked in their fifteen minutes of fame were said to have even gained financially by fleecing gullible tourists or selling their stories to ambitious Eastern journalists. Given the number of alleged survivors, it is a wonder that any bodies were found on the battlefield.

To be fair, the Indians did relate several stories describing soldiers who rode for their lives away from the fighting, but none of these escapees has ever been identified or their freedom substantiated. A couple of sets of bones have been found some distance from the fighting, which may explain the fate of those who fled. In one case, however, a dead cavalry horse was found several weeks after the battle above the mouth of Rosebud Creek, which raised speculation that its rider had escaped—but perhaps by deserting when the column passed that point on the approach to the Valley of the Little Bighorn.

The most famous "lone survivor" was Curly, one of Custer's Crow Indian scouts. Curly had been released prior to the battle but may have witnessed the initial stages as he departed. He later returned to the steamship *Far West* and tried to tell about the fate of Custer but was not understood. For years, however, Curly encouraged researchers with several tantalizing tales of his harrowing escape that day—how he had fooled the hostiles by stripping off his clothing and fashioning his hair Sioux-style, or how he had secreted himself inside the carcass of a dead horse, or how he had crawled under a blanket and hidden in a ravine. None of the stories was true. At the tenth reunion of the battle, Curly was confronted by Sioux chief Gall, who stated that had Curly been on the field that day he would have been dead. The Crow scout did not dare to refute Gall's assertion.

Other alleged former members of Custer's command who offered fanciful stories of a daring escape appeared off and on in the press around the country, but only one has been found to have even a thread of credibility. This claimant was Frank Finkel (aka Frank Hall), a resident of Dayton, Washington, who was the subject of a feature story in the *Walla Walla Bulletin* on March 20, 1921.

Finkel/Hall related in the story that he had been wounded several times that day and escaped when his horse bolted. He happened upon a trapper's cabin the following day and was nursed back to health. At that time, he reported to Fort Benton, where an officer in charge did not believe his story. Finkel/Hall soon thereafter deserted and became a farmer near St. Louis before moving to Dayton, Washington, where he lived for many years. His description of the terrain was said to have been nearly perfect, and his body did show scars from apparent bullet wounds.

Finkel/Hall claimed that he had been a member of Tom Custer's Company C. A check of the official muster rolls reveals a "Sergeant George August Finckle," with Company C, born in Berlin, Germany, in 1844, who had apparently been a captain in the German army before enlisting in the Seventh Cavalry in January 1872. Sergeant Finckle was presumed to have been killed in the battle. There were two cavalrymen named Hall, Edward and John; both were with Company D and known to have survived the battle.

Aliases were a common practice at that time and different spellings of names appeared on various documents, so it is virtually impossible to confirm or debunk the claim by Finkel/Hall. One curious note: he died in 1930 from a malignancy caused by a bullet in his side that had been received decades before—perhaps fired from an Indian rifle at the Little Bighorn battle.

Another more recent claimant to the title of survivor is a farrier with Company L named William H. Heath, an emigrant from Staffordshire, England. His name has been listed as one of the casualties of the battle, but official records in Pennsylvania show that he was buried in Schuylkill County Cemetery on May 2, 1891—after dying of a brain tumor. It has been speculated that Heath in his capacity as a farrier may not have been with Custer's column at all but could have been detailed to care for an injured horse or some other such duty. Heath, who had enlisted in October 1875, may have deserted, leaving behind $1.14 due him for tobacco and $15.00 for clothing. His personal effects were sold at auction in March 1877 and brought $5.

Most of the world had not even been informed about the battle when a cu-

rious document dated July 4, 1876, surfaced. This petition had been allegedly
signed by 235 or 236 of the Seventh Cavalry survivors of the Little Bighorn—
accounts vary but approximately 80 percent of the survivors of Reno's and Benteen's commands were said to have signed.

This document was sent "To His Excellency the President and the Honorable Representatives of the United States."

The text read:

> *We, the enlisted men the survivors of the battle of the Heights of*
> *Little Big Horn River, on the 25th and 26th of June 1876, of the 7th*
> *Regiment of Cavalry who subscribe our names to this petition, most*
> *earnestly solicit the President and Representatives of our Country, that*
> *the vacancies among the Commissioned Officers of our Regiment, made*
> *by the slaughter of our brave, now heroic, now lamented Lieutenant*
> *Colonel George A. Custer, and the other noble dead Commissioned*
> *Officers of our Regiment who fell close by him on the bloody field,*
> *daring the savage demons to the last, be filled by the Officers of the*
> *Regiment only.*
>
> *That Maj. M. A. Reno, be our Lieutenant Colonel vice Custer,*
> *killed; Captain F. W. Benteen our Major vice Reno, promoted.*
>
> *The other vacancies to be filled by officers of the Regiment by*
> *seniority.*
>
> *Your petitioners know this to be contrary to the established rule of*
> *promotion, but prayerfully solicit a deviation from the usual rule in*
> *this case, as it will be conferring a bravely fought for and justly merited*
> *promotion on officers who by their bravery, coolness, and decision on*
> *the 25th and 26th of June 1876, saved the lives of every man now*
> *living of the 7th Cavalry who participated in the battle, one of the most*
> *bloody on record and one that would have ended with the loss of life of*
> *every officer and enlisted man on the field only for the position taken by*
> *Major Reno, which we held with bitter tenacity against fearful odds to*
> *the last.*
>
> *To support this assertion—had our position been taken 100 yards*
> *back from the brink of the heights overlooking the river, we would have*

been entirely cut off from water; and from those heights the Indian demons would have swarmed in hundreds picking off our men by detail, and before midday June 25th not an officer or enlisted man of our Regiment would have been left to tell of our dreadful fate as we then would have been completely surrounded.

With prayerful hope that our petitions be granted, we have the honor to forward it through our commanding officer.

Very Respectfully,

[236 signatures]

At face value this petition would appear innocent enough. The enlisted survivors of the battle—at least 236 of them—in appreciation of the gallant efforts of their senior officers for saving their lives and perhaps in an effort to maintain continuity within the regiment had formally requested that Major Marcus A. Reno and Captain Frederick W. Benteen be rewarded with promotions.

The petition was trumpeted by newspapers and forwarded through military channels until reaching General William T. Sherman, who returned it with his endorsement. Sherman noted, however, that only the president and Senate could grant the petition. The matter never did reach the White House or Congress, and no further action was taken.

The first inclination that there could be a question about the validity of the petition arose years later when General Edward S. Godfrey looked into the matter, and wrote: "There were several men of the 7th Cavalry at Soldiers Home and in Washington in 1921 and 1922 who, when asked if they had signed the petition, denied ever having had such a thought, yet their signatures proved genuine. . . . Not one would admit that he had signed, until shown his signature." Taking into consideration the absolute authority that officers had over enlisted men, perhaps these soldiers had been "ordered" to sign or had signed without knowing the content of the document and had later dismissed the act as inconsequential or were ashamed to admit that they had been coerced.

In 1954, Major Edward S. Luce, the superintendent of Custer Battlefield National Monument, became suspicious about certain irregularities within the petition. He noticed that a number of the signers were not on regimental rolls at the time of the battle and others had always signed the payroll with an "X" but had signed their full names on the document. Luce called in the Federal Bureau of Investigation to determine the authenticity of the signatures in question.

The FBI, although hindered by a lack of handwriting samples from many of the enlisted men, nevertheless concluded that at least seventy-six of the signatures—one-third of the total—were "probable forgeries." Many had purportedly been signed by one man—First Sergeant Joseph McCurry of Company H, which was commanded by Captain Frederick Benteen.

That overwhelming evidence clearly points toward a devious scheme by a person or persons unknown who perhaps had a desire to head off any potential criticism and validate his conduct on June 25, 1876. The finger of guilt, given the fact that First Sergeant McCurry was involved, would point directly at Captain Benteen. Furthermore, McCurry could not have accomplished the task without Benteen's knowledge. And the captain was no stranger to conducting unscrupulous business behind people's backs.

Benteen was indeed popular with the enlisted men and had distinguished himself during the hilltop fight—although his actions beforehand are a subject of controversy—and possibly in the minds of the troops he was deserving of a promotion. Reno was not well liked, but the petition would have been far less credible had his name been left off. Without additional evidence—a "smoking gun"—the guilty party or parties will never be revealed.

The Enlisted Men's Petition, however, stands as a perfect example of the pattern of deception that has created many myths, controversies, and conjectures about the battle while suppressing the true facts and preventing a clear view of actual events to emerge.

Seventeen

Clearing the Smoke from the Battlefield

Even as the smoke still wafted over the battlefield strewn with bodies, fingers of blame pointed and controversial theories abounded. The United States Army simply does not lose that high of a percentage of men in one engagement to not come under fire from countless critics who wanted to know why and how it could happen. The entire nation wanted to know what had happened to the gallant Custer and his brave Seventh Cavalry troopers.

Theories for this battle have ranged from the marginally credible right on down to the ridiculous. Sadly enough, each one of these assumptions has been taken seriously by certain factions of the history community and many have taken root long enough to appear true.

Surprisingly, the order issued by Brigadier General Alfred H. Terry to George Armstrong Custer on June 22, 1876, has become the most enduring misconception. This document has ignited a major controversy over whether or not Custer willfully disobeyed Terry's instructions.

Here is the uncensored copy of those orders:

Camp at Mouth of Rosebud River
Montana Territory

June 22nd, 1876
LIEUT.-COL. CUSTER 7TH CAVALRY
COLONEL:

The Brigadier-General Commanding directs that, as soon as your regiment can be made ready for the march, you will proceed up the Rosebud in pursuit of the Indians whose trail was discovered by Major Reno a few days since. It is, of course, impossible to give you any definite instructions in regard to this movement, and were it not impossible to do so the Department Commander places too much confidence in your zeal, energy, and ability to wish to impose upon you precise orders which might hamper your action when nearly in contact with the enemy. He will, however, indicate to you his views of what your actions should be, and he desires that you should conform to them unless you shall see sufficient reasons for departing from them. He thinks that you should proceed up the Rosebud until you ascertain definitely the direction in which the trail above spoken of leads. Should it be found (as it appears almost certain that it will be found) to turn towards the Little Horn, he thinks that you should still proceed southward, perhaps as far as the headwaters of the Tongue, and then turn toward the Little Horn, feeling constantly, however, to your left, so as to preclude the possibility of the escape of the Indians to the south or southeast by passing around your left flank. The column of Colonel Gibbon is now in motion for the mouth of the Big Horn. As soon as it reaches that point it will cross the Yellowstone and move up at least as far as the forks of the Big and Little Horns. Of its future movements must be controlled by circumstances as they arise, but it is hoped that the Indians, if upon the Little Horn, may be so nearly enclosed by the two columns that their escape will be impossible.

The Department Commander desires that on your way up the Rosebud you should thoroughly examine the upper part of Tulloch's Creek, and that you should endeavor to send a scout through to Colonel Gibbon's column, with information of the result of your examination. The lower part of the creek will be examined by a detachment from Colonel Gibbon's command. The supply steamer will be pushed up the Big Horn as far as the forks if the river is found navigable for that

distance, and the Department Commander, who will accompany the
column of Colonel Gibbon, desires you to report to him not later than
the expiration of time for which your troops are rationed, unless in the
meantime you receive further orders.

> *Very respectfully your obedient servant*
> *E. W. Smith*
> *Captain 18th Infantry*
> *Acting Assistant Adjutant General*

When reading the text of this order, with phrases such as "It is, of course, impossible to give you any definite instructions in regard to this movement," and "the Department Commander [Terry] places too much confidence in your zeal, energy, and ability to impose upon you precise orders which might hamper your action," and "He will, however, indicate to you his views of what your actions should be, and he desires that you should conform to them unless you shall see sufficient reasons for departing from them," one sees that Custer was for all intents and purposes on his own in making decisions about the march after he had ventured up the Rosebud, which he did.

It must also be remembered that Terry had no practical experience fighting Indians; Custer had plenty. Therefore, it would only be logical for Terry to give Custer a free hand with respect to his own initiative depending on what he found in front of him and where the trail led him.

Yet people after the battle and through the ensuing years, mainly fueled by statements from defensive military participants shamed by their own ineptitude, have come to the conclusion that Custer brought about the loss of his command by disregarding those orders. This accusation brings the term "scapegoat" to the forefront.

Even President U. S. Grant made remarks in the public debate following the battle that reflected his malice toward Custer over the Belknap affair when he said: "I regard Custer's Massacre as a sacrifice of troops brought on by Custer himself, that was wholly unnecessary—wholly unnecessary." Grant was no stranger to his own battlefield blunders—his ill-advised frontal assault at Cold Harbor during the Civil War left nearly seven thousand federal soldiers killed or wounded.

At the time of his statement, Grant was dodging barbs for his own actions toward Custer. The pro-Custer faction blamed the president indirectly for Custer's defeat, maintaining that Grant's earlier humiliation of Custer undermined the Seventh Cavalry commander's authority and set the stage for the questionable military behavior of Benteen and Reno.

In addition to his official report that outlined the facts of the battle, General Terry, in an attempt to deflect criticism from himself, wrote a "confidential" report on July 2, 1876. This second explosive report, which was leaked to the press by General William T. Sherman, implied that Custer had disobeyed orders by not following Terry's "plan." Terry's "plan"—whatever that might have been—was never revealed.

The press was quick to engage in sensationalism. Newspapers revealed this shocking story under headlines such as "Custer's Blunder" and "Custer's Fault."

Terry also told reporter Charles S. Diehl that had Custer survived he would have faced a court-martial for disobeying orders. At the time, it must be noted that Terry, the ranking officer who had remained back at the Powder River base camp when Custer marched, was fighting for his military life. His own competence in the matter was being questioned, with at least one newspaper calling for his court-martial.

In addition to the top brass circling the wagons, Custer critic Captain Frederick W. Benteen, no stranger himself to disobeying orders, wrote to his wife on July 4, 1876: "Had Custer carried out order he got from Genl. Terry the command would have formed a junction exactly at the village—and have captured the whole outfit of tepees, etc. and probably any quantity of squaws, pappooses &c. &c. but Custer disobeyed orders from the fact of not wanting any other command—or body to have a finger in the pie, and thereby lost his life."

It would be doubtful that by the time this letter was written Benteen had been privileged to read or know the contents of the order that Custer received to have enough knowledge to determine whether or not the orders had been disregarded. Perhaps Benteen had written his letter from the position that the best defense is a good offense. No doubt Benteen's scheming mind had already dreamed up plenty of excuses why he had not immediately ridden to the sound of firing when Custer sent him the order to "hurry."

Benteen's letter, Terry's order, and other questionable statements have led some historians to suggest that Custer was scheduled to rendezvous with the Terry-Gibbon column on June 26 or at least was required to send a messenger when he found a village and wait for the other column to arrive before attacking. But Terry did write in his order that "its [Gibbon's column's] future movements must be controlled by circumstances as they arise." That column, by the way, did not arrive at the battlefield until the twenty-seventh. By that time, the village would have been vacant whether Custer had attacked or not.

Custer was under the impression that his column had been discovered by the Sioux, as evidenced by the episode of the box of hardtack that had been lost and was subsequently surrounded by Indians. As he knew that it was the Indian custom to flee from a large detachment of approaching soldiers, that would have made it imperative in his mind that he immediately attack.

Similar views were later expressed by many army officers, including Generals Nelson Miles and Phil Sheridan, who were experienced in the ways of the hostiles. The real concern of the campaign participants, which was summed up before the battle in the June 20, 1876, edition of the *St. Paul Pioneer Press,* was that "there is not much probability of these cunning rascals being caught by our more slow-moving forces, for they can break up and fly in a thousand different directions and hide among the hills and gullies, every foot of which is to them familiar ground." This certainly was Terry's concern as well. He wrote to Sheridan on June 21: "My only hope is one of the two columns will find the Indians."

Another factor was the statement made by Custer's cook, Mary Adams, who had accompanied him on the campaign. She claimed in an affidavit dated January 16, 1878, that she overheard Terry tell Custer: "Use your own judgment and do what you think best if you strike the trail."

If Terry's order were followed to the letter of the law, Custer could have chased the Sioux and Cheyenne across the entire country to the streets of New York City if that was where the trail led and would not have been in violation of the order.

Quite simply, the officer who has shouldered the blame, the scapegoat, could not personally defend himself against the charges—he was dead. Therefore, the accusation that Custer disobeyed orders and thereby lost his command has been a convenient excuse for those who may have played a part in the defeat but lived to tell their stories. Those orders, however, tell a different story and serve to clear him of that charge.

But, absurd as it seems, historians to the present day have somehow clung to this fallacy that Custer disregarded orders and charged into the cannon's mouth to obtain glory. He was merely *following* orders, like the professional military man that he was.

While on the subject of Custer rendezvousing with Gibbon—oddly enough, the vanishing act by General George Crook has not come under scrutiny. After his humiliation on the Rosebud, Crook should have dispatched messengers to Terry at the Powder River base camp and informed him of the whereabouts of his one-thousand-man column. Crook should then have taken up the trail of Sitting Bull's village, which would not have been difficult to follow. Terry could have coordinated efforts between Crook and Custer, and at least two prongs of the three-column pincer movement they had designed would have struck the village in force. But Crook was missing in action and became the weak link in the campaign strategy that he had helped devise.

Now that the subject of the orders has been dismissed as a smoke screen, the second most criticized action taken by Custer that day has been his decision to separate his command into three battalions at the mouth of Reno Creek on his advance toward the village. In fact, this subject has been one of the primary reasons many armchair Napoléons have given for the defeat.

Those scholars have argued that Custer's total command of nearly six hundred fighting men would have been quite a formidable force had it swept into the village in force. Consequently, Custer had weakened his ability to contend with the overwhelming number of warriors by separating his command.

Historians have been so intent on treating Little Bighorn as a lone entity—as if it had been the only engagement of Custer's career—that they have failed to factor in the experience he had gained in previous battles. Few cavalry officers throughout American history have charged the cannon's mouth with as much frequency or with as much success as George Armstrong Custer.

Part of the reason for this modern error in judgment can be attributed to the sad fact that a great number of Little Bighorn scholars are ignorant of Custer's tendencies in battle because they have failed to study and dissect his prior battles, mainly those during the Civil War. He became known for the ability to develop a strategy on the field with a moment's notice that would exploit the weakness of his enemy while making use of the terrain.

At Winchester in September 1864, he had even been permitted to countermand an order on the field from General Phil Sheridan, which is unheard of in military protocol. Had junior officers made that request it would have been considered insubordination. But this demonstrates the trust Sheridan had placed in his star field commander. And Custer, outnumbered as usual, prevailed that day, capturing seven hundred prisoners and seven battle flags.

It can be noted that Custer traditionally separated his command before charging into the enemy. He had employed this tactic time and time again in victories during the Civil War and again at the 1868 Battle of the Washita, where he secured a large Cheyenne village within ten minutes of his charge. He would traditionally dispatch one strike force on a frontal assault of his objective while sending one or more detachments on a flanking movement.

Custer's battle plan at Little Bighorn was devised with the thought—and rightly so—that the Indians would flee, which had been their custom. Had he charged into the village with his entire command from the south, where Reno had been ordered to enter, the thousands of occupants would have raced through the tangled maze of lodges toward the north, where the pony herd was located, with the result being that great numbers would have escaped.

Besides that, the warriors would have had the opportunity to organize a solid defense and effective counterattack if afforded the time to gather on the north end. There may have been nearly six hundred cavalrymen, but there were also fifteen hundred to two thousand warriors, a good many armed with Winchester repeaters. The Indians were familiar with the terrain, and groups of warriors could have deployed across the river on the high ground to maintain a withering fire on the bunched-up horsemen.

Those cavalrymen who would have been threading their way through the complex of tepees and other obstacles would have been met with steady resistance as they advanced and assuredly faced a large force of warriors at the end, if they made it that far, who would cover the getaway by their old men, women, and children. Either way, there also was the chance that the cavalrymen could have been driven from the village or at the very least stalled completely while the occupants fled. In either case, casualties for the cavalry would have been high.

As a last resort, the Indians could have stampeded thousands of ponies through the village from the north directly at the oncoming cavalry. This tactic would have stopped the cavalrymen in their tracks. The warriors would have hated to place their precious ponies at risk, but the safety of their families was far more important. And they still would have had plenty of ponies left over in the herd estimated at up to twenty thousand to ride away from the attack—breaking up into small bands and vanishing across the prairie.

Consequently, attacking with the entire command from one direction offered the enemy too many options to save themselves.

With that in mind, it would appear that the only logical method of attacking the village would be by separating the command in order to cover escape routes to the west with Benteen and for Custer's detachments to enter the village from the east and north at various points along the natural pathways created by the ravines when Reno charged from the south.

To charge that village head-on with his total command would have been an outdated and impractical European Napoléonic tactic and would surely have been doomed to failure.

Another issue that has been raised has been the question regarding the readiness, or the lack thereof, of the cavalrymen to effectively fight on June 25, 1876. The theories that many of the troopers were untrained raw recruits and that the unit as a whole had succumbed to fatigue by the time they reached the battlefield have been posed as reasons for the Seventh Cavalry's poor showing against the enemy. In fact, more than one author has claimed that Custer's men just wanted to lay down their weapons and go to sleep instead of fighting this enemy.

The first matter of contention pertains to new recruits who lacked proper training and were said to have been called upon to fight alongside seasoned veterans. There can be no question that poorly trained troops are more vulnerable under combat conditions. The ability to fight effectively was dependent upon learning the skills necessary to be proficient in the ways of warfare. Lessons in weaponry and military discipline are essential in order to engender personal confidence and unit cohesiveness when facing the enemy. This competency requires intense training over a period of time. But did a lack of training apply to those soldiers who rode into the Valley of the Little Bighorn?

Records indicate that approximately 150 recruits joined the Seventh Cavalry in 1875, with about 60 of them having prior service. Another 62 new men were said to have joined the unit in early 1876—although only 54 could be verified from regimental rosters on June 25, 1876. The latter men were more than likely untrained in the ways of a cavalryman, as their daily activities were consumed by guard duty, fatigue duty, and the monotonous post routine.

This lack of training for the new recruits can be placed on the shoulders of Major Marcus A. Reno, who commanded the Seventh Cavalry in Custer's absence during preparations for the campaign. Reno neglected to schedule target practice training or instruction in the rudiments of cavalry tactics. Granted, it did not take an expert to figure out how to aim and fire the Springfield Model 1873 or the Colt .45 revolver. But, with respect to the Springfield trapdoor carbine, there was a technique of loading and extracting that required proper learning and practice in order to fire the maximum number of rounds per minute. Training in horsemanship—other than feeding, grooming, and mucking out stalls—had been lacking as well.

At first glance it would appear that these new recruits were a detriment to the efficiency of the Seventh Cavalry against the Sioux and Cheyenne—if they indeed had been called upon for a combat role.

A check of regimental rosters confirms that at the time of the battle a total of thirty-seven new recruits—those who had signed up in 1876—did not accompany Custer. He had wisely left these recruits on detached duty at the Powder River base camp, with one at Fort Abraham Lincoln, another in confinement, and two en route. Nine had been detailed with the pack train escort, while only four remained with companies assigned to Reno's battalion—including Private Theodore Goldin, who was awarded the Medal of Honor—and two of those had years of prior service with the infantry. No new recruits were members of the companies that comprised Custer's command.

Therefore, the charge that untrained recruits contributed to Custer's defeat can be readily dismissed.

The second allegation concerning readiness charges that the cavalrymen were too fatigued to fight by the time they had arrived in the Valley of the

Little Bighorn. The regiment had traveled approximately 113 miles with little sleep or nourishment between June 22 and 25. A long, hard march such as that can certainly create a state of tiredness that would prevent anyone from functioning at peak performance. Field rations during the previous month had consisted mainly of hardtack and bacon, with the occasional supplement of wild game. Fatigue and malnourishment unquestionably sap the spirit and can result in a breakdown of discipline and morale. These cavalrymen, however, were proud, trained professionals serving in an elite unit and were expected to perform under the most adverse conditions. A number of these troopers had braved freezing temperatures and a blizzard to successfully attack Black Kettle's village at the Battle of the Washita.

There exists another element that must be considered when assessing a soldier's readiness to fight. The one factor that can overcome fatigue and hunger is being under attack and hearing that bullet or arrow zip past your head too close for comfort. As anyone who has experienced combat is aware, adrenaline-fueled energy plays a major role in quickly readying the body and mind for battle. Like a slap in the face, senses and concentration are heightened when the first round has been fired and, although fatigue may become a factor during a prolonged battle, men trained to fight usually respond in an admirable fashion in the short term. Whether Custer's men could have fared better had they enjoyed a good night's sleep and a full belly is a moot point.

Another debate that has ensued for years was over the issue of whether or not the Model 1873 Springfield carbines that the cavalrymen carried into battle malfunctioned and thereby contributed to the defeat. The controversy stems from the fact that the weapon was known after firing to frequently fail to properly extract its spent .45/55-caliber copper cartridge casing, which expanded when hot. That failure, combined with a faulty extractor mechanism and common dirt, could cause the head of the cartridge to be torn away when the block was opened. This would leave the cartridge cylinder remaining inside the chamber, which required manual removal with a pocketknife before reloading and firing. This extraction malfunction problem had been noted in 1872 by the board of officers who selected the carbine for use by the army but at that time was not considered serious enough to scrap the weapon.

There is no doubt that if this malfunction occurred with enough frequency during the battle the troopers would have been seriously affected in firepower. Therefore, the question that must be posed is: With what frequency did this defect occur on June 25, 1876, when it really mattered?

And these numbers have been uncovered and analyzed over the years by Drs. Douglas D. Scott and Richard A. Fox, Jr. These two archaeologists found during the initial study of items from excavations on the battlefield that very few .45/55-caliber cartridge casings displayed any evidence of pry or scratch marks, such as those by a pocketknife that would have permanently scarred a hot casing. On the Custer portion of the field only 3 of 88 casings could have been involved in an extraction jam. Seven out of 257 fit this category on the Reno-Benteen hilltop site.

Sioux chief Gall mentioned that he witnessed soldiers throwing away their long guns in favor of their short guns. There is the likelihood that those men had simply run out of ammunition for their carbines. Each cavalryman carried only fifty .45/55 cartridges in his cartridge belt. Fifty additional rounds were located in his saddlebags, which would have been lost when the Indians stampeded the horses. Fifty rounds fired in the frantic heat of battle could be expended in a very short period of time. The Colt revolvers, for which they carried twenty rounds, may have been more effective at short range, but, again, twenty rounds would not last long.

Custer had dispatched an urgent message to Captain Benteen that emphasized bringing up the ammunition packs in a hurry. Benteen dawdled along the trail, never arriving to assist Custer. There is a distinct possibility that rather than blame any malfunction of the carbine on the defeat, the more logical explanation would be that the cavalrymen simply ran out of ammunition and were overwhelmed by their enemy.

Perhaps that also explains why Custer's command was strung out along Battle Ridge rather than formed in a tight defensive position. The companies to the south, led by First Lieutenant James Calhoun, may have been sent to escort Benteen and the ammunition—or even to locate the pack train themselves—and return with ammo but were stopped in their tracks at that point by an overwhelming number of warriors.

If the numbers of damaged cartridge casings posed by the archaeological digs are representative, and there is no reason to believe otherwise, it would appear that malfunction of the carbine from that source was quite minimal and could not be considered a factor in the defeat. Ammo not arriving in time along with reinforcements could certainly be considered a more relevant factor.

The question has been debated about whether the Indians were better armed than the cavalrymen. There can be no question that the cavalry was outgunned by the Indians that day—and not necessarily due to better firearms but simply by sheer numbers.

Customary Indian tactics called for them to remain a safe distance away—hidden by tall grass, bushes, and terrain features—while they fired an endless stream of arcing arrows at the pinned-down cavalrymen. Add to that arrow barrage the firearms, and the all-important fire superiority certainly favored the Indians in a battle of attrition.

There can also be no doubt that the modern repeaters made quite a difference. General George Crook, in a September 25, 1876, report, stated: "Of the difficulties with which we have had to contend, it may be well to remark, that when the Sioux Indian was armed with a bow and arrow he was more formidable, fighting as he does most of the time on horseback, than when he got the old fashioned muzzle loading rifle. But when he came into possession of the breech loader and metallic cartridge, which allows him to load and fire from his horse with perfect ease, he became at once ten thousand times more formidable."

Some military tacticians who may not be familiar with the rugged terrain leading to the battlefield have suggested that Gatling guns would have provided Custer the firepower necessary to defeat the overwhelming number of Indians that he faced. In fact, Custer had been offered the use of three Gatling guns by General Alfred H. Terry. Custer at first accepted the offer and then about an hour later changed his mind, deciding that the guns would impede his march.

Surely, the formidable firepower that those guns, which were invented in 1861, could have brought into play would have been devastating to any enemy. The Gatling gun, forerunner of the machine gun, worked on the principle of having a soldier turn a crank that fed ammunition from a hopper into either six or ten barrels and could fire up to 350 rounds per minute.

The downside of these guns' operation was that they had not been modified much since their invention and were known to frequently malfunction—often jamming due to residue from black powder or overheating. Also, they were designed to repel a massed attack of the enemy, such as was customary in European warfare, whereas the Indians would not have marched into the line of fire in the tradition of Redcoats. Another disadvantage was that the guns were mounted on large wheels, which meant that during operation the gun crew would be standing upright and this would make them sitting ducks to Indian snipers.

But perhaps the most negative aspect of Gatlings in turning the tide of a battle such as the Little Bighorn was the difficulty in simply getting them to the battlefield. The guns were drawn by four horses, and each obstacle would have required unhitching the horses in favor of manpower to maneuver the guns to an agreeable location, then re-hitching the horses in order to continue. Taking into consideration the difficult terrain on Custer's march, the guns would have greatly impeded his progress.

This fact can be evidenced by Terry's own battery—the one he had offered to Custer. Gibbon's Twentieth Infantry was in charge of the guns and was unable to keep up with the column.

In his defense, General Nelson Miles wrote to General William T. Sherman on July 8, 1876, that Gatlings "are worthless for Indian fighting."

There are also scholars who suggest that Custer would have fared better had he taken the Gatling guns—but not necessarily on account of their firepower. The guns would have delayed Custer's march to the extent that he would have rendezvoused with the Terry-Gibbon column and unified their commands to attack the village.

To be fair, for the disadvantages outlined earlier Custer was justified in his decision to refuse the Gatling guns.

Apparently Custer had discussed artillery with scout Fred Girard prior to the march. Girard was of the opinion that the Indians would not charge the Gatlings or simply stand around getting picked off. The scout told Custer that a twelve-pounder cannon would be a much better choice of artillery. They could destroy a village in quick order by lobbing shells from a mile away.

That theory had already been proven by Colonel Kit Carson in early

November 1864 at Adobe Walls, Texas. Carson had commanded fewer men than Custer and faced more Indians—in fact, more than anyone ever had or would on the plains—and was able to destroy a large Kiowa-Comanche village and extricate himself from being surrounded by several thousand warriors because of the two twelve-pounder mountain howitzers that he had brought along. Otherwise, Carson assuredly would have suffered Custer's fate.

Still, it was not Custer's custom to allow anything to delay his march to the objective. And, in this case, the village would have been packed and gone before he could have fired even one volley.

Thirty-seven years after the Little Bighorn battle an Arikara scout named Red Star through an interpreter stated that George Armstrong Custer told his Ree scouts before departing from Fort Lincoln in May 1876 that a victory against the Sioux would make him the "Great Father" in Washington.

Most famously, author Mari Sandoz used Red Star's statement to outline her idea of Custer's plan to gain the nomination of the Democratic Party, which was meeting in St. Louis June 27–29.

The theory was that Charley Reynolds would duplicate his Black Hills dash to a telegraph office and relay the news of the victory over the Sioux to the floor of the convention, where Custer's supporters would push for his nomination. This ambition would explain the motivation behind Custer's hasty attack.

This account, however, has led some to assume that Custer intended to use the Little Bighorn campaign as a launching pad into the presidency of the United States—perhaps to the extent that he would become reckless in his zeal to erase Grant's insult over the Belknap Scandal and to occupy the office that Grant presently held.

There is no question that at some future date Custer would have made an attractive candidate to the Democratic Party for which he had performed admirable service over the years. Military commanders traditionally were mentioned as qualified contenders for the presidency after winning a major war. And had Custer defeated the Sioux on June 25, 1876, his already high popularity with the public would have soared to presidential heights.

It is doubtful, however, that Custer at that point in his career even remotely dreamed of the presidency. In fact, it is absurd to believe, given his prior embarrassing dabblings in politics, that he thought himself suited as a politician rather than a soldier.

In 1866, he had accompanied President Andrew Johnson on his "Swing Around the Circle," a tour around the country designed to win support for the president's Southern policy. Custer was mercilessly attacked in the North for mingling with Southern traitors, which compelled him to abandon the tour before its end to escape protesters and adverse publicity. Repercussions from his testimony at the Belknap hearings had served to further convince him that he presently lacked adequate political skills for national office.

Another problem would be the timing. Word of a victory over the Sioux—much less Custer in person—could not have reached the convention in St. Louis in time to make any impact on the party's nominee, regardless of whether Charley Reynolds had killed several horses in an effort to reach a telegraph.

If Custer had indeed in early 1876 tendered presidential aspirations the perfect platform for a run had been presented to him. He had been offered a contract by the Redpath Lyceum Bureau, a Boston talent agency, that called for him to make a speech five nights a week for four to five months at an astounding two hundred dollars per lecture. Not only could he have earned more than ten times his annual army salary in that short period, but he also could have placed his carefully constructed views, thrilling war stories, and considerable charm before an already-adoring nationwide audience. Although it had been suggested that the tour would begin in the spring, had Custer been setting sights on the presidency that year he could have pushed up the date to suit his ambitions. He almost certainly could have received a leave of absence and not participated in the Little Bighorn Campaign in order to fulfill the schedule of speaking engagements.

The lecture tour could have concluded with Custer's triumphant entrance at the Democratic Party convention. By that time he would have gained the admiration and confidence of the public and, that combined with his influential party benefactors, his friendship with a number of leading congressmen, his association with New York newspapers, and the fact that he had exposed fraud in the Grant administration and been punished for his actions, perhaps could have resulted in the nomination. But Custer had turned down this lucrative opportunity to gain publicity for himself in order to remain with the army on active duty.

That appealing scenario of lecturing to help gain the nomination, however, may have been in the back of his mind for the distant future. The lecture tour certainly would have been available as a reward after Little Bighorn and beyond. He certainly had tales to tell—and without a doubt wanted to collect more adventures before he was put out to pasture by the army.

He was only thirty-six years old, much too young to seriously consider the staid chief executive position, an old man's job. And another relevant consideration: it would be doubtful that this man of good humor and sensitivity who craved constant activity could picture himself mired down in the daily partisan bickering and boring policy meetings inherent to that high office. Perhaps when he was older he may have entertained a run, but not in 1876 when the West promised excitement for years to come.

If Custer truly had made any statement of that nature to his Arikara scouts before Little Bighorn it was probably little more than playful banter, an indication of the importance that a victory against the Sioux would be for his career. More than likely Custer was envisioning for himself the reward of a brigadier general's star, an appointment made by the president when a vacancy occurred—regardless of seniority—to a worthy recipient. And a victory over Sitting Bull and Crazy Horse would certainly make George Armstrong Custer worthy of promotion. But Custer failed to attain that victory.

This reason for the defeat remains behind an insidious smoke screen to blame the scapegoat who could not defend himself.

Each of these issues has been presented over the years as a reason for Custer's defeat, with most of them pointing the finger of blame at Custer for his personal actions. There can be found, however, the real reason for the defeat—and one must only look to the source of the conspiracy theories for the answers: the military cover-up.

Eighteen

———◆———

What Really Happened?

Contrary to the assumption of many, if not most, modern scholars who believe that George Armstrong Custer's plan of attack was hastily devised, reckless, and destined to fail, his battle plan was in fact well thought out and logical and could have—should have—succeeded. He did not blunder whatsoever but designed a plan with the potential to be as effective as any in his career.

But how do we know what he intended when apparently no one who survived the fight was told the specific details? It does not take a military genius to understand exactly how Custer envisioned the unfolding of his plan. Plenty of evidence exists to support a strategy that was nothing less than brilliant, especially given the terrain.

According to Custer's battle plan, Reno's charge into the village would have caused the Indians to flee blindly into the hands of Custer's command, which had ridden to the east and north. It would then have been a matter of securing the village and deploying a tight perimeter to guard against a counterattack from those who had slipped through the seams, while details of other troopers chased down the stragglers.

By that time, Benteen and his battalion, along with the pack train of ammunition and an additional eighty-five men, would have arrived as reinforcements—as ordered by Custer. Captured Indian women and children would have been held as hostages with which to bargain and assure that a counter-attack in force would not be forthcoming for fear of the captives being in harm's way. A systematic destruction of the village, its valuable contents, and the huge pony herd would then have taken place. Messengers would have been dispatched to hurry the Terry-Gibbon column to the scene. Even if Custer had become surrounded by survivors of the attack, he had enough firepower within the village proper to maintain his position until Terry and reinforcements arrived.

In the preceding scenario, it would not have mattered how many Indians escaped Custer's trap. They would have been demoralized, split into small bands running for their lives, and on the verge of poverty, which would have encouraged many to submit to the reservation.

The conduct of Major Marcus Reno during the period of time that his command remained in a defensive position on the hilltop under siege by the hostile Indians has been the subject of controversy. Suffice it to say, had a man of lesser discipline than Benteen been second-in-command there might have been another bloody retreat similar to one Reno had ordered earlier that day from the timber to the hilltop.

The questions about Reno's behavior after his retreat will never be resolved to everyone's satisfaction—but it is a moot point. It does not matter how Reno handled himself on the hilltop. He and his men should never have been on that hilltop in the first place. At that point, Reno's command should have been within the confines of Sitting Bull's village. Reno was only on the hilltop because he had not executed his orders but decided on his own to shirk his responsibility and retreat to that position.

Major Reno had been ordered by Custer in the person of adjutant W. W. Cooke to cross the river and charge the Indian village, with the alleged parting words to the effect that "you will be supported by the whole outfit." That was all Reno had been told. He had no other knowledge of Custer's overall plan, only his part in it, which was normal military operating procedure. And Reno's part in the plan was to charge the village, not to wonder about Custer's location or how his battalion would be supported by Custer.

By his own admission, during the charge in the valley Reno kept looking behind him for any sign of reinforcement by Custer's command, which, to his dismay, did not appear. This led Reno to believe—according to him—that Custer had abandoned him and he would be obliged to fend for himself. That fate evidently did not appeal to the major. Therefore, he aborted his charge one-quarter of a mile from the village.

It is quite obvious, however, that Custer had never intended for his command to appear behind or even beside Reno. Custer never meant to *follow* Reno's charge into the village with reinforcements, as Reno even acknowledged in his official report. Reno was part diversion, part strike force.

The Indians in the village were unaware of Custer's presence on the eastern bluffs. He had the all-important element of surprise in his favor, just as Reno had enjoyed until he aborted his charge. Custer meant to support Reno when the two commands rendezvoused *inside* the Indian village.

This plan of attack had been Custer's customary tactic during the Civil War and again at Washita. He would execute a frontal assault with one detachment while sending one or two other detachments on a flanking movement. This strategy made it virtually impossible for the enemy to respond quickly enough to effectively repel both attacks.

When Reno charged into that village, which would have caused great chaos within as well as prevented the Indians from organizing any defense or mounting a counterattack, individual units from Custer's command would have by then been descending the various ravines on the field sloping from Battle Ridge and striking the village from a number of locations at once—without any concentrated opposition.

Perhaps all or part of Captain Myles Keogh's detachment would have ridden to strike the village from the north. If not, he would have ridden down the coulees on the upper reaches of the village to strike it at that point. That coordination would have created a massive one-two-three punch—Reno, Custer, and Keogh—and would have made it impossible for the Indians to escape and would have inflicted devastating casualties.

In Reno's defense, apologists have suggested that the Indians that day were just so furious and fed up with the white man that they decided to make a stand and that spelled Custer's doom. The facts do not support this theory.

Reno, who had never witnessed an arrow fired in anger, had every advantage—the upper hand on his charge as well as afterward inside what would have become a chaotic village. This can be evidenced by the fact that not one cavalryman had been shot from his horse by a bullet or an arrow on the approach. Chief Gall had rallied a handful of warriors as a delaying tactic while the women frantically packed the village and there was some return fire, but there had not been time for the Indians to mount a concerted effort to repulse Reno.

If these Indians at the edge of the village had been such a threat, why was it then that Reno subsequently lost only two men whose horses had bolted and taken them into the village during his presence in the valley before retreating and during his indecisive wait in the timber? He suffered no other losses until he failed to maintain control of his command in the timber.

Reno and others have made the case that charging into the village would have been tantamount to suicide. In his imagination, Reno saw too many Indians for him to fight. Where did he conjure up this idea? Few warriors had emerged to confront him. For all he knew, all the men from the village were out hunting or on a war party far distant from that valley. For him to imagine great numbers at that point was sheer folly.

In dissecting a battle plan, it must be noted that every element, every component, every part, must be executed properly for the plan to succeed.

In battles throughout American history, success has been dependent on every component of a battle plan working properly, with or without knowledge of the other components. Attacks by land, sea, and air may be coordinated, but each commander would have only been informed about his own part in that plan. If he takes care of his mission and the other commanders take care of their missions, the battle plan, if drawn up properly, has a good chance of bringing about success.

In 1789, Article I, Section 8, of the United States Constitution provided Congress the power to regulate land and naval forces. On April 10, 1806, the United States Congress enacted 101 Articles of War—military law—that applied to both the Army and the Navy. This system of military justice was in effect at the time of the 1876 battle and continued to operate as the rule of military law until 1951, when the present-day Uniform Code of Military Justice came into effect.

Article 9 of the Articles of War stated: "Any officer or soldier who shall strike his superior officer, or draw or lift up any weapon, or offer any violence against him, being in the execution of his office, on any pretense whatsoever, *or shall disobey any lawful command of his superior officer,* shall suffer death, or such other punishment as shall, according to the nature of his offense, be inflicted upon him by the sentence of a court-martial."

Not surprisingly, disobedience of orders was deemed important enough to be placed right up there with killing the commanding officer—that was how seriously obeying orders from a superior officer was taken. The gravity of an offense of this nature was further reinforced by the recommended punishment—death. And this disobedience was not reserved exclusively for orders delivered in combat—any lawful order in a garrison or in the field held the same serious consequences.

In these days and times, military personnel who disobey even the pettiest or most insignificant order are generally brought up on charges and punished in some manner, losing rank and/or a forfeiture of pay. It is widely known that a soldier today, just as those in 1876, does not have the right to question an order or obey it at his or her discretion. An order from a superior officer is to be carried out without question, or debate, or complaint, or risk—or else.

Custer's battle plan had three basic parts—the most important being Reno's charge on the village and Custer's descent from the eastern slope. Benteen's part in the plan became more relevant when he was ordered to hurry to the field with ammunition.

No one disagrees that Major Reno was issued a lawful order by Custer to charge the village with his battalion.

There was no discretion given in Reno's orders. He was not told to use his best judgment on whether or not to charge the village. Subordinates obey orders from their superior officers—without question—or face punishment. Many a soldier throughout history has charged the cannon's mouth under more desperate circumstances when ordered to do so. Reno was told to charge. It was not by any stretch of the imagination his prerogative to consider the odds or risk before carrying out his orders. It would not have mattered if he had observed two thousand entrenched, heavily armed warriors waiting for him outside that village. He would still have been expected to charge. If Custer had ordered Reno to execute a one-man charge by himself into that hostile village,

Reno would have been obliged to obey. Moreover, Reno should have had faith that his well-trained cavalrymen would be up to the task of attacking that village and being victorious.

On July 3, 1863, George Armstrong Custer, a general for only four days, assumed command of a twenty-three-hundred-man Union cavalry detachment that was poised to charge directly into a force of six thousand Confederate cavalrymen and infantrymen. "Good heavens!" cried one Union officer. "We will all be swallowed up!" Custer led his force from four horse lengths to the front and they slammed into the enemy on what could only be called a suicide mission. He could have left his men entrenched and waited for this oncoming six-thousand-man sledgehammer to pound into them. Instead, he took the initiative, and, amazingly, he beat the odds that day and drove those Rebels back up the hill to their original position. It may have been the turning point of the battle.

But Major Marcus Reno failed to charge the Indian village as ordered by George Armstrong Custer, an inexcusable failure of command.

Further, Reno had no right to know the other components of Custer's battle plan or even how it was intended to unfold. That information was simply none of his business. He only had to understand his own mission, which obviously he did. He should have known that if he carried out his part of the battle plan and every other detachment did the same then there was a good chance that they would prevail.

And what happens when orders by a commander are disobeyed in combat? When a battle plan falls apart—when only one part of it is not executed properly—the odds of total failure rise substantially. It can be a fatal mistake. In such cases, the lives of men are placed in dire jeopardy.

And that was exactly what happened at the Little Bighorn on June 25, 1876. Major Marcus Reno disobeyed the orders of his superior. Consequently, not only many of the men in his detachment were killed, but Custer and his battalion were massacred also—all because Reno did not follow orders.

When Reno halted his charge and formed a line of dismounted skirmishers, he afforded the Indians an opportunity to assemble in numbers sufficient enough to counterattack. Had Reno carried out his orders and charged the village, Custer's troops would have been there to greet him—just as Cooke had indicated. Reno would have been supported by the whole outfit.

Instead, Custer made an attempt to probe the village with a detachment sent down Medicine Tail Coulee, which was forced back by warriors who would not have been available for defense had Reno penetrated the village as ordered. Custer's other detachments were forced to retreat or remain on the eastern bluffs, as sitting ducks, when Reno ran away and left Custer's command high and dry.

Furthermore, had Benteen ridden to the rescue immediately as ordered instead of dawdling along the trail, another 125 troopers would have roared into this chaotic village to wreak havoc upon their enemy. But Benteen, for reasons known only to himself, chose to disobey Custer's order as well. And, when Benteen later met Reno, his order from Custer became Reno's order. In other words, both men should have immediately led their commands to the aid of Custer. Instead, they cowered on the hilltop and shamefully accused Custer of abandoning *them*.

It should be noted that the outcome of the battle decidedly would have been different had Captain Frederick Benteen been in command of the battalion in the valley instead of Reno. In spite of his hatred for Custer, Benteen, a fearless soldier, would have slammed into that village as ordered, which would have permitted Custer's strategy to proceed as planned. But Custer evidently had felt obligated to hand Reno, his second-in-command, the honor and glory of commanding the heroic valley charge.

The battle plan would have followed as such:

Reno charges down the valley into the village.

Custer stealthily descends down the coulees from the eastern bluffs and wades into the village at intervals.

Benteen rushes up with reinforcements and ammunition packs.

Executed vigorously, it was a brilliant plan devised by Custer, using the terrain like a chessboard and moving his pieces to checkmate his opponent. No other theory about this battle makes any sense whatsoever.

The Seventh Cavalry would have routed the Indians that day, killing and capturing great numbers of them, destroying a huge village, its valuable contents, and the pony herd, which would have crippled those who escaped to the extent that eventual submission would have been the only alternative. The victory would have been beneficial to the country by making the territory a more peaceful place for people to travel through or settle.

The portrayal of Custer as a bumbling tactician who led his men into certain death due to his ego and lust for glory is simply not supported by the evidence. The outcome of the battle assuredly would have been different—regardless of the number of Indians—had Custer's subordinate officers simply obeyed their orders.

Reno's guilt cannot be denied. Major Marcus A. Reno committed the ultimate betrayal for an army officer. His disobedience of orders by failing to charge the village cost the Seventh Cavalry almost three hundred lives that day. And punishment should have been doled out according to the Articles of War.

If Reno's subordinate officers would have been more competent or aware of what was happening sooner, one of them should have either shot Reno or placed him under arrest and assumed command for the good of the unit. There is no worse offense in the military than letting down your fellow soldiers under enemy fire. It is *the* ultimate betrayal.

A person enters military service and abruptly forfeits all the freedom and rights granted under the Constitution and lives in a dictatorship in which he or she *must* obey the whims of even the most unreasonable or unstable superior in rank. Such a scenario is difficult for anyone to imagine. A soldier is on duty every minute of the day and night for the remaining years on his or her enlistment, no matter the inconvenience to their personal life. If they are told to jump, they may ask, "How high?" But they *will* jump.

Anyone who has served in the military can attest to the fact that Marcus Reno disobeyed orders. It is an open-and-shut case. But many people think that Reno had an option to carry out his orders or not and therefore did nothing wrong. Foolish thought to anyone who has worn the uniform. The most inconsequential infraction of rules in the minds of civilians could lead to prison time and a dishonorable discharge in military life. This conclusion, however, does not always compute in the equations of those researchers working in the safe confines of a classroom or a library who lack firsthand knowledge.

As a result of this absence of military service, most students of the battle have never experienced combat. If one has never heard a shot fired at them in anger by an enemy trying to kill them, they cannot imagine the effect it has on the behavior and senses of them or their comrades. How men react under enemy fire and what is expected of them, especially in leadership roles, is essential to understanding any battle. There are consequences to every act executed under fire. There is no room for miscalculation or hesitation—or disobedience of orders.

The controlled terror of combat cannot be effectively re-created or simulated in a classroom, or in a video game, or in movies or by reading diaries, journals, or accounts of battles or hearing about it firsthand from veterans. There is no other way, not even extensive military training, that will allow an understanding of what it is to stand on the sanguinary field of man versus man fighting to the death. It must be experienced.

This fact was perhaps summed up best by none other than George Armstrong Custer. On Sunday, July 21, 1861, Custer found himself on the field at Bull Run, the first meaningful battle of the Civil War. His cavalry unit was protecting an artillery battery, which was under fire from enemy artillery.

Custer later wrote: "I remember well the strange hissing and exceedingly vicious sound of the first cannon shot I heard. Of course I had often heard the sound made by cannon balls while passing through the air during my artillery practice at West Point, but a man listens with changed interest when the direction of the balls is toward instead of away from him. They seem to utter a different language when fired in angry battle from that put forth in the tamer practice of drill."

Military service and combat is indeed a different language and a different world, and if one has not learned that language and lived in that reality they will find it almost impossible to comprehend.

Accordingly, it has been rather easy for noncombatants and those inexperienced in military affairs to generate excuses for the malfeasance of Reno and Benteen and to place the blame on Custer, who was not available to defend his true intentions and thereby became a convenient target.

Also, not too many people who delve into the Little Bighorn battle admit to having an intimate familiarity with Custer's incredible Civil War career—possibly due to the lack of readily accessible material—and therefore treat

Little Bighorn as a lone entity. People who wish to comment on the Little Big-horn would be well served to learn those battlefield strategies and tendencies that made Custer a national hero.

By the same token, this battle against the Sioux must be examined through the eyes of 1876, not from the twenty-first-century standards by people who tend to ignore necessary truisms of that distant time and replace them with societal rules of today.

There is a darker, more sinister reason—one rarely proposed for fear of ac-cusations of prejudice—why Custer has been blamed for the tactical decisions that led to this defeat, however. A disgraceful school of alleged scholars have desperately searched for any way to place the blame for this devastating de-feat on George Armstrong Custer. They have grasped at the flimsiest of straws and cited the absurd during this demonization process where one person or entity must be denigrated in order to support the rise of another. Why?

Some so-called revisionists hold to the opinion that they must attempt to absolve the Lakota Sioux from all culpability for their actions that day. In or-der to elevate the role of the Sioux from enemy to honorable in this battle—with the thought that they had been poltically wronged and thereby had a reputable cause—Custer and his Seventh Cavalry must be painted as villains. This methodology is simply a misguided effort of building up wrong by pull-ing down right. It is virtually impossible to accurately analyze evidence when influenced by such a preconceived notion.

These people who believe they are righteously righting some terrible his-toric political wrong have been willing to compromise their integrity and cred-ibility to try to prove their opinion. Those with a bias against Custer believe that the soldiers got what they deserved that day and they are *expected to and indeed must* portray Custer as a bumbling tactician in order to sell that ab-surd misconception.

True revisionism constitutes a continuing dialogue between the past and present that is based on fact and adds to the record without compromising the truth. The process of changing history without regard for the credibility of evidence is not revisionism—it is historical terrorism that cheats the student of an accurate portrayal of events.

Consequently, this pseudo-revisionist agenda that discourages independent research and fails to follow the pathway of evidence leads to faulty conclusions. Myths are accepted in place of evidence and then perpetuated, the result being a subtle form of brainwashing that has been shamefully passed down from one generation of unwitting scholars to the next.

To study this battle is to enter a maze that heretofore may have been deemed without a verifiable outlet. Now gaping holes have been punched through the walls of this maze that lead to a shining vision of that illusive open exit—at least until the next red herrings are brought forth with the hope of condemning Custer and exonerating Reno, and the Sioux and Cheyenne, and the representatives of the government who ordered the military action of 1876.

Nineteen

Heroes and Villains

The initial interest in establishing a lasting memorial for George Armstrong Custer and his men was created by newspapers that began publishing sensational stories soon after the battle about half-buried bodies strewn across the barren field. This revelation caused an outcry from the public and high-ranking army officers, who demanded that Congress allocate funds for a cemetery to properly bury the fallen.

Finally, on August 1, 1879, Custer Battlefield National Cemetery was established by General Order No. 78. Troopers from Fort Custer were called upon to make the field more presentable, which included erecting a log memorial on top of Custer Hill and re-marking the scattered graves with a substantial wooden stake.

In 1881, the log memorial was replaced by a huge white granite monument on which the names of the dead—a number of them misspelled—had been inscribed. The remains of the enlisted troopers were at that time collected from their various graves and reinterred in a mass grave at the base of the monument. White marble headstones replaced the wooden markers in 1890 to designate the places where the cavalrymen had fallen. Three years later, the first superintendent was named to oversee the care of the cemetery.

In 1930, the parcel of land that was the location of the Reno-Benteen hilltop fight was added. The two distant battlefields were connected by a right-of-way road between them. Ten years later the National Park Service of the Interior Department assumed responsibility from the War Department for the area. In 1946, the historic site was renamed Custer Battlefield National Monument and the principal mission became the study of the battle—primarily from the standpoint of the soldiers, although that has gradually changed over the years to include the Indian side of the story.

In 1983, a prairie fire swept across six hundred grassy acres of the battlefield, which removed much of the obscuring vegetation and made the area suitable for examination. James V. Court, the superintendent at that time, had the foresight to wonder what artifacts might have been exposed that could shed new light on the famous battle and thereby enhance the interpretive programs at the battlefield. Court called in a young archaeologist named Richard A. Fox, Jr., who examined the field and prepared two reports indicating that there was a great potential of uncovering items of significance.

Fox submitted his reports to Douglas D. Scott, Chief of the Rocky Mountain Division, Midwest Archaeological Center, National Park Service. Scott also was impressed with the potential and organized a two-year project in which he and Fox would serve as co-principal investigators. National Park Service approval for this dig was obtained, but no funding. The Custer Battlefield Historical & Museum Association, a nonprofit historical interest group, came forward to finance the project. In 1984, Scott, Fox, and about one hundred volunteers embarked on an initial dig that lasted about five weeks.

The battlefield was swept with electronic sensing devices—metal detectors—and each site where a possible relic was indicated was marked with a small plastic flag. That area was then probed with a trowel, and every item found was recorded and coded into a computer with a specific number. Among the four thousand artifacts that the dig unearthed were buttons from various types of clothing, pieces of firearms, a watch, coins, a pocketknife, iron arrowheads, horse trappings, bone fragments, and, most of all, a huge number of bullets and cartridge casings from many different weapons. The computer coding assisted in generating a map that detailed battle events from the position of found bullets and cartridge casings.

One of the more interesting discoveries was that of a nearly complete skeleton they named "Trooper Mike." These remains were examined by famed forensic anthropologist Clyde Snow, who estimated that this trooper was between nineteen and twenty-two years old, five feet eight, and weighed 150 to 160 pounds. Mike had been shot twice in the chest, with one bullet fragment embedded in his left wrist. Post-death mutilation was indicated by his shattered skull, his knocked-out teeth, and his right thighbone gashed by six chopping blows, likely from a hatchet. Trooper Mike's remains were reburied in Custer National Cemetery in June 1985.

There have been subsequent excavations in various areas in and around the battlefield that have resulted in additional artifacts. The discovery of artifacts during these excavations has been most helpful in answering certain questions about the battle, such as identifying weapons used by both sides, with shell casings, bones, buckles, et cetera.

But perhaps too much emphasis has been placed on the specific locations of those finds. The battlefield lies within a ragged terrain of ravines and hillsides that have been exposed to the elements—blizzards, gully-washing downpours, hurricane-force winds, et cetera—for over a century and a quarter.

Anyone who has lived in comparable terrain knows that objects are subject to relocation, often by great distances, during even the most common storm. It has even been documented that the Little Bighorn River itself has changed course in that period of time. Locations where artifacts have been found cannot be discounted as a guide for speculation as to positions of groups or individuals or plotting troops' movements but must be viewed with a skeptical eye.

In 1991, the battlefield was renamed Little Bighorn Battlefield National Monument by an act of Congress. The mandate also provided that an Indian Memorial was to be built in the vicinity of the Seventh Cavalry Monument.

This name change and new monument has provoked an ongoing controversy among those who respect the sacrifice of Custer and his cavalrymen as they served their country. Some people believe that his name should have remained on the battlefield and further that the addition of a monument honoring people hostile to our country is an insult to the United States Army—as well as the other branches—much less to the United States of America.

This change in the official attitude opened the door in 1996 for then battlefield superintendent Gerard Baker, a Mandan-Hidatsa Indian and paid representative of the United States government, to not only permit but also organize what he called an "Attack at Dawn." On June 25, Indians rode horses onto the national monument and "counted coup" by using a stick to hit the stone obelisk that marks the mass grave of over two hundred Seventh Cavalry troopers.

There are those who have worn the uniform of this country who disapprove of this defiling of a resting place of their brave brothers in arms by such a disgraceful act by a former enemy and consider the actions that day to be despicable and cowardly. They hold to the belief that desecrating the memory of these Seventh Cavalry soldiers is tantamount to desecrating every American who has ever fallen in combat. And, in military terms, that is not what this country stands for—and too many flag-draped coffins have attested to that fact.

Today visitors can stroll through portions of the battlefield on walkways and drive the two-lane road from Custer Hill to the Reno-Benteen defense site. Park personnel are available to provide tour information and to offer free lectures during the summer months. The visitor center and historical museum on the grounds feature an interesting array of Custer, Seventh Cavalry, and Indian artifacts, dioramas, artwork, maps, photographs, books for sale, and an impressive collection of documents. Custer's widow, Libbie, donated nearly fifty thousand letters and papers to the museum.

The adjoining cemetery, Custer National Cemetery, holds the remains of such notable figures as Custer's longtime orderly John Burkman; Lieutenant John J. Crittenden; Curly the scout; Dr. George E. Lord; and a mass grave for twenty-one soldiers killed in the 1877 Snake Creek fight against the Nez Percé.

Meanwhile, the living were left to deal with the loss of their loved ones. Maria Custer was understandably grief stricken following the deaths of her three sons, a son-in-law, and a grandson in the Little Bighorn battle. She lamented, "How can I bear it? All my boys gone." For unknown reasons, she did not attend the ceremony at West Point when her oldest son was reinterred on October 10, 1877. Maria passed away in January 1882 at the age of seventy-five.

Emanuel Custer, the man who valued family over everything else in his life, had lost three of his beloved sons, Armstrong, Tom, and Boston; a son-in-law, James Calhoun; and a stepgrandson, Autie Reed. Libbie arranged for Emanuel to have Armstrong's horse Dandy, and for years he would proudly ride his son's favorite mount in parades. Emanuel eventually went to live on son Nevin's farm three miles west of Monroe. He passed away on November 27, 1892—two weeks before his eighty-sixth birthday.

Libbie Custer was only thirty-four years old when she received the news at Fort Abraham Lincoln in Dakota Territory that her husband had been killed. She returned to Monroe, Michigan, and contemplated her future. Her life's mission was soon decided when a debate ensued over Custer's actions during that battle. Libbie worked tirelessly to protect the image of her beloved husband and vigorously defended him against those who brought criticism. Her first act was to assist Frederick Whittaker in the writing of his 1876 *A Complete Life of Gen. George A. Custer* by putting personal correspondence at his disposal. This favorable portrayal of Custer would be the predominant view of her husband for many years to come.

In the summer of 1877, Libbie moved from Michigan to New York City to better her opportunities. She had been faced with considerable family debt that had exhausted her funds, and with only a nine-hundred-dollar donation raised by the *Army and Navy Journal* and a thirty-dollar-a-month pension (raised to fifty dollars in 1882), she would be required to find work to support herself. She also commenced raising money that would eventually pay for monuments honoring Custer in Michigan and at West Point.

Libbie and biographer Frederick Whittaker undertook a relentless effort to convince the government to hold an official inquiry into the circumstances surrounding the Little Bighorn battle. Libbie was interested in clearing her husband's name from those who placed blame on him for the defeat.

Whittaker wrote a letter dated May 18, 1878, to Wyoming congressman W. W. Corlett, which demanded an investigation. The letter included the passage: "Information from participants in the battle is to the effect that gross cowardice was displayed by Major Marcus A. Reno." This letter was leaked to the press, which was the last straw for Reno, who requested that the army convene a court of inquiry to investigate his conduct.

By order of President Rutherford B. Hayes, the court convened at the Palmer House in Chicago on January 13, 1879. The examining committee was comprised of three officers—Colonel John H. King, Ninth Infantry, presiding; Colonel Wesley Merritt, Fifth Cavalry; and Lieutenant Colonel W. B. Royall, Third Cavalry. The court reporter was Lieutenant Jesse M. Lee, Ninth Infantry. Members of the Custer family, including Libbie and Maggie Calhoun, attended every session.

Reno was defended by Lyman Gilbert, the assistant attorney general of Pennsylvania. Reno's primary defense of his actions was to blame Custer for not providing him the complete battle plan. He testified that he had been ordered to charge the village and would "be supported by the whole outfit." He interpreted that to mean that Custer was going to follow him into the village. And because he had not observed Custer behind, Reno claimed that he was justified in not charging into the village on what could be likened to a suicide mission.

An examination of Reno's official report of the battle, however, reveals that he expected Custer to attack on the flank. Therefore, it does not take a lawyer to recognize that Reno's defense was based on a contradiction.

Reno, although evidence indicates otherwise, maintained that his retreat, in which about a third of his men became casualties, was a "charge." He also was asked: "Did you go into that fight with feelings of confidence or distrust [of Custer]?" Reno answered: "Well, sir, I had known General Custer a long time, and I had no confidence in his ability as a soldier." This absurd and insulting statement came from a man who had never commanded troops in battle against Indians about an officer who had faced this enemy on a number of occasions with great success.

Incidentally, at the time of this Court of Inquiry there was no reason for anyone to assume that the Enlisted Men's Petition was not authentic. This phony document was presented as evidence and was a huge boost to Reno's case. Here were 235 or 236 credible eyewitnesses who enthusiastically supported the actions of Reno and Benteen that day—most of them without their knowledge.

Reno was also aided by the fact that fellow officers had closed ranks around the elite Seventh Cavalry and did not desire to bring disgrace upon the unit. Stories were carefully altered and answers were often evasive—some officers did not testify for one reason or another. Only one officer, First Lieutenant (and future general) Edward S. Godfrey, supported the charge of cowardice against Reno by stating that the major had displayed "indecision" and "nervous timidity."

The few disparaging words against Reno came from civilians, scout Fred Girard in particular, who pointed out Reno's mishandling of the retreat, and by two packers who accused Reno of drunkenness. Reno defenders have pointed out that mainly civilians condemned Reno, not fellow officers. These misguided defenders evidently have never served in the armed forces.

Anyone who has worn the uniform to this day knows that unit protocol occasionally calls for "cover-ups" in these situations. You simply do not—cannot—bring discredit upon your unit or organization. The whole truth cannot be revealed at times for the good of the outfit, and anyone who betrays that sacred unwritten law faces repercussions from his comrades. In other words, in this case, the inquiry was little more than a dog-and-pony show performed by career military men who understood the politics of their profession.

In fact, First Lieutenant Charles DeRudio confirmed this attitude by the officers when he told researcher Walter Camp, "There was a private understanding between a number of officers that they would do all they could to save Reno."

Still, it was glaringly evident that Reno had disobeyed Custer's orders by not charging into the village and his subsequent actions were contrary to proper military conduct and discipline.

The testimony of twenty-three veterans of the battle lasted for twenty-six days and filled thirteen hundred pages. The finding of the court was as follows: "The conduct of the officers throughout was excellent, and while subordinates, in some instances, did more for the safety of the command by brilliant displays of courage than did Major Reno, there was nothing in his conduct which requires animadversion [criticism or censure] from this Court."

Amazingly, given the known facts about Custer's orders and strategy and a clear view of the way the battle unfolded, Reno had been cleared of any wrongdoing. The Reno Court of Inquiry, which had been convened in order to establish the facts of the battle, was more farcical than credible and simply served to intensify the debate over the conduct of Custer and Reno that exists to this day.

Libbie Custer was understandably crushed by the decision of the court but said nothing about it in public. Not so Frederick Whittaker. He wrote a scathing letter to the *New York Sun* newspaper that was published on February 26, 1879, in which he called the proceedings a "mockery of justice," and a "whitewash." Whittaker went on to say that Wesley Merritt had been "afterward closeted with the Recorder, [Lieutenant Jesse Lee] alone for several hours, and, it is understood, did most of the work of the decision, the Recorder having no voice save to present the case on trial."

Libbie expressed her feelings about Merritt in an October 16, 1882, letter to General William T. Sherman, in which she wrote: "A wife's love sharpens her eyes and quickens her instinct and years ago I knew (not from my husband) that General Merritt was his enemy. On the plains we entertained him and he seemed to have conquered his enmity and jealousy that was so bitter in the Army of the Republic. But when he was placed at the head of the Court of Inquiry that met to investigate Col. Reno's conduct at Chicago, I saw all through the trial how General Merritt *still* felt toward his dead comrade."

Evidently, Wesley Merritt's envy of Custer—they had been rivals during the Civil War—had been a major influence on the outcome. Or could it have been that higher-ups in the government had stacked the court, privately making their sentiments about the outcome known? In all fairness, no officer who had served as closely with George Armstrong Custer as had Merritt during his career should have been appointed to that inquiry. The court failed to meet the standards of an objective military investigation and possibly from the start never had any intention of placing blame where it belonged. But that is not the end of the story.

Years later, there would be some measure of satisfaction for Libbie Custer, however. General (former lieutenant) Jesse M. Lee, the Reno court recorder, wrote a letter to Libbie, dated June 27, 1897, and confessed to having been influenced during the inquiry "by the prejudicial opinions of those whose motive I did not then understand, and whose sources of information I then had no means of testing." Lee went on to offer the opinion that blame for the defeat should have been placed squarely on Marcus Reno.

The important vindication of Custer by the court recorder, unfortunately, had come eighteen years too late and has had little impact on changing opinions.

Libbie set aside her bitterness about the failure of the inquiry to condemn Reno to become a writer of articles published in the country's most respected magazines as well as the author of three memoirs of note. Each of these books that related her adventures on the frontier and further shaped the heroic image of her husband became exceedingly popular with the public.

Boots and Saddles or, Life in Dakota with General Custer, released in 1885, recounted the story of how her marriage survived the frustrations, dangers, and hardships of living on frontier posts and concludes by blaming the corrupt Indian policy for the tragedy at the Little Bighorn. *Tenting on the Plains; or, General Custer in Kansas and Texas,* 1887, addresses post–Civil War duty in Texas, where a near mutiny occurred, as well as posts in Kansas, including those events pertaining to Custer's 1867 court-martial. *Following the Guidon,* 1890, refutes criticism over the 1868 Washita battle. These fascinating books stand as several of the best ever written about that period in history.

Libbie, who remained unmarried for the rest of her life and lived most of the time in a Park Avenue apartment, traveled the world and was in much demand as a public speaker. The issues she embraced ranged beyond maintaining her husband's image to include the women's suffrage movement and other feminist causes. She invested her money wisely and purchased property in Bronxville, Westchester County, New York, where she spent her later years.

Libbie Bacon Custer died of a heart attack on April 4, 1933—four days short of her ninety-first birthday—and was buried beside her husband two days later at the U.S. Military Academy at West Point, New York. Her obituary appeared in *The New York Times* on April 5, 1933.

Frederick Benteen, the recipient of Custer's last message, has also come under fire for his behavior on June 25, 1876. Instead of hurrying to rescue Custer's command, Benteen lollygagged along the way, which in the opinion of many scholars constituted a disobedience of orders. Had he acted immediately, it has been theorized, he could have reached the battlefield in time to assist Custer. True, statements made by orderly John Martin, who had delivered the message to hurry, were of a reassuring nature, which might have convinced Benteen that the situation was well in hand. But nothing in battle should be assumed, rather it should be confirmed, and Benteen—who had received his orders—neglected to do that.

Benteen stated at the 1879 Reno Court of Inquiry that he believed that it would have been tantamount to suicide to follow Custer's order. "We were at their hearth and homes," he said, referring to the Sioux, "their medicine was working well, and they were fighting for all the good God gives anyone to fight for."

Perhaps that was the case when Benteen finally arrived near the scene of the battle and was met by a terrified Marcus Reno. Had Benteen "Come on" and been "Quick," just the mere presence of his 125 troopers advancing, much less their firepower, might have made a difference in discouraging the fighting spirit of the enemy. Benteen, true to form, also held the opinion that Custer had disobeyed the orders of General Terry and thereby sacrificed his command.

Custer's last message, by the way, has survived. Benteen wrote to his wife on July 4, quoted the message, and said: "I have the original, but it is badly torn and it should be preserved." He brought the document to Reno's Court of Inquiry and later gave it to a friend in Philadelphia, who sold it to a New Jersey collector. At some point Colonel Charles Bates, author of several Custer-related books, noticed the message advertised for sale at an auction. Bates arranged with the owner to have it secured by the U.S. Military Academy at West Point.

Benteen remained with the Seventh Cavalry after Little Bighorn and fought against the Nez Percé at Canyon Creek in 1877, for which he received a brevet to colonel. In 1882, he was promoted to major and transferred to the Ninth Cavalry.

While serving as commander of Fort Duchesne, Utah, in 1886, Benteen, who had a fondness for alcohol, faced a court-martial and was found guilty of various offenses ranging from drunkenness on duty to using obscene and profane language and exposing himself in public. His punishment, dismissal from the army, was later amended by President Grover Cleveland to a one-year suspension in respect for Benteen's long and honorable service.

Benteen established his residence in Atlanta and requested that he be retired on disability following his suspension, which took effect July 7, 1888.

Two years later, he somehow was awarded a brevet of brigadier general for his actions at Little Bighorn and against the Nez Percé.

A portrait of Benteen's sarcastic and critical personality was revealed during his later years. Bitter and vindictive in his old age, Benteen literally blisters the pages of letters written to a number of people, most notably a former Seventh Cavalry private named Theodore Goldin, with hatred of Custer and contempt for most of his old comrades.

Goldin's company was part of Major Marcus Reno's battalion during the Little Bighorn battle. He was said to have been wounded twice while retreating from the valley across the river to the bluffs and during the two-day siege of the hilltop. Goldin participated in the 1877 Nez Percé Campaign until November, when he was discharged as a private of good character. He returned to Wisconsin, where he eventually practiced law with his brother-in-law. Goldin enlisted in May 1888 as a private in the Wisconsin Infantry and was soon promoted to sergeant major, then in January 1889 appointed colonel and aide-de-camp to the governor.

Between the fall of 1891 and the summer of 1896 Goldin and Frederick Benteen exchanged letters. Benteen, who addressed Goldin as "Colonel," perhaps his National Guard rank, would not have remembered the former enlisted man and may not have corresponded with him had he known that Goldin had not been a former regular army officer. Nonetheless, these fascinating accounts bear further witness to the dark side of Benteen, who demonstrated a startling bitterness and sarcasm toward his former comrades, especially George Armstrong Custer.

Incidentally, Goldin applied for the Medal of Honor by claiming that he had been among the volunteers who had risked their lives to carry water to the wounded while trapped on the hilltop in June 1876. The medal was awarded on December 21, 1895—nineteen years after the battle—possibly with assistance from Benteen.

Benteen occasionally rattled his saber by alluding in these letters to great crimes or misdeeds committed by Custer but failed to provide any evidence whatsoever and instead merely repeated camp gossip spiced with his rancorous conjectures. (These letters were compiled into a fascinating book: *The Benteen-Goldin Letters on Custer and His Last Battle*, edited by John M. Carroll.)

Frederick Benteen died on June 22, 1898, from paralysis following a stroke. He was initially buried in Westview Cemetery in Atlanta but reinterred in November 1902 in Arlington National Cemetery.

After the famous battle, Major Marcus A. Reno was the subject of immediate and intense criticism, privately from the officers and men who had witnessed his actions as well as public condemnation from those who could recognize his cowardice.

He was soon assigned (or exiled) to Fort Abercrombie, known as the armpit of the Dakotas. Shortly after arriving, he was accused of cavorting with a fellow Seventh Cavalry officer's wife—Emeline Bell, the wife of Captain James M. Bell. Reno faced a general court-martial on March 8, 1877, on charges of "conduct unbecoming an officer and gentleman" and being drunk on duty. Reno claimed that the charges were simply post politics and that Mrs. Bell had been the aggressor. He was found guilty as charged and sentenced to be dismissed from the service. President Rutherford B. Hayes stepped in to cite Reno's exemplary record, however, and commuted the punishment to two years' suspension, effective May 1, 1877.

At that time, other Seventh Cavalry officers, including McDougall, Moylan, DeRudio, and Bell, charged Reno with striking a junior officer and being drunk on duty, but the charges were eventually dropped.

Reno was restored to duty at Fort Meade and soon found himself in more trouble. A drunken Reno struck another officer over the head with a pool cue and, if that were not enough, while being confined to quarters was accused of a "Peeping Tom" incident. The subject was Ella Sturgis, the twenty-year-old daughter of Colonel Samuel Sturgis, in whom Reno was said to have had a one-sided romantic interest. While strolling on the parade ground on November 10, 1879, Reno inexplicably peeked into the window of the Sturgis parlor and then, upon seeing Ella, tapped on the window. Ella screamed bloody murder, and Colonel Sturgis left his bed to chase Reno with his cane.

Reno's court-martial convened on November 28, and he was once again found guilty and sentenced to be dismissed from the service. This time President Hayes refused to commute the sentence—in spite of a petition for clemency filed by Generals Terry and Sherman. Reno was dishonorably discharged on April 1, 1880, after twenty-three years in the army.

Marcus Reno, who for the rest of his life tried unsuccessfully to clear his name, fell on hard times as a civilian. He married for a second time, but his wife left him after only a few months. Newspaper and magazine editors were not interested in his accounts of the famous battle. He even lacked expenses to travel to his son's wedding. Reno eventually landed a job as a clerk with the Bureau of Pensions in Washington, but that apparently did not last long.

Reno was diagnosed with cancer of the tongue and developed complications following surgery. He died on March 30, 1889, at Providence Hospital in Washington. His brief obituary in *The Washington Star* read: "Reno—In this city died, Marcus A. Reno, late major and Brevet Lt. Col., U.S. Army."

In the mid-1960s, Reno's great-nephew, backed by the American Legion, asked the army to reexamine the final court-martial charges. The judge advocate general's office concluded that Reno had been improperly dismissed from the service, and his records were corrected to reflect an honorable discharge.

On September 9, 1967, Reno was reinterred with full military honors in the Custer National Cemetery at Little Bighorn. Thus, Marcus A. Reno, the officer who had committed the ultimate betrayal of failing to carry out his orders in the face of the enemy and thereby contributed to the loss of hundreds of lives, became the only battle participant honored with such pomp and circumstance at that site.

Custer and Reno's enemy that day, the Lakota Sioux, had merely been doing what came naturally—fighting. The tribe had prevailed at the Little Bighorn, but that victory was the beginning of the end for them. They subscribed to a culture that thrived on warfare, and had taken and held their territory by force. After Little Bighorn, however, they ran into a more powerful enemy in the inspired United States Army and lost this land by force—which the Sioux by their actions had chosen as the only arbiter they respected.

The United States had every right to expand its boundaries to include the Great Plains West. Oddly enough, many modern scholars believe there was something honorable about the Sioux fighting to defend their right to roam free. It is apparent, however, that the great thinkers of today have not been able to develop a practical policy that would have solved the "Indian problem" back then any more than could their counterparts of the nineteenth century.

The West was becoming too small and populated to allow a group advocating violence to close off thousands of square miles, with its resources and potential, and stand in the way of settlers who wanted to work the land, build towns and lives, and raise their families. Peace entreaties had been made and were dismissed. It was indeed unfortunate that a peaceful solution could not have been reached. In the end, the only response to violence was violence—a circumstance that sends American servicemen into battle with regularity right up to this day.

Although the leadership by the officers of Reno's command left much to be desired—other than Benteen on the hilltop—the enlisted soldiers were truly men of courage. It was not their fault that their commander, Major Marcus Reno, had placed them in one precarious situation after another—from a gallant charge of the village to setting up the skirmish line on to the timber and finally that disastrous retreat to the hilltop. None of them panicked as the horror show was being performed in the village during that first night, and they were prepared to fight to the death should the Sioux press the issue.

The volunteers' risking their lives and journeying to the river for water must go down as one of the most heroic acts under fire imaginable. Anyone who has stood overlooking that steep ravine on the battlefield can only marvel at the courage of those men. For their bravery, twenty-four Seventh Cavalry troopers—water carriers and sharpshooters—would be awarded the Medal of Honor, the highest number cited on any one day in United States history.

With respect to the legacy of George Armstrong Custer, fair-minded people should reject the traditional fixation with trying to place the blame for the Little Bighorn debacle on him and allow the evidence to lead them to practical and logical answers. In addition, the portrayal of Custer as the poster boy for the destruction of Indian culture has been based on nothing more than misguided prejudice caused by lack of knowledge and a recent pseudo-revisionist inclination to tarnish heroes.

Custer is an American hero—a man who rose from meager beginnings to attain greatness by his own abilities and talents—and that same resentment that fueled inferior people with weak character like Frederick Benteen to disparage him, sadly enough, continues to this day.

Custer's military career from Bull Run to the Little Bighorn was by any measurement one of the finest in American history. Many military icons immortalized to this day cannot come close to matching the accomplishments of Custer. Yet his image has been sullied by unfair portrayals in silly, historically embarrassing movies and books, and especially in classrooms and textbooks where social and political agendas have supplanted truth.

Heroes and villains? The Battle of the Little Bighorn has no lack of either—but too often the villains have been portrayed as heroes and vice versa. It is time to balance the account, set the record straight, and restore and pay tribute to heroes who have fallen prey to the academic and pop-culture bullies who cannot accept the premise that everyone throughout history has not been equal and that great men have actually walked this earth—and their accomplishments attest to that fact.

Finally, thank God for the bravery and sacrifices of the American military, which has responded without question to their country's call and performed their duty with honor throughout history.

Appendix

———◆◈◆———

Table of Organization and Casualty Report of the
Seventh Cavalry Little Bighorn Campaign

Nearly every source about the battle differs in estimated casualty totals. This Table of Organization and Casualty Report was compiled as best as possible from the official Seventh Cavalry Muster Rolls dated June 30, 1876. Those troopers from companies attached to Custer's battalion listed as wounded in action or who died of wounds were serving with either another company or the pack train at the time of the battle. Consequently, it is extremely difficult to calculate exact strength numbers for individual companies.

Although identification was impossible in some cases due to mutilation, 208 or 210 bodies—accounts vary—were said to have been found and buried on June 27, 1876, on the Custer battlefield. This figure may not account for an undetermined number that may have been missing from the field—excluding Lieutenants Henry M. Harrington, James E. Porter, and James G. Sturgis, who were presumed to have been killed but their bodies never found.

Code: (KIA): Killed In Action; (WIA): Wounded In Action; (DOW): Died Of Wounds; (MIA): Missing In Action.

HEADQUARTERS

Lieutenant Colonel George Armstrong Custer, commanding (KIA)
First Lieutenant William W. Cooke, adjutant (KIA)

Lieutenant George E. Lord, assistant surgeon (KIA)

Mitch Bouyer, interpreter (KIA)

Marcus H. Kellogg, correspondent (KIA)

Harry Armstrong Reed, attached civilian (KIA)

Boston Custer, forage master (KIA)

(3 officers KIA; 2 enlisted KIA; 4 staff KIA)

CUSTER'S BATTALION
Company C

Captain Thomas W. Custer (KIA)

Second Lieutenant Henry M. Harrington (MIA)

(1 officer KIA; 1 officer MIA; 36 enlisted KIA; 4 enlisted WIA; 1 enlisted DOW)

Company E

First Lieutenant Algernon E. Smith (KIA)

Second Lieutenant James G. Sturgis (MIA)

(2 officers KIA; 37 enlisted KIA; 2 enlisted WIA)

Company F

Captain George W. Yates (KIA)

Second Lieutenant William V. W. Reily (KIA)

(2 officers KIA; 36 enlisted KIA)

Company I

Captain Myles W. Keogh (KIA)

First Lieutenant James E. Porter (MIA)

(2 officers KIA; 36 enlisted KIA; 1 enlisted WIA; 1 enlisted DOW)

Company L

First Lieutenant James Calhoun (KIA)

Second Lieutenant John J. Crittenden (KIA)

(2 officers KIA; 44 enlisted KIA; 1 enlisted WIA)

RENO'S BATTALION

Major Marcus A. Reno, commanding

Second Lieutenant Benjamin H. Hodgson, adjutant (KIA)

Company A

Captain Myles Moylan

First Lieutenant Charles DeRudio

(8 enlisted KIA; 7 enlisted WIA; 1 enlisted DOW)

Company G

First Lieutenant Donald McIntosh (KIA)

Second Lieutenant George D. Wallace

(1 officer KIA; 13 enlisted KIA; 6 enlisted WIA)

Company M

Captain Thomas H. French

(12 enlisted KIA; 11 enlisted WIA; 1 enlisted DOW)

Attached

James M. DeWolf, acting assistant surgeon (KIA)

Henry R. Porter, acting assistant surgeon

Second Lieutenant Charles A. Varnum, commanding Indian scouts (WIA)

Second Lieutenant Luther R. Hare, with Indian scouts

Isaiah Dorman, interpreter (KIA)

Frederic Girard, interpreter

George B. Herendeen, scout

Billy Jackson, scout

Bloody Knife, scout (KIA)

Charles Reynolds, scout (KIA)

(Indian scouts—2 KIA; 2 WIA)

BENTEEN'S BATTALION

Captain Frederick W. Benteen, commanding (WIA)

Company D

Captain Thomas B. Weir

Second Lieutenant Winfield S. Edgerly

(3 enlisted KIA; 3 enlisted WIA)

Company H

First Lieutenant Francis M. Gibson

(2 enlisted KIA; 20 enlisted WIA; 2 enlisted DOW)

Company K

First Lieutenant Edward S. Godfrey

(5 enlisted KIA; 3 enlisted WIA)

Pack Train

First Lieutenant Edward G. Mathey

(Civilian packers—1 KIA; 1 WIA)

Company B

Captain Thomas M. McDougall

(2 enlisted KIA; 5 enlisted WIA)

DETACHED SERVICE

Colonel Samuel D. Sturgis; Major Lewis Merrill; Captain Michael V. Sheridan; Captain Charles S. Illsley; Captain John E. Tourtellotte; Captain Owen Hale; First Lieutenant Henry J. Nowlan (with Terry); First Lieutenant William T. Craycroft; First Lieutenant Henry Jackson; Second Lieutenant Charles W. Larned.

LEAVE OF ABSENCE

Major Joseph G. Tilford; First Lieutenant James M. Bell; Second Lieutenant Ernest A. Garlington.

SICK LEAVE

Second Lieutenant Charles Braden; Second Lieutenant Andrew H. Nave.

TOTAL CASUALTIES

KIA—260

WIA—68

DOW—6

MIA—3

Sources

———◆———

Sources for events in the life and times of George Armstrong Custer—and the Little Big-horn Campaign in particular—are so plentiful that selecting one or even several in specific footnotes does not do justice to a subject. Therefore, I have chosen to offer multiple sources when possible accompanied by commentary in order to provide a view of relevant material for casual reading or in-depth research. Every effort has been made to supply readily accessible material in addition to official or obscure documentation. Not every item pertaining to a subject has been listed as a source, only those that are the most helpful and pertinent—others may be found by perusing the bibliography. All quotations have been cited by chapter and verse.

Chapter One
The Wrath of President Grant

The best readily available account of the Belknap impeachment hearings and Custer's involvement can be found in chapter 6 of *Custer's Luck,* by Stewart.

The official report: "Report on Management of the War Department, Rep. Heister Clymer, Chairman of Committee," *House Reports* no. 79, 44th Congress, 1st sess. serial no. 1715 (1876).

Periodicals with interesting contemporary reporting about Custer's involvement in the hearings include: *Nation* (New York), March 16, 1876; *Army and Navy Journal,* April 1, April 8, April 15, May 27, 1876; *New York Herald,* May 2, May 6, May 10, June

6, 1876; *New York World,* May 1, 2, 6, 1876; *New York Times,* May 1, 1876; *Cincinnati Enquirer,* April 5, 1876; and *Cincinnati Commercial,* April 5, 1876.

Another notable source is: "Campaign Against the Sioux in 1876," by Hughes, reprinted in *The Story of the Little Bighorn,* by Graham.

For information about Custer's snub of Belknap at Fort Lincoln, see "Custer's Last Meeting with Secretary of War Belknap at Fort Abraham Lincoln," by Brigham.

The kickback scheme by Belknap and Grant is detailed in *Tales from Buffalo Land,* by Burdick and "The Malfeasance of William Worth Belknap, Secretary of War" by Prickett.

Interesting information about Custer's activities in Washington and New York at the time of the Belknap hearings, including extracts from correspondence with Libbie, is contained in *The Custer Story,* edited by Merington.

Custer's early life is covered in a number of references, including: *Custer Genealogies,* edited by Carroll and Horn; Ronsheim's *Life of General Custer; Custer's Ohio Boyhood,* by Wallace; *General Custer and New Rumley, Ohio,* by Carroll; "Custer's First Romance Revealed" by O'Neil; and Frost's *Custer Legends.*

Custer's boyhood is also predictably found within his biographies. Surprisingly, given the amount of information written about George Armstrong Custer and the famous battle, few notable biographies are available.

Rather than start with the best biography, the first one published still deserves attention. That would be *A Complete Life of Gen. George Armstrong Custer,* by Whittaker. Whittaker, who was a British expatriate and Civil War brevet captain in the Sixth New York Cavalry, had met Custer at the offices of Sheldon and Company where he worked as a dime novelist during the time Custer published his *My Life on the Plains* with that firm. Libbie Custer provided Whittaker with Custer's personal correspondence, and the book was released within six months of Custer's death. The biography was an instant success and played a major role—second only to Libbie—in transforming Custer into an enduring national hero.

That portrayal went unchallenged until 1934—one year after Libbie's death—when Van de Water's *Glory-Hunter* was published. In this iconoclastic work Van de Water, an admirer of Sigmund Freud, attempted to delve beyond the deeds and into the mind of Custer. Van de Water concluded that Custer was a deeply flawed man, a perpetual adolescent, addicted to fame, driven and destroyed by ambition, and responsible for the defeat at Little Bighorn.

A compelling, if not rather unusual, biography is *The Custer Story,* by Merington. Hundreds of excerpts from letters, the majority written by Custer and Libbie, provide a unique, intimate insight into these private lives. Merington, who was a close friend of Libbie Custer in later life, adds a narrative that fills in the blanks and puts the letters in proper perspective. This "firsthand" account stands as one of the better portrayals of Custer, Libbie, and their life and times.

The next biography of note is *Custer,* by Monaghan. This book, which is favorable without exception to Custer and is written with a captivating flair, highlights his Civil War career. Some critics have complained, however, that the book fails to provide a completely satisfying account of the Little Bighorn battle.

One biography barely worth mentioning is Kinsley's two-volume *Favor the Bold,* which offers little of value.

Crazy Horse and Custer, by Ambrose, presents the story with speculation wherever facts are absent. This intriguing book reconstructs a period in history through the eyes of two notable participants and, although some re-creations provoke skepticism, the exciting narrative makes for a good read.

One book of borderline biography is Hofling's *Custer and the Little Big Horn: A Psychobiographical Inquiry.* As the title suggests, this speculative work delves into the deeper recesses of the Custer legend, and therefore is not recommended for the beginner.

One of the best biographies, which was made into a pathetic movie, is Connell's *Son of the Morning Star.* Connell restores Custer's reputation as a heroic figure and does so not in chronological order of his life but by wandering off on research tangents into aspects of white–Indian relations and culture that some have found enlightening while others have deemed maddening. There are several drawbacks to this work, however. One is the brief treatment of certain aspects of Custer's life in order to concentrate on events pertaining to Plains history and characters. Another is the lack of any sort of documentation, which, considering the diversified subject matter, would have been quite helpful for the researcher. Also, the index is relatively sparse, which often requires the reader to leaf through the pages when seeking specific material. Nevertheless, this book is utterly fascinating.

The best biography for the beginner or casual reader—and not to exclude the serious student—is Utley's *Cavalier in Buckskin.* Although this view of Custer can be less than flattering at times, Mr. Utley, an Old West historian without peer, brought a lifetime of knowledge and perspective to this biography.

One "specialty" biography that deserves mentioning is *The Custer Album,* by Frost. This volume not only tells the story in an inspiring narrative by one of the foremost Custer scholars but, as the title suggests, also is chock-full of photographs and drawings that depict just about everyone and everything associated with Custer.

Another book that does not snugly fit into the category of biography but should be noted is *The Custer Reader,* edited by Hutton. Beginning with the Civil War, the reader is presented a series of reprinted articles by Custer, his contemporaries, and noted historians that portray Custer's personality and career and the many myths surrounding his life. Hutton's accompanying excellent commentary places each piece in its historical perspective.

Perhaps the most ambitious biography to date is Wert's *Custer*. This meticulously researched, well-written study covers every aspect of Custer's life in a balanced and thoughtful manner. Wert did not fall victim to the myths and legends perpetuated by earlier biographers but, rather, carefully analyzed each claim to present the most factual portrayal possible and backed up his findings with ample documentation.

One of Custer's modern-day relatives, Brice C. Custer, now deceased, provides interesting family anecdotes and admirably defends his great-great-uncle in his *Sacrificial Lion George Armstrong Custer*. This book not only offers a clear view of Custer's life but also challenges critics of the general who have failed to properly research their subject.

For Custer's West Point career, the best volume would be my *Glorious War,* which portrays the true personality of the young Custer as he matures into a man. Also see *The Class of 1861,* by Ralph Kirshner, which provides an interesting insight into Custer and his West Point contemporaries.

For a fascinating and often unintentially humorous account, read *"Skinned": The Delinquency Record of Cadet George Armstrong Custer U.S.M.A. Class of June 1861,* by Horn. For an official view see: Register of Delinquencies, 1856–61; and also *Regulations for The U.S. Military Academy at West Point, New York; Custer and His Times,* book 2, edited by Carroll; and *4 on Custer by Carroll.*

The quotes of Custer's classmates can be found in Frost's *Custer Legends,* 136; Schaff, *The Spirit of Old West Point;* and Hutton's *Custer Reader,* 9.

Custer's letter about the worries of impending war written to Ann Reed, November 10, 1860, is in the George Armstrong Custer Collection, Monroe Library System.

For a great portrait of the men and traditions of West Point, with amusing Custer anecdotes, one of the best overall books is *The Spirit of Old West Point,* by Schaff.

Custer's West Point court-martial record can be found in Special Orders, no. 21, U.S. Military Academy Archives.

Chapter Two
Glorious War

The definitive account of Custer's Civil War career can be found in my *Glorious War.* From Custer's West Point days to the daring exploits that propelled him to the rank of general and the cavalry charges that gained him national fame, with special attention to his romance with Libbie Bacon, this book encompasses every aspect of his incredible service to the country.

One of the first books to cover Custer's Civil War career was *Custer Victorious* by Urwin. A minor drawback to this well-written work is that—as the title suggests—it concentrates on the battles when Custer was a general and fails to adequately chronicle his first two years of service and associated aspects of his career, including his courtship of Libbie.

Custer's own words in *Custer in the Civil War*, edited by Carroll, provide an insightful glimpse into his early career, and this would have been a major work had it been completed for the period beyond May 1862. This volume also includes all of the official reports written by Custer and provides an extensive bibliography in the appendix that cites every Civil War book the editor could locate that mentions Custer.

Another notable book is *Custer and His Wolverines*, by Longacre, which focuses on the Michigan "Wolverines" with and without Custer. The best memoir is *Personal Recollections of a Cavalryman with Custer's Michigan Brigade in the Civil War*, by Kidd, which was written by one of Custer's officers who had an excellent eye for detail and offers a fascinating portrayal of Custer and his exploits. Other notable sources include: *Last Hours of Sheridan's Cavalry*, by Tremain; *East of Gettysburg*, by Riggs; *From Winchester to Cedar Creek*, by Wert; and *The Union Cavalry in the Civil War*, vol. 1 and vol. 2: *The Union Cavalry in the Civil War in the East*, by Starr.

McClellan's quote about Custer can be found in *McClellan's Own Story*, 364.

The quote from the official report about Custer's action, "the first to cross the stream . . . ," is found in O.R. series 1, vol. 11, pt. 1, 651–54, or more conveniently located in Reynolds, *The Civil War Memories of Elizabeth Bacon Custer*, 75.

Perhaps the most appealing biography of Libbie Custer is *General Custer's Libbie*, by Custer scholar and Libbie admirer Lawrence A. Frost. A close second would be the intriguing and informative *Touched by Fire*, by Barnett. Another biography of note is the meticulously researched and well-written *Elizabeth Bacon Custer and the Making of a Myth*, by Leckie. Excerpts from a sample of Libbie's correspondence, some of which have been donated to the Little Bighorn Battlefield National Monument, can be found in *The Custer Story*, by Merington, which provides an excellent narrative of the Custers' life together. See also: *A Life Within a Life*, by Kines; "Sidesaddle Soldier: Libbie Custer's Partnership in Glory," by Ambrose; "Mrs. General Custer at Fort Riley, 1866," by Millbrook; "The Girl He Left Behind," by Tate; and "Elizabeth Bacon Custer in Japan: 1903," by Wabuda.

Libbie's heartfelt quote "He is noble . . ." can be read in Merington, *The Custer Story*, 50.

Letters and manuscripts of Libbie's are housed at the Detroit Public Library, Lincoln Memorial University, Monroe County Historical Museum, U.S. Military Academy at West Point, and Yale University, as well as Little Bighorn Battlefield National Monument.

Pleasonton's quote about Custer being "the best cavalry general in the world" is on page 60 of Merington, *The Custer Story*.

Major Kidd's quote about Custer taking command is in Kidd's *Personal Recollections*, 125–29.

The quotes by Ballard and Christiancy can be found in the *Grand Rapids Daily Eagle*, July 8, 1876, and Libbie's *Boots and Saddles*, 9–10.

Libbie's "My more than friend . . ." letter is in Merington, *The Custer Story*, 73.

Rebecca Richmond's description of Libbie's wedding dress can be found in Frost's *General Custer's Libbie*, 92.

Custer's exclamation of "Glorious War" is in my *Glorious War*, 202.

New York Times reporter E. A. Paul compared Custer to Napoléon in the October 27, 1864, edition.

The subject of the Surrender table is covered in most Custer biographies and perhaps best by Frost in *General Custer's Libbie*. Sheridan's letter can be found in Merington's *Custer Story*, 165.

Accounts of Custer's temperance lecture from Ann Reed and his religious conversion can be found in most biographies of him but perhaps are best depicted in my *Glorious War*.

Chapter Three
Chasing Shadows on the Plains

Custer's activities during this period of time in Texas and Louisiana are covered in the following: *Tenting on the Plains; or, General Custer in Kansas and Texas,* by Elizabeth Custer; *Custer in Texas: An Interrupted Narrative,* by Carroll; "The Boy General and How He Grew," by Millbrook; and "A Better Time Is in Store for Us: An Analysis of the Reconstruction Attitudes of George Armstrong Custer," by Richter.

Perhaps the most interesting account of the Hancock Expedition, although decidedly biased, was written by George Armstrong Custer in his *My Life on the Plains.* A well-researched reconstruction of events covering the years 1866–67 can be found in two fine articles by Millbrook: "The West Breaks in General Custer," which has been reprinted in Hutton's *Custer Reader,* and "Custer's First Scout in the West," edited by

Dippie. Also, Dippie's footnotes in *Nomad* provide valuable information and Custer's own story about his adventurous buffalo hunt is included in his first "letter" of that volume.

Two views by participants—a cavalry officer and the only doctor accompanying Custer—are also significant: *Life in Custer's Cavalry*, edited by Utley, and *On the Plains with Custer and Hancock*, by Kennedy.

Observations by two representatives of the press who accompanied the expedition are documented in "A Summer on the Plains," by famed illustrator Theodore R. Davis, and *My Early Travels and Adventures in America and Asia*, by Henry M. Stanley of the *New York Tribune*.

A highly critical assessment of Hancock's expedition from an Indian point of view is included in *The Fighting Cheyennes*, by Grinnell. The best source about the Kidder massacre is *A Dispatch to Custer*, by Johnson and Allan. This volume contain important correspondence between those involved—including Custer—as well as excellent photos and maps.

Other notable sources for the expedition include: *Custer, Come at Once!* by Burkey; *Tenting on the Plains*, by Elizabeth B. Custer; and "The Hancock and Custer Expedition of 1867," by White.

The best account of the Seventh Cavalry Regiment is *Of Garry Owen in Glory*, by Chandler. Three fascinating books flavored with amusing anecdotes written by Libbie Custer, who followed the Seventh Cavalry's guidon, offer an insight into post life and personalities: *Boots and Saddles, Tenting on the Plains*, and *Following the Guidon*. The Seventh Cavalry is well represented, with depictions of daily duty, in Utley's *Frontier Regulars*. For a look at the trials and tribulations of a cavalryman see *The Troopers*, by Whitman, and *Forty Miles a Day on Beans and Hay*, by Rickey. A description of the weapons, dress, equipment, horses, and flags of the Seventh Cavalry in 1876 can be found in *Boots & Saddles at the Little Bighorn*, by Hutchins.

Biographical sketches of individual members of the Seventh Cavalry are contained in *They Rode with Custer*, edited by Carroll, and a revised and expanded edition of that book titled *Men with Custer*, edited by Nichols.

More about Winfield Scott Hancock can be found in *Reminiscences of Winfield Scott Hancock, by His Wife*, by Hancock; *The Life of Winfield Scott Hancock*, by Junkin; and *Winfield Scott Hancock*, by Jordan.

Custer describes his inaugural excursion to Denver aboard the Kansas Pacific Railroad in the October 7, 1870, edition of *Turf, Field and Farm*, which has been reprinted in *Nomad*, edited by Dippie. General railroad sources include: "When the Union and Kansas Pacific Built Through Kansas," by Snell and Richmond; *The Story of the*

Western Railroads, by Riegel; *New Tracks in North America,* by Bell; and *Trails, Rails and War,* by Perkins.

For two notable works about railroad and land speculator William Jackson Palmer, see: *Rebel of the Rockies,* by Ahearn and *A Builder of the West,* by Fisher.

The definitive biography of William W. Cooke is *Custer's Forgotten Friend,* by Arnold; see also Arnold's "Cooke's Scrawled Note: Last Word from a Doomed Command." Numerous references to his friend Cooke are made by Custer in his *My Life on the Plains*.

Perhaps the most accurate book about the life of the enigmatic Myles Keogh is *Myles Keogh,* edited by K. Langellier, et al. The most romantic and thought-provoking account is *Keogh, Comanche and Custer,* by former battlefield superintendent Luce. See also: *The Honor of Arms,* by Convis; *Captain Myles Walter Keogh,* by Hayes-McCoy; Hayes-McCoy's "Captain Myles Walter Keogh, the Irish Sword"; "The Man Who Rode Comanche," by Taunton; and "Myles Keogh from the Vatican to the Little Big Horn," by Pohanka.

References to Weir's personal relationship with the Custers can be found in *The Custer Story,* by Merington, as well as *Elizabeth Bacon Custer and the Making of a Myth,* by Leckie.

The best version of Custer's dash across Kansas can be found in "The West Breaks in General Custer," by Millbrook, which has been reprinted in *The Custer Reader,* by Hutton. Also see: *My Life on the Plains,* by Custer and *The Custer Story,* by Marguerite Merington, which contains Libbie's letter and other interesting observations, as does Libbie's *Tenting on the Plains*.

Benteen's theory for Custer's desertion is related in Carroll's *Custer: From the Civil War to the Big Horn,* and Mathey's account was told in an interview with Walter M. Camp, Harold B. Lee Library.

The Court-Martial of George Armstrong Custer, by Frost, includes not only an excellent account of the Hancock Expedition but also a verbatim account—testimony and exhibits—of Custer's court-martial proceedings. Two other notable sources are "The Custer Court Martial," by Murray, and "The Court-Martial of Brevet Major General George A. Custer," by Halsey. Custer's point of view can be found in his *My Life on the Plains* and Libbie's *Tenting on the Plains*. The subject is also covered from various angles in every biography of Custer, but none comes close to matching Frost's work, which allows readers to form their own conclusions regarding Custer's actions and subsequent punishment.

Chapter Four
Death Along the Washita

The debate about the "Indian problem" is described best in *Uncle Sam's Stepchildren*, by Priest, and *American Indian Policy in Crisis*, by Prucha.

The concept and execution of "total war" demonstrated during the Winter Campaign of 1868–69 can be found in *William Tecumseh Sherman and the Settlement of the West*, by Athearn; *Personal Memoirs of Philip Henry Sheridan*, by Sheridan; *Phil Sheridan and His Army*, by Hutton; *General Custer and the Battle of the Washita: The Federal View*, by Carroll; Utley's *Cavalier in Buckskin; Sheridan's Troopers on the Borders*, by Keim; and Hoig's *The Battle of the Washita*.

The best contemporary account of the Beecher Island battle is Monnett's *Battle of Beecher Island and the Indian War of 1867–69*. George A. Forsyth's own romanticized version of the battle can be found in "A Frontier Fight" and in his autobiographies, *Thrilling Days in Army Life* and *The Story of a Soldier*. Eyewitness accounts by participants John Hurst and Sigmund Shlesinger are found in "The Beecher Island Fight." The rescue by the Tenth Cavalry is detailed in *The Buffalo Soldiers: A Narrative of the Negro Cavalry in the West*, by Leckie.

Other notable sources include: *Hero of Beecher Island*, by Dixon; *The Beecher Island Battle*, by Werner; "The Battle of Beecher Island," by White; *The Fighting Cheyennes*, by Grinnell; and *Indian Fights and Fighters*, by Brady.

The best accounts of the march of the Kansas cavalrymen can be found in *Campaigning with Custer and the Nineteenth Kansas Volunteer Cavalry on the Washita Campaign, 1868–69*, by participant David L. Spotts, edited by Brininstool; "Winter Campaigning with Sheridan and Custer," by White; and "The Nineteenth Kansas Cavalry in the Indian Territory, 1868–69," edited by White. Other helpful sources include: "The Nineteenth Kansas Cavalry and the Conquest of the Plains Indians," by Hadley; "The Nineteenth Kansas Cavalry in the Washita Campaign," by Moore; and Hutton's *Phil Sheridan and His Army*.

Benteen's dislike of Custer is demonstrated in one classic volume, *The Benteen-Goldin Letters on Custer and His Last Battle*, edited by Carroll, which best reveals the true personality of the sarcastic and critical army captain. Bitter and vindictive in his old age, Benteen literally blisters the pages of these letters to a former Seventh Cavalry private named Theodore Goldin and others with his hatred of Custer and contempt for most of his old comrades. Benteen occasionally rattled his saber by alluding to great crimes or misdeeds committed by Custer but fails to provide evidence and instead merely repeats camp gossip spiced with his rancorous conjectures.

Benteen was the subject of a rather sympathetic biography, *Harvest of Barren Regrets,* by Mills. His softer yet no less sarcastic side is revealed in *Camp Talk: The Very Private Letters of Frederick W. Benteen of the 7th U.S. Cavalry to His Wife, 1871–1888,* edited by Carroll. *The Custer Myth,* by Graham, dedicates a full chapter to a sampling of Benteen's writings on various topics.

Other notable sources include *Gray Head and Long Hair,* by Karol Asay; *Cavalry Scraps: The Writings of Frederick W. Benteen,* edited by Carroll; and *Benteen's Ordeal and Custer's Field,* by Johnson. The Frederick W. Benteen Collection, which consists of three boxes of material, is located in the University of Georgia Library.

Cheyenne oral tradition contending that Custer and Mo-nah-se-tah were an item can be found in *Cheyenne Autumn,* by Sandoz; *Custer on the Little Bighorn,* by Marquis; and *Custer's Fall: The Indian Side of the Story,* by Miller.

Benteen's allegations about Custer's affair with the Indian girl are contained in his letters of February 14 and 17, 1896, in *The Benteen-Goldin Letters on Custer and His Last Battle,* edited by Carroll; scout Ben Clark's fading memories were recorded in a 1910 interview with Walter Camp in Field Notes, Folder 4, Box 2, Walter M. Camp Papers, Lilly Library, Indiana University.

An analysis by Custer scholars includes: *General Custer's Libbie,* by Frost; *Custer,* by Monaghan; *Son of the Morning Star,* by Connell; Ambrose's *Crazy Horse and Custer,* and Wert's *Custer.* One noted historian, Robert M. Utley, in his biography, *Cavalier in Buckskin,* leaves the door open a crack to the possibility that another child was born late in 1869 and that Custer could have been the father. Mo-nah-se-tah is a prominent figure in Custer's memoir, *My Life on the Plains,* and Elizabeth Bacon Custer's *Following the Guidon.*

For the case of a woman who claims to be a descendent of "Yellow Hair," also known as Josiah Custer, the alleged child of Mo-nah-se-tah and Custer, see: "My Heritage, My Search," by Gail Kelly-Custer.

An opposing view of the relationship within Cheyenne oral tradition is presented by John Stands in *Timber* and Margot Liberty in *Cheyenne Memories,* which dismisses any notion of a liaison between Custer and the girl.

The text of Benteen's scurrilous letter about Custer abandoning Elliott can be found in *The Custer Myth,* by Graham. Benteen's explanation of the incident in Custer's tent is described in his letter of February 22, 1896, to Theodore Goldin in *The Benteen-Goldin Letters on Custer and His Last Battle,* edited by Carroll.

The best accounts of the Joel Elliott affair can be found in *Cavalier in Buckskin,* by Utley; *Custer Legends,* by Frost; *The Battle of the Washita,* by Hoig; and *Sheridan's Troopers on the Borders,* by Keim. Incidentally, Keim, the reporter whom Benteen noted as being a witness to a later confrontation with Custer, makes no mention of that incident in his coverage of Elliott's tragic fate, although he did write that he reported the reason for Custer's officer's call to Sheridan.

The theory about Benteen fearing to confront Myers can be attributed to the author's speculation.

Captive Clara Blinn's message is on display at the National Frontier Trails Center in Independence, Missouri, and has been reprinted in Rister's *Border Captives,* which details the incident. W. T. Harrington's letter to Sheridan dated November 8, 1868, is located in the Records of the U.S. Army, Box 16, Division of the Missouri, Special File, RG 393. For an excerpt of the incident from Custer's official report see *My Life on the Plains,* by Custer. The University of Oklahoma edition of the book also includes an argument by Colonel William B. Hazen with respect to the identity of the Indians who were responsible for the death of Mrs. Blinn.

Custer's own dramatic account of the release of the captured women on Sweetwater Creek can be found in *My Life on the Plains.* His wife, Libbie, adds her perspective to the story in *Following the Guidon.* An eyewitness account by participant David Spotts is contained in his *Campaigning with Custer and the Nineteenth Kansas Volunteer Cavalry on the Washita Campaign, 1868–69.* For two other interesting versions see *California Joe,* by Milner and Forrest and chapter 11, "Deliverance by Deception," of Hoig's *Battle of the Washita.*

The best version of the Battle of Summit Springs can be found in a biography of Major Carr titled *War Eagle,* by King. *The Summit Springs Battle,* by Werner, includes copies of Carr's official reports and several interesting maps. Scout Luther North's interview with Walter Camp about the battle can be found in *Camp on Custer,* edited by Liddic and Harbaugh. An in-depth analysis by Don Russell with respect to who actually killed Tall Bull—in his opinion Buffalo Bill—is contained in his *Lives and Legends of Buffalo Bill.* For support for Frank North as the slayer of Tall Bull, as well as coverage of the battle, see both *Two Great Scouts and Their Pawnee Battalions,* by Grinnell and Danker's *Man of the Plains.* Other notable sources for the battle include: *Summit Springs,* by King; *Across the Continent with the Fifth Cavalry,* by Price; and Sheridan's *Record of Engagements with Hostile Indians Within the Military Division of the Missouri.*

The most factual and dramatic account of the Washita battle, which provides a perspective from the Indian side of the affair without compromising the truth, can be found in my *Black Kettle.* An accurate overall account of the Winter Campaign of 1868–69 can be found in Hoig's *Battle of the Washita.* Another excellent choice would be *Phil Sheridan and His Army,* by Hutton. For a compilation of the official documents see *General Custer and the Battle of the Washita: The Federal View,* edited by Carroll. An eyewitness perspective from a reporter who accompanied the campaign is *Sheridan's Troopers on the Borders,* by Keim. The classic *Indian Fights and Fighters,* by Brady, includes a notable version of the Washita battle. Edward Godfrey, one of Custer's officers, adds interesting details in his "Some Reminiscences, Including the Washita Battle, November 27, 1868," which also appears in Hutton's *Custer Reader.*

Custer's own view of events is included in his memoir, *My Life on the Plains,* in which he reacts to the criticism, and Libbie Custer provides her insight in *Following the Guidon.*

Two of the more critical assessments are Brill's *Conquest of the Southern Plains* and *Custer's Battle of the Washita and a History of the Plains Indian Tribes,* by Epple.

The most balanced debate about the morals of the campaign can be found in Hutton's *Phil Sheridan and His Army.* One of the better arguments for the humanitarian position is covered in detail in chapter 12, "A Quarrel of Conscience," of Hoig's *Battle of the Washita.* Ironically, Hoig concludes that the battle was a massacre but provides more than enough evidence to dispute that finding.

For a reporter's eyewitness point of view that at times both supports and refutes the army's presentation of events and evidence, see *Sheridan's Troopers on the Borders,* by Keim. Sheridan's orders to Custer appear in the works by both Hoig and Keim.

Other sources, for the most part sympathetic to the Indians, include: *The Fighting Cheyennes,* by Grinnell, and *Our Indian Wards,* by Manypenny.

The most powerful narrative of the Sand Creek Massacre can be found in my *Black Kettle,* which provides an evenhanded view of events from both sides of the tragic affair.

Helen Hunt Jackson was a resident of Colorado Springs when she wrote *A Century of Dishonor,* which describes the massacre in great detail and quotes liberally from testimony given before the Congressional Committee. The report of the U.S. War Department was published in 1975 by the Library of Congress under the title *Report of the Secretary of War Communicating, in Compliance with a Resolution of the Senate of February 4, 1867: Copy of Evidence Taken at Denver and Fort Lyon, Colorado by a Military Commission Ordered to Inquire in the Sand Creek Massacre, November 1864.*

Sherman's quote defending the attack on Washita can be found in my *Black Kettle,* 256.

Chapter Five
Battling Sioux in Yellowstone Country

The incident between Tom Custer and Wild Bill is related by O'Conner in his *Wild Bill Hickok* and also in an article titled "Tom Custer: In the Shadow of His Brother," by Reedstrom.

Bird's biography, *In His Brother's Shadow: The Life of Thomas Ward Custer,* provides an evenhanded depiction of Tom's event-filled life.

Henry Capehart's quote about Tom's bravery can be found in my *Glorious War,* 297.

A detailed account of Custer's investment venture and his New York socializing can be found in *General Custer's Libbie,* by Frost. Correspondence about the subject between and by Custer and Libbie has been reprinted in *The Custer Story,* by Merington. Another notable source is Utley's *Cavalier in Buckskin,* which suggests that some of Custer's practices in promoting the mine, although common for the time, were less than honorable.

Between 1867 and 1875, Custer—under the pseudonym Nomad—wrote fifteen letters describing his adventures with horses, hounds, and hunting, which were published in *Turf, Field and Farm.* Five of these stories relate to his experiences in Kentucky. The entire collection has been published with informative anecdotes by editor Brian W. Dippie in a book titled *Nomad.* A chapter in Frost's *General Custer's Libbie* has been dedicated to the Custers' rather uneventful stay in Kentucky. Other notable sources include: *General Custer's Thoroughbreds: Racing, Riding, Hunting, and Fighting,* by Frost; "The Two-Year Residence of General George A. Custer in Kentucky," by McMurtry; and "Custer's Kentucky: General George Armstrong Custer and Elizabethtown, Kentucky, 1871–73," by Crackel.

John Burkman's biography, *Old Neutriment,* by Wagner was based for the most part on Burkman's reminiscences. His memories provide an excellent, if not emotional, insight into the personal life of the Custers and associated events from the viewpoint of an enlisted man who happened to be a hero worshiper of Custer. Libbie Custer also pays tribute to Burkman in her *Boots and Saddles.*

The best account of the Grand Duke's entire U.S. visit, which was compiled from newspaper stories, can be found in *The Grand Duke Alexis in the United States,* by Tucker and Dykes. An excerpt from Libbie Custer's diary can be found in *The Custer Story,* by Merington. Two versions by participants are Cody's *The Life of Hon. William F. Cody, Known as Buffalo Bill,* and "A Royal Buffalo Hunt" by Hadley, a scout who also had been an officer in the Nineteenth Kansas Volunteer Cavalry during the Winter Campaign of 1868–69. "Custer, Cody and the Grand Duke Alexis" by Elizabeth Bacon Custer and John Manion, is also entertaining.

The text of the letter written to Custer by Jimmy Calhoun can be found in Merington's *Custer Story,* 236–37.

The politics of the Union Pacific Railroad are vividly portrayed in Kuberkin's *Jay Cooke's Gamble: The Northern Pacific Railroad, the Sioux, and the Panic of 1873.* Excellent sources about the railroad at that time for the casual reader are *Penny-an-Acre*

Empire in the West, by Stewart, and *Guidebook of the Western United States; Part A: The Northern Pacific Route,* by Campbell, et al. Information and documents pertaining to the Northern Pacific are also contained in the collection of the Minnesota Historical Society.

Stanley covers the scope of his military career in his *Personal Memoirs of Major-General D. S. Stanley, U.S.A.* The appendix of this book includes extracts from Stanley's letters to his wife during the Yellowstone Expedition, which conveys his low opinion of Custer, as well as his official report: *Report on the Yellowstone Expedition of 1873.* Custer's vacillating opinion of Stanley can be found in his correspondence with Libbie in Merington's *Custer Story.* More about the Stanley–Hazen feud can be found in *Great Plains Command,* by Kroeker and *Phil Sheridan and His Army,* by Hutton.

Informative references about George Yates are "Colonel George W. Yates," by Annie Roberts Yates; "George Yates: Captain of the Band Box Troop," by Pohanka; and *A Summer on the Plains,* by Pohanka.

The best biography of Tom Rosser is *Fightin' Tom Rosser, C.S.A.,* by Bushong and McKain. My *Glorious War* contains detailed accounts of those times Custer and Rosser met on the Civil War battlefield. Rosser and Custer on the Yellowstone Expedition, in addition to biographical material on Rosser, are covered in *Custer's 7th Cav and the Campaign of 1873,* by Frost.

Custer's article "Battling with the Sioux on the Yellowstone," which includes the quote about Rosser, can be found in the July 1876 issue of *Galaxy* reprinted in *The Custer Reader,* edited by Hutton.

There has been some question regarding the identity of the Lakota Sioux Indians who attacked Custer's cavalry in the engagements of August 4 and 11, 1873. There are those, including author Stephen Ambrose in *Crazy Horse and Custer* supported by Mari Sandoz in her *Crazy Horse,* who have written that famed warrior Crazy Horse and medicine man Sitting Bull probably participated in at least the first, if not both skirmishes. The tactics employed in that initial skirmish on August 4 certainly resembled those that Crazy Horse had first displayed to the white man during Red Cloud's War. One piece of evidence that may point to Sitting Bull having a hand in the attacks was the presence of Frank Grouard with the Sioux. This future army scout whose treachery indirectly contributed to the death of Crazy Horse at that time was known to have been a member of Sitting Bull's family by adoption.

Custer noted in his report that was reprinted in his wife's book *Boots and Saddles:* "The Indians were made up of different bands of Sioux, principally Uncpapas [*sic*], the whole under command of 'Sitting Bull,' who participated in the fight, and who for once has been taught a lesson he will not soon forget."

Custer, however, does not repeat that assertion in his article "Battling with the Sioux on the Yellowstone." It would seem odd that Custer did not mention Sitting Bull or Crazy Horse, if indeed these by then famous warriors had participated.

Also, another article reprinted in Hutton's *Custer Reader*, "Expedition to the Yellowstone River in 1873: Letters of a Young Cavalry Officer" by Larned, a Seventh Cavalry officer who was a member of the expedition, failed to name any of the Indians who attacked the cavalry.

Custer scholar Frost in his *Custer's 7th Cav and the Campaign of 1873* related the Indian fights without identifying any of the Sioux participants. In his notes, however, Frost quotes Colonel David Stanley as stating that upon the colonel's arrival at Fort Sully he spoke to a man named Antoine Clement who had learned from a Sioux chief named Little White Swan that the leaders in the attacks were Red Ears' son, a Brulé, and Bull Without Hair, a Miniconju.

In the absence of definitive sources, perhaps the romantic view that the eyes of Custer and Crazy Horse had briefly danced together in prelude to their meeting at the Little Bighorn—as Ambrose suggests—adds to the drama and creates a more stirring picture of those two battles on the Yellowstone.

The best account of Bloody Knife's life is *Bloody Knife: Custer's Favorite Scout*, by Innis. Other notable works include: "Bloody Knife," by Collin, and "Bloody Knife, Ree Scout for Custer," by Gray, and for Bloody Knife's controversy with Chief Gall see "Bloody Knife and Gall" by Taylor.

The best accounts of the life and death and usefulness of the American bison can be found in *The Buffalo: The Story of American Bison and Their Hunters from Prehistoric Times to the Present*, by Haines; "Bison Ecology and Bison Diplomacy: The Southern Plains from 1800 to 1850," by Flores; *The Buffalo Hunters*, by Mari Sandoz; *The Buffalo Book*, by Dary; and "Indians as Buffalo Hunters," by Rister.

The best source in the rather lean bibliography of the Yellowstone Expedition is *Custer's 7th Cav and the Campaign of 1873*, by Frost. Another interesting source, which provides excerpts from fifteen of Custer's letters to his wife, is *The Custer Story*, by Merington. For Libbie's personal account and a reprint of Custer's official report see her *Boots and Saddles*. One other source of note is "The Yellowstone Expedition of 1873." For the role of steamboats on this expedition, see "Steamboats on the Yellowstone" by Lass.

Chapter Six
Black Hills, Red Spirits

The best account of the Custers' life at Fort Abraham Lincoln can be found in Libbie's *Boots and Saddles or, Life in Dakota with General Custer*. Another interesting source is chapter 24 in *General Custer's Libbie*, by Frost. Also see *Custer's Seventh Cavalry Comes to Dakota*, by Darling.

Excellent sources for the arrival and domination of the Lakota Sioux in the Black Hills area can be found in *Red Cloud's Folk*, by Hyde; *Spotted Tail's Folk*, by Hyde; *The Sioux: Life and Customs of a Warrior Society*, by Hassrick; and "The Intertribal Balance of Power on the Great Plains, 1760–1850," by Calloway.

The best source for the complete history of the fight over the Black Hills by the Lakota Sioux is *Black Hills/White Justice*, by Lazarus.

Text of the Fort Laramie Treaty of 1868 (from *U.S. Statutes at Large*, vol. 15, 635–40) can be found in *Custer's Gold*, by Jackson, and in volume 2 of *Indian Affairs: Laws and Treaties*, compiled by Kappler.

An excellent account of the treaty and its aftermath based on Indian and white sources is *Red Cloud and the Sioux Problem*, by Olson. Also see *Fort Laramie in 1876: Chronicle of a Frontier Post at War*, by Hedren; *Phil Sheridan and His Army*, by Hutton; and *Frontier Regulars*, by Utley.

The best sources for Red Cloud's War include: *Red Cloud's Folk*, by Hyde; *Fort Phil Kearny: An American Saga*, by Brown; *The Bozeman Trail: Historical Accounts of the Blazing of the Overland Route into the Northwest and the Fights with Red Cloud's Warriors*, by Brininstool and Hebard; *The Fetterman Massacre*, by Brown; *Indian Fights and Fighters*, by Brady; *Red Cloud and the Sioux Problem*, by Olson; *Indian Fights*, by Vaughn; and *My Army Life and the Fort Phil Kearny Massacre*, by Carrington.

Sherman's defense of entry into the Black Hills is in Jackson's *Custer's Gold*, 24; Barrows' quote is in the same volume, 76; McKay's quote can be found in my *Custer Companion*, 146.

Custer's fame as a dead-eyed marksman in large part can be attributed to his own considerable promotion. His articles in *Galaxy* and the sportsman's journal *Turf, Field and Farm* record many memorable hunts and days spent with thoroughbred horses in Kentucky. The *Galaxy* articles were compiled into Custer's book, *My Life on the Plains*, which brought his exploits to the general public. The *Turf, Field and Farm* articles have been reprinted in *Nomad*, edited by Dippie.

For other interesting portrayals of Custer's sporting life, see: *General Custer's*

Thoroughbreds: Racing, Riding, Hunting, and Fighting, by Frost; "Buffalo Hunting with Custer," by Talmadge; and "Big Game Hunting with the Custers," by Millbrook. Many of Custer's hunts and observations are noted by his wife in her three books: *Boots and Saddles, Tenting on the Plains,* and *Following the Guidon.* John Burkman's recollections about tending Custer's hounds can be found in *Old Neutriment,* by Wagner.

Custer's quote about hunting can be found in Merington's *Custer Story,* 274–75. His dispatch to Sheridan about finding gold is in Jackson's *Custer's Gold,* 87–88.

Biographical material about Boston Custer comes from the various biographies of his famous brother. His obituary appeared in the January 11, 1878, edition of *The Monroe Commercial.* Boston's letter to his mother has been reprinted in Graham's *Custer Myth.*

George Bird Grinnell's descriptive books and articles about the Cheyenne, Pawnee, and Blackfoot remain excellent sources of information. Most notable are *The Cheyenne Indians* and *The Fighting Cheyennes.*

Notable books and articles about Charley Reynolds include: the definitive biography *Charley Reynolds: Soldier, Hunter, Scout and Guide,* by John E. and George J. Remsburg; "Charley Reynolds, Hunter & Scout," by Brininstool; "On the Trail of Lonesome Charley Reynolds," by Gray; and Gray's "Last Rites for Lonesome Charley Reynolds." George Bird Grinnell's account of Reynolds and the pronghorn antelope can be found in Grinnell's "The Return of a War Party: Reminiscences of Charley Reynolds."

Reynolds' diary, with entries from May 17 to June 22, 1876, is in the archives of the Minnesota State Historical Society, St. Paul. The text of the diary can be found in Koury's *Diaries of the Little Big Horn.*

The best account of the Black Hills Expedition, which provides an excellent overview with interesting anecdotes, is *Custer's Gold: The United States Cavalry Expedition of 1874,* by Jackson. Newspaper coverage, Custer's reports, and journals maintained by Forsyth and Grant can be found in *Prelude to Glory,* by Krause and Olson. For Custer's official report see *Report of the Expedition to the Black Hills Under Command of Brevet Major General G. A. Custer,* 43rd Cong., 2nd sess., Sen. Exec. Doc. 32.

Diaries of two military participants—one officer and one enlisted—are: *With Custer in '74: James Calhoun's Diary of the Black Hills Expedition,* edited by Frost, and *Private Theodore Ewert's Diary of the Black Hills Expedition of 1874,* edited by Carroll and Frost.

The journal of Theodore Ewert, who was serving as Custer's orderly trumpeter, is especially notable. His record of events provides interesting and relevant information not available in official reports or articles submitted by correspondents. His descriptions of the daily routine include amusing observations and complaints that have been expressed by enlisted men throughout military history. He also had the freedom to state opinions that may have been contrary to those of his superiors, the public, and the mainstream press. Ewert was discharged from the army on April 10, 1876, and therefore did not march with the Seventh Cavalry to the Little Bighorn. Many excerpts from Ewert's journal can be found in *Custer's Gold,* by Jackson.

Another participant's view is in *The Passing of the Great West: Selected Papers of George Bird Grinnell,* edited by Reiger.

For a modern-day photographic reconstruction of Custer's route, see *Following Custer,* by Progulske and Shideler.

Also valuable are: *Gold in the Black Hills,* by Parker; "The Red Man and the Black Hills," by Bates; and "The Black Hills Expedition of 1874," by Gerber.

Chapter Seven
Prelude to War

Plenty of sources where Custer's writing skills can be viewed have been documented in previous chapters. Other works by Custer—personal letters, orders, et cetera—can be found in collections at the Little Bighorn Battlefield National Monument; University of Michigan; Monroe, Michigan County Library System; Monroe County Historical and Museum Association; New York Public Library; Rochester, New York Public Library; U.S. Army Military History Institute; U.S. Military Academy at West Point; and Yale University.

The Custer-Hazen feud is covered in *Penny-an-Acre Empire in the West,* edited by Stewart; *Great Plains Command: William B. Hazen in the Frontier West,* by Kroeker; "Deceit About the Garden: Hazen, Custer, and the Arid Lands Controversy," by Kroeker; and "A Short Evaluation of the Custer-Hazen Debates" in *4 On Custer by Carroll.* Excerpts of letters written by Hazen and Custer—as well as others involved—are contained in *Custer's 7th Cav and the Campaign of 1873,* by Frost. Rosser's letter of February 16, 1874, which requests that Custer respond to Hazen, is in the Elizabeth B. Custer Collection, Little Bighorn Battlefield National Monument.

Custer's close relationship with the railroads can be found in "Fort Desolation: The Military Establishment, the Railroad, and the Settlement on the Northern Plains," by Hutton.

Hazen's "Some Corrections of 'Life on the Plains'" and Custer's opinion of Hazen can be found in *My Life on the Plains.* An attack on Hazen's position, *Major General Hazen on His Post of Duty in the Great American Desert,* was written by former U.S. Surveyor General John O. Sargeant.

The most complete account of Rain-in-the-Face's arrest and escape can be found in *Custer's 7th Cav and the Campaign of 1873,* by Frost. Various versions of the event attributed to Rain-in-the-Face are in "Rain-in-the-Face: The Story of a Sioux Warrior," by Eastman; "The Personal Story of Rain-in-the-Face," by Brady; "Custer and Rain in the Face," by Huggins, and "Captain Yates' Capture of Rain-in-the-Face," by Brady.

Thomas "Tucker" French is the subject of "A Captain of Chivalric Courage," by Johnson and articles in two newspapers: "The Man in Buckskin" in *The Bismarck Tribune,* April 11, 1877, and "Tracking a Custer Indian Fighter" in *The Washington Post,* March 27, 1980. A letter he wrote to the wife of Dr. A. H. Cooke has been reprinted in *The Custer Myth,* edited by Graham.

Every book about the Apache Wars in Arizona contains biographical material about George Crook. An entertaining autobiography is *General George Crook: His Autobiography.* His Civil War career is chronicled in Magid's *George Crook: From the Redwoods to Appomattox.* A well-balanced account of his Western adventures can be found in Robinson's *General Crook and the Western Frontier.* Stories from an unabashed admirer who served as Crook's aide for sixteen years yet offers a fair account of the general's service in Arizona, Wyoming, and Montana are in *On the Border with Crook,* by John G. Bourke.

Walter P. Jenny's *Report on the Mineral Wealth, Climate and Rainfall and Natural Resources of the Black Hills of South Dakota,* which covers his 1875 expedition, can be found in 44th Cong., 1st sess., Exec. Doc. 51.

The best sources for the Allison Commission's attempt to purchase the Black Hills and ensuing events leading to hostilities include: Allison's report: *Annual Report to the Commissioner of Indian Affairs,* 1875; *Red Cloud's Folk* and *Spotted Tail's Folk,* by Hyde; *A History of the Dakota or Sioux Indians,* by Robinson; and "The Majors and the Miners: The Role of the U.S. Army in the Black Hills Gold Rush," by Parker.

President Grant's edict of December 6, 1875, to the Lakota Sioux in the unceded territory is contained in *Report of the Secretary of War, 1876.* Instructions to the various Indian agents have been printed in 44th Cong., 1st sess., Sen. Exec. Doc. No. 52, pp. 5–6, *and* 44th Cong., 1st sess., House Exec. Doc. No. 184.

The complex political intrigue and struggle over the direction of the country's reaction to the "Indian Problem" has a number of valuable sources, including: "The Celebrated Peace Policy of General Grant," by Utley; "Indian Fighters and Indian Reformers: Grant's Indian Peace Policy and the Conservative Consensus," by Levine; "The Argument over Civilian or Military Indian Control, 1865–1880," by D'Elia; *Military and United States Indian Policy, 1865–1903,* by Wooster; and Prucha's *Great Father: The*

United States Government and the American Indians and his *American Indian Policy in Crisis: Christian Reformers and the Indian, 1865–1900.*

Custer's telegram to Grant can be found in virtually every biography and book about the Little Bighorn.

Chapter Eight
First Blood

Notable sources for the life of General Alfred Terry include: *Pacifying the Plains: General Alfred Terry and the Decline of the Sioux, 1866–1890,* by Bailey; *The Field Diary of General Alfred H. Terry: The Yellowstone Expedition—1876;* and *The Terry Letters: The Letters of General Alfred Howe Terry to His Sisters During the Indian War of 1876,* edited by Willert. In addition, nearly every volume published about the U.S. Army's campaigns against the Indians on the Northern Plains includes references to Terry. His official report of the Little Bighorn Campaign can be found in 44th Cong., 2nd sess., House Exec. Doc. 1, part 2, and *Annual Report, 1876,* United States War Department.

The best information about John Gibbon includes *Gibbon on the Sioux Campaign of 1876,* by Gibbon, which reprinted his articles from the April and October 1877 *American Catholic Quarterly Review;* and *On Time for Disaster: The Rescue of Custer's Command,* by McClernand. Generous mentions about Gibbon's role in the Little Bighorn Campaign can be found in *Custer's Luck,* by Stewart and *Custer and the Great Controversy,* by Utley.

The Powder River fight is nicely covered in *The Reynolds Campaign on Powder River,* by Vaughn. Additional information can be found in Battle of the Rosebud sources mentioned later, as well as every book about the Battle of the Little Bighorn.

The most famous and interesting account of Crazy Horse's life is the fictionalized *Crazy Horse: The Strange Man of the Oglalas,* by Sandoz. Another fascinating biography, which fills in blanks with dramatic and believable speculation, is *Crazy Horse and Custer: The Parallel Lives of Two American Warriors,* by Ambrose. Other credible sources include: *The Journey of Crazy Horse: A Lakota History,* by Marshall; *Crazy Horse: The Life Behind the Legend,* by Sajna; *Red Cloud's Folk,* by Hyde; *Spotted Tail's Folk,* by Hyde; *Crazy Horse,* by Brininstool; "Crazy Horse's Story of the Custer Battle," edited by Robinson; "Oglala Sources on the Life of Crazy Horse," by Hinman; and "An Indian Scout's Recollections of Crazy Horse," by Grouard.

The Grattan massacre and subsequent events that affected Crazy Horse can be found in transcripts of interviews with Indian and white residents of the time, along with letters, newspapers clippings, and comments by Judge Daniel Ricker in the Eli Ricker Collection, Nebraska State Historical Society. More convenient sources include: *Spotted Tail's Folk*, by Hyde; *Frontiersmen in Blue: The United States Army and the Indian, 1848–1865,* by Utley; *Red Cloud and the Sioux Problem*, by Olson; and "The Grattan Massacre," by McCann.

Two excellent biographies of Sitting Bull top the list: *The Lance and the Shield: The Life and Times of Sitting Bull,* by Utley, and *Sitting Bull: Champion of the Sioux*, by Vestal. Also see: *Sitting Bull*, by Adams; *Sitting Bull*, by Dugan; *Cry of the Thunderbird,* by Hamilton; and *A Sioux Chronicle*, by Hyde.

The best (and definitive) source for the Rosebud battle is *Battle of the Rosebud: Prelude to the Little Bighorn,* by Mangum. See also: *The Reynolds Campaign on Powder River,* by Vaughn; *Campaigning with Crook,* by King; and *With Crook at the Rosebud,* by Vaughn. For the Indian account, see *Soldiers Falling into Camp,* by Lefthand, Marshall, and Kammen.

Chapter Nine
The March of the Seventh Cavalry

The best source for Grant Marsh and the *Far West* is *The Conquest of the Missouri: Being the Story of the Life and Exploits of Captain Grant Marsh,* by Hanson. See also: Crittenden's *History of Early Steamboat Navigation on the Missouri River.*

A sympathetic biography of Reno is *Faint the Trumpet Sounds,* by Terrell and Walton. Author George Walton joined with Reno's great-nephew and the American Legion in 1967 in the successful petition to have Reno's record reviewed. The result of that review can be found in the June 1, 1967, edition of *The New York Times.* Johnson also wrote "Reno as Escort Commander." Perhaps the one author most blinded by the facts of Reno's betrayal is Ronald H. Nichols, who has written articles and books vigorously defending Reno. These include: "Marcus Albert Reno," *The Reno Court of Inquiry,* and the biography *In Custer's Shadow: Major Marcus Reno.*

Reno's Powder River scout can be found in every book about the battle. In addition, see "The Reno Scout," by Stewart and Luce.

Sources for Terry's final order to Custer can be found listed and discussed in the narrative and sources of chapter 17: "Clearing the Smoke from the Battlefield."

Custer's last letter to Libbie can be read in Merington's *Custer Story,* 307–8.

Everything you need to know about the weapons carried by the soldiers can be found in the following sources: *Custer Battle Guns,* by duMont; *The Springfield Carbine on the Western Frontier,* by Hammer; *Firearms in the Custer Battle,* by Parson and duMont; "The Army's Search for a Repeating Rifle," by Chamberlain; "Firearms at Little Bighorn," by duMont; and "Cavalry Firepower: Springfield Carbine's Selection and Performance," by Nichols.

Mark Kellogg's battlefield notes (May 17 to June 9), which were delivered to Bismarck druggist John P. Dunn, with whom Kellogg played chess, are in the possession of the North Dakota State Historical Society. His final dispatch, published in the *New York Herald* July 11, 1876, has been reprinted in *The Custer Myth,* edited by Graham. For a well-researched chronicle of the life and death of Kellogg, including a reprinting of his diary, see *I Go with Custer,* by Barnard. See also: "Custer's 'Mysterious Mr. Kellogg' and the Diary of Mark Kellogg," by Hixon; "The Mark Kellogg Story," by Vaughn; "Colonel Custer's Copperhead: The Mysterious Mark Kellogg," by Saum; "Mark Kellogg Telegraphed for Custer's Rescue," by Knight; and "The Custer Campaign Diary of Mark Kellogg," by Watson.

Charles Varnum's unfinished memoir was published as *I, Varnum: Autobiographical Reminiscences of Custer's Chief of Scouts,* edited by Carroll and Mills, and *Custer's Chief of Scouts,* edited by Carroll. Also of interest are: "Interview with Charles A. Varnum, May 1909," in *Custer in '76,* edited by Hammer, and "Varnum: The Later Years of Custer's Last Lieutenant," by Kanitz. Varnum wrote: "I Was There: Colonel Charles A. Varnum's Experience" and "Fighting the Indians."

The army had learned over the years that the main problem that plagued cavalry columns when fighting hostile Indians was a lack of mobility. Therefore, excellent intelligence from reconnaissance was essential in order to locate and surprise the Indians in their camps, where they were vulnerable. White frontiersmen who were wise in the ways of the Indian were of great help, but Indian scouts—usually bitter enemies of the hunted—who knew the terrain and could assist in bringing the command within striking distance, were indispensable.

Fifty-one Indian scouts commanded by Second Lieutenant Charles Varnum accompanied the Seventh Cavalry on the Little Bighorn Campaign. These scouts rode ahead of the cavalry column on the approach into the Valley of the Little Bighorn and reported about the numerous fresh trails that they encountered, which appeared to be leading toward a single objective.

On the morning of June 25, evidence of Sitting Bull's huge village, some fifteen miles ahead, was confirmed by the scouts. At that point, many of the Arikara scouts refused to accompany Custer any farther and others were dismissed, their job of locating the village accomplished. In the ensuing battle, two Indian scouts were killed (Bob Tailed Bull and Little Brave) and two were wounded (Goose and White Swan).

For more about the scouts, see: *Wolves for the Blue Soldiers*, by Dunlay; *The Arikara Narrative of the Campaign Against the Hostile Dakotas, June 1876*, by Libby; "The Crow Scouts: Their Contributions in Understanding the Little Big Horn Battle," by Sills; and "Did Custer Believe His Scouts?" by Church.

Chapter Ten
Into the Valley

The author, a Marine Corps Vietnam veteran, felt obligated to defend the diminishing reputation of the Seventh Cavalry, which has suffered at the hands of modern historians who have unfairly condemned these men for their service. The Vietnam conflict may not have been popular for whatever reasons, but military personnel served in that affair with as much honor and patriotism as had their fathers in World War II—and nearly sixty thousand gave their lives. The average soldier or Marine was not versed in the geopolitics of the matter, only that he was fighting to free people from a brutal Communist regime with a murderous and ruthless dictator. They were indeed marching in their father's footsteps and those of the country's military forefathers, including the men of the Seventh Cavalry, who helped make the West safe for Americans with their participation.

A detailed discussion and list of sources with respect to Custer's separation of his command can be found in chapter 17: "Clearing the Smoke from the Battlefield."

Girard's quote "Here are your Indians . . ." comes from page 84 of Nichols' *Reno Court of Inquiry*.

A detailed discussion and list of sources with respect to Custer's order for Major Reno to charge the village can be found in chapter 17: "Clearing the Smoke from the Battlefield."

Estimates on the number of warriors available to fight the Seventh Cavalry from military sources include: Colonel John Gibbon, 2,500; Second Lieutenant Luther Hare, 4,000; scout George Herendeen, 3,000; First Lieutenant Charles DeRudio, 3,000–4,000; and Captain Myles Moylan, 3,500–4,000. Second Lieutenant Charles Varnum reported not less than 4,000; Second Lieutenant George D. Wallace at first estimated the number at 3,000 and then at the 1879 Reno Court of Inquiry testified that there were 9,000. Captain Frederick Benteen initially set the number at 1,500 and then in later years arrived at a figure of 8,000–9,000.

Estimates from historians include: Stanley Vestal, 2,500; Frazier Hunt, 1,800–2,000; Lewis Crawford, 2,000–2,500; Fred Dustin, 3,000–3,500; full-blooded Sioux Dr. Charles Eastman, not more than 1,411; Edgar I. Stewart, 3,000; Robert M. Utley, 2,000; Jeffry D. Wert, 2,000; and George B. Grinnell, 4,500–6,000.

Perhaps the best—and most logical—estimate of the number of lodges in the village has been provided by John S. Gray in his *Centennial Campaign: The Sioux War of 1876:*

Northern Cheyenne—120

Oglala Sioux—240

Blackfoot, Brulé, and Two Kettle Sioux—120

Sans Arc Sioux—110

Miniconjou Sioux—150

Hunkpapa Sioux—235

Yanktonnais and Santee Sioux—25

Gray estimated the total number of lodges at one thousand but does not include any Arapaho, who were known to have members of their tribe in the village.

It has been said that each lodge would be home to two warriors, perhaps more if the older boys were involved. Add to that the wickiups on the north end of the village that housed young warriors who did not live with their families; subtract those men who had reached "retirement" age, which was said to be sometime before their fortieth birthday.

Whatever the exact number of warriors, it would be safe to say that their number far exceeded that of Custer's troops that day.

Sources for these numbers are culled from the pages of the works by the author listed. In addition, an excellent commentary with plentiful references can be found in *Custer's Luck,* by Stewart.

Biographical material and statements about the battle by Lakota chief Gall can be found in a chapter devoted to him, "The Story of War Chief Gall of the Uncpapas," contained in *The Custer Myth,* edited by Graham. That chapter is followed by "General Godfrey's Comments on Gall's Story." For biographical material, see: *The Lance and the Shield,* by Utley; *Sitting Bull,* by Vestal; *Indian Notes on the Custer Battle,* by Barry; "Custer's Last Battle," by Godfrey; and "Gall: Sioux Gladiator or White Man's Pawn?" by Mangum.

Chapter Eleven
The Crimson Trail

As Custer and the Seventh Cavalry engage the hostiles each specific movement will not be referenced because there is an accepted consensus of the big picture about how the battle unfolded—only the presentation, time lines, intentions of the players, and conclusions differ.

The issues that have become a matter of contention—such as disobedience of orders and separation of command—have been covered in depth with sources in subsequent chapters.

To provide the most pertinent and accessible sources for comparison with this version, however, the following works are listed for additional reading. It must be noted that every biography has its own interpretation of the battle.

There is no lack of material about this famous battle for the serious researcher or casual reader. In fact, this bibliography is one of the most voluminous in American history. A number of books, however, rise to the top of the list.

Perhaps the best single volume, although it may be somewhat studious for the beginner, is Gray's *Centennial Campaign.* Gray's well-researched study utilizes time lines, detailed documentation, and careful reasoning and analysis to reconstruct the battle. Gray then expanded on his earlier work in *Custer's Last Campaign: Mitch Boyer and the Little Bighorn Reconstructed.*

Another notable book—a personal favorite for its informative yet entertaining readability—that will satisfy both the researcher and casual reader is *Custer's Luck,* by Stewart.

One book that has been exhaustively researched and presented in a highly satisfying manner is *A Terrible Glory,* by Donovan. This book will be a welcome addition to the library of the casual reader or the serious researcher. Also, a vivid portrayal comes from Philbrick's *Last Stand.*

A must-have volume for students at any level is *The Custer Myth,* edited by Graham. This work offers eyewitness testimony from both white and Indian participants, letters, reports, and other fascinating miscellany, including a comprehensive bibliography, albeit outdated. In the same category is *The Custer Reader,* edited by Hutton.

Another invaluable source of testimony is *Custer in '76,* edited by Kenneth Hammer, and to a lesser extent *Camp on Custer,* edited by Liddic and Harbaugh.

Other reminiscences of note from soldiers can be found in *Troopers with Custer,* by Brininstool; *Diaries of the Little Big Horn,* by Koury; *I Fought with Custer: The Story of*

Sergeant Windolph, edited by Frazier and Robert Hunt; and *I Buried Custer,* edited by Liddic. An interesting memoir written by Richard A. Roberts, who was Captain George Yates' brother-in-law, is *Custer's Last Battle.*

For accounts by Indian eyewitnesses, as well as the Indian side of the story, see: *Custer's Fall,* by David Humphreys Miller; *Soldiers Falling into Camp,* by Kammen, Lefthand, and Marshall; *Warpath,* by Vestal; *Barry's Indian Notes on the Custer Battle;* and *Killing Custer: The Battle of the Little Bighorn and the Fate of the Plains Indians,* by Welch.

The official documents can be found in *General Custer and the Battle of the Little Big Horn: The Federal View,* edited by Carroll, and *The Little Big Horn, 1876: The Official Communications, Documents, and Reports, with Rosters of the Officers and Troops of the Campaign,* by Overfield.

An examination of the day-by-day activities leading up to the battle is the subject of *Little Big Horn Diary: Chronicle of the 1876 Indian War,* by Willert and Van Ess.

An analysis of the legends created by the battle—although most have been debated in every volume about the battle—is best told in *Custer's Last Stand: The Anatomy of an American Myth,* by Dippie; *Custer and the Great Controversy: The Origin and Development of a Legend,* by Utley; and *Custer and the Epic of Defeat,* by Rosenberg.

Other worthwhile sources about the battle not listed elsewhere can be found in the bibliography.

The best sources for confirmation about what weapons were carried that day by the Sioux and the Cheyenne can be found in *Archaeology, History, and Custer's Last Battle,* by Fox. See also: *Archaeological Insights into the Custer Battle,* by Fox and Scott, and *Archaeological Perspectives on the Battle of the Little Bighorn* by Conner, Fox, Harmon, and Scott.

For more about scout George Herendeen, see: "George Herendeen, Montana Scout," by Johnson. His accounts of the battle, which were originally published in the *New York Herald* on July 8, 1876, and January 22, 1878, have been reprinted in *The Custer Myth,* edited by Graham. See also "Interview with George Herendeen" in *Custer in '76,* edited by Hammer.

Jackson's biography is *William Jackson, Indian Scout,* by Schultz. His account of the famous battle can be found in *Battles and Skirmishes of the Great Sioux War, 1876–77: The Military View,* edited by Greene.

Girard is the subject of "Interview with Frederic F. Gerard, January 22 and April 3, 1909," in *Custer in '76,* edited by Hammer; "F. F. Girard, Scout and Interpreter," by Lounsberry; and "F. F. Gerard's Story of the Custer Fight" in *The Custer Myth,* edited by Graham. Girard's criticism of Major Reno at Little Bighorn can be found in the February 22, 1879, edition of *The Bismarck Tribune,* and his quote accusing Reno of drinking can be found in Hammer's *Custer in '76,* 232.

Ryan's quote about Reno's indecisiveness is on page 293 of Barnard's *Ten Years with Custer.*

More about Isaiah Dorman can be found in: "Isaiah Dorman and the Custer Expedition," by McConnell; "Custer's Negro Interpreter," by Ege; Ege's "Braves of All Colors: The Story of Isaiah Dorman Killed at the Little Big Horn"; *Custer's Black White Man,* by Boyes; and *Troopers with Custer,* by Brininstool. The quote by Sioux chief Runs-the-Enemy can be found in *The Vanishing Race,* by Dixon.

Material about Donald McIntosh can be found in "Donald McIntosh: First Lieutenant, 7th U.S. Cavalry," by Lyon. McIntosh is also the subject of numerous references in *The Custer Myth,* edited by Graham.

Biographical material about Hodgson can be found in "In Memoriam. Lieutenant Benjamin H. Hodgson," by Remak and "Who Buried Lieutenant Hodgson?" by Tuttle. The quote about Hodgson's death is in *Of Garry Owen in Glory,* by Chandler. A more flowery version was written by Captain Charles King in his "Custer's Last Battle," which was reprinted in *The Custer Reader,* edited by Hutton.

For Dr. DeWolf: "The Diary and Letters of Dr. James M. DeWolf, Acting Assistant Surgeon, U.S. Army; His Record of the Sioux Expedition of 1876 as Kept Until His Death," by Luce. A notebook belonging to DeWolf was stolen while on display in the museum at Little Bighorn Battlefield National Monument and has never been recovered.

A biography of Dr. Porter is Walker's *Dr. Henry Porter: The Surgeon Who Survived Little Bighorn.* His quote to Reno and Reno's answer on the hilltop about the men being demoralized can be found in Graham's *Reno Court of Inquiry,* 63.

Chapter Twelve
Battle Ridge

In 1908, Kanipe accompanied historian Walter Camp on a tour of the battlefield, which resulted in "Daniel A. Kanipe's Account of Custer Fight Given to Me on June 16 and 17, 1908," in *Custer in '76,* edited by Hammer. Letters written by Kanipe to Camp are in the Walter M. Camp collection, Harold B. Lee Library, Brigham Young University. See also: "A New Story of Custer's Last Stand, by the Messenger Boy Who Survived," by Aiken, and "The Story of Sergeant Kanipe, One of Custer's Messengers," by Kanipe, is in *The Custer Myth,* edited by Graham.

"Interviews with John Martin, October 24, 1908 and May 10, 1910," can be found in *Custer in '76,* edited by Hammer; "John A. Martin—Custer's Last Courier," by Ross; "Custer's Battle Plan," by Graham; a letter from Martin to D. R. Barry, dated April 7,

1907, can be found in the collection at the Little Bighorn Battlefield National Monument; numerous references to Martin, including his own story, are in *The Custer Myth,* edited by Graham.

Another version of the Benteen duel with the young warrior is recounted in Hoig's *Battle of the Washita.*

Although there are several sources for the attitude, reaction, and behavior of soldiers under fire listed in the bibliography, this version can be attributed to the author, based on his experiences and observations as a United States Marine Corps Vietnam veteran.

Custer's quote about praying before each battle is on page 95 of Merington's *Custer Story.* Libbie's quote about the two of them dying together is also in Merington's *Custer Story,* 144.

Chapter Thirteen
The Siege of the Hilltop

Reno's plea to Benteen "For God's sake . . ." can be found in Lonich, "Blacksmith Henry Mechling," 31.

References with respect to Weir's gallant actions at the Little Bighorn are contained in *The Custer Myth,* edited by Graham. See also "Tribute to Colonel Weir," *The Bismarck Tribune,* January 3, 1877, and "Death of Tom Weir" in the *Army and Navy Journal,* December 27, 1876.

For more about Charles DeRudio, see: *Charles C. DeRudio,* by Mills; "Interview with Charles DeRudio, February 2, 1910," in *Custer in '76,* by Hammer; "Carlo di Rudio, 1st Lt. 7th U.S. Cavalry," by Stone; and "Charles DeRudio: European Assassin," by Shoenberger. According to DeRudio, the following article attributed to him was actually written by Major James S. Brisbin: "My Personal Story," *New York Herald,* July 30, 1876, and reprinted in the *Chicago Times,* August 2, 1876.

An autobiography of Frank Grouard, which was written with the assistance of newspaperman Joe DeBarthe in 1894, does not mention Grouard's involvement in the death of Crazy Horse and occasionally suffers from historical inaccuracies but nonetheless offers a fascinating insight into the life and exploits of this colorful character: *The Life and Adventures of Frank Grouard* by Joe DeBarthe, edited by Stewart. Grouard's early life can be found in "Frank Grouard: Kanaka Scout or Mulatto Renegade?" by Gray. His association with Crazy Horse is contained in his own "An Indian Scout's Recollections of Crazy Horse" and the less flattering *Crazy Horse,* by Sandoz.

Eyewitness testimony with respect to Reno's actions on the hilltop can be found in *Reno Court of Inquiry: The Chicago Times Account,* by Utley; and *Reno Court of Inquiry,* edited by Nichols. Reno's admission of being drunk is in *Indian Fights and Fighters,* by Cyrus Townsend Brady. Reno's suggestion to abandon the hilltop is discussed at length in *I Fought with Custer,* by Frazier and Robert Hunt. Reno also told the *Northwestern Christian Advocate* in 1904 that "his strange actions" during and after the battle were "due to drink."

Chapter Fourteen
Bodies on the Field

James Bradley, the man who found the bodies of Custer's battalion, was killed while commanding a mounted detachment at the August 9, 1877, Battle of Big Hole during the Nez Percé Campaign. Bradley was a prolific writer, however, who maintained journals of various military operations in which he participated. His most famous work is an account of Gibbon's Montana Column in 1876, which has been published as *The March of the Montana Column,* edited by Stewart. Other narratives by Bradley have appeared over the years in issues of *Contributions to the Historical Society of Montana.*

The quotes of the Seventh Cavalry officers upon viewing the dead bodies on the field can be found in a letter from Lieutenant Edward S. Godfrey to John Neihardt, January 6, 1924, Francis R. Hagner Collection. See also: Godfrey's article "Custer's Last Stand," first published in *Century Magazine* 43 (January 1892) and reprinted in *The Custer Reader,* edited by Hutton; and "After the Custer Battle," by Partoll. Other testimony and quotes can be found in *The Custer Myth,* edited by Graham.

The controversy over Rain-in-the-Face's assertion that he cut out and ate Tom Custer's heart can be found in *Custer and the Great Controversy,* by Utley.

The statements by Kate Bighead and Wooden Leg have been attributed to Thomas Marquis. The careful researcher should be warned that Marquis occasionally had trouble separating truth from fable in his *Custer Soldiers Not Buried, She Watched Custer's Last Battle, Two Days After the Battle,* and other publications.

For more about William Van Wyck Reily, see "Profile: Lieutenant William Van Wyck Reily, 7th Cavalry," by Pohanka. A ring that Reily wore when he was killed is on display at the Smithsonian Institution.

Biographical material on John J. Crittenden can be found in *The Crittenden Memoirs,* by Crittenden, and "Lt. Crittenden: Striving for the Soldier's Life," by Cecil.

For Dr. Lord, see "Dr. George E. Lord, Regimental Surgeon," by Vaughn and "Custer's Surgeon, George Lord, Among the Missing at Little Bighorn Battle," by Noyes.

David Humphreys Miller, who consulted dozens of Indian participants for his *Custer's Fall: The Indian Side of the Story*, lists the names of only twelve Cheyenne and twenty Lakota Sioux who were said to have been killed. And one of those, Cheyenne chief Lame White Man, was shot and scalped by a Sioux who mistook him for an Arikara or Crow, perhaps because he was wearing a captured cavalry uniform. In addition to the preceding source, an excellent commentary with plentiful references can be found in *Custer's Luck*, by Stewart. Also see *Hokahey! A Good Day to Die!: The Indian Casualties of the Custer Fight*, by Hardorff.

The best account of news of Custer's defeat can be found in "Montana Editors and the Custer Battle," by Myers, which has been reprinted in *The Great Sioux War 1876–77*, edited by Hedren. See also "Why Helena Instead of Bozeman Scooped the News in 1876" in *The Custer Myth*, edited by Graham.

Excellent information about Mitch Bouyer can be found in Gray's *Custer's Last Campaign: Mitch Bouyer and the Little Bighorn Reconstructed*. See also: *Memoirs of a White Crow Indian*, by Marquis; "Mitch Bouyer, a Scout for Custer," by Hickox; and a letter from W. B. Logan, Fort Belknap Agency, to Walter Camp, dated May 17, 1909, in the Walter Camp Collection, Harold B. Lee Library, Brigham Young University. In 1987, it was announced that bone fragments discovered on the battlefield had been identified as belonging to Bouyer.

The remarkable journey of the *Far West* can be found in *The Conquest of the Missouri: Being the Story of the Life and Exploits of Captain Grant Marsh*, by Hanson.

The letter to Libbie Custer from Major Joseph G. Tilford was quoted from *General Custer's Libbie*, by Frost. The original was part of Frost's personal collection.

Final resting places of the officers who were killed on June 25, 1876, are as follows:

First Lieutenant James Calhoun—Fort Leavenworth National Cemetery, August 3, 1877

First Lieutenant William W. Cooke—Hamilton Cemetery, Hamilton, Ontario, Canada

Second Lieutenant John J. Crittenden—Custer National Cemetery, September 11, 1931

Captain Thomas W. Custer—Fort Leavenworth National Cemetery, August 3, 1877

Dr. James M. DeWolf—Woodlawn Cemetery, Norwalk, Ohio, August 1, 1877

Second Lieutenant Henry M. Harrington—body never found

Second Lieutenant Benjamin H. Hodgson—Laurel Hill Cemetery, Philadelphia, October 1877

Captain Myles W. Keogh—Fort Hill Cemetery, Auburn, New York, October 25, 1877

Dr. George E. Lord—Custer National Cemetery

Second Lieutenant Donald McIntosh—Arlington National Cemetery, July 28, 1909

First Lieutenant James E. Porter—body never found

Second Lieutenant William V. W. Reily—Mt. Olivet Cemetery, Washington, D.C., August 3, 1877

First Lieutenant Algernon E. Smith—Fort Leavenworth National Cemetery, August 3, 1877

Second Lieutenant James G. Sturgis—body never found

Captain George W. Yates—Fort Leavenworth National Cemetery, August 3, 1877

Harry "Autie" Reed was killed alongside his three uncles on Custer Hill and temporarily buried on the field. His body was later exhumed and reinterred in Woodlawn Cemetery in Monroe in January 1878. His name on the battle monument is listed as "Arthur Reed." See "Autie Reed's Last Letters," by O'Neil.

Boston Custer was initially buried on the battlefield. His body was exhumed in 1878 and reinterred in the family plot at Woodlawn Cemetery in Monroe, Michigan. See: "Letters from Boston Custer," by O'Neil.

The best source for this subject is *The Custer Battle Casualties: Burials, Exhumations, and Reinterments,* by Hardorff. See also "With the Indian and the Buffalo in Montana," by McClernand, an officer with Gibbon's column who witnessed the burials.

George Armstrong Custer's funeral is covered in "The Funeral of General Custer," *Harper's Weekly* (October 27, 1877), and "Custer's Burial Revisited: West Point, 1877," by Barnard.

Chapter Fifteen
Custer's Avengers

The best overall account of the period immediately following the Little Bighorn battle is in *Frontier Regulars,* by Utley. See also: *Battles and Skirmishes of the Great Sioux War, 1876–77,* by Greene; *War-Path and Bivouac,* by Finerty; and *The Great Sioux War 1876–77,* edited by Hedren. For a detailed account of Colonel Miles' 1876–77 campaign, see *Yellowstone Command,* by Green.

The story of Cody's "duel" can be found in *First Scalp for Custer: The Skirmish at Warbonnet Creek, Nebraska, July 17, 1876,* by Hedren, as well as in any Cody biography.

The Slim Buttes battle is covered nicely in *Slim Buttes, 1876: An Episode of the Great Sioux War,* by Greene and *Campaigning with Crook,* by King.

The text of the Agreement of August 15, 1876, in which the Sioux signed over the Black Hills, has been reprinted from the *U.S. Statutes at Large, 19,* which has been conveniently reprinted in the appendix of *Custer's Gold: The United States Cavalry Expedition of 1874,* by Jackson.

The Dull Knife battle is covered in *Mackenzie's Last Fight with the Cheyennes,* by Bourke, *The Fighting Cheyennes,* by Grinnell, and *The Dull Knife Fight,* by Werner.

The best source for the Wolf Mountain battle is "The Battle of Wolf Mountain," by Rickey; see also *Faintly Sounds the War-Cry: The Story of the Fight at Battle Butte,* by Werner.

For the Lame Deer fight, see "The Last Fight of the Sioux War of 1876–77," by McBlain.

The flight of Dull Knife and Little Wolf has been sympathetically and vividly portrayed in *Cheyenne Autumn,* by Sandoz.

The surrender and death of Crazy Horse can be found in any of the previously mentioned biographies of him. See also: *The Killing of Crazy Horse,* by Clark and Friswold; "Chief Crazy Horse, His Career and Death," by Brininstool; "The Man Who Killed Crazy Horse," by Carroll; and chapter 5, "The Death of Crazy Horse," in *Camp on Custer,* edited by Liddic and Harbaugh.

The Nez Percé War can be found in *The Flight of the Nez Perce: A History of the Nez Perce War,* by Brown.

For Sitting Bull's adventures in Canada, see "Sitting Bull and the Mounties," by Anderson. The surrender and death of Sitting Bull can be found in any of the previously mentioned biographies of him. Also see: *My Friend, the Indian,* by McLaughlin; "The True Story of the Death of Sitting Bull," by Fechet; and "Surrender of Sitting Bull," by Allison.

A few of the better sources for the Ghost Dance and Wounded Knee affair are: *Eyewitness at Wounded Knee,* by Carter, Jensen, and Paul; *Wovoka and the Ghost Dance,* edited by Lynch; *The Ghost Dance Religion and Wounded Knee,* by Mooney; and *Bury My Heart at Wounded Knee,* by Brown.

Chapter Sixteen
Mysteries, Myths, and Legends

The mystery of the missing bodies from Company E has been covered in most books about the battle—in particular Hammer's *Custer in '76* and King's *Massacre*. One 350-page book, Michno's *Mystery of E Troop,* has been dedicated to the subject and should have been condensed into a short article. Michno's conclusion, incidentally, was that the bodies could have been found in an adjoining ravine.

The intriguing story of Harrington is covered in Hammer's *Custer in '76*; "Another Custer Mystery," published in the *Pony Express Courier,* Placerville, California, August 1936; and "Echoes of the Custer Tragedy," by Scott. Another version of Gall's story about a trooper committing suicide is told by King in his "Custer's Last Battle," which has been reprinted in *The Custer Reader,* edited by Hutton. King states that a year after the battle one of the Sioux pursuers of this rider pointed out a skeleton to officers of the Fifth Cavalry. King also writes that three years after the battle Harrington's watch was returned to his father after being traded by a Sioux who had fled to Canada.

There is no lack of information about the horse Comanche, with my "The Story of Comanche" leading the way. See also: *Comanche (the Horse That Survived the Custer Massacre),* by Amaral; *Comanche of the Seventh,* by Leighton; *His Very Silence Speaks,* by Lawrence; and *Keogh, Comanche and Custer,* by Luce.

Red Horse's statement about the bravest man can be found in *The Custer Myth,* edited by Graham. Luce's version is in his *Keogh, Comanche and Custer,* and Stewart's story is in his *Custer's Luck.* The statement by Cheyenne chief Two Moon can be found in the article "General Custer's Last Fight as Seen by Two Moon," by Garland. Cheyenne warrior Wooden Leg's version is in *Wooden Leg: A Warrior Who Fought Custer,* by Marquis.

Those historians who believe Keogh was the bravest man include Kuhlman in his *Legend into History,* Rosenberg in his *Custer and the Epic of Defeat,* and Miller, who interviewed seventy-one Indian survivors of the battle for his *Custer's Fall.*

Curley's story can be found in "Was There a Custer Survivor?" by Brininstool; *Indian Fights and Fighters,* by Brady; and "Unwritten Seventh Cavalry History," by Brininstool.

A collection of newspaper clippings and personal material about Frank Finkel's claim can be found in the Oshkosh, Wisconsin, Public Museum. His story can be found in Stewart's *Custer's Luck.*

The William Heath mystery is covered in *The Billings Gazette,* June 28, 1999.

A list of the signers of the Enlisted Men's Petition can be found in *The Custer Myth,* edited by Graham.

Chapter Seventeen
Clearing the Smoke from the Battlefield

The most convenient reprint of Terry's order to Custer can be found in Stewart's *Custer's Luck*, 249–50.

Just about every volume that chronicles the battle discusses Terry's orders. In addition to those, some of the best sources include: *Did Custer Disobey Orders at the Battle of the Little Big Horn?* by Kuhlman; *"Sufficient Reason?" An Examination of Terry's Celebrated Order to Custer*, by Taunton; *Indian Fights and Fighters*, by Brady; *Custer and the Great Controversy*, by Utley; and "A Modern Look at Custer's Orders," by O'Neil and Vandenberg.

Terry went as far as to delay the departure of the *Far West*, with the wounded aboard, in order to closet himself with his staff to craft a report that would deflect criticism from him as much as possible. That claim can be found in Walker's *Dr. Henry R. Porter*. The statement from Terry that Custer would have faced a court-martial can be found in the *Chicago Times*, September 16, 1876.

The remarks from Mary Adams are in Graham's *Custer Myth*, 279. Graham's work also includes other quotes and opinions about this subject from participants.

The controversy about readiness arose from an article, "Varnum, Reno and the Little Bighorn," written by W. J. Ghent for *Winners of the West*. In this article, battle participant Second Lieutenant Charles Varnum alleged that the number of recruits participating in the battle was greatly exaggerated at the Court of Inquiry in order to aid Reno's case. Varnum went on to claim that most of the new recruits had been left back at the Powder River base camp and that no company had more than two recruits on the march. Regimental records confirm that statement.

The opinion about how soldiers respond under fire can be attributed to the author, a United States Marine Corps Vietnam veteran.

With respect to the malfunction issues concerning the Springfield carbines, the best source is Fox in his excellent *Archaeology, History, and Custer's Last Battle*. See also: "Carbine Extractor Failure at the Little Big Horn," by Hedren and "The Cartridge Case Evidence on Custer Field," by Trinque.

Custer's refusal to drag along Gatling guns has been covered in Noyes' "The Guns 'Long Hair' Left Behind." Kit Carson's battle at Adobe Walls can be found in my *The Blue, the Gray, and the Red*.

A grasping at straws allegation of Custer's ambition to quickly end the battle and arrive triumphantly at the Democratic Convention to accept the presidential nomination is in Sandoz's *Battle of the Little Bighorn*. Red Star's account appears in "The Arikara

Narrative of the Campaign Against the Hostile Dakotas," edited by Libby. Another embellishment of Red Star's alleged statement can be found in *Custer's Fall: The Indian Side of the Story,* by Miller. See also *Custer for President?* by Repass.

Chapter Eighteen
What Really Happened?

The conclusions contained in this chapter are based on the training, experiences, and observations of the author as a United States Marine Corps Vietnam veteran, as well as his lifelong study of military tactics and history.

Custer's quote about the difference between training and actual combat can be found in Carroll's *Custer in the Civil War,* 101–2.

Chapter Nineteen
Heroes and Villains

The best source for the establishment of the battlefield as a national monument is *History of Custer Battlefield,* by Don Rickey, Jr. Rickey, a former historian at the battlefield, provides answers to just about every possible question. See also Rickey's "Myth to Monument: The Establishment of Custer Battlefield National Monument." For material about the controversial name change, see "Whose Shrine Is It? The Ideological Struggle for Custer Battlefield," by Utley. Superintendent Baker's "Attack at Dawn" was reported by *The New York Times* on June 23, 1996.

Biographical information about the Custer family can be found on the pages of every Custer biography, as well as throughout these notes.

The best book utilizing information from the archaeological digs, a true classic of the battle—although not for beginners—remains *Archaeology, History, and Custer's Last Battle,* by Richard Allan Fox. Dr. Fox combines his extensive knowledge of the battle with his expertise in archaeology to present a fascinating, albeit speculative, glimpse into the unfolding of events on June 25, 1876. See also: *Archaeological Insights into the Custer Battle: A Preliminary Assessment,* by Fox and Scott; *Archaeological Perspectives on the Battle of the Little Bighorn,* by Conner, Fox, Harmon, and Scott; *They Died with Custer: Soldiers' Bones from the Battle of the Little Big Horn,* by Conner, Scott, and Wiley; and Scott's *Uncovering History: Archaeological Investigations at the Little Bighorn.*

There are plenty of sources for the Reno inquiry. Some of the better ones are: Utley's *Reno Court of Inquiry: The Chicago Times Account*; *The Reno Court of Inquiry: Abstract of the Official Record of Inquiry,* by Graham; and *The Reno Court of Inquiry,* edited by Nichols. Three other helpful sources are Utley's *Custer and the Great Controversy, The Story of the Little Big Horn,* by Graham, and "The Reno Court Martial," *Bismarck Tribune,* March 21, 1877.

Reno's side of the story can be found in his "Custer Massacre," in *Americana Magazine.* A literary duel between Reno and Custer's friend Tom Rosser, as well as plenty of other material, can be found in *The Custer Myth,* edited by Graham.

DeRudio's statement is in Hardorff's *On the Little Bighorn with Walter,* 241.

The letter from Lieutenant Lee to Libbie, which is in the collection at the Little Bighorn Battlefield National Monument, has been reprinted in *General Custer's Libbie,* by Frost.

The complete story of Benteen and Theodore Goldin can be found in Carroll's *Benteen-Goldin Letters on Custer and His Last Battle.* See also *The Court Martial of Frederick W. Benteen, Major, 9th Cavalry, or Did General Crook Railroad Benteen?,* edited by Carroll.

The list of the men who were awarded Medals of Honor for their action on the hilltop includes:

Company A: Private Neil Bancroft, Private David W. Harris, and Sergeant Stanislas Roy

Company B: Private Thomas J. Callan, Sergeant Benjamin C. Criswell, Private Charles Cunningham, Sergeant Rufus D. Hutchinson, Sergeant Thomas Murray, and Private James Pym

Company C: Sergeant Richard P. Hanley and Private Peter Thompson

Company D: Private Abram B. Brant, blacksmith Frederick Deetline, Private William M. Harris, Private Henry Holden, Private George D. Scott, Private Thomas W. Stivers, Private Frank Tolan, and Private Charles H. Welch

Company G: Private Theodore W. Goldin

Company H: Sergeant George Geiger, blacksmith Henry W. B. Mechlin, Private Otto Voit, and Private Charles Windolph

For the best stories about these heroic men, see: "Account of Edward Pickard," *Oregon Journal;* "Custer Battle Water Party," by Brininstool; *Army and Navy Journal* (July 15, 1876); *Winners of the West* (June 24, 1926); "A Survivor's Story of the Custer Massacre on the American Frontier," by Adams; and *Indian Fights and Fighters,* by Brady.

Bibliography

A listing here does not necessarily mean an endorsement of any kind for the credibility of the work; rather, these are publications cited as sources as well as associated material that have assisted in gathering facts and forming observations and opinions. I apologize if I have omitted any material that a writer or a historian has worked so hard to research and publish—which I am sure I unintentionally have—but the bibliography of George Armstrong Custer and the Little Bighorn is perhaps the most voluminous in American history and can at times seem almost unmanageable.

Newspapers and Journals

Army and Navy Journal
Billings Gazette
Bismarck Tribune
Chicago Daily News
Chicago Daily Tribune
Chicago Evening Journal
Chicago Tribune
Cincinnati Commercial
Cincinnati Enquirer
Detroit Free Press
Grand Rapids Daily Eagle

Harper's Weekly

Helena Herald

Inter-Ocean

Minneapolis Tribune

Monroe Commercial

Monroe Democrat

Monroe [MI] *Evening News*

National Tribune

New York Herald

New York Sun

New York Times

New-York Tribune

New York World

Placerville [CA] *Pony Express Courier*

St. Louis Democrat

St. Paul Pioneer Press

Sioux City Journal

Toledo Blade

Walla Walla Bulletin

Washington Post

Washington Star

Winners of the West

Government Reports and Publications

Annual Report to the Commissioner of Indian Affairs, 1875.

Campbell, Marius, et al. *Guidebook of the Western United States; Part A: The Northern Pacific Route.* Bulletin 611. Washington, D.C.: Government Printing Office, 1916.

Kappler, Charles J., comp. *Indian Affairs: Laws and Treaties.* Washington, D.C.: Government Printing Office, 1904–41.

44th Cong., 1st sess., Sen. Exec. Doc. No. 52.

44th Cong., 1st sess., House Exec. Doc. No. 184.

Records of the U.S. Army, Box 16, Division of the Missouri, Special File, RG 393.

Register of Delinquencies, 1856–61, United States Military Academy Archives, West Point, New York.

Regulations for the U.S. Military Academy at West Point, New York. New York: John F. Trow, Printer, 1857.

Report of the Expedition to the Black Hills Under Command of Brevet Major General G. A. Custer, 43rd Cong., 2nd sess., Sen. Exec. Doc. 32.

Report of the Secretary of War Communicating, in Compliance with a Resolution of the Senate of February 4, 1867: Copy of Evidence Taken at Denver and Fort Lyon, Colorado by a Military Commission Ordered to Inquire in the Sand Creek Massacre, November 1864.

Report of the Secretary of War, 1876.

"Report on Management of the War Department, Rep. Heister Clymer, Chairman of Committee." *House Reports* no. 79, 44th Cong., 1st sess., serial no. 1715 (1876).

Report on the Mineral Wealth, Climate and Rainfall and Natural Resources of the Black Hills of South Dakota, 44th Cong., 1st sess., Exec. Doc. No. 51.

Report on the Yellowstone Expedition of 1873. Washington, D.C.: Government Printing Office, 1874.

Special Orders, no. 21, U.S. Military Academy Archives.

War of the Rebellion: A Compilation of the Official Records of the Union and Confederate Records. 130 vols. Washington, D.C., 1880–1901.

Collections

Benteen, Frederick W., Collection. University of Georgia Library.

Bonner, Robert. Papers. New York Public Library.

Brininstool, Earl Alonzo, Collection. Center for American History, University of Texas, Austin.

Camp, Walter M., Papers. Denver Public Library.

Camp, Walter M., Papers. Harold B. Lee Library, Brigham Young University, Provo, UT.

Camp, Walter M., Papers. Lilly Library, Indiana University, Bloomington.

Campbell, Walter Stanley, Collection. Western History Collection, University of Oklahoma, Norman.

Cartwright, R. G., Collection. Phoebe Apperson Hearst Library, Lead, SD.

Custer, Brice C. W. Private Collection.

Custer File and Scrapbooks. Montana Room, Billings Public Library, Billings, MT.

Custer, Elizabeth, Collection. Detroit Public Library.

Custer, Elizabeth B., Collection. Little Bighorn Battlefield National Monument, Crow Agency. MT.

Custer, George Armstrong, Collection. Monroe County Library System, Monroe, MI.

Frost, Lawrence A., Collection. Monroe County Historical Museum, Monroe, MI.

Ghent, William J., Papers. Library of Congress, Washington, D.C.

Godfrey, Edward S., Papers. U.S. Army Military History Institute, Carlisle, PA.

Grinnell, George Bird, Papers. Braun Research Library, Institute for the Study of the American West, Autry National Center, Los Angeles, CA.

Hagner, Francis R., Collection. New York Public Library.

Hein, Louis, Collection. Special Collections Division, Georgetown University Library, Washington, D.C.

Kellogg Collection. North Dakota State Historical Society.

Kuhlman, Charles, Collection. Harold B. Lee Library, Brigham Young University, Provo, UT.

McCracken Research Library, Buffalo Bill Historical Center, Cody, WY.

Merington, Marguerite, Papers. New York Public Library.

National Archives, Washington, D.C.

Order of the Indian Wars Papers. U.S. Military History Institute, Carlisle, PA.

Oshkosh, Wisconsin, Public Museum.

Ricker, Eli, Collection. Nebraska State Historical Society, Lincoln.

Smith, Nettie Brown, Collection. Bancroft Library, University of California, Berkeley.

Terry Family Collection. Beinecke Library, Yale University, New Haven, CT.

Van de Water, Frederic, Papers. New York Public Library.

Wyoming State Archives, Cheyenne.

Periodicals

Adams, Jacob. "A Survivor's Story of the Custer Massacre on the American Frontier." *Journal of American History* 3 (1909).

Aiken, Will. "A New Story of Custer's Last Stand, by the Messenger Boy Who Survived." *Montana Historical Society Contributions* 4 (1923).

Aimore, Alan. "U.S. Military Academy Civil War Sources and Statistics." *Military Collector and Historian* 54, no. 3 (Fall 2002).

Alfield, Philip L. "Major Reno and His Family in Illinois." *English Westerners' Brand Book,* July 1971.

Allison, E. H. "Surrender of Sitting Bull." *South Dakota Historical Quarterly* 6 (1912).

Ambrose, Stephen E. "Sidesaddle Soldier: Libbie Custer's Partnership in Glory." *Timeline* 7 (August–September 1990).

Anderson, Harry H. "Cheyennes at the Little Bighorn: A Study in Statistics." *North Dakota History* 27, no. 3 (Summer 1960).

———. "Indian Peace Talkers and the Conclusion of the Sioux War of 1876." *Nebraska History,* December 1963.

Anderson, Ian. "Sitting Bull and the Mounties." *Wild West,* February 1998.

Arnold, Steve. "Cooke's Scrawled Note: Last Word from a Doomed Command." *Greasy Grass* 14 (May 1998).

Athearn, Robert G. "War Paint Against Brass." *Montana* 6, no. 3 (July 1956).

Bailey, Edward C. "Echoes from Custer's Last Fight." *Military Affairs* 17, no. 4 (1953).

Baird, Andrew T. "Into the Valley Rode the Six Hundred: The 7th Cavalry and the Battle of the Little Bighorn." *Vulcan Historical Review* 4 (Spring 2000).

Barnard, Sandy. "Custer's Burial Revisited: West Point, 1877." *6th Annual Symposium Custer Battlefield Historical & Museum Association,* 1992.

Barnett, Louise. "Powder River." *Greasy Grass* 16 (May 2000).

Bates, Colonel Charles Francis. "The Red Men and the Black Hills." *Outlook,* July 27, 1927.

Beardsley, J. L. "Could Custer Have Won?" *Outdoor Life* 71, no. 3 (March 1933).

Beck, Paul. "Military Officers' Views of Indian Scouts." *Military History of the West* 23, no. 1 (Spring 1993).

Benham, D. J. "The Sioux Warrior's Revenge." *Canadian Magazine* 43 (September 1914).

Braatz, Timothy. "Clash of Cultures as Euphemism: Avoiding History at the Little Bighorn." *American Indian Culture and Research Journal* 28, no. 4 (2004).

Brackett, William S. "Custer's Last Battle on the Little Big Horn in Montana, June 25, 1876." *Contributions to the Historical Society of Montana* 4 (1903).

Braden, Charles. "An Incident of the Yellowstone Expedition of 1873." *Journal of the United States Cavalry Association* 15, no. 54 (October 1904).

———. "The Yellowstone Expedition of 1873." *Journal of the United States Cavalry Association* 16 (October 1905).

Bradley, James H. "Journal of the Sioux Campaign of 1876 Under the Command of General John Gibbon." *Contributions to the Historical Society of Montana* 4 (1903).

Brady, Cyrus T. "Captain Yates' Capture of Rain-in-the-Face." *The Teepee Book.* Sheridan, WY: June 1916.

Bray, Kingsley M. "Teton Sioux Population History, 1655–1881." *Nebraska History* 75, no. 2 (Summer 1994).

Briggs, Harold E. "The Black Hills Gold Rush." *North Dakota Historical Quarterly* 5, no. 2 (January 1931).

Brigham, Eric. "Custer's Last Meeting with Secretary of War Belknap at Fort Abraham Lincoln." *North Dakota History,* August 1952.

Brininstool, E. A. "Charley Reynolds, Hunter & Scout." *North Dakota Historical Quarterly,* July 1930.

——. "Chief Crazy Horse, His Career and Death." *Nebraska History* 12, no. 1 (January–March 1929).

——. "Custer Battle Water Party." *Hunter-Trader-Trapper* 65 (August 1932).

——. "Unwritten Seventh Cavalry History." *Middle Border Bulletin* (Spring 1945).

——. "Was There a Custer Survivor?" *Hunter-Trader-Trapper,* April 1922.

——. "With Reno at the Little Big Horn." *Hunter-Trader-Trapper,* March, April 1924.

Britt, Albert. "Custer's Last Fight." *Pacific Historical Review* 13, no. 1 (March 1944).

Broome, Jeff. "In Memory of Lt. James Sturgis." *Guidon* 3, no. 3 (June 2000).

Brown, Jerold E. "Custer's Vision." In *Studies in Battle Command.* Fort Leavenworth, KS: Combat Studies Institute, U.S. Army Command and General Staff College.

Brust, James. "Lt. Oscar Long's Early Map Details Terrain, Battle Positions." *Greasy Grass* 11 (May 1995).

Buecker, Thomas R. "Frederic S. Calhoun: A Little-Known Member of the Custer Clique." *Greasy Grass* 10 (May 1994).

Bulkley, John M. "As a Classmate Saw Custer." *New York Evening Post,* May 28, 1910.

Burrows, Jack. "From Bull Run to Little Big Horn." *American West* 5, no. 2 (March 1968).

Calloway, Colin G. "The Intertribal Balance of Power on the Great Plains, 1760–1850." *Journal of American Studies* 16 (1982).

Campsey, William M. "Intuitive Vision Versus Practical Realities: Custer at the Battle of the Little Bighorn." In *Studies in Battle Command.* Fort Leavenworth, KS: Combat Studies Institute, U.S. Army Command and General Staff College.

Carroll, John M. "The Man Who Killed Crazy Horse." *Old West* 27, no. 4 (Summer 1991).

—— and Robert Aldrich. "Some Custer and Little Big Horn Facts to Ponder." *English Westerners' Society Tally Sheet* 40, no. 3 (Summer 1994).

Cecil, Jerry. "Lt. Crittenden: Striving for the Soldier's Life." *Greasy Grass* 11 (May 1995).

Chamberlain, Pierce. "The Army's Search for a Repeating Rifle." *Military Affairs* 32 (1968).

Church, Robert. "Did Custer Believe His Scouts?" *5th Annual Symposium, Custer Battlefield Historical & Museum Association,* 1991.

Collin, Richard E. "Bloody Knife: Custer's Favorite Scout." *Greasy Grass* 13 (May 1997).

Couglan, Colonel T. M. "The Battle of the Little Big Horn: A Tactical Study." *Cavalry Journal* 43, no. 181 (January–February 1934).

Crackel, Theodore J. "Custer's Kentucky: General George Armstrong Custer and Elizabethtown, Kentucky, 1871–73." *Filson Club Historical Quarterly* 48 (April 1974).

Craig, Reginald S. "Custer on the Washita." *Brand Book of the Denver Westerners* 10 (1965).

Custer, Elizabeth Bacon. "Custer's Favorite Photo of Himself." *Tepee Book* 1 (July 1916).

———. "General Custer and the Indian Chiefs." *Outlook Magazine,* July 1927.

———. "The General Custer Statue." *Michigan Historical Commission Historical Collection* 39 (1915).

———. "Home Making in the American Army." *Harper's Bazaar,* September 1900.

———. "An Out-of-the-Way 'Outing.'" *Harper's Weekly,* July 18, 1891.

———. "'Where the Heart Is': A Sketch of Women's Life on the Frontier," *Lippincott's Magazine,* February 1900.

———. and John Manion. "Custer, Cody and the Grand Duke Alexis." *Research Review: The Journal of the Little Bighorn Associates* 4 (January 1990).

Custer, George Armstrong. "Battling with the Sioux on the Yellowstone." *Galaxy* 22 (July 1876).

"Custer's Battle from the Indian Viewpoint." *American Indian Journal* 1 (1929).

Daubenmier, Judy. "Empty Saddles: Desertion from the Dashing U.S. Cavalry." *Montana* 54, no. 3 (Autumn 2004).

Davis, Theodore R. "A Summer on the Plains." *Harper's New Monthly Magazine* 36 (February 1868).

D'Elia, J. "The Argument over Civilian or Military Indian Control, 1865–1880." *The Historian* 24, (February 1962).

Deming, Edwin Willard. "Custer's Last Stand." *Mentor,* July 1926.

DeRudio, Carlo. "My Personal Story." *Frontier and Midland Magazine.* Missoula: Montana State University, January 1934.

DeRudio, Charles C. "My Personal Story." Edited by Clyde McLemore. *Frontier and Midland* 14, no. 2 (January 1934).

Dickson, Ephriam. "Reconstructing the Indian Village on the Little Bighorn." *Research Review* 22 (May 2006).

Dixon, David. "The Sordid Side of the Seventh Cavalry." *Research Review* 1, no. 1 (June 1987).

Donahue, Michael. "Revisting Col. Gibbon's Route." *Greasy Grass* 19 (May 2003).

duMont, John S. "Firearms at Little Bighorn." *Greasy Grass* (May 1990).

———. "Custer's Negro Interpreter." *Negro Digest* (February 1965).

Eastman, Charles A. "Rain-in-the-Face: The Story of a Sioux Warrior." *Outlook,* October 1906.

————. "The Story of the Little Bighorn." *Chautauquan,* no. 31 (July 1990).

Ege, Robert. "Braves of All Colors: The Story of Isaiah Dorman Killed at the Little Bighorn." *Montana* (Winter 1966).

Ellis, Horace. "A Survivor's Story of the Custer Massacre." *Journal of American History 3,* no. 2 (April 1909).

Essin, Emmett M., III. "Mules, Packs, and Packtrains." *Southwestern Historical Quarterly* 74, no. 1 (July 1970).

Ewers, John C. "Intertribal Warfare as the Precursor of Indian-White Warfare on the Northern Great Plains." *Western Historical Quarterly* 6, no. 4 (October 1975).

Farioli, Dennis, and Ron Nichols. "Fort A. Lincoln, July 1876." *Greasy Grass* 17 (May 2001).

Farlow, Ed. "Custer Massacre." *Annals of Wyoming* 4, no. 2 (October 1926).

Fechet, E. G. "The True Story of the Death of Sitting Bull." *Proceedings and Collections of the Nebraska State Historical Society,* 2nd ser. (1898).

Flores, Dan L. "Bison Ecology and Bison Diplomacy: The Southern Plains from 1800 to 1850." *Journal of American History* 78 (September 1991).

Foley, James R. "Walter Camp & Ben Clark." *Research Review* 10, no. 1 (January 1996).

Forsyth, George A. "A Frontier Fight." *Harper's New Monthly Magazine* 91 (June 1895).

Fox, Richard Allan. "West River History: The Indian Village on Little Bighorn River, June 25–26, 1876." In *Legacy: New Perspectives on the Battle of the Little Bighorn,* edited by Charles E. Rankin. Helena: Montana Historical Society Press, 1996.

Frost, Lawrence. "The Black Hills Expedition of 1874." *Red River Valley Historical Review* 4, no. 4 (Fall 1979).

Garland, Hamlin. "General Custer's Last Fight as Seen by Two Moon." *McClure's Magazine* 21, no. 4 (August 1903).

Gerber, Max E. "The Black Hills Expedition of 1874: A New Look." *South Dakota History* 8 (June–July 1970).

Ghent, W. J. "Varnum, Reno and the Little Bighorn." *Winners of the West,* April 30, 1936.

Gibbon, Colonel John. "Hunting Sitting Bull." *American Catholic Quarterly Review,* October 1877.

————. "Last Summer's Expedition Against the Sioux and Its Great Catastrophe." *American Catholic Quarterly Review,* April 1877.

Glease, George W. "The Battle of the Little Big Horn." *Periodical* 20, no. 2 (Summer 1993).

Godfrey, Edward. "Custer's Last Battle." *Contributions to the History Society of Montana* 9 (1921).

Godfrey, Hon. Calvin Pomeroy. "General Edward S. Godfrey." *Ohio Archaeological and Historical Quarterly* 43 (1934).

———. "Some Reminiscences, Including the Washita Battle, November 27, 1868." *Cavalry Journal* 37, no. 153 (October 1928).

Gompert, David C., and Richard L. Kugler. "Custer in Cyberspace." *Defense Horizons* 51 (February 2006).

Graham, W. A. "Custer's Battle Plan." *Cavalry Journal*, July 1923.

Gray, John S. "Arikara Scouts with Custer." *North Dakota History* 35 (Spring 1968).

———. "Bloody Knife, Ree Scout for Custer." *Westerners' Brand Book* 17 (February 1961).

———. "Custer Throws a Boomerang." *Montana* 11, no. 2 (April 1961).

———. "Frank Grouard: Kanaka Scout or Mulatto Renegade?" *Westerners' Brand Book* 16, no. 8 (October 1959).

———. "Last Rites for Lonesome Charley Reynolds." *Montana* 143, no. 3 (July 1963).

———. "Medical Service on the Little Big Horn Campaign." *Westerners' Brand Book* 24, no. 11 (January 1968).

———. "On the Trail of Lonesome Charley Reynolds." *Chicago Westerner's Brand Book* 16, no. 8 (1959).

———. "The Pack Train on George A. Custer's Last Campaign." *Nebraska History* 57, no. 1 (Spring 1976).

———. "The Reno Petition." *Westerners' Brand Book* 24, no. 6 (August 1967).

———. "Suttler on Custer's Last Campaign." *Nebraska History* 43, no. 3.

———. "Veterinary Service on Custer's Last Campaign." *Kansas Historical Quarterly* 43, no. 3 (Autumn 1977).

Green, Meg. "Custer's Last Policy: General George Custer's Life Insurance Policy." *Bert's Review*, November 2006.

Greene, Jerome. "The Hayfield Fight: A Reappraisal of Neglected Action." *Montana* 23, no. 3 (Autumn 1972).

———. "The Uses of Indian Testimony in the Writing of Indian Wars History." *Journal of the Order of the Indian Wars* 2, no. 1 (Winter 1981).

Grinnell, George B. "The Return of a War Party: Reminiscences of Charley Reynolds." *Forest & Stream Magazine*, December 26, 1896, and January 30, 1897.

Grouard, Frank. "An Indian Scout's Recollections of Crazy Horse." *Nebraska History*, no. 12 (January–March, 1929).

Hadley, James Albert. "A Royal Buffalo Hunt." *Transactions of the Kansas State Historical Society* 10 (1907–8).

Halsey, Milton B., Jr. "The Court-Martial of Brevet Major General George A. Custer." *Trail Guide* 13 (September 1968).

Hammer, Kenneth. "The Glory March: A Concise Account of the Little Bighorn Campaign of 1876." *English Westerners' Brand Book* 8, no. 4 (July 1966).

Hanson, Charles E. "The Post-War Indian Gun Trade." *Museum of the Fur Trade Quarterly* 4, no. 3 (Fall 1968).

Hardorff, Richard. "Some Recollections of Custer: His Last Battle." *Research Review* 4, no. 2 (June 1990).

Harnsberger, John L. "Land Speculation, Promotion, and Failure: The Northern Pacific Railroad." *Journal of the West* 9, no. 1 (January 1970).

Hart, John P. "Custer First Stand: The Washington Fight." *Research Review* 12, no. 1 (Winter 1998).

Hatch, Thom. "Custer vs. Stuart." *America's Civil War Magazine* (November, 2013).

———. "Custer vs. Stuart: The Clash at Gettysburg." *Columbiad: A Quarterly Review of the War Between the States* (Winter 1998).

———. "The Story of Comanche: A True American Hero," *Western Horseman* (April 1996).

Hayes-McCoy, G. A. "Captain Myles Walter Keogh, the Irish Sword." *Journal of the Military Historical Society of Ireland,* 1951.

Hedren, Paul L. "Carbine Extractor Failure at the Little Big Horn." *Military Collector and Historian,* Summer 1973.

Heski, Thomas M. "'Don't Let Anything Get Away'—the March of the Seventh Cavalry, June 24–25, 1876: The Sundance Site to the Divide." *Research Review* 21, no. 2 (Summer 2007).

Hickox, R. G. "Mitch Bouyer . . . a Scout for Custer." *Gun Report,* March 1980.

Hilger, Sister M. Inez. "The Narrative of Oscar One Bull." *Mid-America* 28, no. 3 (July 1946).

Hinman, Eleanor. "Oglala Sources on the Life of Crazy Horse." *Nebraska History* 57, no. 1 (Spring 1976).

Hixon, John C. "Custer's 'Mysterious Mr. Kellogg' and the Diary of Mark Kellogg." *North Dakota History* 17, no. 3 (1950).

Holmes, Thomas A. "The Little Big Horn—Benteen: An Unpublished Letter." *Research Review* 7, no. 1 (January 1993).

Horn, W. Donald. "Custer's Turn to the North at the Little Big Horn: The Reason." *Research Review* 8, no. 1 (January 1994).

———. "The Tainted Testimony of Captain Frederick Benteen." *Research Review* 15, no. 2 (Summer 2001).

Hudnutt, Dean. "New Light on the Little Bighorn." *Field Artillery Journal* 26, no. 4 (July–August 1936).

Huggins, Eli L. "Custer and Rain in the Face." *American Mercury* 11, no. 35 (November 1926).

Hughes, Robert. "Campaign Against the Sioux in 1876." *Journal of the Military Service Institution of the United States* 18 (January 1896).

Hutchins, James S. "Mounted Riflemen: The Real Role of Cavalry in the Indian Wars." *El Palacio* 69 (Summer 1962).

Hutton, Paul A. "Fort Desolation: The Military Establishment, the Railroad, and the Settlement on the Northern Plains. *North Dakota History* 56 (Spring 1989).

———. "From Little Bighorn to Little Big Man: The Changing Image of the Western Hero in Popular Culture." *Western Historical Quarterly* 7 (January 1976).

Jacker, Edward. "Who Is to Blame for the Little Big Horn Disaster?" *American Catholic Quarterly Review* 1 (January–October 1876).

———. "United States vs. Major M. A. Reno." *English Westerners' Brand Book* 9, no. 4 (July 1967), 10, no. 1 (October 1967), 10, no. 2 (February 1968).

Johnson, Barry C. "A Captain of Chivalric Courage." *English Westerners' Brand Book,* 1988.

———. "George Herendeen, Montana Scout." *English Westerners' Brand Book* 2, nos. 3 and 4 (April and July 1960).

———. "Reno as Escort Commander." *English Westerners' Society Brand Book,* September 1972.

Jordan, Robert P. "Ghosts on the Little Bighorn." *National Geographic* 170, no. 6 (December 1986).

Kanipe, Daniel A. "A New Story of Custer's Last Battle; Told by a Messenger Boy Who Survived." *Contributions to the Historical Society of Montana* 9 (1923).

Kanitz, Jay F. "Varnum: The Later Years of Custer's First Lieutenant." *5th Annual Symposium, Custer Battlefield Historical & Museum Association,* 1991.

Kelly-Custer, Gail. "My Heritage, My Search." In *Custer and His Times,* book 5, edited by John P. Hart. El Paso, TX: Little Big Horn Associates, 2008.

King, Captain Charles. "Custer's Last Battle." *Harper's,* August 1890.

Knight, Oliver. "Mark Kellogg Telegraphed for Custer's Rescue." *North Dakota Historical Society* 27, no. 2 (1960).

Kroeker, Marvin E. "Deceit about the Garden: Hazen, Custer, and the Arid Lands Controversy." *North Dakota Quarterly* 38 (Summer 1970).

Krott, Rob. "Was Custer Outgunned?" *Military Illustrated,* no. 139 (2004).

Larned, Charles W. "Expedition to the Yellowstone River in 1873: Letters of a Young Cavalry Officer." *Mississippi Valley Historical Review* 39 (December 1952).

Lass, William E. "Steamboating on the Missouri: Its Significance on the Northern Great Plains." *Journal of the West* 7, no. 1 (1967).

Levine, Richard R. "Indian Fighters and Indian Reformers: Grant's Indian Peace Policy and the Conservative Consensus." *Civil War History* 31, no. 4 (December 1985).

Libby, Orin G., ed. "The Arikara Narrative of the Campaign Against the Hostile Dakotas." *North Dakota Historical Collections* 6 (Bismarck, 1920).

Lonich, David W. "Blacksmith Henry Mechling: From Pennsylvania to Little Bighorn." *Greasy Grass* 17 (May 2001).

Lounsberry, Clement. "F. F. Girard, Scout and Interpreter." *The Record,* July 1896.

Luce, Edward S. "The Diary and Letters of Dr. James DeWolf, Acting Assistant Surgeon, U.S. Army: His Record of the Sioux Expedition of 1876 as Kept Until His Death." *North Dakota History* 25, no. 3 (April–July 1958).

———. Review of *Echoes from the Little Big Horn Fight. Montana* 3, no. 4 (Autumn 1953).

MacLaine, Bob. "Our 1876 'Injun Fightin'' Cavalry." *Little Big Horn Associates Newsletter* 1 (August 1967).

MacNeil, Rod. "Raw Recruits and Veterans." *Little Big Horn Associates Newsletter* 21 (October 1987).

Mangum, Neil. "Gall: Sioux Gladiator or White Man's Pawn?" *5th Annual Symposium, Custer Battlefield Historical & Museum Association,* 1991.

———. "Reno's Battalion in the Battle of the Little Big Horn." *Greasy Grass* 2 (May 1996).

Marquis, Thomas B. "Indian Warrior Ways." *By Valor and Arms* 2, no. 2 (1977).

Mattingly, Arthur H. "The Great Plains Peace Commission of 1867." *Journal of the West* 15, no. 3 (July 1976).

McBlain, John F. "The Last Fight of the Sioux War of 1876–77." *Journal of the United States Cavalry Association* 10 (1897).

———. "With Gibbon on the Sioux Campaign of 1876." *Journal of the United States Cavalry Association* 9, no. 33 (June 1896).

McClernand, Edward J. "With the Indian and the Buffalo in Montana." *Cavalry Journal,* no. 36 (January–April 1927).

McConnell, Roland C. "Isaiah Dorman and the Custer Expedition." *Journal of Negro History* 32, no. 3 (July 1948).

McGinnis, Anthony. "A Contest of Wits and Daring: Plains Indians at War with the U.S. Army." *North Dakota History* 48, no. 2 (Spring 1981).

McMurtry, R. G. "The Two-Year Residence of General George A. Custer in Kentucky." *Kentucky Progress Magazine,* Summer 1933.

Meketa, R. T. "The Press and the Battle of the Little Big Horn." *Research Review* 1, no. 1 (March 1984).

Merrick, Henry S. "Was There a White Survivor of Custer's Command?" *Military Affairs* 20, no. 1 (Spring 1956).

Millbrook, Minnie Dubbs. "Big Game Hunting with the Custers." *Kansas Historical Quarterly* 41 (Winter 1975).

———. "The Boy General and How He Grew: George Custer After Appomattox." *Montana* 23, no. 2 (April 1973).

———. "Godfrey on Custer." *Research Review* 6, no. 4 (Winter 1972).

———. "Mrs. General Custer at Fort Riley, 1866." *Kansas Historical Quarterly* 40 (Spring 1974).

Miller, David Humphreys. "Echoes of the Little Bighorn." *American Heritage* 22, no. 4 (June 1971).

Moore, Colonel Horace L. "The Nineteenth Kansas Cavalry in the Washita Campaign." *Chronicles of Oklahoma* 2, no. 4 (December 1924).

Morris, Major Robert E. "Custer Made a Good Decision: A Leavenworth Appreciation." *Journal of the West* 16, no. 4 (October 1977).

Murphy, James P. "The Campaign of the Little Big Horn." *Infantry Journal* 34 (June 1929).

Murray, Robert A. "The Custer Court Martial." *Annals of Wyoming* 36, no. 2 (October 1964).

Myers, Rex C. "Montana Editors and the Custer Battle." *Montana* 26 (Spring 1976).

Myers, Steven W. "Roster of Known Hostile Indians at the Battle of the Little Big Horn." *Research Review* 5, no. 2 (June 1991).

Nesbit, Paul. "Battle of the Washita." *Chronicles of Oklahoma* 3, no. 1 (1924).

Newcomb, W. W., Jr. "A Re-Examination of the Causes of Plains Warfare." *American Anthropologist* 52 (July–September 1950).

Nichols, Ron. "Cavalry Firepower: Springfield Carbine's Selection and Performance." Custer Battlefield Historical & Museum Association. *Greasy Grass* (May 1999).

———. "Marcus Albert Reno." *Greasy Grass* (1986).

Nicolls-Kyle, Joanna R. "Indian Picture Writing and Drawings of Custer's Massacre." *Ainslee's Magazine* 3, no. 3 (April 1899).

Noyes, C. Lee. "The Battle of the Little Big Horn: Reno, Terry and a Variation of a Major Theme." *13th Annual Symposium.*

———. "Captain Robert P. Hughes and the Case Against Custer: An Early Perspective of the Little Big Horn." *Little Big Horn Associates Newsletter* 33, no. 1 (February 1999).

———. "Custer's Surgeon, George Lord, Among the Missing at Little Bighorn Battle." Custer Battlefield Historical & Museum Association. *Greasy Grass* 16 (May 2000).

———. "A Dispatch from the Battlefield." *Research Review* 18, no. 2 (Summer 2004).

———. "The Guns 'Long Hair' Left Behind: The Gatling Gun Detachment and the Little Big Horn." *Brand Book* 33, no. 2 (Summer 1999).

O'Neil, Thomas E. "Custer's First Romance Revealed." *Newsletter, Little Big Horn Associates* 28, no. 2 (March 1994).

O'Neil, Thomas E., and Hoyt S. Vandenberg. "A Modern Look at Custer's Orders." *Research Review* 8, no. 2 (June 1994).

Ostler, Jeffrey. "They Regard Their Passing as *Wakan:* Interpreting Western Sioux Explanations for the Bison's Decline." *Western Historical Quarterly* 30, no. 4 (Winter 1999).

Parker, Watson. "The Majors and the Miners: The Role of the U.S. Army in the Black Hills Gold Rush." *Journal of the West* 11 (January 1972).

Partoll, Albert J. "After the Custer Battle." *Frontier and Midland* 19, no. 4 (1938–1939).

Pearson, Carl L. "Sadie and the Missing Custer Battle Papers." *Montana* 26 (Autumn 1976).

Pennington, Robert. "An Analysis of the Political Structure of the Teton-Dakota Indian Tribe of North America." *North Dakota History* 20, no. 3 (July 1953).

Pohanka, Brian. "George Yates: Captain of the Band Box Troop." *Greasy Grass* (May 1992).

———. "Letters of the Seventh Cavalry." *Little Big Horn Associates Newsletter* 10 (February 1976).

———. "Myles Keogh from the Vatican to the Little Bighorn." *Military Images*, September-October, 1986.

———. "Profile: Lieutenant William Van Wyck Reily, 7th Cavalry." *Greasy Grass* (1986).

Prickett, Robert C. "The Malfeasance of William Worth Belknap, Secretary of War." *North Dakota History* 17, no. 1 (January 1950).

Ralston, Alan. "The Yellowstone Expedition of 1876." *Montana* 20, no. 2 (Spring 1990).

Rector, William G. "Fields of Fire: The Reno-Benteen Defense Perimeter." *Montana* 16, no. 2 (Spring 1966).

Reedstrom, E. Lisle. "Tom Custer: In the Shadow of His Brother." *True West Magazine* 41, no. 11 (November 1994).

Reno, Marcus A. "The Custer Massacre." *Americana Magazine* 7 (March–April 1912).

Richter, William L. "A Better Time Is in Store for Us: An Analysis of the Reconstruction Attitudes of George Armstrong Custer." *Military History of Texas and the Southwest* 11 (1973).

Rickey, Don Jr. "The Battle of Wolf Mountain." *Montana* 13 (Spring 1963).

———. "Myth to Monument: The Establishment of Custer Battlefield National Monument." *Journal of the West* 7 (April 1969).

Rister, Carl Coke, "Indians as Buffalo Hunters." *Frontier Times* 5 (September 1928).

Robinson, Doane, ed. "Crazy Horse's Story of the Custer Battle." *South Dakota Historical Collections* 6 (1912).

Rolston, Alan. "The Yellowstone Expedition of 1873." *Montana* 20 (April 1970).

Ross, Raymond J. "John A. Martin—Custer's Last Courier." *The West,* April 1967.

Sage, Walter N. "Sitting Bull's Own Narrative of the Custer Fight." *Canadian Historical Review* 16, no. 2 (June 1935).

Saindon, Bob. "Sitting Bull: Old Fort Peck's Famous Visitor." *Hoofprints* 18, no. 2 (Fall–Winter 1988).

Saum, Lewis O. "Colonel Custer's Copperhead: The Mysterious Mr. Kellogg." *Montana* 28, no. 4 (Autumn 1978).

———. "Private John F. O'Donohue's Reflections on the Little Bighorn." *Montana* 50, no. 4 (Winter 2000).

Schulenberg, Dale T., ed. "A Trooper with Custer: Augustus DeVoto's Account of the Little Big Horn." *Montana* 40, no. 1 (Winter 1990).

Scott, Douglas. "Cartridges, Bullets and Bones." *Research Review* 18 (May 2002).

Scott, Elmo. "Echoes of the Custer Tragedy." *Winners of the West,* July 1936.

Scott, General Hugh. "Custer's Last Fight." *New York Times,* January 6, 1935.

Shoemaker, Colonel John O. "The Custer Court-Martial." *Military Review* 51, no. 10 (October 1971).

Shoenberger, Dale. "Charles DeRudio: European Assassin." *Research Review,* September, 1980.

Sills, Joe Jr. "The Crow Scouts: Their Contributions in Understanding the Little Big Horn Battle." *5th Annual Symposium, Custer Battlefield Historical & Museum Association,* 1991.

Sklenar, Larry. "Captain Benteen's Ugly Little Secret Exposed." *Research Review* 12, no. 2 (Summer 1998).

———. "Theodore Goldin: Little Big Horn Survivor and Winner of the Medal of Honor." *Wisconsin Magazine of History* 80, no. 6 (1996–97).

———. "The 'Wallace Factor' at the Reno Court of Inquiry." *Research Review* 14, no. 1 (Winter 2000).

Smith, Jay. "Custer Didn't Do It." *Little Big Horn Associates Newsletter* 9, no. 2 (February 1975).

Smits, David D. "The Frontier Army and the Destruction of the Buffalo, 1865–1883." *Western History Quarterly* 25, no. 3 (Autumn 1994).

Snell, Joseph W., and Robert W. Richmond. "When the Union and Kansas Pacific Built Through Kansas." *Kansas Historical Quarterly* 32 (Summer and Autumn 1966).

Standing, Percy Cross. "Custer's Cavalry at the Little Big Horn." *Cavalry Journal*, 1914.

Stewart, Edgar I. "I Rode with Custer!" *Montana* 4, no. 3 (Summer 1954).

———. "The Reno Court of Inquiry." *Montana* 2, no. 3 (July 1952).

———. "Treaty Obligations and the Sioux War of 1876." *English Westerners' Brand Book* 13, no. 3 (April 1971) and no. 4 (July 1971).

———. and E. S. Luce. "The Reno Scout." *Montana* 10, no. 3 (July 1960).

———. "The Reno Scout." *Montana* 10, no. 3 (Summer 1960).

Stone, Melville. "Carlo di Rudio, 1st Lt. 7th U.S. Cavalry." *Collier's Weekly*, May 15, 1920.

Swift, Eben. "General Wesley Merritt." *Journal of the United States Cavalry Association*, March 1911.

Talbot, James Joseph. "Custer's Last Battle." *Penn Monthly*, September 1877.

Talmadge, Frank. "Buffalo Hunting with Custer." *Cavalry Journal*, January 1929.

Tate, Michael. "The Girl He Left Behind: Elizabeth Custer and the Making of a Legend." *Red River Valley Historical Review* 5 (Winter 1980).

Taunton, Francis B. "The Man Who Rode Comanche, Sidelights of the Sioux War." *English Westerners*, Special Publication no. 2.

Taylor, Joseph Henry. "Bloody Knife and Gall." *North Dakota Historical Quarterly* 4, no. 3 (April 1930).

———. "Lonesome Charley." *North Dakota Historical Quarterly* 4 (July 1930).

Tilford, James D. Jr. "Life in the Old Army." *Research Review* 4, no. 1 (January 1990).

Trinque, Bruce A. "The Cartridge Case Evidence on Custer Field." *5th Annual Symposium, Custer Battlefield Historical & Museum Association*, 1991.

———. "The Defense of Custer Hill." *Research Review* 8, no. 2 (June 1994).

Utley, Robert M. "The Celebrated Peace Policy of General Grant." *North Dakota History* 20, no. 3 (July 1953).

———. "The Custer Battle in the Contemporary Press." *North Dakota History* 22, nos. 1 and 2 (January–April 1955).

———. The Gatlings Custer Left Behind." *American West* 11, no. 2 (March 1974).

——. "Origins of the Great Sioux War." *Montana* 42, no. 4 (Autumn 1992).

——. "Whose Shrine Is It? The Ideological Struggle for Custer Battlefield." *Montana* 42 (Winter 1992).

Varnum, Charles A. "I Was There: Colonel Charles A. Varnum's Experience." *Winners of the West* (April 1936).

Vaughn, J. W. "Dr. George E. Lord, Regimental Surgeon." *New Westerners' Brand Book*, 1962.

—— "The Mark Kellogg Story." *Westerners New York Posse Brand Book* 7, no. 4 (1961).

Vestal, Stanley. "The Man Who Killed Custer." *American Heritage* 8, no. 2 (February 1957).

Wabuda, Susan. "Elizabeth Bacon Custer in Japan: 1903." *Manuscripts Magazine* 35 (Winter 1983).

Walker, H. P. "The Enlisted Soldier on the Frontier." In *The American Military on the Frontier: The Proceedings of the 7th Military History Symposium,* edited by James P. Tate. Washington, D.C.: Office of Air Force History, 1978.

Walker, L. G., Jr. "Military Medicine at Little Bighorn." *Journal of the American College of Surgeons* 202, no. 1 (January 2006).

Walter, Denton. "Terry and Custer: Was There a Plan?" *Little Big Horn Associates Newsletter* 22 (October 1988).

Watson, Elmo. "The Custer Campaign Diary of Mark Kellogg." *The Westerners' Brand Book, 1945–46* (Chicago, 1947).

Welty, Raymond L. "The Indian Policy of the Army, 1860–1870." *Cavalry Journal* 36, no. 148 (July 1927).

White, Lonnie J. "The Battle of Beecher Island: The Scouts Hold Fast on the Arickaree." *Journal of the West* 5 (January, 1966).

——. "The Hancock and Custer Expedition of 1867." *Journal of the West* 5, no. 3 (1966).

——. "Winter Campaigning with Sheridan and Custer: The Expedition of the Nineteenth Kansas Volunteer Cavalry." *Journal of the West* 6 (July 1966).

White, Richard. "The Winning of the West: The Expansion of the Western Sioux in the Eighteenth and Nineteenth Century." *Journal of American History* 65, no. 2 (September 1978).

Whittaker, Frederick. "General George A. Custer." *Galaxy,* September 1876.

Willert, James. "The Wedding Ring of Lieutenant Donald McIntosh." *Research Review* 10, no. 2 (June 1996).

Wiltsey, Norman B. "We Killed Custer." *Real West* 11, no. 60 (June 1968).

Windolph, Charles. "The Battle of Little Big Horn." *Sunshine Magazine,* September 1930.

Yates, Annie Roberts. "Colonel George W. Yates." *Research Review,* September 1981.

Books

Adams, Alexander B. *Sitting Bull.* New York: G. P. Putnam's Sons, 1973.

Amaral, Anthony A. *Comanche (The Horse That Survived the Custer Massacre).* Los Angeles: Westernlore, 1961.

Ambrose, Stephen. *Crazy Horse and Custer: The Parallel Lives of Two American Warriors.* New York: Doubleday, 1975.

Anders, Frank L. *The Custer Trail.* Glendale, CA: Arthur H. Clark, 1983.

Anderson, Gary C. *Sitting Bull and the Paradox of Lakota Nationhood.* New York: Longman, 1946.

Andrist, Ralph K. *The Long Death: The Last Days of the Plains Indian.* New York: Collier, 1964.

Arnold, Steve. *Custer's Forgotten Friend: The Life of W. W. Cooke.* Howell, MI: Powder River Press, 1993.

Asay, Karol. *Gray Head and Long Hair: The Benteen-Custer Relationship.* New York: Mad Printers of Mattituck, 1983.

———. *William Tecumseh Sherman and the Settlement of the West.* Norman: University of Oklahoma Press, 1956.

Athearn, Robert G. *Forts of the Upper Missouri.* Lincoln: University of Nebraska Press, 1982.

———. *Rebel of the Rockies: A History of the Denver and Rio Grande Western Railroad.* New Haven: Yale University Press, 1962.

Bailey, John Wendell. *Pacifying the Plains: General Alfred Terry and the Decline of the Sioux.* Contributions in Military History 17. Westport, CT: Greenwood Press, 1979.

Barnard, Sandy. *Digging into Custer's Last Stand.* Terre Haute, IN: AST Press, 1998.

———. *I Go with Custer: The Life and Death of Reporter Marl Kellogg.* Bismarck, ND: Bismarck Tribune, 1996.

———. *Speaking About Custer: A Collection of Lectures.* Terre Haute, IN: AST Press, 1991.

———, ed. *Ten Years with Custer: A Cavalryman's Memoirs.* Terre Haute, IN: AST Press, 2001.

Barnett, Louise. *Touched by Fire: The Life, Death, and Mythic Afterlife of George Armstrong Custer.* New York: Henry Holt, 1996.

Barry, David F. *Indian Notes on the Custer Battle*. Baltimore: Proof Press, 1939.

Bates, Colonel Charles Francis. *Custer's Indian Battles*. Bronxville, NY: Privately printed, 1936.

Bell, William A. *New Tracks in North America*. London: Chapman and Hall, 1869.

Berthrong, Donald. *The Cheyenne and Arapaho Ordeal*. Norman: University of Oklahoma Press, 1975.

Bettelyoun, Susan Bordeaux, and Josephine Waggoner. *With My Own Eyes: A Lakota Woman Tells Her People's Story*. Lincoln: University of Nebraska Press, 1998.

Beyer, W. F., and O. F. Keydel, eds. *Deeds of Valor*. Vol. 2. Detroit: Perrian-Keydel, 1907.

Billings, John D. *Hardtack and Coffee: The Unwritten Story of Army Life*. Lincoln: University of Nebraska Press, 1993.

Bird, Roy. *In His Brother's Shadow: The Life of Thomas Ward Custer*. Paducah, KY: Turner Publishing, 2002.

Bookwater, Thomas E. *Honor Tarnished*. West Carrollton, OH: Little Horn Press, 1979.

Bourke, John G. *Mackenzie's Last Fight with the Cheyennes*. Bellevue, NE: Old Army Press, 1970.

———. *On the Border with Crook*. New York: Charles Scribner's Sons, 1981.

Boyd, O. B. *Cavalry Life in Tent and Field*. Lincoln: University of Nebraska Press, 1982.

Boyes, W., ed. *The Cheyenne Tribal Historian John Stands-in-Timber's Account of the Custer Battle*. Little Big Horn Associates, 1991.

———. *Custer's Black White Man*. Washington, D.C.: South Capitol Press, 1972.

———, ed. *Surgeon's Diary with the Custer Relief Column*. Washington, D.C.: South Capitol Press, 1974.

Bradley, James H. *The March of the Montana Column: A Prelude to the Custer Disaster*. Edited by Edgar I. Stewart. Norman: University of Oklahoma Press, 1961.

Brady, Cyrus Townsend. *Indian Fights and Fighters*. New York: McClure, Philips, 1904.

Branch, Edward Douglas. *The Hunting of the Buffalo*. New York: Appleton, 1929.

Bray, Kingsley M. *Crazy Horse: A Lakota Life*. Norman: University of Oklahoma Press, 2006.

Brill, Charles J. *Conquest of the Southern Plains: Uncensored Narrative of the Battle of the Washita and Custer's Southern Campaign*. Oklahoma City: Golden Saga Publishing, 1938.

Brininstool, E. A. *Campaigning with Custer*. Reprint. Lincoln: University of Nebraska Press, 1988.

———. *Crazy Horse*. Los Angeles: Wetzel Publishing, 1949.

———. *Troopers with Custer: Historic Incidents of the Battle of the Little Big Horn*. Reprint. Lincoln: University of Nebraska Press, 1989.

Brown, Dee. *Bury My Heart at Wounded Knee: An Indian History of the American West.* New York: Henry Holt, 2001.

——. *Showdown at Little Big Horn.* Lincoln: University of Nebraska Press, 2004.

Brown, Jesse, and A. M. Willard. *The Black Hills Trails: A History of the Struggles of the Pioneers in the Winning of the Black Hills.* Rapid City, SD: Rapid City Journal Company, 1924.

Brown, Joseph Epes. *The Sacred Pipe: Black Elk's Account of the Seven Rites of the Oglala Sioux.* Norman: University of Oklahoma Press, 1953.

Brown, Mark H. *The Flight of the Nez Perce: A History of the Nez Perce War.* New York: G. P. Putnam's Sons, 1967.

——. *The Plainsmen of the Yellowstone.* Lincoln: University of Nebraska Press, 1961.

——, and W. E. Felton. *The Frontier Years: L. A. Huffman, Photographer of the Plains.* New York: Henry Holt, 1955.

Brust, James, Brian C. Pohanka, and Sandy Barnard. *Where Custer Fell: Photographs of the Little Bighorn Battlefield Then and Now.* Norman: University of Oklahoma Press, 2005.

Buecker, Thomas R., and Eli Pauls, eds. The *Crazy Horse Surrender Ledger.* Lincoln: Nebraska State Historical Society, 1994.

Buell, Thomas B. *The Warrior Generals.* New York: Three Rivers Press, 1997.

Burdick, Usher L., ed. *David F. Barry's Notes on "The Custer Battle."* Baltimore: Wirth Brothers, 1949.

——. *The Last Battle of the Sioux Nation.* Fargo, ND: Worzalla Publishing, 1929.

——. *Tales from Buffalo Land: The Story of Fort Buford.* Baltimore: Wirth Brothers, 1940.

——. *Tragedy in the Great Sioux Camp.* Baltimore: Proof Press, 1936.

Burkey, Blaine. *Custer, Come at Once!* Hays, KS: Society of Friends of Historic Fort Hays, 1991.

Burt, Struthers. *Powder River: Let 'Er Buck.* New York: Farrar & Rinehart, 1938.

Bushong, Millard K., and Dean McKain *Fightin' Tom Rosser, C.S.A.* Shippensburg, PA: Beidel Printing House, 1983.

Byrne, P. E. *Soldiers of the Plains.* New York: Minton, Balch, 1926.

Carrington, Colonel Henry B. *Ab-sa-ra-ka: Land of Massacre.* Wife Margaret's narrative. Philadelphia: J. B. Lippincott, 1879.

Carroll, John M., ed. *The Arrest and Killing of Sitting Bull: A Documentary.* Mattituck, NY: Amereon Press, 1986.

——, ed. *The Benteen-Goldin Letters on Custer and His Last Battle.* New York: Liveright, 1974.

———, ed. *Camp Talk: The Very Private Letters of Frederick W. Benteen of the 7th U.S. Cavalry to His Wife, 1871–1878*. Edited by John Melvin Carroll. Mattituck, NY: J. M. Carroll, 1983.

———, ed. *Cavalry Scraps: The Writings of Frederick W. Benteen*. East Stroudsburg, PA: Guidon Press, 1979.

———, ed *The Court Martial of Frederick W. Benteen, Major, 9th Cavalry, or Did General Crook Railroad Benteen?* Bryan, TX: Privately printed, 1981.

———, ed. *The Court-Martial of Thomas M. French*. Bryan, TX: Privately printed, 1979.

———, ed. *Custer: From the Civil War to the Little Bighorn*. Bryan, TX: Privately printed, 1981.

———, ed. *Custer and His Times*, book 2. Forth Worth, TX: Little Big Horn Associates, 1984.

———, ed. *A Custer Chrestomathy*. Bryan, TX: Privately printed, 1981.

———, ed. *Custer in the Civil War: His Unfinished Memoirs*. San Rafael, CA: Presidio Press, 1977.

———. *Custer in Texas: An Interrupted Narrative*. New York: Sol Lewis & Liveright, 1975.

———, ed. *Custer's Chief of Scouts*. Lincoln: University of Nebraska Press, 1982.

———, ed. *The Eleanor Hinman Interviews on the Life and Death of Crazy Horse*. New Brunswick, NJ: Garry Owen Press, 1976.

———. *4 on Custer by Carroll*. N.p.: Guidon Press, 1976.

———, ed. *The Frank L. Anders and R. G. Cartwright Correspondence*. 3 vols. Bryan, TX: Privately printed, 1982.

———, ed. *General Custer and New Rumley, Ohio*. Bryan, TX: Privately printed, 1978.

———, ed. *General Custer and the Battle of the Little Big Horn: The Federal View*. Mattituck, NY: J. M. Carroll, 1986.

———. *Roll Call on the Little Bighorn*. Fort Collins, CO: Old Army Press, 1974.

———. *General Custer and the Battle of the Washita: The Federal View*. Mattituck, NY: Guidon Press, 1978.

———, ed. *The Two Battles of the Little Big Horn*. Bryan, TX: J. M. Carroll, 1974.

———? *They Rode With Custer: A Biographical Directory of the Men That Rode with General George A. Custer*. Mattituck, NY: J. M. Carroll & Co., 1993.

———. *The Seventh Cavalry Scrapbook*. Nos. 1–13. Bryan, TX: J. M. Carroll, 1978–80.

———, ed. *The Sunshine Magazine Articles by John P. Everett*. Bryan, TX: Privately printed, 1979.

———, and Lawrence A. Frost. *Private Theodore Ewert's Diary of the Black Hills Expedition of 1874*. Piscataway, NJ: CRI Books, 1976.

Carroll, John M., and Donald Horn. *Custer Genealogies*. Bryan, TX: Guidon Press, n.d.

Chambers, Lee. *Fort Abraham Lincoln, Dakota Territory*. Atglen, PA: Schiffer Publishing, 2008.

Chandler, Lieutenant Colonel Melbourne C. *Of Garry Owen in Glory: The History of the 7th U. S. Cavalry*. Annandale, PA: Turnpike Press, 1960.

Chorne, Laudie J. *Following the Custer Trail of 1876*. Bismarck, ND: Printing Plus, 1997.

Clark, George M. *Scalp Dance: The Edgerly Papers*. Oswego, NY: Heritage Press, 1985.

Clark, Robert A., and Carroll Friswold. *The Killing of Crazy Horse*. Lincoln: University of Nebraska Press, 1976.

Cody, William F. *The Life of Hon. William F. Cody, Known as Buffalo Bill*. Lincoln: University of Nebraska Press, 1978.

Coffeen, Herbert. *The Teepee Book, Parts I and II*. New York: Sol Lewis, 1974.

Coffman, Edward M. *The Old Army*. New York: Oxford University Press, 1986.

Connell, Evan S. *Son of the Morning Star: Custer and the Little Bighorn*. New York: Harper Perennial, 1991.

Convis, Charles L. *The Honor of Arms: A Biography of Myles W. Keogh*. Tucson, AZ: Westernlore, 1990.

Cook, John R. *The Border and the Buffalo*. Chicago: R. R. Donnelley & Sons, 1938.

Coppee, Henry. *Field Manual for Courts-Martial*. Philadelphia: J. B. Lippincott, 1863.

Coughlan, Colonel T. M. *Varnum: The Last of Custer's Lieutenants*. Bryan, TX: J. M. Carroll, 1980.

Cox, Kurt Hamilton, and John Langellier. *Custer and His Commands, from West Point to Little Bighorn*. Philadelphia: Chelsea House, 2002.

Cozzens, Peter Gould, ed. *Eyewitness to the Indian Wars, 1865–1890*. Vol. 3, *Conquering the Southern Plains*. Mechanicsburg, PA: Stackpole, 2003.

———, ed. *Eyewitness to the Indian Wars, 1865–1890*. Vol. 4, *The Long War for the Northern Plains*. Mechanicsburg, PA: Stackpole, 2004.

———, ed. *Eyewitness to the Indian Wars, 1865–1890*. Vol. 5, *The Army and the Indian*. Mechanicsburg, PA: Stackpole, 2005.

Crawford, Lewis F. *Rekindling Camp Fires*. Bismarck, ND: Capital Book, 1926.

Crittenden, H. H. *The Crittenden Memoirs*. New York: G. P. Putnam's Sons, 1936.

Crook, George. *General George Crook: His Autobiography*. Norman, OK: University of Oklahoma Press, 1946.

Cross, Walt. *Custer's Last Officer: The Search for Lieutenant Henry Moore Harrington, 7th Cavalry*. Stillwater, OK: Cross Publications, 2006.

Custer, Brice C. *The Sacrificial Lion: George Armstrong Custer: From American Hero to Media Villain.* El Segundo, CA: Upton & Sons, 1999.

Custer, Elizabeth B. *Boots and Saddles or, Life in Dakota with General Custer.* New York: Harper and Brothers, 1885.

——. *Following the Guidon.* New York: Harper and Brothers, 1890.

——. *Tenting on the Plains; or, General Custer in Kansas and Texas.* New York: Harper and Brothers, 1887.

Custer, George Armstrong. *My Life on the Plains or, Personal Experiences with Indians.* Reprint. Norman: University of Oklahoma Press, 1962.

Danker, Donald F. *Man of the Plains: Recollection of Luther North 1856–1882.* Lincoln: University of Nebraska Press, 1961.

Darling, Roger. *Benteen's Scout-to-the-Left: The Route from the Divide to the Morass (June 25, 1876).* El Segundo, CA: Upton and Sons, 1987.

——. *Custer's Seventh Cavalry Comes to Dakota.* El Segundo, CA: Upton & Sons, 1989.

——. *General Custer's Final Hours: Correcting a Century of Misconceived Mystery.* Vienna, VA: Potomac-Western Press, 1992.

——. *A Sad and Terrible Blunder: Generals Terry and Custer at the Little Big Horn.* Vienna, VA: Potomac-Western Press, 1990.

Dary, David A. *The Buffalo Book: The Full Saga of the American Animal.* Chicago: Swallow Press, 1974.

Davis, Karen, and Elden Davis, eds. *The Reno Court of Inquiry: The Pioneer Press, St. Paul and Minnesota, 1878–79.* Howell, MI: Powder River Press, 1992.

——. *That Fatal Day: Eight More with Custer.* Howell, MI: Powder River Press, 1992.

Davis, William C. *Frontier Skills: The Tactics and Weapons That Won the American West.* Guilford, CT: Lyons Press, 2003.

Day, Carl. *Tom Custer: Ride to Glory.* Spokane, WA: Arthur H. Clark, 2002.

DeBarthe, Joe. *The Life and Adventures of Frank Grouard.* Norman: University of Oklahoma Press, 1958.

Deland, C. E. *The Sioux Wars.* 2 vols. Pierre: South Dakota Historical Collections, 1930, 1934.

Deloria, Vine, Jr. *Custer Died for Your Sins: An Indian Manifesto.* Norman: University of Oklahoma Press, 1988.

De Trobriand, Regis. *Military Life in Dakota.* Lincoln: University of Nebraska Press, 1982.

Diedrich, Mark S. *Famous Chiefs of the Eastern Sioux.* Minneapolis: Coyote Books, 1987.

DiMarco, Louis A. *War Horse: A History of the Military Horse and Rider.* Yardley, PA: Westholme Publishers, 2008.

Dippie, Brian W. *Custer's Last Stand: The Anatomy of an American Myth.* Lincoln: University of Nebraska Press, 1994.

——, ed. *Nomad: George A. Custer in Turf, Field and Farm.* Austin: University of Texas Press, 1980.

Dixon, David, *Hero of Beecher Island: The Life and Military Career of George A. Forsyth.* Lincoln: University of Nebraska Press, 1994.

Dixon, Dr. Joseph K. *The Vanishing Race.* Garden City, NY: Doubleday, 1913.

Dixon, Norman. *On the Psychology of Military Incompetence.* London: Pimlico, 1994.

Donahue, Michael. *Drawing Battle Lines: The Map Testimony of Custer's Last Fight.* El Segundo, CA: Upton and Sons, 2008.

Donovan, James. *A Terrible Glory: Custer and the Little Bighorn—the Last Great Battle of the American West.* New York: Little, Brown and Company, 2008.

Downey, Fairfax. *Indian-Fighting Army.* New York: Bantam, 1957.

duBois, Charles G. *The Custer Mystery.* El Segundo, CA: Upton and Sons, 1986.

——. *Kick the Dead Lion: A Casebook of the Custer Battle.* El Segundo, CA: Upton and Sons, 1987.

Dugan, Bill. *Sitting Bull.* San Francisco: HarperCollins, 1994.

duMont, John S. *Custer Battle Guns.* Fort Collins, CO: Old Army Press, 1974.

Dunlay, Thomas W. *Wolves for the Blue Soldiers: Indian Scouts and Auxiliaries with the United States Army, 1860–90.* Lincoln: University of Nebraska Press, 1982.

Dunn, J. P. *Massacres of the Mountains.* New York: Harper and Brothers, 1886.

Dustin, Fred. *The Custer Tragedy: Events Leading up to and Following the Little Big Horn Campaign of 1876.* Reprint. El Segundo, CA: Upton and Sons, 1987.

Eastman, Charles. *Indian Heroes and Great Chieftains.* Boston: Little, Brown, 1918.

Ege, Robert J. *Curse Not His Curls.* Fort Collins, CO: Old Army Press, 1974.

Ellis, John. Cavalry: *The History of Mounted Warfare.* Barnsley, S. Yorkshire, UK: Pen and Sword, 2004.

Ellison, Douglas W. *Mystery of the Rosebud.* Medora, ND: Western Edge, 2002.

Epple, Jess C. *Custer's Battle of the Washita and a History of the Plains Indian Tribes.* New York: Exposition Press, 1970.

Evans, David C. *Custer's Last Fight: The Story of the Battle of the Little Big Horn.* El Segundo, CA: Upton and Sons, 1999.

Ewers, John Canfield. *Indian Life on the Upper Missouri.* Norman: University of Oklahoma Press, 1968.

———. *Plains Indian History and Culture: Essays on Continuity and Change.* Norman: University of Oklahoma Press, 1997.

Farrow, Edward S. *Mountain Scouting: A Handbook for Officers and Soldiers on the Frontier.* Norman: University of Oklahoma Press, 2000.

Fay, George E. *Military Engagements Between United States Troops and Plains Indians, Part IV, 1872–1890.* Greeley: University of Northern Colorado, 1973.

Finerty, John G. *Warpath and Bivouac: or the Conquest of the Sioux.* Chicago: Chicago Times, 1890.

Fiske, Frank B. *The Taming of the Sioux.* Bismarck, ND: Bismarck Tribune, 1917.

Forrest, Earle R. *Witnesses at the Battle of the Little Big Horn.* Monroe, MI: Monroe County Library System, 1986.

Fougera, Katherine Gibson. *With Custer's Cavalry.* Caldwell, ID: Caxton Printers, 1940.

Fox, Richard Allan. *Archaeology, History, and Custer's Last Battle.* Norman: University of Oklahoma Press, 1993.

Frost, Lawrence. *The Custer Album: A Pictorial Biography of General George A. Custer.* Reprint. Norman: University of Oklahoma Press, 1990.

———. *Custer Legends.* Bowling Green, OH: Bowling Green University Popular Press, 1981.

Frost, Lawrence A. *The Court-Martial of George Armstrong Custer.* Norman, OK: University of Oklahoma Press, 1968.

———. *Custer's 7th Cav and the Campaign of 1873.* El Segundo, CA: Upton and Sons, 1986.

———. *General Custer's Libbie.* Hesperia, CA: Superior Publishing, 1976.

———. *General Custer's Thoroughbreds: Racing, Riding, Hunting, and Fighting.* Bryan, TX: J. M. Carroll, 1986.

———, ed. *With Custer in '74: James Calhoun's Diary of the Black Hills Expedition.* Provo, UT: Brigham Young University, 1979.

Gibbon, John. *Gibbon on the Sioux Campaign of 1876.* Bellevue, NE: Old Army Press, 1970.

Godfrey, Edward. *Custer's Last Battle.* 1892. Reprint, Olympic Valley, CA: Outbooks, 1976.

———. *The Field Diary of Lt. Edward Settle Godfrey.* Portland, OR: Champoeg Press, 1957.

Goldin, Theodore. *With the Seventh Cavalry in 1876.* N.p.: Privately printed, 1980.

Grafe, Ernest, and Paul Horsted. *Exploring with Custer: The 1874 Black Hills Expedition.* Custer, SD: Golden Valley Press, 2005.

Graham, Colonel William A. The *Custer Myth: A Sourcebook of Custeriana.* Harrisburg, PA: Stackpole, 1953.

———. *The Official Record of a Court of Inquiry Convened at Chicago, Illinois, January 13, 1879, by the President of the United States upon the Request of Major Marcus A. Reno, 7th Cavalry to Investigate His Conduct at the Little Big Horn, June 25–26, 1876.* Pacific Palisades, CA: Privately printed, 1951.

———. *The Reno Court of Inquiry: Abstract of the Official Record of Inquiry.* Harrisburg, PA: Stackpole, 1954.

———. *The Story of the Little Big Horn: Custer's Last Fight.* New York: Century, 1926.

Gray, John S. *Arikara Scouts with Custer.* Brooklyn: Arrow and Trooper., n.d.

———. *Centennial Campaign: The Sioux War of 1876.* Norman: University of Oklahoma, 1988.

———. *Custer's Last Campaign: Mitch Bouyer and the Little Bighorn Reconstructed.* Lincoln: University of Nebraska Press, 1991.

Greene, Jerome. *Battles and Skirmishes of the Great Sioux War, 1876–77: The Military View.* Norman: University of Oklahoma Press, 1993.

———. *Evidence and the Custer Enigma: A Reconstruction of Indian-Military History.* Kansas City, MO: Kansas City Posse of Westerners, 1973.

———. *Indian War Veterans.* New York: Savas Beatie, 2007.

———. *Lakota and Cheyenne: Indian Views of the Great Sioux War, 1876–1877.* Norman: University of Oklahoma Press, 1994.

———. *Morning Star Dawn: The Powder River Expedition and the Northern Cheyennes, 1876.* Norman: University of Oklahoma Press, 2003.

———. *Slim Buttes, 1876: An Episode of the Great Sioux War.* Norman: University of Oklahoma Press, 1982.

———. *Stricken Field: The Little Big Horn Since 1876.* Norman: University of Oklahoma Press, 2008.

———. *Washita: The U.S. Army and the Southern Cheyennes, 1876–79.* Norman: University of Oklahoma Press, 2004.

Grinnell, George Bird. *The Fighting Cheyennes.* New York: Charles Scribner, 1915.

———. *Two Great Scouts and Their Pawnee Battalions.* Lincoln: University of Nebraska Press, 1973.

Haines, Francis. *The Buffalo: The Story of American Bison and Their Hunters from Prehistoric Times to the Present.* New York: Thomas Y. Crowell, 1976.

Hamilton, Charles. *Cry of the Thunderbird.* Norman: University of Oklahoma Press, 1972.

Hammer, Kenneth, ed. *Custer in '76: Walter Camp's Notes on the Custer Fight*. Norman: University of Oklahoma Press, 1990.

——. *The Springfield Carbine on the Western Frontier*. Fort Collins, CO: Old Army Press, 1971.

Hancock, Almira R. *Reminiscences of Winfield Scott Hancock, by His Wife*. New York: Charles L. Webster & Co., 1887.

Hanson, Joseph Mills. *The Conquest of the Missouri: Being the Story of the Life and Exploits of Captain Grant Marsh*. Chicago: A. C. McClurg, 1910.

Harcey, Dennis W., and Brian R. Croone, with Joe Medicine Crow. *White-Man-Runs-Him: Crow Scout with Custer*. Evanston, IL: Evanston Publishing, 1991.

Hardorff, Richard G. *Camp, Custer, and the Little Bighorn: A Collection of Walter Mason Camp's Research Papers on General George A. Custer's Last Fight*. El Segundo, CA: Upton and Sons, 1997.

——. *Cheyenne Memories of the Custer Fight*. Spokane, WA: Arthur H. Clark, 1995.

——, ed. *Cheyenne Memories of the Custer Fight*. Lincoln: University of Nebraska Press, 1998.

——. *The Custer Battle Casualties: Burials, Exhumations, and Reinterments*. El Segundo, CA: Upton and Sons, 1989.

——. *The Custer Battle Casualties II: The Dead, the Missing, and a Few Survivors*. El Segundo, CA: Upton and Sons, 1999.

——. *Hokahey! A Good Day to Die!: The Indian Casualties of the Custer Fight*. Spokane, Arthur H. Clark, 1993.

——. *Indian Views of the Custer Fight: A Source Book*. Spokane, WA: Arthur H. Clark, 2004.

——. *Lakota Recollections of the Custer Fight*. Spokane, WA: Arthur H. Clark, 1991.

——. *Markers, Artifacts and Indian Testimony: Preliminary Findings on the Custer Battle*. Short Hills, NJ: Don Horn Publications, 1985.

——. *The Oglala Lakota Crazy Horse*. Mattituck, NY: J. M. Carroll, 1985.

——. *On the Little Bighorn with Walter Camp: A Collection of Walter Mason Camp's Letters, Notes and Opinions on Custer's Last Fight*. El Segundo, CA: Upton and Sons, 2002.

——. *The Surrender and Death of Crazy Horse*. Spokane, WA: Arthur H. Clark, 1998.

——. *Walter M. Camp's Little Bighorn Rosters*. Spokane, WA: Arthur H. Clark, 2002.

——. *Washita Memories: Eyewitness Views of Custer's Attack on Black Kettle's Village*. Norman: University of Oklahoma Press, 2006.

Hart, John P., ed. *Custer and His Times*. Book 4. LaGrange Park, IL: Little Big Horn Associates, 2002.

——, ed. *Custer and His Times. Book 5*. El Paso, TX: Little Big Horn Associates, 2008.

Hassrick, Royal. *The Sioux: Life and Customs of a Warrior Society*. Norman: University of Oklahoma, 1962.

Hatch, Thom. *Black Kettle: The Cheyenne Chief Who Sought Peace but Found War*. Hoboken, NJ: John Wiley & Sons, 2004.

——. *The Blue, the Gray, and the Red: Indian Campaigns of the Civil War*. Mechanicsburg, PA: Stackpole, 2003.

——. *Glorious War: The Civil War Adventures of George Armstrong Custer*. New York: St. Martin's Press, 2013.

Hayes-McCoy, G. A. *Captain Myles Walter Keogh, the United States Army, 1840–1876*. Dublin: National University of Ireland, 1965.

Hedren, Paul L. *First Scalp for Custer: The Skirmish at Warbonnet Creek, Nebraska, July 17, 1876*. Lincoln: University of Nebraska Press, 1980.

——. *Fort Laramie and the Great Sioux War*. Norman: University of Oklahoma Press, 1998.

——. *Fort Laramie in 1876: Chronicle of a Frontier Post at War*. Lincoln: University of Nebraska Press, 1988.

——, ed. *The Great Sioux War 1876–77: The Best from Montana: The Magazine of Western History*. Helena: Montana Historical Society Press, 1991.

——. *Sitting Bull's Surrender at Fort Buford*. Williston, SD: Fort Union Association, 1997.

——, ed. *We Trailed the Sioux: Enlisted Men Speak on Custer, Crook, and the Great Sioux War*. Mechanicsburg, PA: Stackpole, 2003.

Hoebel, E. Adamson. *The Cheyennes: Indians of the Great Plains*. New York: Holt, Reinhart & Winston, 1960.

Hofling, Charles. *Custer and the Little Big Horn: A Psychobiographical Inquiry*. Detroit: Wayne State University Press, 1981.

Hoig, Stanley. *The Battle of the Washita: The Sheridan-Custer Indian Campaign of 1867–69*. Garden City, NY: Doubleday, 1976.

Holmes, Richard. *Acts of War: Behavior of Men in Battle*. New York: Free Press, 1986.

Hoopes, Alban W. *The Road to the Little Big Horn—and Beyond*. New York: Vantage Press, 1975.

Horn, W. Donald. *Portrait of a General*. West Orange, NJ: Don Horn Publications, 1998.

——. *"Skinned": The Delinquency Record of Cadet George Armstrong Custer U.S.M.A. Class of June 1861*. Short Hills, NJ: W. Donald Horn, 1980.

Huls, Don. *The Winter of 1890*. Chadron, NE: Chadron Record, 1974.

Hunt, Frazier, and Robert Hunt, eds. *I Fought with Custer: The Story of Sergeant Windolph, Last Survivor of the Battle of the Little Big Horn.* New York: Charles Scribner's, 1947.

Hutchins, James S., ed. *The Army and Navy Journal on the Battle of the Little Bighorn and Related Matters, 1876–1881.* El Segundo, CA: Upton and Sons, 2003.

———, ed. *Boots & Saddles at the Little Bighorn.* Fort Collins, CO: Old Army Press, 1976.

Hutton, Paul Andrew, ed. *Custer and His Times.* El Paso, TX: Little Big Horn Associates, 1981.

———, ed. *The Custer Reader.* Lincoln: University of Nebraska Press, 1992.

———, ed. *Garry Owen 1976.* Seattle, WA: Little Big Horn Associates, 1977.

———. *Phil Sheridan and His Army.* Norman: University of Oklahoma Press, 1995.

Hyde, George E. *Red Cloud's Folk: A History of the Oglala Sioux.* Norman: University of Oklahoma Press, 1975.

———. *A Sioux Chronicle.* Norman: University of Oklahoma Press, 1980.

———. *Spotted Tail's Folk: A History of the Brule Sioux.* Norman: University of Oklahoma Press, 1974.

Innis, Ben. *Bloody Knife! Custer's Favorite Scout.* Fort Collins, CO: Old Army Press, 1973.

Irwin, Lee. *Native American Spirituality: A Reader.* Lincoln: University of Nebraska Press, 2000.

Jackson, Donald. *Custer's Gold: The United States Cavalry Expedition of 1874.* New Haven, CT: Yale University Press, 1966.

Jackson, Helen Hunt. *A Century of Dishonor.* Norman: University of Oklahoma Press, 1995.

Jackson, Royal G. *An Oral History of the Battle of the Little Bighorn from the Perspective of the Northern Cheyenne Descendants.* Laramie: University of Wyoming National Park Service Research Center, 1987.

Jamison, Perry D. *Crossing Deadly Ground: United States Army Tactics, 1865–1899.* Tuscaloosa: University of Alabama Press, 1994.

Jensen, Richard, R. Eli Paul, and John E. Carter. *Eyewitness at Wounded Knee.* Lincoln: University of Nebraska Press, 1991.

Johnson, Barry. *Benteen's Ordeal and Custer's Field.* London: Johnson-Taunton Military Press, 1983.

———. *Custer, Reno, Merrill and the Lauffer Case.* London: English Westerner's Society, 1971.

———. "Dr. Paulding and His Remarkable Diary." In *Sidelights of the Sioux Wars,* edited by Francis Taunton. London: English Westerner's Society, 1967.

———. *Merritt and the Indian Wars.* London: Johnson-Taunton Military Press, 1972.

———, and Francis Taunton. *More Sidelights of the Sioux Wars.* London: Westerners' Publications, 2004.

Johnson, Randy and Nancy Allen. *A Dispatch to Custer: The Tragedy of Lieutenant Kidder.* Missoula, MT: Mountain Press, 1999.

Jones, Douglas C. *The Court-Martial of George Armstrong Custer.* New York: Scribner's, 1976.

———. *The Treaty of Medicine Lodge: The Story of the Great Treaty as Told by Eyewitnesses.* Norman: University of Oklahoma Press, 1966.

Jordan, David M. *Winfield Scott Hancock: A Soldier's Life.* Bloomington: Indiana University Press, 1988.

Junkin, D. X. *The Life of Winfield Scott Hancock.* New York: Appleton, 1880.

Kammen, Robert, Frederick, Lefthand and Joseph Marshall. *Soldiers Falling into Camp: The Battles of the Rosebud and the Little Bighorn.* Encampment, WY: Affiliated Writers of America, 1991.

Katz, D. Mark. *Custer in Photographs.* New York: Bonanza Books, 1985.

Kaufman, Fred S. *Custer Passed Our Way.* Aberdeen, SD: North Plains Press, 1971.

Keeley, Lawrence H. *War Before Civilization: The Myth of the Peaceful Savage.* New York and Oxford, UK: Oxford University Press, 1996.

Keim, DeB. Randolph. *Sheridan's Troopers on the Borders: A Winter Campaign on the Plains.* 1870. Reprint. Williamstown, MA: Corner House, 1973.

Keller, Julia. *Mr. Gatling's Terrible Marvel: The Gun That Changed Everything and the Misunderstood Genius Who Invented It.* New York: Viking, 2008.

Kennedy, W. J. D. *On the Plains with Custer and Hancock: The Journal of Isaac Coates, Army Surgeon.* Boulder, CO: Johnson Books, 1997.

Kidd, James H. *Personal Recollections of a Cavalryman with Custer's Michigan Brigade in the Civil War.* Reprint. Alexandria, VA: Time-Life Books, 1983.

Kime, Wayne R., ed. *The Black Hills Journals of Colonel Richard Irving Dodge.* Norman: University of Oklahoma Press, 1996.

Kines, Pat. *A Life Within a Life: The Story and Adventures of Libbie Custer.* Commack, NY: Kroshka Books, 1998.

King, Charles. *Campaigning with Crook.* Norman: University of Oklahoma Press, 1988.

———. *Summit Springs.* Ft. Collins, CO: Old Army Press, 1984.

King, James T. *War Eagle: A Life of General Eugene Carr.* Lincoln: University of Nebraska Press, 1963.

King, W. Kent. *Massacre: The Custer Cover-up.* El Segundo, CA: Upton and Sons, 1989.

———. *Tombstones for Bluecoats.* Vols. 1–4. Marion Station, MD: Privately printed, 1980–81.

Kinsley, D. A. *Favor the Bold.* 2 vols. New York: Holt, Rinehart and Winston, 1967–68.

Kirshner, Ralph. *The Class of 1861: Custer, Ames, and Their Classmates After West Point.* Carbondale: Southern Illinois University Press, 1999.

Knight, Oliver. *Following the Indian Wars.* Norman: University of Oklahoma Press, 1963.

———. *Life and Manners in the Frontier Army.* Norman: University of Oklahoma Press, 1969.

Koenig, Arthur. *Authentic History of the Indian Campaign Which Culminated in Custer's Last Battle, June 25, 1876.* Milwaukee, WI: Anheuser-Busch Brewing Association, 1896.

Koury, Michael. *Diaries of the Little Big Horn.* Fort Collins, CO: Old Army Press, 1968.

———, ed. *Gibbon on the Sioux Campaign of 1876.* Fort Collins, CO: Old Army Press, 1969.

Kraft, Louis. *Custer and the Cheyennes: George Armstrong Custer's Winter Campaign on the Southern Plains.* El Segundo, CA: Upton and Sons, 1995.

Krause, Herbert, and Gary Olson. *Prelude to Glory: A Newspaper Accounting of Custer's 1874 Expedition to the Black Hills.* Sioux Falls, SD: Brevet Press, 1976.

Kroeker, Marvin E. *Great Plains Command: William B. Hazen in the Frontier West.* Norman: University of Oklahoma Press, 1976.

Kuberkin, M. John. *Jay Cooke's Gamble: The Northern Pacific Railroad, the Sioux, and the Panic of 1873.* Norman: University of Oklahoma Press, 2006.

Kuhlman, Charles. *Did Custer Disobey Orders at the Battle of the Little Big Horn?* Harrisburg, PA: Stackpole, 1951.

Landenheim, J. C. *Custer's Thorn: The Life of Frederick Benteen.* Westminster, MD: Heritage Books, 2007.

Langellier, John. *Custer: The Man, the Myth, the Movies.* Mechanicsburg, PA: Stackpole, 2000.

———. *Sound the Charge: The U.S. Cavalry in the American West.* Mechanicsburg, PA: Stackpole, 1998.

———, Kurt Hamilton Cox, and Brian C. Pohanka, eds. *Myles Keogh: The Life and Legend of an "Irish Dragoon" in the Seventh Cavalry.* El Segundo, CA: Upton and Sons, 1999.

LaPointe. Ernie. *Sitting Bull: His Life and Legacy.* Layton, UT: Gibbs Smith, 2009.

Larson, Robert W. *Gall: Lakota War Chief.* Norman: University of Oklahoma Press, 2007.

———. *Red Cloud: Warrior-Statesman of the Lakota Sioux.* Norman: University of Oklahoma Press, 1997.

Lass, William E. *A History of Steamboating on the Upper Missouri River.* Lincoln: University of Nebraska Press, 1962.

Lawrence, Elizabeth Atwood. *His Very Silence Speaks: Comanche, the Horse Who Survived Custer's Last Stand.* Detroit: Wayne State University Press, 1989.

Lazarus, Edward. *Black Hills/White Justice: The Sioux Nation Versus the United States, 1775 to the Present.* New York: HarperCollins, 1991.

Leckie, Shirley A. *Elizabeth Bacon Custer and the Making of a Myth.* Norman: University of Oklahoma Press, 1993.

Leckie, William H. *The Buffalo Soldiers: A Narrative of the Negro Cavalry in the West.* Norman: University of Oklahoma Press, 1967.

LeForge, Thomas H., as told by Thomas B. Marquis. *Memoirs of a White Crow Indian.* Reprint. Lincoln: University of Nebraska Press, 1993.

Leighton, Margaret. *Comanche of the Seventh.* New York: Berkley, 1959.

Lewis, Thomas H. *The Medicine Men: Oglala Sioux Ceremony and Healing.* Lincoln: University of Nebraska Press, 1990.

Libby, Orin G., ed. *The Arikara Narrative of Custer's Campaign and the Battle of the Little Bighorn.* Norman: University of Oklahoma Press, 1998.

Liddic, Bruce, ed. *I Buried Custer: The Diary of Pvt. Thomas W. Coleman, 7th U.S. Cavalry.* Bryan, TX: Creative Publishing, 1979.

———. *Vanishing Victory: Custer's Final March.* El Segundo, CA: Upton and Sons, 2004.

———, and Brian Harbaugh. *Camp on Custer: Transcribing the Custer Myth.* Spokane, WA: Arthur H. Clark, 1995.

———. *Custer and Company: Walter Camp's Notes on the Custer Fight.* Lincoln: University of Nebraska Press, 1995.

Longacre, Edward G. *The Cavalry at Gettysburg.* Lincoln: University of Nebraska Press, 1993.

———. *Custer and His Wolverines: The Michigan Cavalry Brigade, 1861–1865.* Conshocken, PA: Combined Publishing, 1997.

Lounsberry, Clement A. *Early History of North Dakota.* Washington, D.C.: Liberty Press, 1919.

Luce, Edward S. *Keogh, Comanche and Custer.* Ashland, OR: Lewis Osborne, 1947.

Lynch, Don, ed. *Wovoka and the Ghost Dance.* Carson City, NV: Grace Foundation, 1990.

Mackintosh, John D. *Custer's Southern Officer: Captain George D. Wallace, 7th U.S. Cavalry.* Lexington, SC: Cloud Creek Press, 2002.

Magnussen, Daniel O. *Peter Thompson's Narrative of the Little Bighorn Campaign, 1876.* Glendale, CA: Arthur H. Clark, 1974.

Magrid, Paul. *George Crook: From the Redwoods to Appomattox*. Norman: University of Oklahoma Press, 2004.

Mails, Thomas E. *The Mystic Warriors of the Plains*. New York: Marlowe, 1995.

Mangum, Neil C. *Battle of the Rosebud: Prelude to the Little Bighorn*. El Segundo, CA: Upton and Sons, 1996.

Manion, John S. *General Terry's Last Statement to Custer*. El Segundo, CA: Upton and Sons, 2000.

Manypenny, George W. *Our Indian Wards*. Cincinnati: Robert Clarke Co., 1880.

Marquis, Thomas B. *Cheyenne and Sioux: The Reminiscences of Four Indians and a White Soldier*. Stockton, CA: Pacific Center for Western Historical Studies, University of the Pacific, 1971.

———. *Custer, Cavalry and Crows*. Fort Collins, CO: Old Army Press, 1975.

———. *Custer on the Little Bighorn*. Lodi, CA: End-Kian Publishing, 1967.

———. *Custer Soldiers Not Buried*. Hardin, MT: Privately printed, 1933.

———. *Keep the Last Bullet for Yourself*. Algonac, MI: Reference Publications, 1976.

———. *Memoirs of a White Crow Indian*. New York: Century Co., 1928.

———. *She Watched Custer's Last Battle*. Hardin, MT: Privately printed, 1933.

———. *Sitting Bull and Gall the Warrior*. Hardin, MT: Custer Battlefield Museum, 1934.

———. *Two Days After the Battle*. Hardin, MT: Privately printed, 1935.

———. *A Warrior Who Fought Custer*. Minneapolis: Midwest Publishing, 1931.

———. *Wooden Leg: A Warrior Who Fought Custer*. Bison Press, 2003.

Marshall, Joseph M., III. *The Day the World Ended at Little Bighorn: A Lakota History*. New York: Viking, 2007.

———. *The Journey of Crazy Horse: A Lakota History*. New York: Viking, 2004.

Masters, Joseph J. *Shadows Fall Across the Little Big Horn: Custer's Last Stand*. Laramie: University of Wyoming Library, 1951.

McChristian, Douglas. *An Army of Marksmen*. Fort Collins, CO: Old Army Press, 1981.

———, and John P. Langellier. *The U. S. Army in the West, 1870–1880: Uniforms, Weapons, and Equipment*. Norman: University of Oklahoma Press, 1995.

McClellan, George B. *McClellan's Own Story: The War for the Union*. London: Sampson, Low, Marston, Searle & Rivington, 1887.

McClernand, Edward J. *On Time for Disaster: The Rescue of Custer's Command*. Lincoln: University of Nebraska Press, 1989.

McCreight, M. I. *Chief Flying Hawk's Tales: The True Story of Custer's Last Fight*. New York: Alliance Press, 1936.

McFeely, William S. *Grant: A Biography*. New York: W. W. Norton, 1981.

McGillycuddy, Julia. *McGillycuddy, Agent.* Stanford, CA: Stanford University Press, 1941.

McGinnis, Anthony. *Counting Coup and Cutting Horses.* Evergreen, CO: Cordillera Press, 1990.

McGregor, James H. *The Wounded Knee Massacre: From the Viewpoint of the Sioux.* N.p. Fenwyn Press, 1969.

McLaughlin, James. *My Friend the Indian.* Reprint. Seattle: Superior Publishing, 1970.

McMurtry, Larry. *Crazy Horse.* New York: Lipper/Viking, 1999.

——. *Oh What a Slaughter: Massacres in the American West, 1846–1890.* New York: Simon and Schuster, 2005.

Meketa, Ray. *Luther Rector Hare: A Texan with Custer.* Mattituck, NY: J. M. Carroll, 1983.

Merington, Marguerite. *The Custer Story: The Life and Intimate Letters of General George A. Custer and His Wife Elizabeth.* New York: Devin-Adair, 1950.

Merk, Frederick. *History of Westward Movement.* New York: Knopf, 1978.

Merkel, Captain Charles E., Jr. *Unravelling the Custer Enigma.* Enterprise, AL: Merkel Press, 1977.

Merrill, James M. *Spurs to Glory.* Chicago: Rand McNally, 1966.

Michno, Gregory. *Lakota Noon: The Indian Narrative of Custer's Defeat.* Missoula, MT: Mountain Press Publishing, 1998.

——. *The Mystery of E Troop: Custer's Gray Horse Company at the Little Bighorn.* Missoula, MT: Mountain Press Publishing, 1997.

Miles, Nelson. *Personal Recollections and Observations of General Nelson A. Miles.* New York: Werner, 1896.

Miller, David Humphreys. *Custer's Fall: The Indian Side of the Story.* New York: Duell, Sloan, and Pearce, 1957.

Milligan, Edward Archibald. *High Noon on the Greasy Grass.* Bottineau, SD: Bottineau-Courant Printing, 1972.

Mills, Anson. *My Story.* Washington, D.C.: Byron S. Adams, 1918.

Mills, Charles K. *Charles C. DeRudio.* Mattituck, NY: J. M. Carroll, 1983.

——. *Harvest of Barren Regrets: The Army Career of Frederick William Benteen.* Glendale, CA: Arthur H. Clark, 1985.

Milner, Joe E., and Earle R. Forrest. *California Joe: Noted Scout and Indian Fighter.* Lincoln: University of Nebraska Press, 1987.

Mishkin, Bernard. *Rank and Warfare Among the Plains Indians.* Monographs of the American Ethnological Society 3. New York: J. J. Augustin, 1940.

Monaghan, Jay. *Custer: The Life of General George Armstrong Custer.* Boston: Little, Brown, 1959.

Monnett, John. H. *The Battle of Beecher Island and the Indian War of 1867–69.* Niwot: University of Colorado Press, 1992.

Mooney, James. *The Ghost Dance Religion and the Sioux Outbreak of 1890.* Reprint. Lincoln: University of Nebraska Press, 1991.

Moore, Donald. *Custer's Ghost and Custer's Gold.* El Segundo, CA: Upton and Sons, 2007.

Mulford, Ami Frank. *Fighting Indians in the 7th United States Cavalry, Custer's Favorite Regiment.* Corning, NY: Paul Lindsey Mulford, 1878.

Neihardt, John G. *Black Elk Speaks: Being the Life Story of a Holy Man of the Oglala Sioux.* Lincoln: University of Nebraska Press, 2000.

Nichols, Ronald H. *In Custer's Shadow: Major Marcus Reno.* Fort Collins, CO: Old Army Press, 1999.

———, ed. *Men with Custer.* Hardin, MT: Custer Battlefield and Museum Association, 2000.

———. *The Reno Court of Inquiry.* Hardin, MT: Custer Battlefield Historical and Museum Association, 1992.

Nolan, Louis Edward. *Cavalry: Its History and Tactics.* Yardley, PA: Westholme, 2006.

Northrop, Henry D. *Indian Horrors; or Massacres by the Red Men.* Philadelphia: National Publishing, 1891.

Oaks, George W. *Man of the West.* Tucson, AZ: Arizona Pioneer Historical Society, 1956.

O'Conner, Richard. *Wild Bill Hickok.* New York: Konecky & Konecky, 1959.

Olson. James C. *Red Cloud and the Sioux Problem.* Lincoln: University of Nebraska Press, 1965.

O'Neil, Alice Tomlinson. *My Dear Sister.* New York: Arrow and Trooper, 1993.

O'Neil, Tom, ed. *Custer Chronicles.* Vols. 1–10. New York: Arrow and Trooper, 1998.

———. *Custer Conundrums.* Brooklyn, NY: Arrow and Trooper, 1991.

———. *Custer Massacred!—How the News First Reached the Outside World.* New York: Arrow and Trooper, 1995.

———, ed. *Custeriana.* Vols. 1–10. New York: Arrow and Trooper, 1995.

———. *Fort Abraham Lincoln.* New York: Arrow and Trooper, 1996.

———, ed. *Garry Owen Tidbits.* Vols. 1–10. New York: Arrow and Trooper, 1989.

———, ed. *The Gibson-Edgerly Narratives of the Little Big Horn.* New York: Arrow and Trooper, 1993.

———. *In Reply to Van de Water.* New York: Arrow and Trooper, 1994.

O'Neil, Thomas E. *Letters from Boston Custer.* Brooklyn, NY: Arrow and Trooper, 1993.

———, and Alice T. O'Neil. *The Custers in Monroe.* Monroe, MI: Monroe County Library System, 1991.

Overfield, Lloyd, II. *The Little Big Horn, 1876: The Official Communications, Documents, and Reports, with Rosters of the Officers and Troops of the Campaign.* Glendale, CA: Arthur H. Clark, 1971.

Parker, Watson. *Gold in the Black Hills.* Lincoln: University of Nebraska Press, 1982.

Parson, John E., and John S. duMont. *Firearms in the Custer Battle.* Harrisburg, PA: Stackpole, 1953.

Pennington, Jack. *The Battle of the Little Bighorn: A Comprehensive Study.* El Segundo, CA: Upton and Sons, 2001.

———. *Custer, Curley, Curtis: An Expanded View of the Battle of the Little Big Horn.* El Segundo, CA: Upton and Sons, 2005.

Peters, Joseph P., ed. *Indian Battles and Skirmishes on the American Frontier, 1790–1898.* New York: Argonaut Press, 1966.

Philbrick, Nathaniel. *The Last Stand: Custer, Sitting Bull, and the Battle of the Little Bighorn.* New York: Viking, 2010.

Pohanka, Brian. *A Summer on the Plains, 1870: From the Diary of Annie Gibson Roberts.* Mattituck, NY: J. M. Carroll, 1983.

Poole, D. C. *Among the Sioux of Dakota.* 1881. Reprint. St. Paul: Borealis Books, 1988.

Powell, Peter J. *People of the Sacred Mountain.* San Francisco: Harper & Row, 1981.

———. *Sweet Medicine.* Norman: University of Oklahoma Press, 1998.

Powers, William K. *Oglala Religion.* Lincoln: University of Nebraska Press, 1977.

Price, George F. *Across the Continent with the Fifth Cavalry.* New York: Antiquarian Press, 1959.

Price, S. Goodale. *Saga of the Hills.* Los Angeles: Cosmo Press, 1940.

Priest, Loring Benson. *Uncle Sam's Stepchildren: The Reformation of the United States Indian Policy, 1865–1887.* New York: Octagon Books, 1969.

Progulske, Donald R., and Frank J. Shideler. *Following Custer.* Brookings: Agricultural Experiment Station, South Dakota State University, 1974.

Prucha, Francis Paul, *American Indian Policy in Crisis: Christian Reformers and the Indian, 1865–1900.* Chicago: University of Chicago Press, 1977.

———. *American Indian Treaties: Documents of U.S. Indian Policy.* Berkeley: University of California Press, 1994.

———. *The Great Father: The United States Government and the American Indians.* Lincoln: University of Nebraska Press, 1986.

Rankin, Charles, ed. *Legacy: New Perspectives on the Battle of the Little Bighorn.* Helena: Montana Historical Society Press, 1996.

Reedstrom, E. Lisle. *Bugles, Banners and War Bonnets: A Study of George Custer's Seventh Cavalry from Fort Riley to the Little Big Horn.* Caldwell, ID: Caxton Press, 1977.

———. *Custer's 7th Cavalry: From Fort Riley to the Little Bighorn.* New York: Sterling, 1992.

Reiger, John F., ed. *The Passing of the Great West: Selected Papers of George Bird Grinnell.* New York: Scribner, 1972.

Riegel, Robert Edgar. *The Story of the Western Railroads: From 1852 Through the Reign of the Giants.* Lincoln: University of Nebraska Press, 1964.

Remsburg, John E., and George J. Remsburg. *Charley Reynolds: Soldier, Hunter, Scout and Guide.* Kansas City, MO: H. M. Sender, 1931.

Repass, Craig. *Custer for President?* Fort Collins, CO: Old Army Press, 1985.

Reynolds, Arlene. *The Civil War Memories of Elizabeth Bacon Custer.* Austin: University of Texas Press, 1994.

Reynolds, Art. *Collision of Cultures.* Bloomington, IN: 1st Books, 2003.

Ricker, Eli S. *The Indian Interviews of Eli S. Ricker, 1903–1919.* Lincoln: University of Nebraska Press, 2005.

———. *The Settler and Soldier: Interviews of Eli S. Ricker, 1903–1919.* Lincoln: University of Nebraska Press, 2005.

Rickey, Don, Jr. *Forty Miles a Day on Beans and Hay.* Norman: University of Oklahoma Press, 1963.

———. *History of Custer Battlefield.* Hardin, MT: Custer Battlefield Historical & Museum Association, 1998.

Rister, Carl Coke. *Border Captives: The Traffic in Prisoners by Southern Plains Indians.* Norman: University of Oklahoma Press, 1940.

———. *Border Command: General Phil Sheridan in the West.* Norman: University of Oklahoma Press, 1944.

Roberts, Richard A. *Custer's Last Battle: Reminiscences of General Custer.* Monroe, MI: Monroe County Historical Society, 1978.

Robinson, Charles M. *General Crook and the Western Frontier.* Norman: University of Oklahoma Press, 2001.

———. *A Good Year to Die: The Story of the Great Sioux War.* Norman: University of Oklahoma Press, 1995.

Robinson, Doane. *A History of the Dakota or Sioux Indians.* 1906. Reprint. Minneapolis: Ross and Haines, 1956.

Rodenbough, Theodore, ed. *Uncle Sam's Medal of Honor: Some of the Noble Deeds for Which the Medal Has Been Awarded, Described by Those Who Have Won It 1861–1886.* New York: G. P. Putnam's Sons, 1886.

Roe, Charles F. *Custer's Last Battle.* New York: Robert Bruce, 1927.

Roe, Francis. *Army Letters from an Officer's Wife.* New York: Appleton, 1909.

Ronsheim, Milton L. *The Life of General Custer.* Cadiz, OH: Cadiz Republican, 1929.

Rosenberg, Bruce A. *Custer and the Epic of Defeat.* University Park: Pennsylvania State University Press, 1974.

Russell, Don. *The Lives and Legends of Buffalo Bill.* Norman: University of Oklahoma Press, 1973.

Ryan, John. *Ten Years with General Custer Among the American Indians.* Edited by John M. Carroll. Bryan, TX: April 1980.

Sajna, Mike. *Crazy Horse: The Life Behind the Legend.* New York: John Wiley and Sons, 2000.

Sandoz, Mari. *The Battle of the Little Bighorn.* Philadelphia and New York: J. B. Lippincott, 1966.

——. *The Buffalo Hunters: The Story of the Hide Men.* New York: McGraw-Hill, 1954.

——. *Cheyenne Autumn.* Lincoln: University of Nebraska Press, 1992.

——. *Crazy Horse: The Strange Man of the Oglalas.* Lincoln: University of Nebraska Press, 1942.

Sarf, Wayne Michael. *The Little Bighorn Campaign.* New York: Combined Publishing, 1993.

Sargeant, John O. *Major General Hazen on His Post of Duty in the Great American Desert.* New York: G. P. Putnam's Sons, 1874.

Sarkesian, Sam C. *Combat Effectiveness: Cohesion, Stress and the Volunteer Military.* Conshohocken, PA: Combined Books, 1993.

Schaff, Morris. *The Spirit of Old West Point, 1858–1862.* Boston: Houghton Mifflin, 1907.

Schivelbusch, Wolfgang. *The Culture of Defeat: On National Trauma, Mourning, and Recovery.* Translated by Jefferson Chase. New York: Henry Holt, 2003.

Schmitt, Martin, ed. *General George Crook: His Autobiography.* Norman: University of Oklahoma Press, 1946.

Schneider, James. *Behind Custer at the Little Big Horn: Lieutenant Edward C. Mathey.* Fort Wayne, IN: n.p., 1981.

Schoenberger, Dale. *End of Custer: The Death of an American Military Legend.* Blaine, WA: Hancock House, 1995.

Schultz, James Willard. *Blackfeet and Buffalo: Memories of Life Among the Indians.* Norman: University of Oklahoma Press, 1962.

——. *William Jackson, Indian Scout.* Boston: Houghton Mifflin, 1926.

Scott, Douglas. *Uncovering History: Archaeological Investigations at the Little Bighorn.* Foreword by Bob Reece. Norman: University of Oklahoma Press, 2013.

———, Melissa A. Conner, and Dick Harmon. *Archaeological Perspectives on the Battle of the Little Bighorn.* Norman: University of Oklahoma Press, 1989.

Scott, Douglas D., and Richard Fox Jr. *Archaeological Insights into the Custer Battle: A Preliminary Assessment.* Norman: University of Oklahoma Press, 1987.

Scott, Douglas D., P. Wiley, and Melissa A. Connor. *They Died with Custer: Soldiers' Bones from the Battle of the Little Big Horn.* Norman: University of Oklahoma Press, 1998.

Scott, Hugh Lennox. *Some Memories of a Soldier.* New York: Century, 1928.

Scudder, Ralph E. *Custer Country.* Portland, OR: Binfords and Mort, 1963.

Sheridan, Philip H. *Record of Engagements with Hostile Indians Within the Military Division of the Missouri, from 1868 to 1882, Lieutenant-General P. H. Sheridan, Commanding.* Fort Collins, CO: Old Army Press, 1972.

———, and Michael V. Sheridan. *Personal Memoirs of Philip Henry Sheridan, General United States Army.* 2 vols. New York: S. Appleton, 1904.

Sklenar, Larry. *To Hell with Honor.* Norman: University of Oklahoma Press, 2000.

Smalley, Vern. *Little Bighorn Mysteries.* Bozeman, MT: Little Buffalo Press, 2005.

———. *More Little Bighorn Mysteries.* Bozeman, MT: Little Buffalo Press, 2005.

Smith, DeCost. *Indian Experiences.* Caldwell, ID: Caxton Printers, 1943.

Smith, Jean Edward. *Grant.* New York: Simon and Schuster, 2001.

Smith, Sherry. *Sagebrush Soldier: Private William Earle Smith's View of the Sioux War of 1876.* Norman: University of Oklahoma Press, 1989.

Snelson, Bob. *Death of a Myth.* Snelson Books, 2002.

Spotts, David L. *Campaigning with Custer and the Nineteenth Kansas Volunteer Cavalry on the Washita Campaign, 1868–69.* Edited by E. A. Brininstool. Reprint. Lincoln: University of Nebraska Press, 1988.

Standing Bear, Luther. *My People the Sioux.* Boston: Houghton Mifflin, 1928.

Stands in Timber, John, and Margot Liberty. *Cheyenne Memories.* New Haven, CT: Yale University Press, 1967.

Stanley, General D. S. *Personal Memoirs of Major-General D. S. Stanley, U.S.A.* Cambridge, MA: Harvard University Press, 1917.

Stanley, Henry M. *My Early Travels and Adventures in America and Asia.* Lincoln: University of Nebraska Press, 1982.

Starr, Stephen Z. *The Union Cavalry in the Civil War in the East, from Gettysburg to Appomattox, 1863–1865.* Baton Rouge: Louisiana State University Press, 1979, 1981.

Steffen, Randy. *The Horse Soldier: The Frontier, the Mexican War, the Civil War, the Indian Wars, 1851–1880*. Norman: University of Oklahoma Press, 1992.

Stewart, Edgar I. *Custer's Luck*. Norman: University of Oklahoma Press, 1955.

———, ed. *Penny-an-Acre Empire in the West*. Norman: University of Oklahoma Press, 1968.

———. *"Sufficient Reason?" An Examination of Terry's Celebrated Order to Custer*. London: English Westerners' Society, 1977.

Sully, Landon. *No Tears for the General: The Life of Alfred Sully*. Palo Alto, CA: American West Publishing, 1974.

Swanson, Glenwood J. *G. A. Custer: His Life and Times*. Agua Dulce, CA: Swanson Productions, 2004.

Tate, Michael L. *The Frontier Army in the Settlement of the West*. Norman: University of Oklahoma Press, 1999.

Tatum, Lawrie. *Our Red Brothers and the Peace Policy of President Ulysses S. Grant*. Lincoln: University of Nebraska Press, 1968.

Taunton, Francis B. *Army Failures Against the Sioux in 1876*. London: Westerners' Publications, 2004.

———. *Custer's Field: A Scene of Sickening, Ghastly Horror*. London: Johnson-Taunton Military Press, 1989.

———, ed. *No Pride in the Little Big Horn*. London: English Westerners' Society, 1987.

———. *"Sufficient Reason?": An Examination of Terry's Celebrated Order to Custer*. London: English Westerners' Society, 1977.

Taylor, Joseph Henry. *Frontier and Indian Life, and Kaleidoscopic Lives*. Reprint. Valley City, ND: Washburn's Fiftieth Anniversary Committee, 1932.

Taylor, Rev. Landon. *The Battlefield Reviewed*. Chicago: Privately printed, 1881.

Taylor, William O. *With Custer on the Little Bighorn*. New York: Viking, 1996.

Terrell, John Upton, and George Walton. *Faint the Trumpet Sounds*. New York: David McKay, 1966.

Terry, Alfred H. *The Field Diary of General Alfred H. Terry: The Yellowstone Expedition—1876*. Bellevue, NE: Old Army Press, 1969.

———. *The Terry Letters: The Letters of General Alfred Howe Terry to His Sisters During the Indian War of 1876*. Edited by James Willert. La Mirada, CA: James Willert, 1980.

Thorndike, Rachel Sherman. *The Sherman Letters*. New York: Da Capo, 1969.

Tibbles, Thomas Henry. *Buckskin and Blanket Days*. New York: Doubleday, 1957.

Trinka, Zena Irma. *Out Where the West Begins*. St. Paul, MN: Pioneer Company, 1920.

Trobriand, P. R. *Army Life in Dakota*. Chicago: Lakeside Press, 1941.

Trout, M. D., ed. *Joseph Culbertson's Indian Scout Memories, 1876–1895*. Anaheim, CA: Van-Allen Publishing, 1984.

Tucker, William, and Jeff C. Dykes. *The Grand Duke Alexis in the United States*. Reprint. New York: Interland Publishing, 1972.

Upton, Emory. *Cavalry Tactics, United States Army*. New York: D. Appleton, 1874.

Upton, Richard. *The Custer Adventure: As Told by Its Participants*. El Segundo, CA: Upton and Sons, 1990.

Urwin, Gregory, J., ed. *Custer and His Times*. Book 3. El Paso, TX: Little Big Horn Associates, 1987.

———. *Custer Victorious: The Civil War Battles of General George Armstrong Custer*. Edison, NJ: Blue and Gray Press, 1983.

Utley, Robert M. *Cavalier in Buckskin: George Armstrong Custer and the Western Military Frontier*. Norman: University of Oklahoma Press, 1988.

———. *Custer and the Great Controversy: The Origin and Development of a Legend*. Pasadena, CA: Westernlore Press, 1962.

———. *Frontier Regulars: The United States Cavalry and the Indian, 1866–1890*. New York: Macmillan, 1973.

———. *Frontiersmen in Blue: The United States Army and the Indian, 1848–1865*. New York: Macmillan, 1973.

———. *The Indian Frontier of the American West, 1846–1890*. Albuquerque: University of New Mexico Press, 1984.

———. *The Lance and the Shield: The Life and Times of Sitting Bull*. New York: Holt, 1993.

———. *The Last Days of the Sioux Nation*. New Haven, CT: Yale University Press, 1963.

———. *Life in Custer's Cavalry: Diaries and Letters of Albert and Jennie Barnitz, 1867–1868*. Lincoln: University of Nebraska Press, 1987.

———. *Little Bighorn Battlefield: A History and Guide*. Washington, D.C.: Division of Publications, National Park Service, 1988.

———. *The Reno Court of Inquiry: The Chicago Times Account*. Fort Collins, CO: Old Army Press, 1972.

———, and Wilcomb E. Washburn. *Indian Wars*. Boston: Houghton Mifflin, 1977.

Van de Water, Frederic. *Glory-Hunter: A Life of General Custer*. New York: Bobbs-Merrill, 1934.

Varnum, Charles A. *Custer's Chief of Scouts: The Reminiscences of Charles A. Varnum*. Edited by John M. Carroll. Lincoln: University of Nebraska, 1987.

———, and Charles K. Mills. *I, Varnum: The Autobiographical Reminiscences of Custer's Chief of Scouts*. Edited by John Meluni Carroll. Mattituck, NY: J. M. Carroll, 1982.

Vaughn, J. W. *The Reynolds Campaign on Powder River.* Norman: University of Oklahoma Press, 1966.

———. *With Crook at the Rosebud.* Harrisburg, PA: Stackpole, 1956.

Vestal, Stanley. *New Sources of Indian History, 1850–1891.* Norman: University of Oklahoma Press, 1934.

———. *Sitting Bull: Champion of the Sioux.* Norman: University of Oklahoma Press, 1957.

———. *Warpath: The True Story of the Fighting Sioux.* Boston: Houghton Mifflin, 1934.

———. *Warpath and Council Fire.* New York: Random House, 1948.

Viola, Herman J., ed. *Diplomats in Buckskins: A History of Indian Delegations in Washington City.* Washington, D.C.: Smithsonian Institution Press, 1981.

———. *Little Bighorn Remembered: The Untold Indian Story of Custer's Last Stand.* New York: Crown, 1999.

———, with Jan Shelton Danis. *It Is a Good Day to Die: Indian Eyewitnesses Tell the Story of the Battle of the Little Bighorn.* Lincoln: University of Nebraska Press, 1998.

Wagner, Glendolin Damon. *Old Neutriment.* Lincoln: University of Oklahoma Press, 1989.

Walker, James R. *Lakota Belief and Ritual.* Edited by Raymond DeMallie. Lincoln: University of Nebraska Press, 1991.

———. *The Sun Dance and Other Ceremonies of the Oglala Division of the Teton Dakota.* Washington, D.C.: American Museum of Natural History, 1917.

Walker, Judson. *Campaigns of General Custer.* Reprint. New York: Promontory Press, 1966.

Walker, L. G., Jr. *Dr. Henry R. Porter: The Surgeon Who Survived Little Bighorn.* Jefferson, NC: McFarland, 2008.

Wallace, Charles B. *Custer's Ohio Boyhood: A Brief Account of the Early Life of Major General George Armstrong Custer.* Cadiz, OH: Harrison County Historical Society, 1987.

Walter, Dave, ed. *Speaking Ill of the Dead.* Guilford, CT: Twodot, 2000.

War of the Rebellion: The Official Records of the Union and Confederate Armies. Washington, D.C.: Government Printing Office, 1896.

Weibert, Don. *Custer, Cases and Cartridges: The Weibert Collection Analyzed.* Billings, MT: Weibert, 1989.

Weibert, Henry, and Don Weibert. *Sixty-six Years in Custer's Shadow.* Billings, MT: Falcon Press, 1988.

Welch, James, with Paul Stekler. *Killing Custer: The Battle of the Little Bighorn and the Fate of the Plains Indians.* New York: Penguin, 1995.

Wengert, James. *The Custer Dispatches.* Manhattan, KS: Sunflower University Press, 1987.

Werner, Fred H. *The Beecher Island Battle.* Greeley, CO: Werner Publications, 1989.

———. *The Dull Knife Fight.* Greeley, CO: Werner Publications, 1981.

———. *Faintly Sounds the War-Cry: The Story of the Fight at Battle Butte.* Greeley, CO: Werner Publications, 1983.

———. *The Summit Springs Battle.* Greeley, CO: Werner Publications, 1991.

Wert, Jeffrey D. *Custer: The Controversial Life of George Armstrong Custer.* New York: Simon and Schuster, 1996.

———. *From Winchester to Cedar Creek: The Shenandoah Campaign of 1864.* Carlisle, PA: South Mountain, 1987.

Wheeler, Homer W. *Buffalo Days: Forty Years in the Old West.* Reprint. Lincoln: University of Nebraska Press, 1990.

Whitman, S. E. *The Troopers: An Informal History of the Plains Cavalry.* New York: Hastings House, 1962.

Whittaker, Frederick. *A Complete Life of Gen. George A. Custer.* New York: Sheldon and Company, 1876.

Wilbert, James. *March of the Columns: Chronicle of the 1876 Indian War.* El Segundo, CA: Upton and Sons, 1994.

———, and Warren Van Ess. *Little Big Horn Diary: Chronicle of the 1876 Indian War.* El Segundo, CA: Upton and Sons, 1997.

Windolph, Charles. *I Fought with Custer: The Story of Sergeant Windolph, Last Survivor of the Battle of the Little Big Horn as Told to Frazier and Robert Hunt.* Lincoln: University of Nebraska Press, 1987.

Winthrop, William. *Military Law and Precedents.* Reprint. New York: Arno Press, 1979.

Wooster, Robert. *The Military and United States Indian Policy, 1865–1903.* New Haven, CT: Yale University Press, 1983.

Yenne, Bill. *Indian Wars: The Campaign for the American West.* Yardley, PA: Westholme, 2006.

———. *Sitting Bull.* Yardley, PA: Westholme, 2008.

Zeisler, Karl. *Custer Observed: General Custer as Seen Through the Eyes of the Monroe Evening News.* Monroe, MI: Monroe County Library System, 1988.

Index